BRAZIL

A book in the
Brasiliana Collection of the
series Latin America in Translation / en
Traducción / em Tradução

*Sponsored by the
Consortium in Latin American Studies
at the University of North Carolina at
Chapel Hill and Duke University*

BRAZIL

A Century of Change

EDITED BY

Ignacy Sachs,

Jorge Wilheim, and

Paulo Sérgio Pinheiro

TRANSLATED BY

Robert N. Anderson

FOREWORD BY

Jerry Dávila

THE UNIVERSITY OF

NORTH CAROLINA PRESS

Chapel Hill

Translation of the books in the series Latin America in Translation /
en Traducción / em Tradução, a collaboration between the Consortium
in Latin American Studies at the University of North Carolina at Chapel Hill
and Duke University and the university presses of the University of North
Carolina and Duke, is supported by a grant from the Andrew W. Mellon
Foundation. Publication of this book was also supported by a grant from the
Brazil Information Center of the Brazilian Embassy in Washington, D.C.

Originally published in Portuguese in São Paulo, Brazil, by Companhia
das Letras as *Brasil: Um século de transformações*, © 2001 by Os autores

The paper in this book meets the guidelines for permanence and
durability of the Committee on Production Guidelines for Book Longevity
of the Council on Library Resources.

The University of North Carolina Press has been a member of the
Green Press Initiative since 2003.

Library of Congress Cataloging-in-Publication Data
Brasil. English
Brazil : a century of change / edited by Ignacy Sachs, Jorge Wilheim, and Paulo
Sérgio Pinheiro ; translated by Robert N. Anderson ; foreword by Jerry Dávila.
p. cm. — (Latin America in translation/en traducción/em tradução.
Brasiliana collection)
Includes bibliographical references and index.
ISBN 978-0-8078-3130-4 (cloth : alk. paper)
ISBN 978-0-8078-5927-8 (pbk. : alk. paper)
1. Brazil—Civilization—20th century. 2. Brazil—Forecasting.
3. Twenty-first century—Forecasts. I. Sachs, Ignacy.
II. Wilheim, Jorge, 1928– III. Pinheiro, Paulo
Sérgio de M. S. (Paulo Sérgio de Moraes Sarmento) IV. Title.
F2538.3.B6313 2001
982.06—dc22
2008036712

cloth 13 12 11 10 09   5 4 3 2 1
paper 13 12 11 10 09   5 4 3 2 1

Contents

CONTENTS

JERRY DÁVILA

Foreword

Brazil is the country of the future and always will be. This common refrain captures three basic sides of Brazilian identity: a sense of tremendous potential; anxiety about the country's problems, particularly the problem of deep social inequality; and a sense that Brazil is in process—that change is constant. This book focuses on those challenges, examining patterns of change and continuity in the twentieth century. The contributors to this volume have all been involved in Brazil's transition to democracy, either in policy making or in policy analysis. They represent an intellectual cross-section of Brazilian governance stretching from the first civilian government since military rule to the administration of President Luiz Inácio Lula da Silva. They reflect an emerging consensus in diagnosing and defining potential solutions for Brazilian problems of economic, regional, and racial integration. This consensus is particularly remarkable because it spans the center-right governments of Sarney and Collor, the social democratic Cardoso government, and the leftist Lula government, despite a culture of intense political competition.

Because of their leading academic and policy roles, there is no better group of observers than the contributors to this volume to comment on Brazil's post-dictatorship political consensus and on the unfinished challenge of unraveling the country's inequalities. The authors offer a range of interpretations of Brazil's potential, of its patterns of social exclusion, and of the means to manage the country's transformation. These interpretations are revealing both because of the picture they draw of twentieth-century Brazil and because of the types of understanding they show about governance and public policy going into the twenty-first century.

Brazil faces an ongoing transition to democracy. Democratization does not mean simply that the generals have returned to the barracks and that civilian leaders have been elected. It also means that a society has been created in which rights are equally shared and in which all members of the society share an active responsibility for the functioning of public institutions. Enduring poverty, wide-spread violence (particularly directed at the poor), and the persistence of informal work arrangements (over half of Brazilian workers are in the informal sector, which includes street vendors and day laborers) are the major challenges in Brazil's redemocratization.

Two of the ways in which Brazil is different from the United States stand out in this book. First, scholars and intellectuals play a much more prominent role in public policy, moving between university and government posts. Second, even those Brazilians most committed to free markets and to a limited role for the government believe that the state should play a strong (and sometimes a leading) role in mediating desirable social and economic goals. Nearly all the contributors to this volume have held senior positions in government. Four have been cabinet ministers; three have been federal institute or agency directors; one has been a governor and later a presidential candidate; several have been state secretaries; and several have held senior positions at the United Nations or in nongovernmental organizations. All emphasize the role of the state in their interpretations of problems and their analyses of solutions.

The theme of this book is that Brazil has experienced significant changes in the twentieth century (involving industrialization, urbanization, the integration of previously isolated regions, and patterns of demographic change dominated by population movements) but also confronts historical continuity in the form of trenchant social inequalities. These inequalities are rooted in an arcane system of rural land tenure and production, in development policies that have privileged increases in production rather than distribution, in the patterns of dependent integration into the world economy, and in state planning that has focused on long-term change rather than on immediate social needs. Given the involvement of many of the contributors in either administering public policy or formulating the intellectual framework for redemocratization since military rule ended in 1985, beyond their scholarly merit, the essays in this volume offer considerable insight into the paradigms of governance and policy making in contemporary Brazil.

The authors promote a reading of Brazilian society and of the role of public policy that incorporates a critique of the neoliberal economic policies of the 1980s and 1990s, and they assert a "neodevelopmentalist" vision defending the idea that the state should be active in managing patterns of economic growth with a mind to engineering greater social inclusion. This vision balances the neoliberal perception that the country needs to develop greater productivity and global economic integration with the developmentalist notion that state planning should shape the nation's direction. This postneoliberal critique frames 1980s and 1990s neoliberalism not as a definitive step away from Brazil's historical circumstances of mixed development and large gaps in income distribution but as another moment in the conversation about Brazil's development. For the authors here, neoliberalism is a moment whose paradigms share space with both the goals and the tools of developmental nationalism. In his essay on globalization in this volume, Gilberto Dupas expresses this idea in the following terms: "As we can see, it is essential that strategies for national growth contain redistributive policies that address the chronic problems of wealth concentration and poverty. . . . It is essential that Brazil create conditions under which economic growth results in real improvement in distribution of wealth and breaks historical patterns."

This volume was published in Brazil at the end of the two terms of Fernando Henrique Cardoso's centrist Social Democratic presidency (1995–2002), a period when the visions articulated in these essays became the foundations of Brazilian federal policies. Since its publication, the leftist opposition Workers' Party leader Lula (2003–) has succeeded Cardoso. Over its two terms, Lula's government has continued many of the economic, social, and developmental policies of its predecessor. Here lies the significance of the essays contained in this book: the ideas expressed reflect the emerging consensus among political groups about the paradigms of governance, economic, and social policy.

Brazil's Twentieth Century

During the long twentieth century, Brazil had six constitutions (1891, 1934, 1937, 1946, 1967, and 1988). This number illustrates several aspects of the country's experience: Almost all these constitutions were enacted following abrupt regime changes, signaling the political turbulence of the century. The constitutions reflected cycles of political centralization and decentralization, authoritarianism and democracy. They also reflected widening social goals. In 1934, for instance, women gained the right to vote, workers gained a labor code, and the constitution mandated public expenditure on education.

At the beginning of Brazil's twentieth century, coffee was king. The country was predominantly rural, and in the countryside, land was concentrated in the hands of large landowners rather than small farmers. Cities were predominantly commercial and administrative centers with little manufacturing. Coffee exports paid for the importation of manufactured goods. Not only was Brazil the world's largest coffee producer, but if its states were independent countries, five southeastern Brazilian states, led by São Paulo, would have been the top five coffee exporters in the world. Export production structured the patterns of wealth and power, and the planter families of the Southeast concentrated both. The 1891 constitution, modeled on European and U.S. political liberalism, decentralized power into the hands of regional oligarchs. The Northeast and West of Brazil stagnated economically. Though slavery ended in 1888, former slaves and their descendants had little access to land, education, or capital. New immigrants to Brazil's South and Southeast, coming mostly from the Mediterranean but also emigrating in significant numbers from Japan and central and eastern Europe, found better terms for work and improved chances for mobility than those experienced by Brazilians of color.

During the first decades of the twentieth century, conditions combined to stimulate the growth of manufacturing. These included the concentration of capital from coffee exports, the need to substitute imports during World War I, and the growth of the urban (particularly immigrant) labor force. The Depression and World War II accelerated import-substitution industrialization, which gained a powerful boost when the Brazilian government negotiated a wartime military alliance with the United States in exchange for the construction of a vertically integrated steel production complex in southeastern Brazil. By the 1950s, economic planning had evolved from its origins in schemes to boost the international price of coffee into complex schemes to promote industrialization through both state ownership and investment, as well as the attraction of multinational companies.

Growing political pressure, particularly from groups previously excluded from the political process, accompanied the growing state intervention in the economy. At the beginning of the century, a single political party, the Republican Party, controlled all levels of government. Suffrage was limited, political bosses fixed elections, and São Paulo dominated presidential politics. The tightly restricted system channeled discontent into protests like urban strikes, riots, and rural uprisings. By the 1920s, discontent spread to the officer corps of the military, which embraced nationalist critiques of the regime that suggested that Brazil was falling behind industrial countries, was unable to defend itself militarily, and lacked internal political, social, and economic cohesion. Urban workers, regional oligarchs shut out of power by the ascendant São Paulo planter class, and nationalist intellectuals dissatisfied with laissez-faire liberalism joined forces to challenge the outcome of the 1930 presidential election. Their movement culminated in a military coup that installed Getúlio Vargas as president.

During Vargas's first years in power, a new constitution was drafted that included many of the social and political reforms sought by politically excluded groups. It restricted Vargas's term in office, but he evaded this restriction by replacing his own government, promulgating a new authoritarian constitution modeled on Fascist regimes in Europe, and ruling by decree. The military supported his 1937 self-coup but deposed him in 1945. The 1946 constitution returned to the framework enacted in 1934, opening a window of democratic politics colored by sometimes violent political confrontations. This window was closed by a military coup in 1964.

Vargas returned to the presidency in 1950, elected with the support of a workers' party he had organized in the 1940s. Governing as a populist nationalist, he generated resentment within conservative groups and the military, which tried to force him from office in 1954. He resisted by committing suicide, generating widespread popular hostility toward his political opponents, which permitted the election of a political protégé, Juscelino Kubitschek, as president in 1955. Kubitschek was the last popularly elected president to serve a constitutional term in office until Cardoso was elected in 1994. Kubitschek responded to the increasingly confrontational Brazilian political environment by constructing a new national capital in the center of the country. The construction of Brasília created jobs, built infrastructure, stimulated the economy, and placated the military. It also increased Brazil's debt and spurred inflation.

By the 1960s, Brazil looked very different than it had at the beginning of the century. Each of its two largest cities, São Paulo and Rio de Janeiro, had over 3 million inhabitants. Cars, trucks, and buses rolled off Brazilian assembly lines. Within another decade, manufactured goods would become Brazil's major export. Roads, electricity, and telephone lines stretched through the once sparsely populated interior. Cities boasted growing networks of public schools, hospitals, and clinics. Still, the country faced a deep political crisis: debt and inflation had become politically unmanageable, and the political Right mistrusted those politicians whose populist rhetoric and practices made them best able to gain votes. In 1961, after eight months in office, President Jânio Quadros abruptly resigned. Vice President João Goulart succeeded him despite objections by the military, which believed his ties to workers made him a Communist. After supporting organizations of rural workers and a strike by navy sailors, Goulart was overthrown by the military.

The generals who seized power in 1964 were divided. Moderates believed their role should be the same as it was in 1889, 1930, 1937, 1945, and almost in 1954: to act as a mediating force that would execute a transfer of power from one political group to another. Hard-liners believed that the military was apolitical and should govern in the national interest. Tension between these groups maintained a political inertia that kept the military in power until 1985. The 1967 constitution served military governance by giving the armed forces authority over the electoral process, over so-called national security crimes, and over a national congress whose powers were limited. The military regime relied on widespread torture, detention, and harassment of political opponents. The military, police, and paramilitary death squads were responsible for hundreds of disappearances. Several of the authors in this collection were victims of detention or harassment, and several went into exile.

The military regime presided over an "economic miracle" in which the Brazilian economy grew at an average annual rate of 11 percent from 1968 to 1973. But the regime also borrowed heavily to support economic development and to offset the cost of oil imports during the 1973 and 1979 oil crises. By 1980, Brazil faced the largest foreign debt in the developing world, and the combination of rising interest rates and global recession plunged the country into a protracted economic crisis. Between 1981 and 1983, the Brazilian economy actually contracted at a rate of 2 percent per year.

Since much of the military regime's initial public support came from the credit it received for Brazil's economic performance, the financial crises of the late 1970s and 1980s helped shape the country's return to civilian rule. In 1985, the last general to be indirectly elected president, João Baptista Figueiredo (1979–85), handed power to an indirectly elected civilian president, José Sarney (1985–90). Brazil's transition to democracy was hampered by economic instability and high inflation. Between 1985 and 1994, inflation exceeded 3,000 percent per year, and political and economic difficulties caused several currency stabilization plans to fail. Luiz Carlos Bresser Pereira, a contributor to this volume, authored one of the plans to combat hyperinflation during the Sarney presidency. Inflation was finally controlled in 1994 with the Real Plan authored by Cardoso. The success of the plan helped elect Cardoso president in 1994.

In the 1990s, Brazil's economy was opened by reforms enacted by President Fernando Collor (elected in 1989 and impeached in a corruption scandal in 1992) and continued by his successors, Itamar Franco (1992–94) and Cardoso. These reforms extinguished the bureaucracies discussed in this volume by Afrânio

Garcia and Moacir Palmeira, privatized state-owned companies and utilities, and reduced barriers to imported goods. These neoliberal reforms helped sustain Brazil's currency stability but failed to stimulate economic growth, especially because cheaper imports stressed Brazilian industrial production. And even after the reduction in state ownership of industry, the Brazilian government was still intensely involved in the economy.

Brazil's current constitution, ratified in 1988, reacted to the military regime's repressive centralization by broadly, and sometimes very specifically, defining and defending civil rights. The new constitution spells out minority rights, such as the land rights of indigenous peoples and communities formed by the descendants of runaway slaves. It also guarantees human rights, such as the right of imprisoned nursing mothers to breastfeed their infants. A high level of social violence endures in Brazil, particularly directed at the poor and often including action by police, illustrating the limits on the rights defined in the new constitution.

At the end of the twentieth century, Brazil was characterized by remarkable continuities amid its dramatic changes. São Paulo, which for a half century had been Brazil's largest city, had over 20 million inhabitants. Rio de Janeiro had ceased to be the capital and Brazil's largest city but still had world-famous beaches and a population of just over 10 million inhabitants. Migrations from the Northeast to the Southeast and into the Amazonian region have swelled cities and driven expanding western and northern agricultural frontiers. Brazil exports jet aircraft but struggles to maintain the capital flows that allow it to sustain its debt obligations. Brazil avoided segregation and widespread racial violence, even to the point of celebrating the idea that it was a racial democracy, free from intolerance. Yet racial inequalities in Brazil remain as deep as in any other country that once relied on African slaves. The dynamics of redemocratization have spurred a new consciousness about racial inequality that has led to the creation of quota and affirmative action programs in education and government hiring.

In 2002, the political, economic, and intellectual consensus that emerged after the dictatorship was considerably—and surprisingly—reinforced by the election of Lula. The Workers' Party (Partido dos Trabalhadores, PT) that Lula helped found as a São Paulo metalworker in the 1970s sustained opposition to both the military regime and the civilian governments that followed it. But, to the frustration of many of the longest-standing members of the party, the PT government largely has continued the policies of its predecessors, especially in the area of economic policy. As Paulo Sérgio Pinheiro explains in this volume, "Radical reformism ceases to exist the instant that these parties shift from opposition to government." Indeed, some leading members of the PT left the party both because of the centrist policies it pursued in government and because of a series of corruption scandals involving congressional vote buying. One of the contributors to this volume, Cristovam Buarque, was a PT governor of Brasília in the 1990s and the minister of education in the first Lula government but left the party and ran as an opposition presidential candidate in 2006.

Brazil: A Century of Change and Brazil's Century of Changes

This book opens with a statistical portrait to help readers appreciate the magnitude of demographic change that took place in the twentieth century. One of the two non-Brazilian contributors to this volume, Hervé Thery, profiles the intense movement of peoples within this country of continental proportion — the largest population flow within Latin America in its history. This movement was induced both by the dramatic population explosion of the middle decades of the century, based on high birth rates and longer life expectancies, and by the deep disparities of opportunity between North and South and between the countryside and cities. Thery also helps readers get a broad sense of Brazil by the numbers, presenting social indicators about race mixture, television ownership, education rates, and patterns of economic growth.

At the beginning of the century, Brazil was predominantly rural. Over continental expanses of farmland, patterns of land concentration and rural labor inherited from slavery and from Portugal's colonial settlement continued to shape the productive and social order of the countryside. Afrânio Garcia and Moacir Palmeira discuss the systems of production, patterns of social inequality, and sets of values that shaped rural Brazil. Their chapter frames the basic dynamics of continuity and change that characterized twentieth-century Brazil. Rural production was transformed over the century, but this only reshaped rather than diminished inequalities. Garcia and Palmeira trace the evolution of the plantation system under the state policies created during the Vargas era to combat the effects of the Great Depression. These policies, including the creation of state institutes intended to protect agricultural production and exports, helped large planters hold on to their land. A rural labor code also transformed seigneurial relations by requiring that rural workers be paid cash wages for their work. In the balance, state policy preserved the arcane land tenure structure that concentrated land in the hands of established and capitalized planters at the same time that it created a more fluid labor force. The outcome was widespread rural to urban migration and rural poverty.

Agricultural policy reflected broader trends in the expansion of the Brazilian state and its involvement in the economy and production. Paulo Singer examines the cycles between free-market economic liberalism and state intervention, as well as the tension between internal and external markets. Singer suggests that prior to the Vargas era, Brazilian production was capital extensive rather than intensive, meaning that economic development was based on a large number of small, lightly capitalized producers. After 1930, state planners began to defy the notion of a free market, embracing job creation and business development programs and protections. Like Garcia and Palmeira, Singer argues that the creation of state institutes intended to protect agricultural producers reinforced inequitable rural power structures. Singer believes intervention in industry and agriculture was beneficial to Brazil because it helped stimulate industrialization. The growth of Brazil's automotive industry is one example of this success.

Brazilian foreign policy has frequently been harnessed to the goal of promoting Brazilian industry and agriculture. Celso Lafer, the Brazilian foreign minister at the time of this volume's publication in Brazil, traces the principles that guided Brazilian foreign relations in the twentieth century: the definition of Brazil's borders, the cultivation of a longstanding alliance with the United States, and the promotion of Brazilian exports. Lafer discusses the role of the Baron of Rio Branco, the foreign minister at the beginning of the century, in creating the patterns of modern Brazilian diplomacy, beginning with the negotiation of borders with Brazil's neighboring countries that has allowed for peaceful relations with its ten neighbors. Lafer also examines the politics of cultivating a special relationship with the United States as a way of offsetting Brazil's lack of diplomatic leverage in relation to more developed nations. For instance, Brazil's diplomatic relations with the rest of Latin America have been largely negotiated through Washington. During the second half of the century, the Brazilian foreign ministry also aimed to build autonomy from Cold War pressures and to build markets for Brazilian goods. Lafer's chapter offers a good sense of the neodevelopmentalist tone of the volume, suggesting that "in a country with Brazil's characteristics, development will not result automatically from just the right combination of fiscal, monetary, and exchange policies. . . . Development requires a broad array of public policies that are congruent and compatible with the broad macroeconomic balances that ensure currency stability, reduce inequality, and drive national development."

Renato Ortiz examines Brazilian culture, focusing on such media as books, periodicals, radio, cinema, and television. This is one of the areas of greatest change, starting from limited means of cultural production at the beginning of the century, constrained by geographic isolation, poverty, and high levels of illiteracy. But widening education, state policies beginning in the Vargas era that promoted a unified national identity, and the spread of radio, cinema, and, later, television expanded the possibilities for national cultural and artistic production. Ortiz suggests that while the Vargas regime failed to build a civic identity through new media, it succeeded in promoting a Brazilianness rooted in carnival, samba, and soccer.

Following the chapters that trace the economic, social, and cultural landscape of Brazil, several authors look more closely at politics and public policy. Luiz Carlos Bresser Pereira, for instance, examines the transition in Brazil from a paternalist administrative culture inherited from the Portuguese to the professional bureaucratic culture that took root in the Vargas era. Bresser Pereira is a particularly appropriate author for this discussion because of the federal and state ministerial positions he has held since the 1980s. He was the architect of one of the economic plans that attempted to curb the runaway inflation of the 1980s.

Paulo Sérgio Pinheiro, one of the volume's editors, looks at Brazil's recurring authoritarian streak. He suggests that the long periods of authoritarian rule, such as the first Vargas regime and the military dictatorship (together spanning over a third of the century), have left vestiges that have constrained Brazil's democratic intervals. As a result, democratic opposition movements have failed to carry out far-reaching reforms in the nature of government and society that would be capable of consolidating Brazilian democracy. Pinheiro examines the inability of democratic governments to extend effective civil rights to the entirety of Brazil's population. In doing so, he adds a crucial political rights dimension to the discussions about enduring social inequality, which other contributors to the volume also stress.

Aspásia Camargo examines the cycles of political centralization and decentralization that have characterized Brazilian history. Camargo suggests that the political and constitutional framework in place since the end of military rule has created, for the first time, the conditions for grassroots political democracy. She suggests that past periods of decentralization have cast power into the hands of rural oligarchs and that past periods of political centralization have replaced the power of oligarchs with that of an authoritarian state. By contrast, the political framework defined by the 1988 constitution shifted considerable political power

to municipal governments, where decision making can be most clearly account-
able.

The chapters on politics and policy are followed by essays that focus on region
and demographics. José Seixas Lourenço discusses the economic, environmental,
and demographic issues of the Amazonian region, focusing on cycles of production such as the rubber boom of the first decades of the century, the road building and expansion of agriculture during the middle of the century, the creation
of an industrial park and free trade zone in the river port city of Manaus during
the military regime, and the efforts to develop ecologically sustainable projects
in conjunction with global environmental protection initiatives at the end of the
century. Lourenço argues that cycles of economic production have not developed
or sustained the employment base necessary to support the region's population
and asks whether current economic conditions, framed by the Kyoto Protocol,
can change this pattern through reforestation and sustainability projects.

Cristovam Buarque's chapter on Brazil's Northeast builds on the commonly
held vision of the region as impoverished and underdeveloped, suggesting that
ill-conceived development projects, as well as intensive patterns of northeastern
emigration to other regions of the country have made "the northeast" into a national rather than a regional condition. In this analysis, schemes to develop the
Northeast failed because they were inconsistent and badly managed and because
they worked within a national policy framework that favored the consumer-
driven industrialization of southeastern Brazil. Buarque argues that the problems that the Northeast symbolizes (faulty distribution of income and wealth,
poverty, poor education and health) are ultimately national issues that need to
be solved with national policies. These problems, according to Buarque, should
be addressed through a "feminization" of social policy, meaning that alongside
long-range planning for development, short-term, outcome-driven social welfare
projects need to be undertaken. An example of this type of policy was developed
by Buarque when he was governor of the Federal District in the 1990s: Bolsa Escola, a program that gives poor families a financial supplement for keeping their
children in school.

The last four chapters of this volume turn their sights on Brazil's future. The
aptly titled "When the Future Arrives" was written by Celso Furtado, the dean
of Brazilian developmental nationalism. Furtado served as the federal minister
of planning prior to the military regime and the minister of culture in the first
government after military rule. Furtado reflects on Brazil's national development
projects and policies used to combat inflation. He argues that anti-inflation pro-

grams have focused exclusively on the monetary aspect of inflation control, neglecting the social costs of both inflation and inflation-fighting measures. As a result, Furtado notes, both inflation and the tools to combat it have reinforced social inequality. He suggests that future Brazilian economic policy making needs to weigh the social costs of free-market globalization against the legacy of inequality of past experiences with state economic policy making.

Gilberto Dupas focuses on globalization and its implications for Brazil. Dupas discusses the consequences of Brazil's integration into global markets by both promoting exports and making the country more open to imports. These outcomes include greater vulnerability to the speculative entry and exit of capital, a greater presence of multinational corporations (particularly in ownership of privatized industries and utilities), high interest rates (upward of 20 percent), and a significant gap in the cost of capital inside and outside Brazil. The cost of a loan for a Brazilian national company is significantly higher than the cost of a loan obtained abroad by a multinational company, placing national companies at a competitive disadvantage.

Jorge Wilheim, one of the editors of the volume, examines the end-of-the-century growth of cities in the frontier areas of western Brazil. Whereas Brazilian cities have historically hugged the coast, migration to western Brazil and the expansion of export agriculture, particularly of soybean production, have driven the explosive growth of previously small cities in Brazil's West. These cities have grown as transportation hubs, production sites, and commercial centers, dramatically shifting Brazil's demographic and economic landscape. Wilheim suggests that the growth of these cities has been less regulated and more predatory than that of the established cities of coastal and southeastern Brazil, making them into "frontier metropolises."

The volume closes with an essay by volume coeditor Ignacy Sachs, the other non-Brazilian contributor, who asks where Brazil is headed. Sachs reflects on the meaning of unequal development in Brazil, a country that experienced fantastic growth and positive change in the twentieth century without alleviating the serious problems of exclusion it has faced for centuries. For Sachs, part of the problem is an unwillingness to redistribute income and wealth, and the solution does not lie in the traditional invocation of the need for economic growth, which has stagnated for over twenty years. Sachs argues that economic growth is insufficient to alleviate unemployment and underemployment. Instead, he argues, the solution lies in a comprehensive land reform based not only on the redistribution of farmland but on the preparation of technically trained, market-integrated small farmers. This solution relies on the redistribution of land and the development of technical education and infrastructure in the countryside, and it would result in gains of employment and social welfare.

Brazil: A Century of Change is an opportunity to reflect on Brazil's twentieth century and to understand the way scholars and policy makers of the century's end understand Brazil's challenges. The authors of this volume reflect a remarkable consensus in Brazilian thought about the complexity and endurance of social inequality. Whether this legacy can be undone is now a question for the twenty-first century.

Translator's Note

"Language is etiquette," writes Brazilian historian Emília Viotti da Costa in her preface to *The Brazilian Empire: Myths and Histories* (UNC Press, 1985), which she herself translated into English from the Portuguese original. I have learned from her not only in resolving dilemmas of word choice and disciplinary discursive traditions but also in converting the rhetorical and stylistic features typical of Brazilian expository prose into something that U.S. readers would find comfortable and familiar. The work of the translator is always one of editing, re-creating, and inventing, though the degree of intervention may vary. This anthology presented some of the usual challenges of translating Brazilian academic prose: straightening the syntax, breaking up lengthy sentences with embedded verbal phrases, and finding equivalents for or deleting some of the rhetorical mannerisms common in this expository tradition. In the case of this collection, though, the task was daunting because the authors and their work are broadly known, and in some cases their writing has already been translated into English. The essays speak with such scholarly authority and practical experience that I wanted their voices to transpire. At the same time, the most important goal was to create a harmonious and readable collection of synthetic scholarly essays that a U.S. public with limited familiarity with Brazil could readily use and enjoy.

The constituent essays, almost all written by Brazilians, come from a range of scholarly fields. They reveal disciplinary and national traditions of discourse that reflect both their intellectual lineages and their approaches to the study of society on Brazil. The challenge has been to enhance intelligibility and legibility without sacrificing too much subtlety. This really entails two sorts of interventions. The first is to reflect the theoretical framework of the essay, whether the roots are in Marx or Weber, for example, without succumbing to jargon that would be needlessly obscure or pedantic for the U.S. reader. As an example, I have rejected the word "conjuncture" (*conjuntura*) because it is too limited in English currency. At the same time, I have tried to be faithful to the Weberian discourse of Luiz Carlos Bresser Pereira's chapter, beginning with the term "managerial state." Because of recent critiques of political liberalism, notably Paul Edward Gottfried's *After Liberalism: Mass Democracy in the Managerial State* (Princeton University Press, 1999), "managerial" has acquired a negative connotation and, I suspect, a new denotation as a form of mannerist liberalism. The reader should thus understand this term in its earlier, descriptive sense, unburdened by value judgments. I have also chosen to keep the usual English translation of Weber's *Stand* as "status group" since this term is more precise than "group," has a different meaning than the broader "class," and is not connotatively bound to the Middle Ages like the word "estate."

The second sort of intervention is to elucidate details of the Brazilian context that the original essay may have taken as general knowledge. Thus I have frequently made interpolations in the original texts—rearrangements and substitutions for the sake of the readership. I have added contextual information either in the running text or in notes for the sake of the U.S. public. Such additions are meant to illuminate, not change, the original essays, and, of course, any errors in these are mine and not the editors' or authors'.

I have usually opted for a common English expression over a Brazilian term, even if the latter is justified by the practice of Brazilian studies. Where the original Portuguese word or phrase presents difficulties in translation or where the original Portuguese wording is crucial, I have noted this, usually providing both an English gloss and the original Portuguese word or phrase. A few Portuguese terms are increasingly familiar to readers of English and are especially expressive. Thus the terms *favela* (the hillside urban shantytowns) and *telenovela* (the serial prime-time drama) are preferred in the running text.

Some recurring terms demand explanation at the outset. Specialists understand that, despite many similarities in our histories, race, ethnicity, and color are constructed and negotiated differently in Brazil and the United States. The anthologized essays and many works in the field of Brazilian studies address this matter. These differences in how Americans and Brazilians think about race, ethnicity, and color are inscribed, therefore, in words that superficially resemble each other across languages. In recent decades, the Brazilian census has used the following "color or race" categories: *branca* (white), *parda* (brown), *preta* (black), *amarela* (yellow, referring to persons mostly of Japanese, Chinese, and Korean descent), and *indígena* (Indian). In popular usage, *pardo* is usually replaced by *mulato* (mulatto) if the person is of mixed European and African descent, *caboclo* if the indigenous presence is noticeable, or *moreno* (more generically—and euphemistically—brown). Intellectuals will often substitute "mestizo" or "mixed" (*mestiço*) for *pardo*, *mulato*, *caboclo*, and *moreno*. I extend the use of the terms "mestizo" and "mixed" as defaults, avoiding "mulatto" as it is a pejorative and frequently misused term. The disadvantage of "mestizo," however, is its denotation in Spanish America, which tends to include an indigenous root. In fact, the term is vague in Brazil, though statistically, most mestizos there are partially African descended. Both historically and in recent designations of African-descended group and political identity, *negro* (Black) is used, though often ambiguously. *Negro* thus basically subsumes *preto* and *pardo* as shorthand for "African descended." In the translation, I use the English terms above, and because both *negro* and *preto* translate as "black," I use "Black" for the former and "black" for the latter.

One should be aware, though, that by using the English terms, I am not conflating U.S. and Brazilian color or race constructs. The readers should know, for example, that in Brazil "white" and "brown" cover a wide range of phenotypes and identifications, while "black" is a category shrinking proportionally. What lies behind this is a tripartite color distinction that underlies and even competes with biracial, "color blind," and multicolor formations in Brazil.

The terms *indígena* and *índio* appear as "Indian," following common current usage in the United States. These, like *negro* and *amarelo*, are pan-ethnic and even political constructions, with implications of descent as well. They refer to those who have chosen to identify primarily with indigenous Brazilian descent and who might credibly convince others to identify them as such based on cultural and residential criteria.

Some terms have conventional, accepted translations in the scholarly literature in Brazil. I use the standard translations of the Brazilian regions (see map). I have rendered *município* as "municipality," the basic unit of local government in the "trinitary" federation (see chapter 8). The reader should understand, though, that this is essentially the city or town and the suburban and rural areas under its control. This might be understood as a "township" in the American context, but such a translation would obscure its fundamental importance in the structure of government. To render *município* as "city" or "county" would be technically inaccurate.

Other conventional translations are for the categories within the Brazilian police system, which include several terms that are admittedly misleading. For example, the "Military Police" (Polícia Militar) is not the army's police force but rather a state-level law enforcement force, funded by the federal government but now run by the states. Its function resembles that of the U.S. National Guard in some respects. The state Civil Police (Polícia Civil) has an investigative role like that of the U.S. state bureaus of investigation. The functions of the Federal Police (Polícia Federal) resemble those of the Federal Bureau of Investigation. The federal and state enforcement forces receive the most attention in this anthology.

Renato Ortiz and some others use Celso Furtado's neologism *mundialização*, coined in the 1950s, in contrast to *globalização* (globalization), which other authors use. The latter term currently carries economic and ideological connotations that some would like to avoid in certain contexts. I have, however, rendered both as "globalization," hoping that readers will avail themselves of the fruitful debate on the denotations and connotations of the terms. Moreover, "globalization of culture" (cf. Ortiz's *mundialização de cultura*) is in general use in the literature in English.

It is my hope that the public will find the collection both informative and accessible and so increase its awareness about the United States' largest neighbor in the hemisphere and the world's fifth-largest nation in both area and population. If the reader finishes this book with a deeper appreciation of twentieth-century Brazil, I will have met my goal.

IGNACY SACHS, JORGE WILHEIM, & PAULO SÉRGIO PINHEIRO

Preface

At the beginning of the twenty-first century, Brazil looks quite different from how it did in 1900. The extraordinary course of its history in the last century reveals deep transformations. Not only has Brazil experienced modernization, changes in habits and customs, and growth in population (especially in cities) — phenomena shared with countries around the world — but Brazil's very character has changed. What was once an agrarian nation that was sparsely populated, technologically backward, and economically and politically dependent now has a large, diversified economy, an integrated industrial complex, a considerable network of world-class cities, and artistic and intellectual production of high quality. Nevertheless, Brazil is still dependent on a globalized world. Brazil's trajectory also shows that the modernization of the country's structural foundation remains unfinished and is subject to tensions. In addition to foreign and public debts, there also persists a social debt — an unnecessary and unjust inequality in income distribution. This collection of essays presents the dynamics of changes that have occurred and the main characteristics of these transformations — in other words, the courses of change in the twentieth century. The authors, who have expertise in a variety of fields, have undertaken to describe and analyze these changes from the points of view of their respective disciplines.

The end of the century also signals the beginning of a new one. It is a future that, for now, seems nebulous, one that we discuss using terms from the past, for the concepts that will yield new words and expressions have not yet been created. Thus the authors complement their portrayals of the past with visions of Brazil for the twenty-first century, trying to bring the future into better focus at a time when it seems uncertain. These are scenarios, speculations, and reflections that contain strategies and proposals from authors who do not stint in asserting ways to overcome the perplexities of the present, which are the results of past changes and current global conditions.

The contributors make their comments with optimism based on awareness of Brazil's immense resource potential, both natural and human. In the past, Brazil has had visionaries who have proposed concrete policy solutions. In light of this optimism about the future and confidence borne of the past, the present lack of a national plan that is original and appropriate for Brazil is striking. Such a plan would steer Brazil through the passages of historical transition, with its ruptures and possibilities, within a globalized world. It would take up again the essential theme of development, which, in Brazil, must be oriented toward economic "homogenization of society"—a task that can be neither avoided nor delayed. Brazil must overcome the economic injustice that is the crux of its relatively delayed development. Thus this collection of essays contributes to a needed accounting of Brazil at the end of the twentieth century and to a debate that may result in proposals for a more just future. These proposals must be more than mere extrapolations of the trajectories described, since the future is not a prisoner of the past. In the words of the late economist Celso Furtado, "Development is invention."

This book was made possible through assistance from the National Program for the Support of Culture (Programa Nacional de Apoio à Cultura, PRONAC), the Brazilian Ministry of Culture's Secretariat of Books and Reading (Secretaria do Livro e Leitura, Ministério da Cultura), and the Brazilian Postal and Telegraph Company (Empresa Brasileira de Correios e Telégrafos, ECT), for which we are very grateful. We wish to thank for their determined support all those who made this project a reality: Egydio Bianchi, ex-president of the ECT; Ambassador Sérgio Silva Amaral; Ambassador Sérgio Augusto de Abreu e Lima Florêncio Sobrinho; and Maria Teresa de Andrade Carvalho Salgado. We also thank Beatriz Stella de Azevedo Affonso and Tatiana Amendola Barbosa Lima Didion, dedicated assistants in coordinating the original project, and Fernando Faria, our support in the financial office.

BRAZIL

Brazil: States and Regions

HERVÉ THERY

A Cartographic and Statistical Portrait of Twentieth-Century Brazil

The word "transformation" covers a broad semantic field, with many synonyms and varied connotations, indicating a transition to another state, whether better or worse. Among the synonyms and near synonyms are alteration, apostasy, change, conversion, degeneration, degradation, development, deterioration, evolution, expansion, growth, improvement, metamorphosis, modification, mutation, perfection, progress, rectification, reinforcement, reform, renovation, revolution, and "twists and turns." Unfortunately, while this list may capture the sorts of transformations that Brazil experienced in the twentieth century (perhaps even including apostasy), it does little to illuminate the case of Brazil. Even so, resorting to this list can help characterize what happened in each area that this essay seeks to examine.

Looking back over the past century, we see that Brazil has progressed in most of these areas. To borrow Conservative English politician Harold Macmillan's slogan during the 1958 parliamentary elections (which was received with indignation by the Labourites, of course), "You never had it so good." That is, Brazil has never been so populous (growing twelvefold), so urbanized (now around 80 percent), or so wealthy (the per capita income now thirteen times what it was). Nevertheless, Brazil has probably never been so diverse, divided, or unequal as it is today.

The thread, therefore, of this brief cartographic and statistical introduction is to show the size and kinds of economic, demographic, and social transformations that have occurred in the country. Special emphasis is given to the transformations in territorial organization that reflect the deep change Brazil experienced

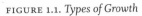

FIGURE 1.1. *Types of Growth*

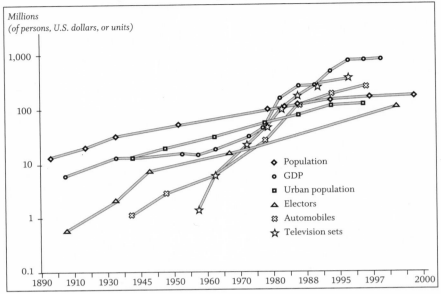

in growing from an "archipelago" of small, poorly connected agricultural regions into a nation. The national territory was unified by government actions and by the integrating forces of the domestic market. In size and economic importance, São Paulo has grown daily, and, at the same time, new foci of growth have appeared, a fact that could change the map of the future.

Types of Growth and Change

The most spectacular and easily measured evolution is in the population. Even so, economic growth has been even greater, as some indicators below will show.

Economic Growth

Figure 1.1 juxtaposes urban, electoral, and total population growth curves and some indicators of wealth (gross domestic product [GDP], number of automobiles, number of television sets). Using a semilogarithmic scale to transform a regular progression into a linear one, the graph shows that whereas the population grew nearly rectilinearly (with the number of urban dwellers and voters reducing the difference with the total), the GDP grew even more rapidly through-

TABLE 1.1. *Growth in Population, GDP, Income, and Equipment*

	Population (millions)		GDP (millions of US$)		Per Capita Income (US$)		Automobiles (thousands)		Television Sets (thousands)	
1890	14	*1*								
1900					380	*1*				
1910										
1920	30	*2*			400	*1*				
1930										
1940	41	*3*			900	*2*	120	*1*		
1950			19	*1*			280	*2*		
1956									141	*1*
1960	70	*5*			1,800	*5*	650	*5*	600	*4*
1966									2,300	*16*
1970	93	*7*	45	*2*			2,600	*22*	4,600	*33*
1976									11,600	*82*
1980	119	*9*	250	*13*	4,710	*12*	10,800	*90*	18,300	*130*
1986									26,500	*188*
1990	146	*10*	463	*20*			18,300	*153*		
1995									31,600	*224*
1996	157	*11*	774	*40*			26,200	*218*		
1997					5,030	*13*				
2000	166	*12*								

Source: Veja, 7 October 1998.
Note: The italicized numbers signify the rates of multiplication of the baseline figures in the columns to their left.

out the century, in spite of the ups and downs caused by crises. Closely following are the curves for the technology that most changed Brazilians' daily lives. As in other countries, the equipment diffusion curves approximate a logistical curve, with sharp inclines at the beginning, in the 1960s and 1970s, followed by flatter segments as market saturation began to occur. This stage seems to have begun in the 1990s, at least within the current pattern of income distribution. Taking 1940 and 1956 as the respective starting points for automobiles and television sets, the total number of automobiles and television sets grew more than 200-fold. Still, with 26 and 31 million units, these are far from representing the total number of

Brazilian families. If income were better distributed, there would still be a large margin of progression.

The economic trends of the twentieth century are treated by other authors in this volume. We limit ourselves here to tracing the profiles of some basic indicators: global and annual variations in GDP, and inflation. There is an undeniable tendency for continuous growth, accelerated in recent decades. Industrial countries had nearly thirty years of glory, the *trente glorieuses*, as the French called them, between 1945 and 1973. In the case of Brazil, the century-long growth trend was not altered by the "lost decade" of the 1980s or by the Collor years (1990–92; see chapter 3). Periodic crises could provisionally bend or even invert the curves, but the rise overall is strong, especially since the 1970s. At the same time, inflation has been a familiar presence in the Brazilian economic panorama for a long time.

Demographic Changes

Figures 1.3 and 1.4 show the twentieth-century changes in the Brazilian population.

Between the country's first census, held in 1872, and the most recent as of the time of this essay, the 1996 National Household Sample Survey (Pesquisa Nacional por Amostra de Domicílios, PNAD), the population grew nearly sixteen-fold, from 9.9 million to 157 million inhabitants. In the twentieth century alone, it grew nearly tenfold. The qualitative transformations of the population are as striking as the quantitative. As shown in figure 1.3, the demographic transition that the country experienced was from a pattern of high birthrates and high mortality to the current pattern of low birthrates and low mortality. The intermediate phase of low mortality and high birthrates caused the rapid population growth from 1940 to 1980. Simultaneously, ethnic composition, at least insofar as it can be seen through census questions about skin color, seems to have evolved in the direction of growing miscegenation, with an increase in the proportion of browns and a decrease in the proportions of both whites and blacks. One explanation could be that the number of marriages between whites and browns (measured by the skin color of the head of household and that of the spouse or partner when there is one) has been larger than any other combination. Or could it be the social acceptability of miscegenation that has grown, leading census interviewees to declare more easily what observation with the naked eye, to say nothing of DNA analysis, has already made very clear?

FIGURE 1.2. *Economic Evolution*

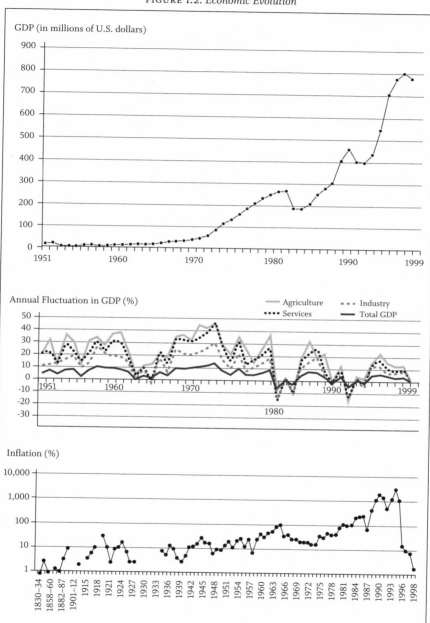

FIGURE 1.3. *Demographic Metamorphoses*

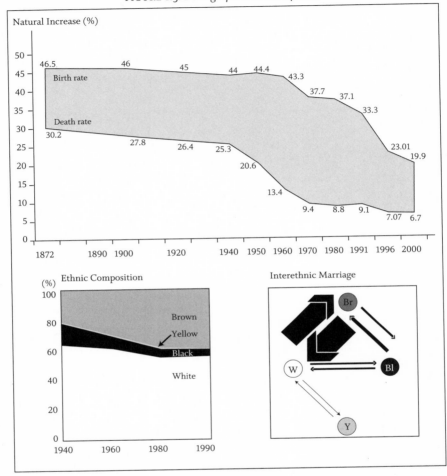

No phenomenon can compare with the wave of urbanization that inverted the proportion of Brazilians living in cities and in the country (figure 1.4). At the beginning of the twentieth century, less than one in five lived in the cities. São Paulo had only a little more than 30,000 inhabitants. Today, nearly four out of five Brazilians live in urban areas. This is a deep movement that has touched every region of the country. The urban and rural population curves crossed at different dates in the various regions, first in the Southeast, next in the South, and later in the Northeast; still in every region urban dwellers are the more numerous,

FIGURE 1.4. *Changes in the Urban and Rural Worlds*

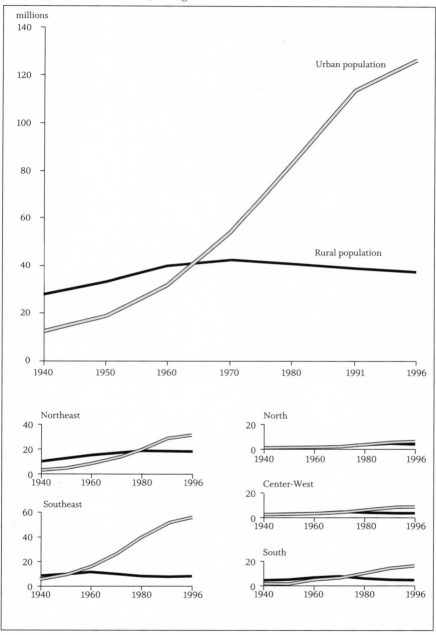

Source: Instituto Brasileiro de Geografia e Estatística.

TABLE 1.2. *Growth in Rates of Urbanization*

	1940	1960	1980	1991	1996
Brazil	31	45	68	75	78
North	28	38	52	58	62
Northeast	23	34	50	61	65
Southeast	39	57	83	88	89
South	28	37	62	74	77
Center-West	22	34	68	84	84

Source: Instituto Brasileiro de Geografia e Estatística.

TABLE 1.3. *Improvement in Social Indices*

	Life Expectancy (years)	Illiteracy (%)	Infant Mortality (per thousand)	Fertility Rate (children per family)
1940	43	56	158	6.1
1950	46	50	138	6.2
1960	52	40	118	6.3
1970	54	30	117	5.5
1980	60	25	88	4.4
1990	65	19	50	2.7
1996	67	17	41	2.1

Source: Instituto Brasileiro de Geografia e Estatística.

even in Amazonia (see chapter 9), which geographer Bertha Becker has called an "urbanized forest."

Without a doubt, the massive transfer of population to the cities was an important factor in the improvement in social indicators that Brazil has enjoyed since 1940 (table 1.3), although other causes contributed. In 1996, life expectancy was 56 percent higher, illiteracy was 70 percent lower, and infant mortality was 74 percent lower than fifty-six years earlier. The demographic structure of the country changed completely, as shown by the fertility rate, which, in the same period, went from 6.1 to 2.1 children per family. This has meant a transition from a population explosion to a situation in which, once the dynamic of growth inherited from prior periods of increase has passed, the population will remain level.

FIGURE 1.5. *Progression of State Population Growth, 1890–1980*

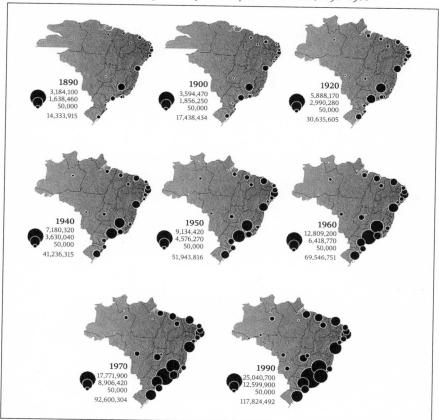

Territory

The overall configuration of the national territory did not change much in the twentieth century. At the end of the nineteenth century, Brazil already had approximately its current shape, although some adjustments would be made to the Amazonian borders and divisions among the states. Its content, however, has changed profoundly, revealing at the same time a concentration of population in the Southeast and South and the settlement of new lands—a unification of the national space that has transformed the country (figure 1.5).

Concentration of Population

The distribution of the rates of population increase among the states has changed radically. The population gains have also radically altered the states' shares of the total population. At the beginning of the twentieth century, the most populous state was Minas Gerais, followed by Bahia. Until 1930, the populations of the Northeast and the Southeast were balanced. In the second half of the century, the rapid natural growth of the Southeast was accompanied by a large migration of northeasterners into the region, attracted by the prospects of employment on the coffee plantations or in the factories of São Paulo or seduced by the mirage of the "big city." This migration pattern was repeated on a smaller scale in the states of Rio de Janeiro and Minas Gerais. These phenomena led to a new national population distribution in which the predominance of São Paulo and the neighboring states came to be a basic feature of Brazil's geography.

Nothing better reflects this change than the differing growth of state capitals throughout the century. Figure 1.6 shows the shift in the hierarchy and the size profiles of the cities. The white center denotes the main urban centers of 1872, dominated by Rio de Janeiro, then the federal capital, and then Salvador, Bahia. The darker cities are of more recent origin, including the new federal capital, Brasília; the capitals of former territories, Macapá in Amapá, Porto Velho in Rondônia, and Boa Vista in Roraima; and the capitals of the recently created states, Campo Grande in Mato Grosso do Sul and Palmas in Tocantins. Both the sizes of the circles, which are proportional to the population, and the concentric circles, indicating growth rates like tree rings, reveal the differences between the old capitals and the faster-growing cities. Among the earlier cities are the old capitals of Rio and Salvador, whose past glory has not been maintained. Even so, Salvador's growth rate has resumed recently, thanks in part to the petrochemical industry, surpassing Belo Horizonte as Brazil's third-largest city. Among the faster-growing cities, one must note those whose growth rates have been sustained throughout the century, especially São Paulo, and those whose growth has resumed more recently, such as Fortaleza and Manaus.

Expansion

Parallel with these movements of population concentration, there has been an opposite movement—that of territorial expansion, occupation, and incorporation. The old image of the Brazilian "archipelago" composed of "islands" formed

FIGURE 1.6. *Population Explosion of State Capitals, 1872–1996*

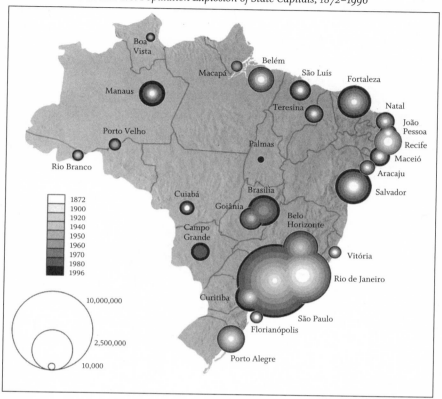

during Brazil's succession of economic cycles has been progressively substituted by that of a politically and economically integrated national territory (see chapter 2).

If we compare the situation in fifty-year periods (figure 1.7), we see that, initially, in the 1890s, there were only a few, isolated economic nuclei, centered on cities that had developed during the successive booms in sugar, gold, coffee, and rubber. In fact, the nation's economic space was organized in two separate blocs, the Northeast and the Southeast, connected mostly through coastal navigation. The major population movement was the emigration of northeasterners, driven from their homes by drought, into Amazonia, then in the middle of its rubber boom (see chapter 9). The coffee culture pioneer frontier was still embryonic, spreading in the Paraíba Valley (see chapter 2).

In the 1940s, the economic area that was truly integrated into the nation had

FIGURE 1.7. *Transformation of an Archipelago into a Continent*

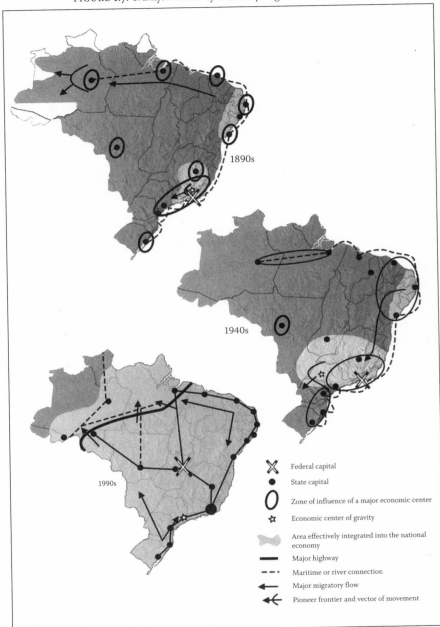

1890s

1940s

1990s

✗ Federal capital

● State capital

⬭ Zone of influence of a major economic center

☆ Economic center of gravity

Area effectively integrated into the national economy

— Major highway

--- Maritime or river connection

◄— Major migratory flow

◄◄— Pioneer frontier and vector of movement

expanded. The major pioneer frontier was no longer in Amazonia but in western São Paulo and northern Paraná, with the expansion of coffee culture. The main migratory flow brought northeasterners to the Southeast, fueling enormous urban growth.

In the 1990s, the economic area was coterminous with the borders of the nation, with the exception of upper Amazonia. The migratory flows were both regional and national. The national migration flows were in some cases centripetal, maintaining the traditional flows from the South and the Northeast to the Southeast, and in other cases centrifugal, such as southern migration to western Amazonia and northeastern migration to eastern Amazonia. The zones of influence of the main economic center, São Paulo, and of the national capital, Brasília, coincide in effect with the national borders and even go beyond, as into eastern Paraguay.

The highway network has been and continues to be one of the essential means of this national integration. Its recent development can be seen by comparing the two maps of figure 1.8. In 1965, only the state of São Paulo had a true network of paved roads. Aside from this, there was a partially paved coastal highway, built after the Second World War, and networks of unpaved highways in the South and Northeast. Several new highways converged in Brasília, linking the new capital, which was opened in 1960, to the big cities of the Southeast as well as to Belém and to Acre. By 1995, the situation had totally changed. Brazil had a network of paved highways that covered the country and was especially dense in the Southeast and Northeast. This network even included Amazonia, where various north-south corridors joined the older Trans-Amazon Highway.

Have Brazil's territorial integration and overall economic growth led to an overall improvement of living conditions and a reduction in regional inequality? Here, another source affords a partial answer, at least for the last twenty years of the century. The United Nations Development Programme (UNDP) publishes annually the human development index (HDI) for all of the countries of the world, calculated to take into account the elements that the gross national product does not, such as education and health. In September 1998, a similar study was published for all of Brazil's municipalities.[1] Figure 1.9, based on this synthetic index for 1970 and 1991 (the year of the most recent information available when the figure was created), shows undeniable progress. In 1970, the upper tier, above 0.65 on a scale of 0 to 1, included only Brasília and a few municipalities in Rio de Janeiro and São Paulo. By 1991, that tier included a large portion of the country.

FIGURE 1.8. *Expansion of the Highway Network*

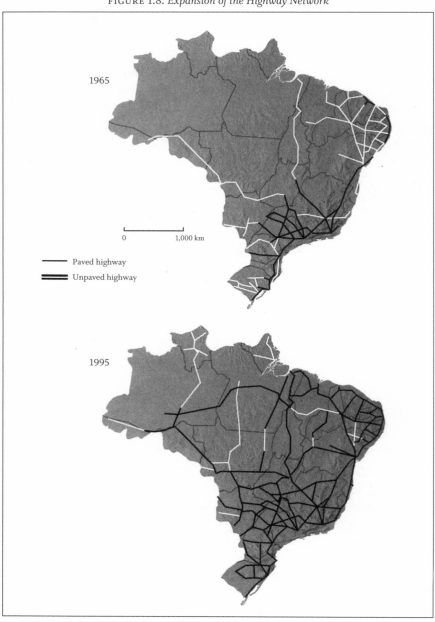

1965

0   1,000 km

——— Paved highway
▬▬▬ Unpaved highway

1995

Source: Quatro Rodas, *Guia rodoviário 1995* (São Paulo: Editora Abril, 1995), on the occasion of
Quatro Rodas magazine's thirtieth anniversary.

FIGURE 1.9. *Changes in the HDI, 1970–91*

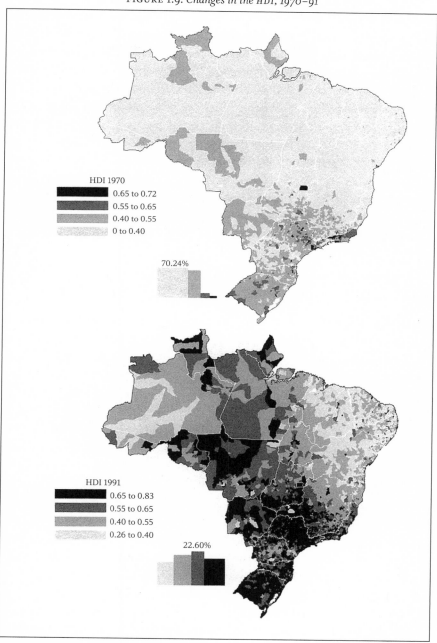

HDI 1970
- 0.65 to 0.72
- 0.55 to 0.65
- 0.40 to 0.55
- 0 to 0.40

70.24%

HDI 1991
- 0.65 to 0.83
- 0.55 to 0.65
- 0.40 to 0.55
- 0.26 to 0.40

22.60%

Source: United Nations Development Programme, 1995.

On the other hand, in 1991, the contrasts were stronger than in 1970. Upper Amazonia, the Northeast, and the north of Minas Gerais were clearly in the rear guard, while the Southeast, the South, Mato Grosso do Sul, southern Goiás, and the Federal District formed a solid bloc of high indices. The exception was Paraná, which in the 1980s suffered a large rural exodus because of frosts that hurt the coffee plantations. A good number of migrants moved to new lands in the Center-West and North (Mato Grosso, Rondônia, and southern Pará). The second map in figure 1.9 reflects this change, as these migrants brought with them their high HDIs. The maps of the breakdowns of these indices on which the synthetic maps are based detail this overall picture without changing it much. For example, life expectancies show both important overall progress and strong contrasts between, on the one hand, the Southeast and South and, on the other hand, the North and Center-West, where, once again, the pioneer zones along the Cuiabá–Porto Velho Highway (BR-364), fed by immigration from the South, stand out.

What Now?

By way of taking account of a century of transformations, we conclude with three images. The first, figure 1.10, underscores the predominance of the state of São Paulo in the Brazilian economy. In this three-dimensional representation of wealth generated, São Paulo literally stands out from the rest of the country, not only from the poorer regions of the North and Northeast but even from the South and the rest of the Southeast, which surround it but still lag behind (or, rather, below). Such dominance and its evolution appear in figure 1.11, which compares the areas of influence of the metropolises in 1971 and 1993.[2] While the areas of influence of all the other cities shrank, that of São Paulo grew considerably. It increased to include most of Amazonia and the Center-West, where it competes only with Goiânia, and even expanded into the Northeast by way of Maranhão.

The future, however, could look somewhat different: more diversified and with more centers. Figure 1.12 shows the "engines of future growth." While modern industry continues strong in São Paulo state, it is decentralized into the interior of the state and into the Mineiro Triangle of southwestern Minas Gerais. At the same time, there are factors that lead us to expect diversified growth in several other regions of the country, from the Center-West, in the wake of modern agriculture, to the Northeast, where irrigated fruit cultivation and tourism offer

FIGURE 1.10. GDP by State, 1996

Source: Confederação Nacional do Comércio, *Synthesis of the Brazilian Economy*.

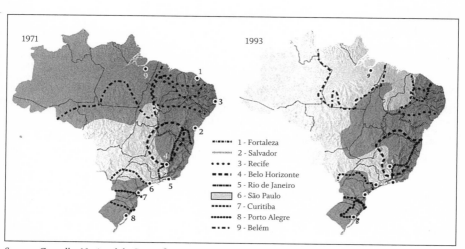

1971   1993

1 - Fortaleza
2 - Salvador
3 - Recife
4 - Belo Horizonte
5 - Rio de Janeiro
6 - São Paulo
7 - Curitiba
8 - Porto Alegre
9 - Belém

Sources: Conselho Nacional de Geografia, 1971; Instituto Brasileiro de Geografia e Estatística, 1993.

FIGURE 1.12. *Engines of Future Growth*

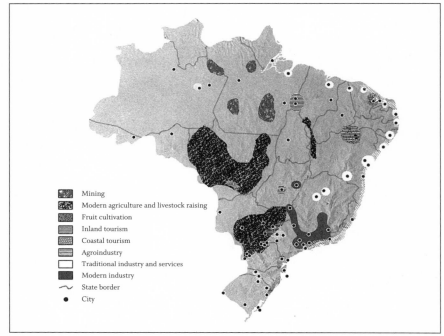

Source: *Brasil em ação*, 1998.

promises of revitalization. Most likely, Brazil has many other surprises for us in the new century.

Notes

This chapter was written in collaboration with Neli Aparecida de Mello.

1. *Índice de desenvolvimento humano* (CD-ROM) (Fundação João Pinheiro, 1998).

2. For the sake of comparison, the area of influence of Goiânia, which is not represented in the 1971 map, is also not included in the 1993 map.

Bibliography

Becker, Bertha, and Claudio Egler. *Brazil: A New Regional Power in the World Economy.* Cambridge: Cambridge University Press, 1992.

Instituto Brasileiro de Geografia e Estatística. *Divisão do Brasil em regiões funcionais urbanas.* Rio de Janeiro: Instituto Brasileiro de Geografia e Estatística, 1972.

Quatro Rodas. *Guia rodoviário 1995*. São Paulo: Editora Abril, 1995.

Rochefort, Michel. "Villes et organisation de l'espace au Brésil." In *La régionalisation de l'espace au Brésil*, 127–35. Paris: Centre National de la Recherche Scientifique, 1971.

Thery, Hervé. "Couleur de peau et revenus." In "Les inégalités socio-économique au Brésil: Cartographie de quelques indicateurs." *Cahiers du Brésil contemporain*, no. 37 (1999): 81–94.

———. "L'équipement des ménages." In "Les inégalités socio-économique au Brésil: Cartographie de quelques indicateurs." *Cahiers du Brésil contemporain*, no. 37 (1999): 47–57.

———. "Indice de développement humain (IDH)." In "Les inégalités socio-économique au Brésil: Cartographie de quelques indicateurs." *Cahiers du Brésil contemporain*, no. 37 (1999): 119–23. In collaboration with Neli Aparecida de Mello.

———. *Le Brésil*. Paris: Armand Colin, 2000.

2

AFRÂNIO GARCIA & MOACIR PALMEIRA

Traces of the Big House and the Slave Quarters: Social Transformation in Rural Brazil during the Twentieth Century

Rural Brazil changed profoundly in the course of the twentieth century. Yet these changes renewed the social hierarchy and inequality that have characterized the rural world since the beginning of colonization. Change has not been simply linear or mechanical. At the beginning of the twentieth century, land and social power were concentrated in the hands of the owners of large plantations devoted to crops bound for international markets, especially in Europe and the United States. Agricultural products such as coffee, sugarcane, cotton, rubber, cacao, and tobacco made up more than 85 percent of Brazilian exports, as they had since the first half of the nineteenth century (Eisenberg 1977, 31, table 1). Planters, sugar mill owners, and farmers recruited labor under various forms of personal domination to carry out the tasks of agricultural production (Palmeira 1971, 1976). This was the condition of sugar plantation dwellers (Sigaud 1980), coffee plantation tenant farmers (Martins 1979), and servants and ranch hands all over the country.

The plantation's activities dictated the appropriation of physical space. The rise of small farmers occurred only in areas peripheral to the large plantations (Heredia 1979; A. Garcia 1983) and in regions expressly set aside for European immigrants. These immigration flows were drawn to Brazil by policies that had both economic ends and the goal of promoting population "whitening," as seen in the Itajaí Valley in the state of Santa Catarina or in the highlands of the state of Rio Grande do Sul (Tavares dos Santos 1978).

The majority of Brazilians lived in the rural world. As late as 1940, 70 percent of Brazil's population was rural. Even so, the various regions of large farms were not interconnected in such a way as to constitute integrated economic circuits. To travel from the regions where coffee predominated, such as the states of São Paulo and Rio de Janeiro, to the cacao-producing areas of the state of Bahia or to the sugarcane areas of Pernambuco, one had to travel by ship along the coast. Thus Brazil's territory was segmented into different regions, each more centered on an exporting port than linked to each other by a networked transportation system. This gave rise to the image of the nation as an "archipelago" whose "islands" were the different agricultural and mining regions. The image of the archipelago contrasts with that of the same territory as an integrated "continent" after the establishment of industrial infrastructure between the 1930s and the 1980s (Thery 2000; see chapter 1).

By the end of the twentieth century, however, the population was concentrated in the cities. The second half of the century saw continuous migration from the country to the city. By 1980, nearly 70 percent of Brazil's population lived in urban areas; in 2000, only 22 percent resided in rural areas. As a result of accelerated industrialization between 1930 and 1980, the dynamic core of the economy, along with social, cultural, and political power, is now located in the large metropolises. This shift accompanied the restructuring of the state, the expansion of state intervention in the economy, the creation of more universities, the reorganization of basic education, and the rise of political parties and movements on a national scale. The forms of social life characteristic of the rural universe now find themselves responding increasingly to lifestyles, worldviews, decision processes, and labor modes developed and modified beyond their horizons. Thus it is no surprise that, at the turn of the millennium, there have been open disputes over the very meanings of "the future of the rural world" and "modernity" when Brazilians have reflected on the transformations of the countryside, especially the relationship between urban and rural worlds. Social transformations do not follow inexorable itineraries. There are alternative paths, as shown in recent debates about "family agriculture" versus "corporate agriculture" and about the growth of the "agroindustrial complex." In any case, it is important to note that today the "agricultural world" is no longer conceived as a cohesive whole, as monolithic throughout Brazil's vast territory. The image of unity of the agricultural world sought at the beginning of the twentieth century is cross-cut by actors from "family agriculture," "corporate agriculture," and so forth. This reveals a competition for land, for financial resources, for the workforce, and, ultimately, for the right to decide the future of relationships both within the rural world and between city and country.

We will examine these profound changes over this long period of time by dividing our analysis into three distinct periods. We first study the particular dynamic of the great traditional plantations, which was responsible for long-lived patterns of social life. We also consider the marginal role of the peasantry. Next we observe the different pathways of change seen in the course of the twentieth century. Finally, we examine the forms of competition, the debates, and the alternative plans for modernization of the countryside that currently frame perceptions about the future of the rural world.

Large Plantations and Small Farmers

The great coffee, sugarcane, cacao, and cotton plantations and the cattle ranches—often with roots in colonial Brazil—were the fundamental units of economic, social, cultural, and political processes at the beginning of the twentieth century. This does not mean that they can be thought of as "isolated rural communities," given that these groups of population arose to produce commodities of value to the international market. An image of the physical space in which the large plantations were established necessarily includes the coastal town where the port and, often, the administrative, religious, and cultural centers were based. This was the case in Recife and Goiânia for the sugarcane region of the Northeast (Eisenberg 1977), in Salvador for the Recôncavo region of Bahia (Mattoso 1992), in Rio de Janeiro for the coffee plantations of the Paraíba Valley (Stein 1957), and in Santos for the coffee plantations of São Paulo (Holloway 1968; Dean 1977), to mention only a few of the key import-export cities. In these centers were the large commercial houses, such as the coffee commission houses (casas-comissárias; Stein 1957; Holloway 1968) and sugar wholesalers (Eisenberg 1977). Here the most imposing churches were built and most of the religious institutions were established, especially for education. These ports were linked to intermediary towns by rivers, wagon roads, and trails wherever there were not yet railroads. For their part, these midsize urban communities were interconnected with vast numbers of small towns and villages. The rural universe, dominated by large plantations surrounded by numerous smaller farms, was, as a consequence, constantly in communication with an urban network that ensured the development of commercial activities in addition to serving as the pole of political, religious, and cultural activity.

The relation of the plantations to the web of cities that connected them to the ports was, therefore, an integral part of the conditions of existence for each large plantation. Thus changes in the transportations system, such as the establishment of the railway network at the end of the nineteenth century, made the expansion of the agricultural frontier possible and allowed for parts of the Atlantic Forest to be appropriated for new coffee estates. This completely transformed the competitive conditions between the "old" areas such as the Paraíba Valley (Stein 1957) and the new areas of the São Paulo Plateau (Monbeig 1952; Dean 1977; Silva 1976). Such changes in the commercial circuits not only altered the daily life of the large plantations and of the myriad of medium-size and small farms subordinate to them but also caused the decay of the network of towns that once had been the links to the port cities and administrative centers. José Bento Monteiro Lobato (1882–1948), a major author of fiction and nonfiction, owned a farm in São Paulo. He described the social climate of these "dead towns" after the dislocation of the "green wave" of coffee expansion into areas where there had been virgin forest. The system of relations that made existence on the large plantations viable presupposed that each unit, old or new, be linked to the ports and administrative centers more or less intensively depending on the condition of the international market in agricultural commodities.

Until the middle of the twentieth century, the large plantations were rather specific economic, social, cultural, and political units. From the economic point of view, these were the settings for the agricultural labor that combined cultivation of crops bound for export, such as coffee, sugarcane, cotton, and cacao, with crops intended mainly for the food supply of the proprietor's family as well as the families of the resident workers.[1] The latter cultivation included manioc, corn, and beans, as well as small livestock (poultry, hogs, sheep, and goats). Since the plantations were geared to producing agricultural goods bound for the long-distance market, they had facilities for processing the raw materials into the products to be sold. The sugar mills were run with animal power or water wheels. The sugar refineries that replaced the mills with large factories amid the cane fields entailed investments in such valuable materials and the acquisition of such broad knowledge and skills that they came to be early symbols of agroindustrial units and emblems of the power of the landowners. Such power is evidenced by the term *senhor de engenho*, which literally means "master of the mill" (Antonil 1711; Correia de Andrade 1964).[2]

Facilities requiring less capital and know-how, such as coffee-drying terraces, cotton gins, and sisal shredders, were also part of the plantations. Thus, since the earliest days of colonization, there existed a sort of integrated agroindustrial complex within sugarcane and coffee plantations, though these were quite different from the agroindustries that would emerge in the 1980s in the production of dairy, fruit pulp, poultry, and pork products. By the middle of the twentieth century, the association of agricultural and industrial capital came to predominate: whoever controlled the labor processes controlled both the agricultural and industrial spheres, and from this joint activity came their profits. Modern agroindustries such as those mentioned above, established at the time of Brazil's industrialization, entail the concentration of capital in an industrial firm that can create a dependable network of suppliers of agricultural goods within established parameters of quality (Wilkerson 1996). The industrial firm subordinates the agricultural entities to its demands but does not concentrate the agricultural labor process in its own hands. The term "agroindustry" therefore has one meaning when referring to the entities established beginning in the late nineteenth century, such as sugar factories located among the plantations, and another meaning when referring to the urban factories created since the end of the twentieth century, such as Parmalat in the dairy sector and Perdigão and Sadia in the meat sector.

The large plantation was, however, much more than just a basic unit in the agroindustrial process. It was also the basis of social life for the rural world in the first half of the twentieth century. The large estate was the place of residence of the large property owner—the "big house" (Freyre 1933). It was also the site of the homes of the resident workers (Palmeira 1976). The estate was where family life took place: procreation, births, marriages, and often burials. The chapels within the wealthiest big houses or on their grounds are reminders that religious practices grouped and ordered the estate's inhabitants. The religious practices of subalterns, such as the African descendants' Candomblé and Xangô (Bastide 1958) and the Protestantism of the European coffee workers (Davatz 1941), were targets of recrimination and censure when not performed under the strict watch of the landowners. The annual calendar was marked by feasts, such as those of Saint John's Day and Christmas, as well as the *botada* and *pejada* that signaled the start and end of the workday in the mills and plants. As social and cultural life were inscribed within the daily routine of the large estates, where almost everything took place under the watchful eye of the head of the big house, it is not surprising that these estates were also political centers—"electoral corrals," to use a term of the day. Accordingly, the resident laborers' votes followed the landowner's prescription and were seen as a mark of loyalty to the "boss," to whom the most essential elements of daily life were owed: the dwelling, the plot of land for foodstuffs, wood and water for domestic purposes, and support in times of illness and need. Thus the hierarchical social structure was inscribed in all planes of social life, from work to family and home, from festivities to religious and political practices. On the one hand, the landowner's extended family, as well as dependents through ties of friendship and godparentage, lived in the big house. On the other, the array of workers' families lived in small, miserable houses of wattle and daub. On the one hand were the endless fields planted in commercial crops under the control of the large landowner. On the other hand was the subsistence agriculture on small plots or between the rows of developing coffee fields. The hierarchy was evident even in posture and voice (Cunha 1902). The erect bodies of owners contrasted with the appearance of workers, bowed when standing or walking, crouched on their heels when resting. Owners shouted for dependents to carry out orders while workers dared not direct even a word to their superiors (Almeida 1976).

Observations recorded in the sociological and historical literature of the 1930s and early 1940s stress the basic character of social patterns inherited from the colonial slave-owning universe that imposed themselves on the country with the growth of urbanization and the acceleration of industrialization. Cultural critic Antônio Cândido described a trilogy of foundational works by three Brazilian sociologists and historians (1967). The first of these was Gilberto Freyre's *The Masters and the Slaves*.[3] Even in the title of his major work, Freyre suggested that the rural estate was a slave-based institution maintained after the abolition of slavery in 1888 and that the concentration of economic, religious, cultural, and political power in the hands of one person was the organizing principle of the social world re-created among the descendants of those masters and slaves, through a logic that presupposes complementarity and irreducible difference. The central argument of Freyre's book deals with sexuality in the slave-owning regime. White patriarchs yielded numerous offspring both through Catholic marriages with white wives and through various forms of amorous relations of varying degrees of stability with Black, Indian, and mestizo women. According to Freyre, miscegenation was related to the sociocultural matrix: the polygamy of the masters and the subordination of Catholic morality to the desires and interests of the slave owners. Freyre's exploration of the history of miscegenation and its positive role in Brazilian social formation broke with the scientific racism, biological eugenics, and cultural whitening valued in the elite discourse of the preceding decades. The rupture that this author introduced into the debates over the meaning of miscegenation in Brazilian society went only halfway, however. Descent from the same patriarch did not attribute to the children of different mothers the same legal or social stature. Even on the strictly emotional plane, this situation could heighten interpersonal conflicts rather than smooth them over, as Freyre repeatedly suggested. The study of actual estates in the Northeast, such as sugar plantations (Sigaud 1980) and factories (Leite Lopes 1976; M. F. Garcia 1977), shows that the uniqueness of the big house contrasted with the multiplicity of resident workers. The offspring of the slave quarters were frequently mestizo. It would be naive to think that a worker who happened to be a sibling on the father's side of a member of the big house's family could be that person's social equal in all respects. Freyre at times highlighted the violence inscribed in the patriarchal power of the slave master but at other times wrote about the attenuation of opposition between slaves and masters because of the sexual exchange. This ambivalence in his examination of the practice of miscegenation did not lead Freyre to deny the present-day perpetuation of the hierarchy of slavery's early days: his second volume, *The Mansions and the Shanties*, demonstrated how old social differences were re-created in urban frameworks.[4]

Alongside Freyre's *The Masters and the Slaves*, *The Roots of Brazil* by Sérgio Buarque de Holanda (1936) would come to influence a whole generation of intellectuals, according to Cândido. Buarque de Holanda also investigated the traces of the old hierarchy of the rural estate, based on the enslavement of the Black African population, in the private lives of his fellow Brazilians. Unlike Freyre, however, Buarque de Holanda was interested in how the hierarchy was projected onto public life and political behavior. He analyzed how this constituted an obstacle for a modern, democratic state. Buarque de Holanda's "cordial man" of Brazil was a slave to his passions, and thus he did not accept norms that transcended his desires. No modern political sphere can rest on this foundation. The Brazilian dilemma in building a state with a modern and democratic basis is the opposition between servants of freely contracted laws and servants of the individual desires of those who are accustomed to being served by slaves. Buarque de Holanda's contribution, however, was not limited to the analysis of the social origins of the elite Brazilian leadership's political ethos. It also included interesting analyses of the subordination of cities and towns to the countryside in the colonial era.

It was the rhythm of country life, the climatic seasons, and the fluctuations between prosperity and decline that made the cities pulse. The urbanization of the twentieth century that had begun to accelerate at the moment that Buarque de Holanda published his book gave the urban centers their own dynamic, driven by industrialization and the intensified development of systems of transportation and communication. These were independent of the rhythm and the pulse of agricultural activities. Since then, it is the urban activities that have tended to subordinate the agricultural activities. The growth of the Brazilian *urbs* came to reflect the social diversification that the country was experiencing. Such change was a necessary but not sufficient condition for the new political ethos of the rule of law to impose itself on the urban setting. Former slave owners, used to living like kings on their estates, had to accept the preeminence of transcendent norms that would be valid for all. Such was the dilemma of Brazilian society as it took root in modernity.

The third work in the classic trilogy that Cândido examined was Caio Prado Jr.'s *The Colonial Background of Modern Brazil*.[5] This book focused on the large rural estate as a basic unit of a *colonial* economy, whose dynamic was wholly governed by forces from the international centers that were the destinations of its commercial crops. For Prado, the construction of a *national* economy, in which domestic industries lead an entire national system of production, implied overcoming the main characteristics that the large estate had imprinted on the economy of the country. The urban world that was expanding and industrializing was the bearer of new potential, but its energy and direction depended on restructuring the way of operating that it had inherited from the agricultural world.

One can see, then, in the trilogy that Cândido highlighted that the legacy of rural social organization weighed heavily on the present, as much more than simply a tradition to be overcome. The very effort that these authors made in studying this tradition, both in its structural aspects and in its projections onto the psychology of every Brazilian, shows that they were convinced that the task of understanding the traditional rural world was an integral part of the effort to imagine new directions for the nation.

In-depth studies of the enormous price fluctuations from the end of the nineteenth century to the 1970s effectively demonstrate that the workings of the Brazilian plantation showed great flexibility in the face of such fluctuations (see Bacha 1992 for coffee and Eisenberg 1977 and Szmrecsanyi 1979 for sugar). It is in the very specificity of the traditional plantation's operational mechanisms that we find the basis of its plasticity, longevity, and strength (Palmeira 1971; Wolf and Mintz 1957). The first of its main characteristics was the form of labor recruitment and the wide array of practical arrangements that allowed the balancing of price drops and commercial crop sales. In fact, most labor on the plantation was provided by resident workers (see Palmeira 1976 for sugar and Martins 1979 and Stolcke 1976 for coffee). These forms of recruitment, established during the era of slavery (Correia de Andrade 1964; Eisenberg 1977; Davatz 1941), ensured the re-creation of the power of coffee and sugar plantation masters after abolition. The arrangement implied that there were contracts, that is, voluntary agreements between distinct people, but these individual contracts were instituted within lasting forms of submission of the worker's family to the wishes of the large property owner. By "requesting residence," a head of a household demonstrated to a plantation owner that he lacked the basic means to provide for his domestic group (Palmeira 1976). He neither owned land to work to provide subsistence nor had a house to shelter his dependents. Thus, by moving onto the estate, he contracted with the owner a moral debt whose value greatly exceeded the material worth of the necessities of life that he received from his new patron. He would receive a house for his family around which he would clear a compound where his wife would raise small animals, such as hogs and fowl. Some workers might plant fruit trees to better mark off their *sítio*, or small farm—a sign of confidence in and durability of the relationship with the boss. Each year, the worker would be allowed to clear small plots for planting. Here he would usually plant manioc, beans, and corn. He would have the use of water sources and the wood that he could collect on the property. He would have access to millhouses where he could turn his manioc into an edible product—varieties of "bitter" manioc must be processed to remove the toxic cyanide in them. He could also buy supplies at the plantation stores, where the credit for the debt was loaned as a form of payment for his work (Palmeira 1970; M. F. Garcia 1977). These "gifts" from the boss must have been a source of help and protection in times of difficulty, especially burials, illnesses, births, and disputes with persons outside the estate. They corresponded to various work obligations. These included the worker's labor in the commercial exploitation of the property, paid in salary calculated either by workday or by production (Sigaud 1977; A. Garcia 1980), and shares of production, as in partnerships in commercial crops such as cotton and coffee. There was also demand for labor to bring crops to market when the estate was the intermediary for leased or allotted farms. The worker also had to participate in building and repairing the estate infrastructure, for example dams, roads, and trails—work performed for free, as in the *cambão* of the northeastern coastal forest zone (Julião 1968). Finally, the resident worker was supposed to serve loyally in any combat in which the boss might be involved, especially in cases of family honor and political disputes.

These agreements between large landowners and heads of households who were resident workers affected a range of interpersonal relations that took the form of mutual give-and-take. It is a wonder that they did not become more codified, with the exception of the names of the types of labor provided: *condicei-ros*, *foreiros*, *eiteiros*, *parceiros*, *meeiros*, *terceiros*, *lavradores*, and so on. In contrast to these designations of specific work relationships, the systematic observation of clientelistic relationships in play in the wider sphere of life shows that it is possible to understand each particular transaction between resident worker and patron only if we take into consideration the history of exchanges between the two individuals from the time that they met each other (in many cases, since birth). The parameters within which such relations were conceived were never reducible to the mere monetary value attributed to the work performed. There-fore, when faced with adverse fluctuations in the international market for cash crops, landowners could always make arrangements in the worker-patron part-nership that reduced labor costs and thus increased the profit margin. In the same way, conversion of cash crops—for example, replacing sugarcane or coffee with cotton, sisal, or cattle—could take advantage of rearrangements in the worker-patron relationship to improve profits for the landowners (A. Garcia 1990).

A basic characteristic of the traditional plantation economy found in the sugar-cane, coffee, cotton, and other regions was the complementary relation between the cycles of work on the commercial crop and on subsistence agriculture. Cane cutting and coffee picking occurred in the dry season, when there was little to do in the workers' manioc, corn, and bean fields (Correia de Andrade 1964). Con-versely, in the Northeast, the rainy season, which runs from March to June and is called winter, the labor required for cleaning and clearing the cane fields was much less than in the cutting season. This was when the family plots of manioc, corn, and beans received attention. Thus there was intensive use of the depen-dent labor on the plantations: at peak times of the commercial harvest, there was little to do in the family plots; in the peak season for the subsistence crops, there was little to do in the commercial fields. It is important to note that this complementarity permitted the use not only of resident workers but also of sal-aried seasonal labor from off the plantation, including from smaller neighboring farms. The agricultural calendar of these small property owners on the periphery of the plantation followed the same rhythm of the family plots of the resident workers (Correia de Andrade 1964; Ringuelet 1977). Thus even the peasants on the margins of the large plantation found themselves subject to the pulse of the plantation economy (Heredia 1979, 1989; Ringuelet 1977; A. Garcia 1990).

Such temporal arrangements were also reflected in the intensive use of space. Planting food crops between the rows of maturing coffee fields, or planting cot-ton in the same space as corn and beans, shows that one of the possible worker-patron arrangements was to delegate to the dependents responsibility for the land for the entire agricultural cycle, since they used the same space for commercial and food crops. In these cases, the landowner monopolized the commerce in the cash crop and established various forms of partnerships or tenancy for the others. The use of the food crops would then normally remain the responsibility of the resident worker's family.

These spatial and temporal arrangements allowed plantation owners to lower labor costs for commercial cultivation and gave them flexibility in expanding and contracting production. Detailed studies of the sugar and coffee plantations show economic mechanisms similar to those of Polish grain farms between the sixteenth and seventeenth centuries (see Kula 1970 for Poland and Heredia 1989 and A. Garcia 1989 for Brazil). In periods of low crop prices, production could be expanded to earn the same income in foreign exchange, since the commercial farmers aimed to be able to buy goods available only as imports: metal equipment, fine clothing, luxury furniture, footwear, and so forth. The drop in prices could be compensated by increasing production as long as the costs of new land under cultivation and employed labor were kept low. Conversely, the drop in income derived from cash crops would cause a decline in the cosmopolitan lifestyle of the plantation owners because of their reduced purchasing power in foreign currency. These fluctuations did not necessarily mean bankruptcy, however. The food supply of the resident workers and of the big house was assured through the systematic cultivation of food crops. The contraction of plantation activities was more frequent than one might think. Long-term drops in prices could result in the substitution of cash crops, for example coffee and sisal for sugarcane, without causing any more than a short-term reduction in the plantation family's spending (A. Garcia 1990). Thus we see that the organization of planting in time and space as well as the various arrangements in sharecropping and work obligations meant that the plantation was blessed with the ability to function on its own even in the face of price fluctuations, in a way similar to Kula's Polish model. We will see below how these mechanisms were ruptured and how the operations of the large plantations were severely altered after the systematic expulsion of resident labor beginning in the 1950s.

Ruy Miller Paiva (1968) studied conditions of the technical modernization of Brazilian agriculture, including mechanization, use of fertilizers, and seed selection, in the period preceding its more systematic advance in the 1970s and 1980s. Paiva saw in the system of residency, in the specific forms of combining abundant land and labor, one of the most powerful restraints on the introduction of technical innovations that could have broken down the barriers created by the decline in cash crop prices. The author also related the low added cost of traditional plantation labor to its capacity to reckon with unfavorable price fluctuations without a breakdown of its basic operating mechanisms. The resident labor force was condemned to a form of productive underemployment that gave the large plantation idle productive capacity beyond its immediate agricultural and agroindustrial activities. Paiva later noted that the replacement of resident labor with systematic recruitment of nonresident labor under new salary arrangements (for example, migrants in São Paulo and clandestine workers in Pernambuco) resulted in higher labor prices for the landowners. This contributed to the accelerated use of new machinery and industrial agricultural procedures (Paiva 1972).

Understanding the specific forms of traditional plantation management is without a doubt fundamental for understanding its endurance throughout the twentieth century. No less important, though, is an understanding of the political efforts of the agricultural elites since the end of the nineteenth century, which resulted in the creation and development of institutional mechanisms of price supports for export crops (see Holloway 1968 and Bacha 1992 for coffee and Szmrecsanyi 1979 for sugar). The realization that Brazil was responsible for a large portion of the world's coffee supply led some of the largest producers, associated with export businessmen and political elites, to try to force a more favorable growth in international prices through supply control practices. It was the policies conceived and put into practice through the initiative of São Paulo coffee growers that introduced the neologism "valorization" to world commodity exchanges. By 1930 coffee price supports were the work of the state of São Paulo, which sought to manage certain basic controls of the national economy to guarantee the success of the policies it had put into place. The world economic crisis begun with the 1929 New York stock market crash caused unprecedented overproduction. It was the new national elites, composed of regional oligarchies under the leadership of Getúlio Vargas and allied with junior army officers in revolt since the 1920s, that created national institutions to regulate the coffee market, including the Brazilian Coffee Institute (Instituto Brasileiro do Café, IBC), which minutely controlled the mechanisms of the internal market and was an actor on the international stage until the 1990s (Fausto 1970).[6] Thus one can say that the large-scale coffee production throughout almost all of the twentieth century depended on instruments of economic policy that tried to regulate the international market through supply control practices, at first statewide, in the case of São Paulo until 1930, then nationwide, though the IBC. In the second half of the twentieth century, this control became effective with the elimination of coffee fields through crop conversion subsidized by the government.

Vargas's coffee policies gained notoriety with the destruction of unsold coffee stocks, which were burned or thrown into the sea (Bacha 1992). Economist Celso Furtado analyzed the policy of purchase and destruction of unmarketable coffee stocks in the 1930s as a means of income protection for the large planters, who, without the foreign exchange that exports ensured, unintentionally provoked import-substitution industrialization and chronic inflation (Furtado 1959). Later discussions of the financing of Brazilian industrialization have raised the issue of the diversion of earnings from commercial farms for the establishment or support of nascent industries, especially through successive political changes after 1945, the end of Vargas's Estado Novo (New State; Rangel 1962, 1963; Tavares 1972; Abreu 1990). Certain analyses echo the coffee growers' representatives' claim that they have always been the injured parties in the management of the national economy. Such views ignore or at least do not duly emphasize that the large coffee plantation owners relied on a specific institution protected within the state apparatus, financed in any emergency by the national treasury, that amortized any negative impact from world market fluctuations and that directly administered crop conversions for coffee plantations.

After 1930, other export crops, especially sugarcane and cacao, had public institutions for the regulation of their trade similar to the IBC. The Institute for Sugar and Alcohol (Instituto do Açúcar e do Álcool, IAA) was created in the early 1930s to deal with the acute crisis in international markets and lasted until the early 1990s, when it was closed along with the IBC. Szmrecsanyi's detailed study of the IAA (1979) demonstrates that, as a public institution established under pressure from sugar plantation and mill owners, it instituted precise control over cane production: the area planted and the area harvested, the quantities processed in the mills, the quantity of sugar and alcohol produced in each mill through a quota system, and the market prices of the products. This organization was also behind several of the technical modernization programs of the sugar agroindustry. The sugar policy of the IAA constantly regulated the numbers of plantations and mills. The old sugar aristocracy, therefore, like the coffee growers with the IBC, had the benefit of a public organization that established the parameters of competition among the suppliers and fostered the conversion of less productive agroindustrial entities. Even when a sugar mill went under, the IAA intervened to administer it, solving its financial problems and making investments for its modernization. The sugar mill was sold only once the business reached the level of other entities under normal operation.

The case of the IAA reveals that the plantation owners had public institutions at their disposal that protected them from national and international competition. From 1930 to 1990, the difference in productivity of agricultural incomes was constant between the Southeast and the Northeast (Szmrecsanyi 1979; A. Garcia 1990). This difference did not lead, however, to the liquidation of less productive agroindustrial units, as should have occurred under the "pure and perfect" competition envisioned by neoclassical economic theory. The IAA instituted a segmentation of the markets in the Southeast and the Northeast, systematically fixing higher prices in the latter region in proportion to higher costs there. There were, then, for more than half a century, subsidies for sugarcane prices. The IAA functioned as a large cartel underwritten by the national treasury that relieved less efficient businesses of the burdens of their relative inefficiency (A. Garcia 1990). This went on until the last decade of the twentieth century, as if public institutions that had been created to keep overproduction of cash crops from undermining prices had instead contributed to the perpetuation of traditional ways of managing plantations. It is important to stress that public institutions like the IBC and the IAA were much more geared to the continuation of the "patrimonial state" than to the construction of a modern state that could promote contemporary capitalism's standards of business efficiency (Faoro 1958; Weber 1971). With organizations like the IBC and IAA, the wielders of economic power had strong leverage for steering history toward conservative modernization at the same time that they prevented outcomes that might have benefited the less privileged classes subordinate to them. Nevertheless, social transformation found a variety of pathways, as we will see.

The Many Paths of Rural Transformation

The abolition of slavery meant the loss of planters' capital tied up in slaves, and this appears to have been significant in some regions, such as the Paraíba Valley (Stein 1957). Even so, the analyses discussed so far show that abolition in no way led to the destruction of the mechanisms that allowed the authority of the old planter families to prevail. Relationships of personal dependency and subordination were re-created, allowing the perpetuation of earlier practices in the exercise of power on the large estates, including the power to inflict corporal punishment on subordinates. These forms of personal domination that become widespread at the end of the nineteenth century were based on an extremely unequal distribution of rural wealth. Yet it was through the very practice of granting the use of this wealth that the large landowners created groups of families of workers under their command. The large plantation owners offered the means for ensuring the material survival of workers' families. They also promoted social and cultural activities on their estates, such as religious events, festivities, meetings, and all sorts of interpersonal exchanges in the vicinity of the big house — not to mention the family life of the dependents themselves. In doing so, the large plantation owners succeeded in attracting significant contingents of people to live under their authority and daily control. At the same time, recruiting resident workers entailed not only knowing how to provide living and working conditions for families lacking the means for survival but also having the credibility to be recognized, at least potentially, as a protector and a "good boss." Therefore, belonging to one of the traditional families of large landowners and bearing the name of a family known in the region where the farm, plantation, or mill was located was a basic trump in establishing one's authority as a head of a big house. The accumulation of credibility, the symbolic capital of the traditional masters, only rarely occurred within the span of one generation.

The historical and sociological literature has conceived of the mass of dependents on the large estates as a "rural proletariat" rather than as "subordinated peasants" (Palmeira 1971). Paradoxically, however, this proletarian mass, which had nothing of its own, is described as constantly undergoing a process of "proletarization." Each new arrangement in the resident worker's relationship with the boss that involved the loss of an earlier benefit, such as the right to plant a grove of fruit trees or to raise livestock on the property, is seen as a marker of "proletarization." In fact, though, resident workers constantly and commonly circulated among the estates. A falling-out between patron and resident worker was often solved by the working family's leaving the estate either voluntarily or involuntarily. This circulation was one of the key mechanisms of competition among patrons for the most productive and loyal laborers. As a consequence, changes in resident-patron relations could occur in the course of a long-term relationship on one estate or as a result of a working family's moving in search of a more effective protector. This circulation of dependents, an ongoing feature of the plantation after abolition, differed completely from the situation after 1950, when contingents of rural workers coming from the regions of large-scale plantation agriculture took up residence on the outskirts of small, midsize, and large cities. It was the second half of the twentieth century that saw the waves of *bóias-frias* (migrant laborers; literally, "cold chows," referring to the meals that they took into the fields) in the Southeast (Incao 1975) and the clandestine day laborers on street corners in the Northeast (Sigaud 1979). The families of dependents continued to leave rural estates without necessarily wanting to abandon agricultural work. However, the landowners were no longer disposed to absorb new families or even maintain the prior forms of labor recruitment. What happened to cause such changes in the practices of rural patronage and their procedures for managing the old groups of workers?

The practices of recruitment and administration of the plantation workforce became ineffective or even counterproductive in the face of the combined effects of developments in the international markets for cash crops, the possibility of migrating to the cities in the Southeast that were industrializing, the rise of peasant social movements resulting in rural unionizing and the establishment of a new legal and institutional framework, and the broadening of educational and health services in the urban milieu.

Let us review the various factors responsible for the greatest changes in the rural-urban relationship. In 1950, 64 percent of the Brazilian population lived in rural areas, whereas in 1980, only 32 percent still lived the country. A change in the way of life and work for so many cannot be explained by a supposed "liberation of the rural workforce" because a constant of this process was the impoverishment of large portions of the newly urbanized populations and the high level of verified unemployment in the cities (Palmeira et al. 1977). This veritable mutation in Brazilian society requires more than a simplistic discussion of how an industrialized Brazil reached "modernity" in the second half of the twentieth century. It requires an examination of the modes of changes in the social horizon for millions of people and their families. These changes are connected to transformations in forms of power, both rural and urban. So how did the individuals who went through this process conceive of the experience of having their social networks changed — networks over which the very beliefs that shaped their daily existence had previously been laid? What efforts were they obliged to make to acquire new competencies and thus insert themselves into new situations and reconstruct the meaning of their existence? What happened in this new context to the preexistent forms of social hierarchy and to the cultural categories that had given them support and legitimacy?

The first explanatory factor has already been discussed: the unfavorable developments in commodity prices. This essay is not the place to go into detail about specific crops; these are found in specialized studies (Bacha 1992; Szmrecsanyi 1979; A. Garcia 1990). Suffice it to highlight here the basis for the constant tendency to overproduce: the Atlantic Forest and other regions not yet settled by the colonists served until the mid-twentieth century as agricultural frontiers to be exploited through the establishment of new plantations (Monbeig 1952; Rangel 1962). The superior fertility of the new lands under cultivation gave planters a compelling reason to relocate to the new areas, especially because the new means of transportation, such as railways from the late nineteenth century and highways from the end of World War II, made it cheaper to get products to market. As we have already seen, the decline of the "old" areas did not necessarily mean that landowners abandoned growing cash crops there; rather, it entailed a more austere lifestyle for the descendants of the big house, since the income earned from agroindustry tended to be lower. Improvements in estate management standards could be postponed whenever it was possible to reduce labor costs through adjustments in the forms of resident labor. Thus the expansion of agricultural frontiers became associated with low indices of productivity in the old areas and the creation of an enormous idle productive capacity (Paiva 1968). This had a bearing on the long-range evolution of terms of trade in agricultural commodities (Rangel 1962, 1963). As we have already summarized, detailed studies of the coffee valorization practices of the IBC and the control of sugar and alcohol supply by the IAA showed that the public institutions never managed to reduce the idle farming capacity in the long term. On the contrary, they crystallized that idle capacity, protecting the most inefficient planters from bankruptcy. Lest we forget the political power of rural landowners throughout the process of industrialization, the Special Group for Rationalization of the Northeastern Sugar Agroindustry (Grupo Especial para a Racionalização da Agroindústria Canavieira do Nordeste, GERAN) of 1962 proposed that publicly funded support for the technical modernization of agroindustries be directed to less productive food-producing lands, which gave rise to the expansion of the peasantry that had resulted from the expulsion of resident workers (Gomes da Silva 1987). These policies were systematically discarded even though they were vigorously applauded upon their release. As a retrospective on Brazilian capitalism has shown, it was not the lack of political imagination, of social movements, or of struggles that prevented the modernization of the traditional plantation from following courses other than the antipeasant "Prussian way" (Palmeira and Leite 1997). Instead, through federal policies, the rural aristocracy sought a "conservative modernization," a bourgeois revolution that assured an alliance between the bourgeoisie and the old landed aristocracy.

A second decisive factor in the change in traditional forms of domination beginning in the 1930s was mass migration to the rapidly industrializing metropolises, mainly São Paulo, Rio de Janeiro, and Belo Horizonte. Migration provided the new industrial capitalists with extremely cheap labor that was willing to accept painful daily conditions, such as those job sites where workers "sleep in hammocks hung in any corner," "eat out of cans," and cover themselves "in any old rag"—"urban standards" of the modern metropolises that would have been unacceptable if these heads of households had had to submit their entire families to them (Oliveira 1972). At the same time, however, migrant urban workers began to accumulate material and cultural resources, at great physical and psychological sacrifice, that allowed many descendants of agricultural workers to escape from the traditional trap of submission through plantation residence—to escape from subjugation in their regions of origin—by becoming small urban property owners, small businessmen, or self-employed tradesmen (masons, firefighters, electricians, and so forth; A. Garcia 1989, 1990). It was not by chance that, beginning in the 1950s, northeastern towns that were sources of migrant labor were also stages for picketing by large landowners trying to prevent waves of "parrot perch" trucks from taking workers to the South.[7] Migration contributed in two ways to eroding the power of large rural property owners: It reduced the stock of those workers who might be forced to accept their impositions. It also exposed workers to the world of the minimum wage, established in 1939, and other workers' rights under Getúlio Vargas's 1943 Consolidation of Labor Laws (Consolidação das Leis do Trabalho, CLT). The large cities, therefore, came to represent a world where workers had rights, against which the countryside could look only like a place of deprivation, a realm of arbitrariness, and a world of subjugation and captivity (Sigaud 1979; Leite Lopes 1976; A. Garcia 1989).

The third factor that drove change in the urban-rural configuration was the establishment of the aforementioned labor rights, inherited from two centuries of social struggle in Europe (Castel 1995). In the case of Brazil and other South American countries, such as Chile (Gómez 1982), there was a split in the institution of norms and a judicial framework for regulating the labor market. In the cities, laws were passed, for example under the CLT, and courts and regulatory offices were created at the moment that import-substitution industrialization picked up pace. In contrast, the countryside was considered a world of "practices and customs"—that is, the traditional practices of domination by the large landowners. In fact, Vargas's original plan seems to have been to extend to rural workers the advantages granted to urban workers. Opposition from political representatives tied to large planters, however, was tenacious. Even when the proposal reappeared in 1953 and 1954, when the progressive João Goulart was labor minister during Vargas's elected term, it suffered such opposition that it was one of the reasons for Goulart's dismissal (Camargo 1979). Only in 1963, with the passage of the Rural Worker Statute, were rights such as minimum wage, paid leave, and formalized work contracts extended to rural workers. The Rural Worker Statute was itself a maneuver that postponed a vote on the Land Statute and the constitutional amendment that would have opened the doors to agrarian reform. Those who today talk of the "flexibilization" of labor regulations to cope with the globalized economy would do well to realize that the "future" that they want to impose — of unstable conditions for wage earners and managerial discretion — has a long tradition in rural Brazil. They are of the very ilk of the "cordial man" that Buarque de Holanda analyzed so well as the opposite of political modernity. Indeed, between 1945, the end of World War II and the redemocratization of the country after Vargas's Estado Novo, and the coup of 1964, the great divide in Brazilian politics during the legislative debates about the new constitution was, without a doubt, whether or not to grant to the president broad powers to promote massive agrarian reform. The constitutional article that was finally approved stated that any land expropriation could take place only through "prior and just" cash indemnification. This effectively blocked any large-scale initiative since it was a period of strong inflationary pressures. Modification of the measure dominated legislative debates until the military government of Castelo Branco, which virtually shut down any civic debate on land reform (Camargo 1979).

The creation of the Peasant Leagues (Ligas Camponesas) by Francisco Julião in the mid-1950s (Julião 1968), along with organizations close to the Brazilian Communist Party in the Brazilian Agricultural Workers' Union (União dos Lavradores e Trabalhadores Agrícolas do Brasil, ULTAB; Grynszpan 1987; Martins 1981; Medeiros 1989), gave a decisive push for Congress finally to vote for the Rural Worker Statute in 1963. These organizations, together with the directions taken by the Cuban Revolution in 1960, contributed to the panic that spread through the landowning class (Palmeira 1977). The members of the Peasant Leagues, however, were not rural wage earners but rather *foreiros*, resident workers of the plantations abandoned by descendents of the landowners who had been granted title, *foro*, to the land (Julião 1968; Heredia 1979; A. Garcia 1983). When the planters' descendents attempted to regain control of the abandoned estates, they tried to resume the traditional practice of the *cambão*, requiring free service on the estate infrastructure, without having fulfilled for years the role of protector, which workers deemed necessary to consider the landowner a "good boss." The threatened *foreiros* approached Julião, who was a young lawyer and deputy from the Brazilian Socialist Party (Partido Socialista Brasileiro, PSB), about bringing the case to court. Julião initially used only the legal provisions of the Civil Code of 1916, both to portray the *cambão* as abusive and to fight the withdrawal of the land grant. Thus the judicial efforts preceded the legislative decisions. That various subaltern groups had gone to court against the landowners gave a weight to the public voice of the peasants equal to that of their "masters." The court proceedings dramatized the equality of citizens before the law. Julião recalled that there was violence against those who had brought cases to court and even against witnesses after the first hearing. The plantation masters, "cordial men" par excellence, were surprised and humiliated when they saw that their court depositions had the same value as those of their adversaries. The rule of law was distasteful to those who considered themselves the sole lords of their domains.

Even though the Peasant Leagues had dominated the peasant movement's political scene in the 1950s, they were not the most influential group in ensuring the enforcement of rural workers' laws or in creating rural workers' unions (Camargo 1973; Palmeira 1977). The major agents in these actions were the Catholic and Communist labor union groups (Bezerra 1979; Pureza da Silva 1982). Competition to monopolize the professional representation of a new political actor—the peasants and rural workers—provoked a large-scale consolidation of peasant unionism, with the creation of state confederations and of the National Confederation of Workers in Agriculture (Confederação Nacional dos Trabalhadores na Agricultura, CONTAG) in 1963. This consolidation contributed decisively to putting the new legal provisions into practice.

The establishment of labor law radically changed the constructs of personal domination prevalent up to then since it introduced a system of monetary value for everything that before had been a matter of exchange, of mutual quid pro quo. The new laws rendered the traditional strategies of the old planters dangerous and even threatening, insofar as they had the goal of driving the rural worker materially and morally into debt. In accordance with the new system of legal norms, any work done for the planter was to be compensated with the minimum wage and all the related benefits—vacation, paid leave, and the "thirteenth salary,"[8] all duly calculated. There were also limits on deductions for lodging, and the granting of lots for subsistence planting and livestock could not take the place of monetary compensation. The collection of traditional practices could not put the workers and dependents in debt to the landowner; rather, the landowner was now their debtor. The landowner might not pay daily what the law prescribed, but if he did not, he could be taken to court by his workers and be obliged to pay his debts with interest and adjustment for inflation. There were several cases in which the recovered value of the house and lot was less than the debt owed. Thus traditional strategic practices in which the planter showed generosity to be considered a "good patron" tended to be radically modified. If landowners did not expel the resident worker families from their estates, they at least no longer granted residency to new families—neither to those coming from other estates nor to descendants of those families already living on the property. This veritable movement on the part of landowners to dismantle social relations had effects throughout society because even smallholders and small businessmen saw their social positions altered. Therefore, all of the participants in the traditional plantation complex had to manage the conversion of their social positions, their practices, their ways of thinking, and their very perceptions of society. They did this, moreover, under unequal conditions, according to the material and symbolic resources that each possessed.

Beginning in the 1950s, most of the former resident workers suffered impoverishment because they had seen their traditional conditions of existence taken away without undergoing transformation into a rural proletariat, a class endowed with new rights and responsibilities. Unable to continue as resident workers on other plantations under the protection of other patrons, they had to leave the large estates. The destiny of a good part of the families of former resident workers was migration to the cities nearest to the estates that had once sheltered them. These cities swelled extraordinarily in the second half of the twentieth century, for example those of the Atlantic Forest zone of Pernambuco (Sigaud 1979) and those of the coffee-growing regions of São Paulo and Paraná. Ignacy Sachs (2000) notes that this process warrants the term "deruralization," in that it is completely different from the process of gaining new lifestyles and perceptions known as "urbanization."

The planters were keen to rid themselves of resident labor so as not to be subject to the rising monetary costs of labor. The exodus from the plantations was massive, but there was not a simultaneous expulsion of all dependent families. Rather, there were isolated cases. Even so, the possibility that a suit would be brought in labor court limited the landowner's ability to send a worker away. It is interesting that wherever rural unionism was the most combative and thus imposed the greatest respect for labor laws, expulsion of resident workers took place on a smaller scale. In these places, respect for labor law served as a brake on the impoverishment caused by the elimination of benefits that before had been provided at no monetary cost.

When the worker left the estate, he was forced to take on the material expenses of a new dwelling, whether paying rent in a building in the city, buying a small lot to build a home, or invading land where he might establish title, however precarious. He no longer had use of water and wood as on the old property. The new situation turned these into commodities that had to be bought. He no longer had access to land for planting food crops during the rainy season. The use of all agricultural land entailed rental or sharecropping. Land, too, became a commodity for all. The land around an urban dwelling was neither ample nor open as before. Women could no longer raise goats, hogs, and chickens. Everything that before was as available as the air one breathed and that cost only the effort of and disposition for heavy work now was a commodity that required the accumulation of monetary resources. One can see that the economic conversion demanded of rural workers and their families was significant: the material and psychological investment required a personal history of accumulation of material goods and of autonomous management of family economics that only a few had (A. Garcia 1990). Forced relocation to the cities, because the boss had "fallen on hard times" and was no longer "generous" as in the past, was experienced in most cases as a process of loss, of downfall. For this reason, workers and their families often held an idealized image of the past as a time of bounty and harmony, as opposed to their conception of the present as a time of privation and uncertainty (Sigaud 1979). In concrete terms, the simple maintenance of past wages, even accounting for current purchasing power, could not cover the prior levels of consumption. The mere maintenance of prior standards of living demanded supplemental work that allowed one to earn money equivalent to the goods and services granted before at no monetary cost but rather in exchange for loyalty and submission. The experience of liberty had real costs. Thus the threat of absolute impoverishment always hovered over the families of resident workers, and sooner or later most experienced it. Poverty was all the more painful because the migrants' constant confrontations with other subaltern urban groups, especially semiskilled and skilled workers, lower-level public servants, and small businesspeople, made their own relative poverty apparent in their daily lives.

For most of the population, the experience of liberty was associated with a material impoverishment that limited cultural investment and the development of subjectivity. In *The Masters and the Slaves*, Freyre portrayed the plight of the nineteenth-century "pariahs of the mills" as worse than that of plantation slaves. This hypothesis merits a more rigorous empirical study. It is a widely documented fact, however, that the mid-twentieth-century transition from resident worker on a coffee estate to urban migrant, or from resident worker on a sugar plantation to clandestine day laborer, entailed an absolute and relative impoverishment for a majority of the population who suffered such a transition. The move from the old system of relations, in which the boss positioned himself as a "protector" who had to provide for the needs and survival of his dependents and who imposed his norms on daily life, to a new system characterized by the interdependence of individuals with no formal connection among them required that all parties develop self-discipline (Elias 1973). We can only imagine the tensions resulting from the imperious new need of having to create one's own existence. One had to do this with no help, subject to immediate emergencies, such as hunger. It is no surprise that such a situation sometimes led to the reactivation of old forms of personal dependence, in which the quest for a new all-encompassing protection might be exchanged for limitless loyalty. This reciprocal exchange might occur in religious organizations, networks of political clientelism, or even in drug-trafficking gangs.

Nevertheless, the massive transformation of rural resident workers into urban migrant laborers did not mean that there was no other social path for those who left the dependency of the plantation. Migration both to the metropolitan centers and to the lands opened up for settlement in the Center-West and the North in the 1970s provided upward mobility, allowing the formation of groups of small businesspeople, self-employed professionals, and frontier farmworkers (Velho 1974). Analysis of social practices and representations of migrant families reveals that those who moved to the industrial centers of São Paulo, Rio de Janeiro, and Belo Horizonte could experience several outcomes. It was possible that, among the same group of siblings, some might secure formal employment in the Southeast, where they might stay permanently. At the same time, other siblings might, by means of temporary employment in the industrial, commercial, or service sector, gain the skills and resources necessary to buy a small rural property or become small businesspeople in their region of origin (A. Garcia 1990). The economic shift caused by migration depended on circumstances at the point of departure, such as the networks of contractors, families, and generational cohorts mobilized for the success of the move. It also depended on the market and living conditions at the destination. Results for individuals could differ widely: depending on gender, age, family condition, group position, and past investments in culture and education, two journeys between the same two points could have completely different outcomes. Migration studies that limit themselves to considering only demographic flows inevitably homogenize practices that are quite different and impede sociological understanding of the diversity of relocation experiences (Palmeira and Wagner de Almeida 1977; Sayad 1991). The fact, nevertheless, is that the experience and material resources acquired in the big cities allowed a significant number of migrants to ensure positions as peasants or as small businesspeople (A. Garcia 1990).

An option for economic improvement for those faced with changes in the "old" rural areas was migration to the agricultural frontier, especially to the Amazonian region (Velho 1970, 1974; Tavares dos Santos 1978; Musumeci 1988; see chapter 9). The intensity of migration loomed large after 1960 with the construction of the highway linking Brasília in the middle of the country and Belém at the mouth of the Amazon, and especially with the building of the Trans-Amazon Highway in the 1970s. Such road construction was directly connected to public policies to deal with the effects of drought in the Northeast. The Brazilian pioneer frontier, however, was not limited to the expansion of small farming, as was the case in the West of the United States (Velho 1974). Finance minister Defim Neto and the economic authorities of the military government quickly used fiscal incentives to attract major domestic and international capital to clear grazing land where there had been tropical forest. As a result, between 1970 and 1990, there developed a concentration of large properties in the Center-West and North even greater than in the areas of early colonization. This is an example of the systematically antipopular character of public policies during the military dictatorship. Overall, policies were used to favor accumulation of land by large business groups, as seen in the conversion of large properties in the "old" areas. The large-scale deforestation in the Amazonian region was another effect of the military authorities' allocation of public lands in areas of virgin forest. Current projects to recover devastated areas and to promote sustainable development (Sachs 2000) seek to redirect and redefine a historical tendency that would have had neither the profile nor intensity it did without the actions of the "wizards" of the Brazilian "miracle."[9]

In practice, during the twenty-one years of military government, land conflicts only grew and spread throughout the country. At the beginning of the 1980s, the Amazonian region had the most violent confrontations (Wagner de Almeida 1980). After 1964, the military harshly repressed Peasant Leagues militants, Com-

munist unionists, and Catholic unionists, especially those furthest to the left—
the Grassroots Education Movement (Movimento de Educação de Base, MEB)
and Popular Action (Ação Popular, AP). Even so, the military did not destroy the
rural unions or repeal the new labor laws (Palmeira 1977). Step by step, Catholic
union activists assumed control of municipally based unions and in 1968 won
elections in nationally strategic federations, as in the states of Pernambuco, Rio
Grande do Norte, and Rio de Janeiro. They even took back control of CONTAG.
Until the Third National Congress in 1979, this new leadership fought for both
respect for rural labor regulations and enforcement of guidelines for leasing and
partnership contracts established by the 1964 Land Statute. They also struggled
to block expulsion of squatter families that were cultivating abandoned lands
and to expropriate real estate where there were land disputes. The military governments tried to control the daily life of the rural unions with provisions of the
CLT that tied them to the Ministry of Labor and, after 1972, sought to make these
unions simply one of the elements in the government's extension of social welfare
through its Rural Worker Assistance Fund (Fundo de Assistência ao Trabalhador
Rural, FUNRURAL). Notwithstanding the subordination of the many unions and
federations to government authority, the rural union activists still became important agents of the promotion of the new social rights that afforded a minimum of
protections for peasants and rural wage earners.

In the 1970s, during the military regime, a new actor began to help peasants
and rural workers mobilize: the Catholic Church. The church organized peasants
and rural workers to improve their living conditions and even to acquire permanent landholdings throughout the country, but especially in the Center-West.
Without a doubt, the change in the attitude of the Catholic Church in the second
half of the twentieth century was one of the most significant factors in Brazilian
politics. As Julião has pointed out, the Catholic Church had a virtual monopoly
on the diffusion of worldviews and of religious practices until the 1950s. It was
not by chance that Socialists and Communists allied themselves with Protestant
pastors, like João Pedro Teixeira of the Sapé League in the state of Paraíba, to
create rural unionism. Thus during the 1950s and the beginning of the 1960s,
the agenda of the church hierarchy was guided by discomfort with the crack in
its absolute political and cultural hegemony as a religious institution. Beginning
in the state of Rio Grande do Norte, Catholic bishops promoted the formation of
Catholic leadership and attracted lawyers and educators who would help create a
new trend in unionism. Because the rural bosses reacted violently to any restriction of their personal power and to any enforcement of laws applicable to rural

workers, many of the Catholic rural leaders, lawyers, and educators moved closer to the Communist and Socialist leagues even before the 1964 coup. At the same time, however, the Catholic hierarchy played a key role in the popular mobilization that opened the doors for the military coup, notably in the 1964 Marches of Godly Families for Liberty (Marchas da Família com Deus pela Liberdade; Dreyfus 1981). By the end of the 1960s, Institutional Act no. 5 (Ato Institucional no. 5, AI-5), along with subsequent legislation, had struck down most basic freedoms, and the military regime began systematic torture of its enemies. After this, the church hierarchy started to criticize the dictatorship and concern itself more about the popular classes, both in the country and in the city (Novaes 1985, 1987). This reorientation of the hierarchy owed much to the coordination of the National Council of Brazilian Bishops (Conselho Nacional de Bispos Brasileiros, CNBB). At the same time, Christian Base Communities (Comunidades Eclesiais de Base, CEBs) were established throughout the country. Inspired by liberation theology, the CEBs fostered group discussions out of which came mobilization initiatives for achieving more dignified living conditions. The creation of the Pastoral Land Commission (Comissão Pastoral da Terra, CPT) in 1975 systematized the mobilization work of priests, bishops, and other religious and lay catechists among peasants and rural workers. The CPT acted as an autonomous source of peasant mobilization and was an agent in many struggles against the expulsion of squatters and for farm expropriations, especially in the states of Mato Grosso and Maranhão and in the Amazonian region. It was an aiding force in CONTAG's union organizing after CONTAG's 1979 convention, where it was more combative especially in cases of occupation of abandoned farms and in rural wage-earner strikes. Within the CPT, opposition groups renewed the leadership of official unions even after the military dictatorship ended, and from these groups came the leadership of the current Landless Workers' Movement (Movimento dos Trabalhadores Rurais Sem Terra, MST), the most powerful Latin American social movement in the 1990s (Fernandes 1996).

During the 1970s, a time of fierce dictatorial repression, the Catholic Church, which, aside from the military, was the only institution with a nationwide presence, made possible a systematic, ongoing discussion of the social problems caused by the social transformations of the day through its new forms of recruitment and proselytizing. Even non-Catholics, including students, intellectuals, political militants, and members of other religions, saw in the church's new activity a safe space within which to take up again the attempts at popular mobilization. Upon their release from prison, a number of political prisoners joined CPT and

CEB efforts among the popular sectors. Many nongovernmental organizations active today in Brazil's rural areas have their roots in the militancy of university students and professors, lawyers, priests, nuns, and pastoral workers from groups formed by the CPT and in the CEBs in the 1970s and 1980s. The change in the Catholic Church's orientation at the end of the 1960s was an essential factor for restructuring Brazilian politics, and it weighed decisively in favor of the growth of the peasant movement and of restoring the legitimacy of the theme of land reform during the last three decades of the twentieth century.

In addition to the Catholic Church, many other religious groups arose and spread around the country, recruiting their faithful from among the poorest strata of the population. Diversification of religion contributed strongly to forging new perceptions of the future, both individually and collectively. The growth of Pentecostalism among peasants who were finding their way in the new social order showed how religious competition could engender new ways of working out an ethos and could help sanctify associations of solidarity that were different from the old patriarchal clientelism (Novaes 1985).

It was not only the churches that saw growth in their institutions and diversification of their activities. The growth of the national government was huge, and the implications for public management of the changes in the countryside were great. Particularly important was the establishment of federal universities throughout Brazil and of institutions specializing in biotechnology research, such as the Brazilian Agricultural Research Institute (Empresa Brasileira de Pesquisa Agropecuária, EMBRAPA), or in its diffusion, such as the Rural Extension and Technical Assistance Initiatives (Empreendimentos de Assistência Técnica e Extensão Rural, EMATER). These organizations helped to train professional scientists in a wide range of disciplines, and the social sciences benefited as much as the earth and life sciences. Thus were forged the tools for charting new directions in the transformation of the rural world. In contrast to entities such as the IAA and the IBC, these public institutions undertook scientific research that was not subordinate to the interests of professional elites or large landowners. The array of pathways to change appears to have broadened.

The Future of the Rural World: New Horizons

Nothing shows better how Brazil's redemocratization in the 1980s is related to the broadening horizons of rural transformation than the retrospective debate on the relevance of agrarian reform in that period. Succinctly put, Tancredo

Neves, the opposition candidate for president in 1985 and a respected senior politician, considered agrarian reform an essential tool for incorporating millions of impoverished families into the economic life of the nation and for giving them real chances to take advantage of the results of industrial modernization between 1930 and 1980 (Gomes da Silva 1987). Neves considered this reform a basic means for consolidating democracy. The 1985 National Agrarian Reform Plan (Plano Nacional de Reforma Agrária, PNRA) was developed under Neves's sponsorship, and he planned to launch it at the start of his term. The progress and setbacks in the implementation of this plan show that the political elites coming out of the parties formed by the military conceived of the alliance between the government party and the opposition merely as a way of perpetuating their own power. After the 1964 coup, the military leaders had established a government party, the National Renewal Alliance (Aliança Renovadora Nacional, ARENA), but also allowed one legal opposition party, the Brazilian Democratic Movement (Movimento Democrático Brasileiro, MDB). The goal of the military government, of course, was to assure that the MDB remained the opposition, and a loyal one at that. Even during the transition to democracy in 1985–88, the populist forces of the opposition were not quite strong enough to create sweeping agrarian reform. The leadership of the large landowning interests, through the creation of a new lobbying organization, the Rural Democratic Union (União Democrática Rural, UDR), dominated the political scene and imposed on the Constitutional Assembly legal language that restricted provisions of the 1964 Land Statute.

It was only the mobilization unleashed by the MST that tipped the balance in favor of land reform. The resumption of land occupations led by the MST since the late 1980s and the acceleration of these actions in the 1990s demonstrate that land conflicts exist everywhere in the country. There are millions demanding land on which to live and from which to extract at least a part of their subsistence, but this demand, which does not have a place in the real estate market, finds its expression in the sacrifices of the squatter camps, the long marches, and the pilgrimages led by the MST. In the most varied ways the descendants of the slave quarters, or their successors, have made public their poverty as well as their stubbornness in not allowing their exclusion from society. It was the old masters that gained freedom after abolition—freedom over their old workers, the freedom to deny them shelter and material sustenance, the freedom to deny them the social acknowledgment that they deserved to have a dignified existence just like any other citizen of a democratic state. Should not the end of the "cordial man" that Buarque de Holanda preached mean the rise of the "man of solidarity"?

The truth is that, in addition to the MST's mobilization, economic factors contributed to agrarian reform's becoming a central issue in the political arena during the last decade of the twentieth century. In the first place, to contain inflation, various focal points of the public deficit had to be battled. This was the reason for the liquidation of the IBC and the IAA and the treasury-financed subsidies that perpetuated large agricultural entities that had been condemned by the marketplace. The same worry about inflation led officials to do away with policies of rural credit with negative interest that had been the basis for all of the technical modernization of the rural economy implemented during the military dictatorship (Delgado 1985). With the end of these state benefits, the attraction of capital to rural real estate speculation disappeared. The price of land, which from the time of the opening of new frontiers in the savannahs of Amazonia and the Center-West had risen faster than the value of any other asset, now started to fall. Prices fell even more precipitously after the implementation of Cardoso's 1994 Real Plan for economic stabilization. Great rural entrepreneurs, such as "Soy King" Olacir de Moraes, now seemed interested in letting go of their rural estates. Several sugar plants in the Northeast were now proposing to liquidate their debts to the Bank of Brazil by relinquishing their landholding. These could be transferred to the new National Settlement and Agrarian Reform Institute (Instituto Nacional de Colonização e Reforma Agrária, INCRA) and be available for distribution. In this case it would be the failure of mechanisms of the "painful, conservative modernization" that would open the way for land reform (Graziano da Silva 1982).

During the military regime, all of the emphasis was on developing visions of the future of the countryside based on rural companies, as defined by the Land Statute, or on their more recent version, the "agroindustrial complex." Technical modernizations that included the use of machinery, chemical fertilizers, and breeder seeds required credit subsidies as incentives for their diffusion. The reality of prices imposed by monetary stabilization under the Real Plan, however, gave a dose of humility to those who saw in rural firms with salaried employees the only model for future commercial agriculture. Even the most virulent defenders of the agroindustrial complex conceded that the transformation of the Brazilian countryside could follow diverse routes (Abramovay 1991).

With the growth in the number of plantations converted into settlements thanks to land distribution, the debate over the viability of the family farm has intensified. What are the strategies of agricultural conversion that entail intensive use of domestic labor or even the development of small to medium properties that use primarily domestic labor? The creation of a credit policy for such purposes, such as through the National Program for Strengthening Family Agriculture (Programa Nacional de Fortalecimento da Agricultura Familiar, PRONAF), has made new modes of agriculture legitimate. The range of terms to describe agricultural units shows that now various actors compete, both in the countryside and in the political arena, for recognition of plans for the future that coincide with their interests. The new official construct, born of current economic principles and technical modernization, labeled the "new rural world" (*novo mundo rural*), is not exempt from these sorts of competition when it says the future of the countryside is a collective one.

The lessons of a century's history show that futures that do not re-create the hierarchies and social distances founded in the era of masters and slaves, that do not re-create the power of "cordial men," require us to pay close attention to the experiences of those who have tried to imagine and seek out forms of social life in which the equality of citizens of a democracy is more than a beautiful literary image.

Notes

1. Resident workers in the sugar region are *moradores*; in the coffee regions they are *colonos*.

2. Throughout much of the history of Brazilian sugar production, however, the sugar plantation was self sustaining and vertically integrated, producing the cane crop as well as extracting and partially refining the sugar or producing secondary products, such as molasses or liquor (*cachaça*). The extraction was done in the on-site mill, or *engenho*, which required specialized skills for its operation. By extension, then, *engenho* came to refer to the entire plantation complex, and the *senhores de engenho* were the plantation owners. True *senhores de engenho* held noble titles under the monarchy. New technologies eventually supplanted the animal- and water-powered mills and their specialized manual laborers on the plantation site. *Usina* means a factory or plant, including those for sugar refining. *Usineiros de açúcar* are, then, the sugar plant or mill owners. These factories were still located on or near the sugar plantations.

3. *Casa-grande e senzala*, 1933. The original title means "the big house and the slave quarters." The English translation, first published by Knopf in 1946, bears the title *The Masters and the Slaves*. Both titles, however, convey the structural opposition that Freyre describes and that is relevant here.

4. *Sobrados e mocambos*, 1936. The English translation, whose title *The Mansions and the Shanties* is more or less equivalent, was published by Knopf in 1963.

5. *Formação do Brasil contemporâneo*, 1942. It was first published in English in 1967.

6. For more on the Vargas government's role in economic policy, see chapter 3.

7. *Pau-de-arara*, literally, "macaw poles," so named because the migrating workers that crowded into the beds of these trucks seemed like birds perched on the framework.

8. The *décimo terceiro* is a bonus equivalent to a month's salary paid in December. Provisions for this bonus, paid to qualifying wage earners, were a feature of Vargas-era labor law.

9. The *milagre brasileiro* was the proposals, and their results, that characterized the development policies of the military governments especially between 1968 and 1974. Through attraction of capital investments, intensification of import-substitution industrialization alongside promotion of the agricultural export sector, and public policies and infrastructure projects of the sort described here, the Brazilian economy saw impressive growth. However, the policies were neither sustainable nor friendly to the "popular" classes. Outcomes included a widening of the income gap and the stimulation of inflation, both through public debt and a "hot" private sector. The hyperinflation and recession of the 1980s were the results.

Bibliography

Abramovay, A. *Paradigmas do capitalismo agrário em questão*. Campinas: Editora da Universidade Estadual de Campinas, 1991.

Abreu, M. *A ordem do progresso: Cem anos de política econômica republicana*. Rio de Janeiro: Campus, 1990.

Almeida, J. A. *Memórias: Antes que me esqueça*. Rio de Janeiro: Francisco Alves, 1976.

Antonil, A. J. *Cultura e opulência do Brasil*. Lisbon: Oficina Real Deslandesiana, 1711. New ed. Paris: Institut des Hautes Études de l'Amérique Latine, Université de Paris, 1968.

Bacha, E. *150 anos de café*. Rio de Janeiro: Marcellino Martins/Johnston Exportadores, 1992.

Bastide, R. *Le candomblé de Bahia*. Paris, La Haye: Mouton, 1958.

Bezerra, G. *Memórias*. 2 vols. Rio de Janeiro: Civilização Brasileira, 1979.

Buarque de Holanda, S. *Raízes do Brasil*. Rio de Janeiro: José Olympio, 1936.

Camargo, A. *Brésil Nord-Est: Mouvements paysans et crise populiste*. Thèse de 3ème cycle. Paris: École des Hautes Études en Sciences Sociales, 1973.

———. *A questão agrária: Crise de poder e reformas de base*. Rio de Janeiro: Fundação Getúlio Vargas, 1979.

Cândido, A. "O significado de *Raízes do Brasil*." In *Raízes do Brasil*, by S. Buarque de Holanda. Rio de Janeiro: José Olympio, 1967.

Castel, R. *Les métamorphoses de la question sociale: Une chronique du salariat*. Paris: Fayard, 1995.

Correia de Andrade, M. *Terra e homem no Nordeste*. São Paulo: Brasiliense, 1964.

Cunha, E. da. *Os Sertões*. Rio de Janeiro: Laemmert, 1902.

Davatz, T. *Memórias de um colono no Brasil (1850)*. São Paulo: Martins, 1941.

Dean, W. *Rio Claro: Um sistema brasileiro de grande lavoura 1820–1920*. Rio de Janeiro: Paz e Terra, 1977.

Delgado, G. C. *Capital financeiro e agricultura no Brasil 1965–1985*. São Paulo: Ícone/ Editora da Universidade Estadual de Campinas, 1985.

Dreyfus, R. *1964: A conquista do Estado, ação política, poder e golpe de classe*. Petrópolis: Vozes, 1981.

Eisenberg, P. *Modernização sem mudança: A indústria açucareira em Pernambuco 1840– 1910*. Rio de Janeiro/Campinas: Paz e Terra/Editora da a Universidade Estadual de Campinas, 1977.

Elias, N. *La civilisation des mœurs*. Paris: Calmann-Lévy, 1973.

Faoro, R. *Os donos do poder: Formação do patronato político brasileiro*. São Paulo: Companhia Editora Nacional, 1958.

Fausto, B. *A revolução de 1930: Historiografia e história*. São Paulo: Brasiliense, 1970.

Fernandes, B. M. *MST: formação e territorialização*. São Paulo: Hucitec, 1996.

Freyre, G. *Casa-grande & senzala*. Rio de Janeiro: Maia Schmidt, 1933.

―――. *Sobrados e mocambos*. São Paulo: Companhia Editora Nacional, 1936.

―――. *The Masters and the Slaves [Casa-grande & senzala]: A Study in the Development of Brazilian Civilization*. 2nd ed. New York: Knopf, 1946.

―――. *The Mansions and the Shanties*. New York: Knopf, 1963.

Furtado, C. *Formação econômica do Brasil*. Rio de Janeiro: Fundo de Cultura, 1959. *The Economic Growth of Brazil: A Survey from Colonial to Modern Times*. Berkeley: University of California Press, 1963.

Garcia, A., Jr. "Salário e campesinato." In *Encontros sobre a realidade nordestina*, edited by R. Novaes. Campina Grande: Editora da Universidade Federal do Paraíba, 1980.

―――. *Terra de trabalho*. Rio de Janeiro: Paz e Terra, 1983.

―――. *Libre et assujetis*. Collection Brasília. Paris: Éditions de la Maison des Sciences de l'Homme, 1989.

―――. *O sul: Caminho do roçado*. São Paulo: Marco Zero/Universidade de Brasília/ Conselho Nacional de Desenvolvimento Científico e Tecnológico, 1990.

Garcia, M. F. *O Bacurau*. Master's thesis, Universidade Federal do Rio de Janeiro. Rio de Janeiro: Museu Nacional, 1977.

Gomes da Silva, J. *Caindo por terra: Crises da reforma agrária na Nova República*. São Paulo: Busca Vida, 1987.

Gómez, S. *Instituciones y procesos agrarios en Chile*. Santiago: Facultad Latinoamericana de Ciencias Sociales, 1982.

Graziano da Silva, J. *A modernização dolorosa*. Rio de Janeiro: Zahar, 1982.

Grynszpan, M. "Mobilização camponesa e competição política no estado do Rio de Janeiro." Master's thesis, Universidade Federal do Rio de Janeiro. Rio de Janeiro: Museu Nacional, 1987.

Heredia, B. *Morada da vida*. Rio de Janeiro: Paz e Terra, 1979.

———. *Formas de dominação e espaço social*. Rio de Janeiro: Paz e Terra, 1989.

Holloway, T. *Vida e morte do convênio de Taubaté*. Rio de Janeiro: Paz e Terra, 1968.

Incao, M. C. *O bóia-fria: Acumulação e miséria*. Petrópolis: Vozes, 1975.

Julião, F. *Cambão, la face cachée du Brésil*. Paris: Maspero, 1968.

Kula, W. *Théorie économique du système féodal*. Paris, La Haye: Mouton, 1970.

Leite Lopes, J. S. *Vapor do diabo: O trabalho dos operários do açúcar*. Rio de Janeiro: Paz e Terra, 1976.

Martins, J. S. *O cativeiro da terra*. São Paulo: Ciências Humanas, 1979.

———. *Os camponeses e a política no Brasil*. Petrópolis: Vozes, 1981.

Mattoso, K. *Bahia, uma província no Império*. Rio de Janeiro: Record, 1992.

Medeiros, L. *História dos movimentos sociais no campo*. Rio de Janeiro: FASE, 1989.

Monbeig, P. *Pionniers et planteurs à São Paulo*. Paris: Armand Colin, 1952.

Musumeci, L. *O mito da terra liberta*. São Paulo: Associação Nacional de Pós-Graduação e Pesquisa em Ciências Sociais/Vértice, 1988.

Novaes, R. *Os escolhidos de Deus*. Rio de Janeiro: Marco Zero/Instituto de Estudos da Religião, 1985.

———. "De corpo e alma." Ph.D. diss., Universidade de São Paulo, 1987.

Oliveira, F. "A economia brasileira: Critica à razão dualista." *Estudos CEBRAP* 2 (October 1972): 3–82.

Paiva, R. M. "Reflexões sobre as tendências da produção, da produtividade e dos preços do setor agrícola no Brasil" and "Bases para uma política para a melhoria da agricultura brasileira." In *Agricultura subdesenvolvida*, edited by F. Sá, 167–261. Petrópolis: Vozes, 1968.

———. "Os baixos níveis de renda e salários na agricultura." *Estudos Agrários* 0 (1972).

Palmeira, M. "Feira e mudança econômica." *Simpósio de Pesquisas do PPGAS*. Rio de Janeiro: Museu Nacional, 1970. Mimeograph copy.

———. *Latifundium et capitalisme: Lecture critique d'un débat*. Ph.D. diss., École des Hautes Études en Sciences Sociales, 1971.

———. "Casa e trabalho: nota sobre as relações sociais na *plantation* tradicional." *Congrès International des Américanistes*. Paris, 2–9 September 1976, no. 42.

———. "The Aftermath of Peasant Mobilization: Rural Conflicts in the Brazilian Northeast since 1964." In *The Structure of Brazilian Development*, edited by N. Aguiar. New York: Transaction Books, 1977.

Palmeira, M., and S. Leite. "Debates econômicos, processos sociais e lutas políticas:

reflexões sobre a questão agrária." *Debates CPDA*, no. 1. Rio de Janeiro: Universidade Federal do Rio de Janeiro, 1997.

Palmeira, M., and A. Wagner de Almeida. "A invenção da migração." In *Projeto Emprego e mudança sócio-econômica no Nordeste*, final report of the Universidade Federal do Rio de Janeiro/Finciadora de Estudos e Projetos/Instituto de Pesquisa Econômica Aplicada/Instituto Brasileiro de Geografia e Estatística consortium, vol. 1. Rio de Janeiro: Museu Nacional, 1977.

Palmeira, M., et al. "Projeto Emprego e mudança sócio-económica no Nordeste." *Anuário Antropológico*, no. 76. Rio de Janeiro: Tempo Brasileiro, 1977.

Prado, C., Jr. *Formação do Brasil contemporâneo*. São Paulo: Martins Fontes, 1942.

————. *The Colonial Background of Modern Brazil*. Berkeley: University of California Press, 1967.

Pureza da Silva, J. *Memória camponesa*. Edited by O. Dwyer. Rio de Janeiro: Marco Zero, 1982.

Rangel, I. *A questão agrária brasileira*. Recife: Comissão de Desenvolvimento de Pernambuco, 1962.

————. *A inflação brasileira*. Rio de Janeiro: Tempo Brasileiro, 1963.

Ringuelet, R. *1977 — Los migrantes estacionales del Nordeste*. Master's thesis, Universidade Federal do Rio de Janeiro. Rio de Janeiro: Museu Nacional, 1977.

Sachs, I. "Amazônia: Problema e solução." *Política Externa* 10, no. 2 (2000).

————. "Brésil: Tristes tropiques ou terre de bonne espérance?" In "La Nation Brésil." *Hérodote* 98 (September 2000).

Sayad, A. *L'immigration ou les paradoxes de l'altérité*. Brussels: De Boeck-Wesmael, 1991.

Seyferth, G. *A colonização alemã no vale do Itajaí-mirim*. Porto Alegre: Movimento, 1974.

Sigaud, L. "A percepção dos salários entre trabalhadores rurais." In *Capital e trabalho no campo*, edited by P. Singer. São Paulo: Hucitec, 1977.

————. *Os clandestinos e os direitos*. São Paulo: Duas Cidades, 1979.

————. "A nação dos homems." *Anuário Antropológico*, no. 78. Rio de Janeiro: Tempo Brasileiro, 1980.

Silva, S. *Expansão cafeeira e origens da indústria no Brasil*. São Paulo: Alfa-Omega, 1976.

Stein, S. *Vassouras: A Brazilian Coffee County, 1850–1900*. Cambridge, Mass.: Harvard University Press, 1957.

Stolcke, V. *Cafeicultura*. São Paulo: Brasiliense, 1976.

Szmrecsanyi, T. *O planejamento da agroindústria canavieira do Brasil (1930–75)*. São Paulo: Hucitec/Editora da Universidade Estadual de Campinas, 1979.

Tavares, M. C. *Da substituição da importação ao capitalismo financeiro*. Rio de Janeiro: Paz e Terra, 1972.

Tavares dos Santos, J. V. *Colonos do vinho*. São Paulo: Hucitec, 1978.

Thery, H. *Le Brésil*. Paris: Armand Colin, 2000.

Velho, O. *Frente de expansão e estrutura agrária*. Rio de Janeiro: Zahar, 1970.

————. *Capitalismo autoritário e campesinato*. São Paulo: Difusão Européia do Livro, 1974.

Wagner de Almeida, A. *Getat: A segurança nacional e o revigoramento do poder regional*. São Luís: CPT-Maranhão, 1980.

Weber, M. *Economie et société*. Paris: Plon, 1971.

Wilkinson, J. *Estudo da competitividade da indústria brasileira: O complexo agroindustrial*. Rio de Janeiro: Forense Universitária, 1996.

Wolf, E., and S. Mintz. "Haciendas and Plantations in Middle America and the Antilles." *Social and Economic Studies* 6, no. 3 (1957).

3

PAULO SINGER

Economic Evolution and the International Connection

Brazil, a country with a huge land area and, at least since the mid-twentieth century, a large population, has long had an economy based on its domestic market. Big countries like Brazil hold a significant share of the world's labor force and production within their borders. This is evident if we imagine what Portuguese America would have been like if it had, like Spanish America, splintered into various countries. In that hypothetical case, the separate countries would not have crystallized around one great metropolitan area, as happened with the Brazilian states in relation to São Paulo. Rather, each country would probably have developed its own industrial center with its own small domestic market, and each economy would have been much more oriented toward foreign markets. Instead, Brazil is a federative republic, somewhat like the United States, with individual states having limited political and administrative autonomy and arising, in part, like those of the United States, from colonial administrative divisions. Though Brazil's political integration occurred much earlier than that of the United States, with the creation of a colonial viceroyalty, its economic integration lagged behind that of the United States. Still, Brazil has developed dense productive and commercial integration among its separate states, in contrast with the externally oriented economies of its neighbors on the continent.

Although Brazil is big, it is underdeveloped. After gaining independence in 1822, Brazil joined the global economy structured around Great Britain, the industrial powerhouse of the time, as a producer of primary products. Dependent on slave labor imported from Africa, Brazil specialized in the production of tropical crops—especially coffee, sugar, cacao, and rubber—bound for Europe and the United States, which were already well ahead in the industrialization process. Brazil's dependent position in the global economy as a producer of primary products and a consumer of manufactured goods delayed the development of its economy for at least eighty years. Before the abolition of slavery in 1888, Brazil was an agrarian country, technically backward because of its dependence on slave labor, which cost so little that there was no incentive to replace it with machinery. Furthermore, plantation owners generally could not entrust to slaves any but the simplest and cheapest equipment for fear of damage or sabotage.

Economic backwardness eventually forced Brazil to turn outward. From abroad came the consumer goods that the dominant classes (naturally dominant, by their reckoning) deemed to be the basis of a civilized standard of living, goods that distinguished them from the primitive, miserable masses. Along with the perfumes, jewelry, clothing, footwear, books, magazines, canes, and snuffboxes came ideas and ideals that were, as Roberto Schwarz has rightly observed, "misplaced" in a society based on plantation slavery. Also from abroad came the capital that allowed Brazil to begin to build an urban services infrastructure for energy, transportation, and communications.

Throughout the twentieth century the Brazilian economy was painfully polarized between the large domestic market that gradually came into being and the advanced foreign capitalist centers, which were the source of progressive aspirations. The republic's flag reflects these ideals, bearing the positivist slogan "Order and Progress." We will see in the course of this essay how each of these poles — the internal and the external — both confronted and joined forces with each other in the social and political conflicts that drove the evolution of Brazil's economy.

From Speculative Frenzy to the Great Depression (1889–1930)

The abolition of slavery (1888) and the proclamation of the republic (1889) set the foundation for contemporary Brazil. Abolition made possible the spread of wage labor, the basis for the accumulation of industrial capital, since wage labor provides both a sufficient workforce and a domestic market that absorbs production. Abolition could have dealt a fatal blow to the oligarchies that were based on agricultural exports, as their spokesmen never tired of predicting. Just the opposite occurred, however. Before abolition, the great streams of European immigration flowed to the United States, Argentina, and Canada, avoiding Brazil. In the 1890s, however, both the United States and Argentina were in economic crisis, which redirected the migratory flow to Brazil. This immigration was organized and financed by the largest of the coffee-producing states, São Paulo. By 1890, European immigration provided an ample labor supply to meet the shortage created by the mass departure of slaves from the plantations.[1] The immigrants were taken directly to the plantations, where they suffered a dual exploitation. There, in addition to the hardships of harvest labor, they were forced to incur debt to subsist until the coffee harvest.

The branch of government that the constitution of 1824 vested in the emperor gave him a discretionary moderating power over the executive, legislative, and judicial branches, over the provinces, and over political parties. The republic abolished the moderating power and, in its place, instituted more political autonomy for the states and municipalities. In the place of a hereditary monarchy exercising power through manipulation of the two parties, the Conservative and the Liberal, the republic established the domination of the *coronéis*—the local oligarchs who chose the state governors, from whose alliances arose the official and opposition candidates for president. During most of the First Republic (1889–1930) the presidency alternated between politicians from the states of São Paulo and Minas Gerais, not coincidentally the two largest coffee-producing states. Because Minas Gerais also produced dairy products, this arrangement became known as "café au lait" (*café com leite*). While not properly democratic, the First Republic decentralized power and opened the system to new classes and new ideologies.

In addition to an ample supply of free labor, what sustained the growth of the Brazilian economy in the years after abolition and the early years of the republic was the increased international demand for coffee and a change in monetary policy favoring the creation of more private banks. Monetary policy since the 1860s had been strictly based on gold reserves. The Bank of Brazil, a private bank controlled by the government, at that time exercised the functions of a central bank, and it had the exclusive right to issue paper currency. This centralization had led to weak expansion of credit and high interest rates, well in accord with the interests of the owners of loan capital. At the time of abolition, however, the Brazilian government set out to aid export agriculture by eliminating the restrictions on the issue of notes by private banks. The change in monetary policy led to an expansion of credit to agriculture and, later, to industrial companies and speculators on the Rio de Janeiro Stock Exchange. With the liberalization of monetary policy after 1888, not only planters but also those engaged in other activities benefited from cheap and abundant credit. The country witnessed a wave of industrial and commercial business establishment: "Between May 1888 and October 1890, the capital of corporations established in Brazil grew approximately 377 percent" (Pelaez and Suzigan, 143–44). It was a typical financial boom marked by intense speculation whose center stage was the Rio de Janeiro Stock Exchange.

This period of speculation became known as the Encilhamento (saddling-up). "The nickname is a neologism from horseracing. In the stables at the Derby or the Jockey Club, where the horses were saddled, the gaming, the buzz of betting tips, the combination of elegance and luck of the racetrack were all on display. Thus, the term was applied to the financial craze that, between 1889 and 1891, infested Rio de Janeiro" (Calmon quoted in Vieira, 176).

Even in the late twentieth century, a hundred years later, the Encilhamento elicited varied interpretations. The partisans of orthodox neoclassicism such as Pedro Calmon viewed the Encilhamento with horror: "The consequences of the monetary disorientation that characterized the Encilhamento were quite harmful. The extraordinary increase in currency issue led to a rise in prices; the reduction in buying power of the currency was all the greater as a result of the counterfeiting of bank notes. Gold reserves emptied out. Speculation made itself felt in all areas: it contributed to the creation of fantastic trade activity, favored playing the stock market, disrupted agriculture, provoked bankruptcies, and, in the end, caused the banks to go broke in 1900" (Calmon quoted in Vieira, 191).

The twentieth-century developmentalists, who themselves saw public and private spending as a key to economic growth in the mid-twentieth century, disagreed. They tended to consider growth and modernization of the economy more important than monetary stability: "The Encilhamento was more than just another South Sea Bubble[2] and . . . it marked a significant step forward in this period. What is more, reform of the laws for creating corporations and of monetary policy (permitting more rapid growth in the money supply) constituted necessary measures for progress. The country had been restricted by excessively austere monetary policies that impeded the institutional change so essential to the process of economic development" (Pelaez and Suzigan, 144).

This sort of polemic has marked Brazilian economic evolution from the founding in 1852 of the second Bank of Brazil, which annulled all of the note-issuing private banks, up to today. On one side are those who represent new productive sectors (coffee, cacao, and rubber in the second half of the nineteenth century and import-substitution industry in the twentieth century) that are developing the economy and need cheap and abundant credit for their primary accumulation of capital. This need for credit has led them to extol the virtues of increasing the money supply beyond the strict limits imposed by the size of gold reserves during the gold standard era (in Brazil, up to 1931) and beyond the limits set by the fear of inflation in the era of fiduciary money (from 1931 on). On the other side are the representatives of the old wealth, of income-earning capital, of those who hold most of their property in the form of financial assets in domestic currency. For them, it is vital that the money supply be scarce not only to prevent any inflation from eroding the value of their assets but also to keep interest rates high, since that is the source of their income. They condemn, therefore, any excess issue of currency and always preach cuts in public spending and reduction in credit supply by the banks.

The ups and downs of development in Brazil during the twentieth century were a result of the alternating dominance of these factions. When the developmentalists (whose nineteenth-century counterparts were called *papelistas*, "paperists") are in power, they let the banks increase the credit supply and loan money for long terms at low interest rates to finance investments. As a result, development accelerates, and after a while prices rise, as does the exchange rate. This is an indication that the economy is about to overheat. The most important consequence is the shortage of hard currency (pounds until 1930, dollars after World War II) for importing equipment and other inputs and servicing the foreign debt.

In general, developmentalist governments try to contain inflation and foreign devaluation of the currency through price and foreign spending controls, which end up provoking a reaction from those most affected: domestic and foreign capitalists. These capitalists then support economic liberals (in the nineteenth century, called *metalistas*, "metalists"), who favor combating inflation and exchange devaluation through cuts in governmental spending and tightened credit. When they assume power, they deeply cut public investment and monetary supply, which can produce financial crises on the one hand and excess supply on the other. The economy plunges into recession, and part of the capital is lost because of business failures. Unemployment increases, which aggravates the recession, since those who have lost their jobs or fear losing them reduce their spending to the minimum necessary. The reduction in private consumer spending heightens the excess production originally caused by the reduction in public spending.

The classic episode of an economic "fix" from the First Republic was the policy introduced by Joaquim Murtinho, finance minister under Campos Sales, who was president from 1898 to 1902. Murtinho instituted the payment of import taxes in gold to prevent inflation from lowering their value, and he negotiated a moratorium on amortization of the foreign debt for thirteen years, with financing from the House of Rothschild, which was to be guaranteed by customs revenues. Brazil earned this demonstration of confidence from a large international bank through an extremely rigorous monetary policy. The funding contract for consolidation and postponement of the foreign debt required the periodic incineration of Brazilian government banknotes, which resulted in a gradual reduction of money supply.

During the first two years of Murtinho's term in the Finance Ministry (1899–1900), the monetary base (defined here as paper currency issued) fell 5.9 percent and 4.6 percent, the reductions in the money supply were 5.0 percent and 3.8 percent, and prices dropped 14.4 percent and 15.7 percent. This was in contrast with the inflation experienced since 1889. Since there are no estimates of economic productivity prior to 1900, evaluation of the impact of deflation on economic activity must be based on qualitative evidence. The commercial review section of the *Jornal do Comércio*, for example, observed that no one had seen the likes of the shrinkage in Rio de Janeiro's commercial climate in the past twenty-five years. The same feeling of pessimism was probably occurring in the rest of the country (Neuhaus 1975, 18).

Murtinho's economic "fix" was so profound that it led to the closing of most of the banks and caused even the Bank of Brazil to suspend payments. The recession resulting from this policy was so violent that it continues in the collective consciousness. Brazil would not witness anything analogous until nearly a century later, when in 1990 the Collor Plan paralyzed the domestic economy by freezing access to savings accounts, effecting a drastic reduction of the means of payment to put the brakes on the runaway inflation of the time (see below).

These economic ups and downs constituted cycles in Brazil's peripheral economy, which was largely conditioned by foreign circumstances. This conditioning was eased only after the 1930s, when the Great Depression led to the relative closing of the economy and the domestic market began to control the economic dynamic. In the period under consideration, though, the dynamic core of the Brazilian economy was foreign trade, especially coffee exports, which followed the fluctuations of the importing countries' markets.

During the nineteenth century the world industrial capitalist economy followed a cycle in which approximately every ten years, the developed economies suffered a collapse, usually unleashed by a financial crisis that soon affected the real economy. The crisis would provoke a fall in demand, which in turn caused excess supply, a widespread fall in prices, and unemployment. Next, there would be another drop in purchasing, both among the wealthy, because of their hope for a further fall in prices, and among workers, because of unemployment or their fear thereof. The vicious cycle of excess supply, deflation, and unemployment would cause a drop in consumption and, therefore, in prices of commodities imported from the economic periphery, for example of rubber, coffee, or cacao from Brazil.

In this way, when crisis gripped the center it quickly spread to the periphery because of the fall of export earnings. This deprived Brazil of the foreign exchange needed to import capital and consumer goods, service the foreign debt, and support the international value of its currency. A foreign exchange scarcity was made worse by the flight of capital abroad. This drain was a result in part of foreign capital's returning to the countries of origin, where it could alleviate the financial distress of the developed economies that had been caused by the crisis in the first place. Finally, the value of imports also shrank, reducing customs receipts, which were the main source of public revenue at the time.

In the face of such crises, which would later be called "foreign shocks," the Brazilian economy could react in two ways. The liberal or *metalista* reaction, as we have seen, forced a reduction in public spending in the same proportion that revenues shrank. It tightened the money and credit supplies to reduce domestic consumption, thus "fitting" it to the availability of foreign exchange for importing consumer goods. This brought the crisis into the country, forcing the slowdown of economic activities until the developed economies began to grow again and increase imports from Brazil. Only then would Brazilian authorities allow the domestic economy to resume growth.

Liberal policies led to a drop in prices and so preserved the foreign value of the currency, since they reduced the demand on reserves at the same rate that the supply fell. This passive adjustment of the domestic economy to international economic conditions imposed a heavy price in loss of production and income for both entrepreneurs and workers. This outcome would usually provoke a strong reaction among the injured parties, who would then begin to clamor for policies that supported production and employment. These were the interventionist or *papelista* policies, which consisted basically of supporting production for the foreign market by financing retention of excess inventories of merchandise. These policies also maintained public spending by means of deficit financing by expanding the public debt, issuing currency, or both. These measures softened the impact of the international crisis on the domestic economy by creating conditions for the substitution of imports, which could no longer be afforded, with domestic products. This allowed the domestic economy to continue to grow, driven no longer by exports but by growth in the demand of the internal market.

Of course, interventionist policies had the undesirable side effects of inflation and increase in the exchange rate. Consumers of above-average income complained that they had to pay more for Brazilian merchandise, which they considered inferior to the previously imported goods. The moneyed class complained about the losses in value of assets caused by inflation, especially when workers, encouraged by the rise in employment, pushed for wage increases to offset the higher cost of living. This in turn led to new price increases.

Until 1914, these cycles modulated the rhythm of Brazilian economic growth, which nevertheless moved forward with building transportation, communications, and energy infrastructures, financed largely by foreign investments. The economy continued to move toward import-substitution industrialization. In addition, the new infrastructure made possible continued growth of commodity production for export.

Coffee, for example, continued its march from the Paraíba Valley near the southeast coast to the western part of the state of São Paulo. This shift required construction of railroads, ports, telegraph and telephone lines, and new cities and towns. Light and Power, a Canadian company, garnered British capital to build dams and hydroelectric power plants, power transmission and distribution lines, public lighting systems, telephone lines, and gas companies in Rio and São Paulo, the two largest cities at the turn of the century. The Electric Bond and Share Company engaged in similar projects elsewhere in the country.

The Amazonian region enjoyed great prosperity thanks to rubber exports, whose demand was driven by the automobile industry. Railways were built and steamship lines established to transport the rubber from the latex plantations in Acre and other places far from the port city of Belém. Rubber export taxes supported the creation of urban service networks in the cities of Belém and Manaus. This lasted until the sudden intrusion of rubber from Southeast Asia into the market after 1910. The resulting excess supply and drop in prices soon eliminated native latex extraction and plunged Amazonia into a long crisis of decline from which it rebounded only during World War II (see chapter 9).

Even so, the same infrastructure that made possible the growth in production for the global market also served to unite physically the domestic market and constantly open it to consume the production from import substitution. This expansion progressed throughout the First Republic, although it suffered contractions during periods of crisis whenever the government implemented liberal economic policies. World War I (1914–18) made it clear that a forced reduction in imports did not have to result in an equivalent decrease in consumption. The consumer demand could just as well be met by domestic production even if at first it was not equal in price and quality. It began to dawn on Brazil that it was much better to have domestic production than none at all.

Roberto Simonsen has summarized the history of Brazilian economic development from abolition and the Encilhamento to 1930 as follows:

> In the last year of the monarchy (1889) there were in the country more than 636 industrial firms with 401,630,600 mil-réis[3] in capital (in 1920 terms), or about 25 million pounds. There were about 65,000 in horsepower and about 54,169 employed workers. Total production is estimated at 507,092,587 mil-réis.
>
> The rhythm of growth was maintained until 1895. Between 1890 and 1895, 452 factories were founded, with 213,714,736 mil-réis in capital. From 1894 to 1904, the country was wracked by political, economic, and financial crises and suffered moreover the consequences of the deflationist policies of the Campos Sales administration (1898–1902).
>
> After 1905, Brazil witnessed an ever-increasing pace of industrial development, especially evident between 1910 and 1914, and even more accelerated between 1915 and 1919, due to the European firestorm. . . . The 1920 national census revealed that at that time there were 13,336 industrial establishments in the country with 1,815,156,011 mil-réis in capital, employing 275,512 workers and with production worth 2,989,176,281 mil-réis. (Simonsen, 16–17)

Note that the capital of Brazilian industrial firms created between 1890 and 1895 was 53.2 percent of all of those in existence in 1889; that is, in six years, the industrial capital grew at a rate of 7.4 percent, not counting any growth in the existing firms. Between 1889 and 1920 Brazilian industrial capital grew 450 percent, at an average annual rate of 5.2 percent. This all confirms without a doubt that the Encilhamento gave a powerful push to industrialization.

A more recent estimate of the total real product and the real industrial product is from Cláudio Haddad. His results for the period in question are summarized in table 3.1.

These data show that both the total and industrial products grew intensely in the first three decades of the twentieth century. In the first two decades, industry grew faster than the economy as a whole, which is to be expected in a developing country. In the third decade, however, the overall economy grew faster than in the first two decades, and industry grew less. From these data we might conclude

TABLE 3.1. *Growth of Real Product and Real Industrial Product, 1901–30*

Decade	Total Real Product		Real Industrial Product	
	Ten-year (%)	Annual (%)	Ten-year (%)	Annual (%)
1901–10	56.9	4.6	70.7	5.5
1910–19	44.0	3.7	80.3	6.6
1921–30	71.3	5.5	54.0	4.4

Source: Disaggregated data, Haddad 1974, transcribed in Neuhaus 1975, table 43.

that industrialization weakened in the 1920s because of the 1929 crisis, which in Brazil affected industry more than other sectors of the economy in 1929 and 1930. From 1921 to 1928 the real industrial product grew 68.8 percent, an annual rate of 6.8 percent, practically equal to that of the prior decade (6.6 percent). In the last two years of the decade, however, the industrial product decreased by 8.8 percent, much more than the total, which fell only 1.1 percent. We should conclude, therefore, that the rate of industrialization remained quite brisk from 1910 to 1928.

There is another interesting conclusion from the data in table 3.1 in light of Simonsen's information. In 1889 industry employed 54,169 workers, whose production was worth over 500 million mil-réis. In 1920, industrial employment reached 275,512 and output was worth nearly 3 billion mil-réis. In these three decades, employment quintupled and output increased sixfold. The industrial per capita product thus rose from 9,361 mil-réis in 1889 to 10,850 mil-réis in 1920. Since per capita output measures productivity, we can conclude that productivity grew only 15.9 percent in thirty-one years. This reveals that industrial growth in Brazil during this period was mainly extensive, with an increase in the number of firms that were, however, often small and lightly mechanized, producing mostly crafts. Warren Dean describes the situation in more detail:

> Analyses of the beginnings of industrialization usually center on the question of the degree to which domestic manufactures are able to supplant imports. This is indeed an important subject, but it is not particularly relevant to the early stages of industrial development, if São Paulo is a typical case. The very first products to be manufactured there were those whose weight-to-cost ratio was so high that even with the most rudimentary technique they cost less to produce than to buy them from Europe. At least until the 1920's, the Paulistas were producing, with very few ex-

ceptions, only goods that were quite bulky and intrinsically low in value. (Dean, 9)

Annibal Villela and Wilson Suzigan have observed that

until 1945 in Brazil there was not a policy with a coordinated set of measures that could stimulate industrial development. Industrialization, in fact, was never a basic goal of government economic policy. . . . It was monetary policy, however, that was mostly responsible for the limited industrial growth in Brazil before 1945, even more so until the end of the 1920s. In addition to the frequent policies of stabilization and even reduction of paper money in circulation, there were not financial institutions up to the task of financing industrial development. The banking system operated within the traditional functional limits of commercial banks. The absence of a development bank kept there from being a domestic supply of long-term credit to finance new industrial ventures. (Villela and Suzigan, 78–79)

This lack explains, more than any factor, the extensive character of Brazilian industrialization before 1930. Accumulation of industrial capital in Brazil depended entirely on unspent profits at a time when mass production already prevailed in more developed countries. This required an ample concentration of capital to make large-scale earnings possible. The so-called second industrial revolution, in full swing since 1880, had caused a large expansion of fixed capital in the form of nearly automatic systems of continuously flowing production in the processing industries for petroleum, grain, animal and plant fibers, food and beverages, tobacco, and so forth. In addition, the manufacturing chains in the metalworking and mechanical industries — for example, automobiles and sewing machines — were costly. Amortizing this capital required large-scale production, complemented by the establishment of extensive networks of distribution and retail, consumer finance, and, in the case of durable goods, technical assistance.

This pattern of industrialization could not rely solely on the accumulation of profits; rather, it required financing sources from outside the company. In the United States and England, this role was largely played by the stock markets, where companies could capitalize themselves through the sale of stocks. In Germany and in the rest of continental Europe, the task fell to the large industrial banks, which allied themselves with the firms that they financed. In Brazil before 1930, no institution financed the establishment of industrial giants. As a result, the industries that expanded in general produced consumer goods in limited runs in modest factories.

In the social realm, the hegemonic portion of the dominant classes was still the agroexporting oligarchies, mostly coffee growers. The industrial bourgeoisie thrived in their shadow, profiting from the domestic market that the agricultural export economy continued to expand. Domestic industry also continued to depend on the import capacity supported by the export economy. These imports were indispensable because the industries of the time were little more than processors, transformers, or mere assemblers of imported raw materials and components.

In conclusion, when Brazil arrived at the end of the 1920s, it had diversified light industry of relatively high volume, spread throughout the country to exploit local and regional markets. In São Paulo, national industry began to take off when coffee growing, in its endless quest for new lands for cultivation, invaded neighboring states. Nonetheless, the industrial sector continued to be subordinate to the agroexporting oligarchy. As coffee's junior partner, it was always on the lookout for opportunities that interventionist policies in support of the coffee sector might afford it.

From Import Substitution to Manufacturing Exports (1930–80)

The Great Depression of the 1930s took up half of the period between the two world wars and was a great watershed of the twentieth century. It was the longest and deepest economic crisis of the century. It struck the world's strongest capitalist economy, that of the United States, and spread from there to the rest. Its social and political impact was so vast that it provoked a profound change in the relationship between the state and the market economy of every country. Up to this point, economic liberalism prevailed in the economically dominant countries. The role of the state was reduced to maintenance of external order — diplomacy and national defense — and of internal order: preservation of civil and criminal law, support of the judicial and legal enforcement systems, government operations, and so forth. Interventions in the economy, such as setting customs tariffs or organizing cartels, occurred in some countries, but these were generally viewed as violations of good political conduct.

To deal with the Depression, which affected the national economies by way of the world markets, governments were moved to raise tariff barriers against imports, subsidize exports, and devalue currency to make exports cheaper and raise the prices of imports. They also promoted import substitution with more vigor. A growing number of governments created new employment through social spending and public investments, in addition to greatly increasing payments to the unemployed and to other poor citizens.

"Official economic science" saw all of these activities as violations of the prerogatives of the marketplace: all of the production promoted by the state would, inevitably, have to replace that of the marketplace since demand for merchandise was a given and nothing would be added by state action. In the same way, any jobs created by the state would only take the places of some in the market economy. The point of departure of this reasoning was that the market economy always strikes a balance in full employment. If there are unemployed persons—and at the time, there were millions of them—they are all voluntarily so in the sense that they could all get work if they were willing to accept wages that the employers "rationally" could pay. Therefore, the only way to reduce unemployment is for those who are out of work to change their own attitudes and become willing to sell their labor at a lower price.

During the 1930s, the new interventionist position (which earlier had not been that uncommon in the peripheral countries) resulted in a revision of economic science—the Keynesian revolution. John Maynard Keynes, the inventor of macroeconomics, proved that the laws that explain the individual behavior of companies and consumers do not apply when considering all of them together. Macroeconomic balance can be reached with *involuntary* unemployment since employers' demand for workers is not determined by the value of wages as compared to the marginal productivity of the labor, as the orthodox position holds. Rather, it is determined by the total demand for merchandise. This demand depends on the total of savings (equal to unspent income) and the proportion of these savings absorbed by investments. If growing pessimism takes hold of business leaders and dissuades them from investing, overall demand will fall, forcing companies to let go part of their workforce. This in turn will reduce consumption, which will reinforce pessimism, causing a new drop in investments, and so on.

Keynes showed that when the macroeconomic balance keeps some workers involuntarily unemployed, added public spending expands the overall demand in an amount equal to its value times a multiplier representing the additional consumer spending of those who gain employment and income. This spending generates new employment and, therefore, new spending in a decreasing spiral because a portion of each increase in overall income is saved. According to this new theory, each additional dollar or mil-réis spent by the government is multiplied by a factor greater than one, driving up total demand and income. Economic recovery would be reinforced by an expansionist monetary policy because abundant credit and currency supplies would facilitate investment. The Keynesian revolution launched an era of great economic growth in both the center and periphery of capitalism. Interventionism had already been a frequent practice in Brazil, and probably for this reason Brazil was a pioneer in the adoption of development policies before *The General Theory of Employment, Interest, and Money* was published in 1936.

The crisis struck the Brazilian economy, as always, through an abrupt drop in the price and volume of coffee and other primary goods exported. The government of President Washington Luís was strictly orthodox and reacted by cutting credit and limiting public spending: "Under the government's restrictive fiscal policy, which had produced surpluses in 1928 and 1929, Treasury figures once again showed a revenue surplus in the first semester of 1930. . . . The pernicious effort to achieve a surplus in the midst of the Depression was great, since the import taxes, traditionally an important source of revenue, were weakened due to the foreign crisis" (Neuhaus 1975, 102–3).

Without going into detail, it was clear that the government of Luís would do nothing to defend the national economy from being swept up in the global market. This must have contributed to the success of the Revolution of 1930, about which there is more discussion in the next section. This does not mean that the coalition of forces around Getúlio Vargas that came to power in 1930 was in any way Keynesian before the term existed. On the contrary, this coalition, just like Luís's finance minister, implemented orthodox policies: "During the early years of the Vargas era (until 1937, and especially in 1930–31) the orthodox conception of economic policy appeared somewhat shocking in light of the abnormal economic circumstances, and historians have characterized it as incompatible with a regime that declared itself to be 'revolutionary'" (Neuhaus 1975, 105).

The Revolution of 1930 eventually led, however, to a transformation of the Brazilian state's role in economic development. First, it destroyed the prior political leadership, which had been firmly entrenched in financial orthodoxy, replacing it with a heterogeneous and more pragmatic cadre of politicians and technocrats. The break with liberal orthodoxy came in practice, if not in doctrine, in 1932. The Paulista Revolution, in which São Paulo's elites revolted against Vargas's centralization efforts, and a drought in the Northeast forced the provisional government to abandon any pretense of balancing the budget or of stabilizing exchange. From then on, the government followed interventionist policies supporting various regions and sectors of society that were victims of the crisis. Sociologist Octavio Ianni interprets the Revolution of 1930 as follows:

> Little by little it became what it had not been at the beginning. It took on the character of a definite bourgeois revolution, in spite of not having been so initially. After coming to power, the indecisive revolutionaries brought themselves up to date and felt their way toward the formulation of a new economic policy. Or rather, faced with new situations, which appeared continuously, they took concrete, innovative measures. Since they had dislodged an important part of the old rulers and bureaucrats, they found themselves in the position to make decisions that went against tradition and crystallized interests. . . . In addition, they sought to establish a dialogue with the social classes that had helped them to come to power and now were making demands. They were sensitive to the claims and interests of the nascent proletariat and bourgeoisie, of the middle class, and of the civil and military bureaucracy. (Ianni, 133–34)

Coffee, which had been the target of valorization policies before 1930, came to be protected in new ways. The government bought excess crops, paid for with revenues from a tax on coffee exports, and warehoused the product. It later had to destroy the surplus: storage costs became prohibitive because coffee harvests increased when the new fields that had been planted before the crisis began to produce. The government then created the National Coffee Council (Conselho Nacional do Café), which started to implement policies to eliminate the excess supply of beans, such as a one mil-réis tax on each new coffee plant to discourage new planting. In November 1932, the council forbade the planting of new coffee fields in Brazil except in the state of Paraná and in states with fewer than 50 million coffee bushes. Once these states had reached this limit, new planting would be prohibited (Villela and Suzigan, 191–95).

Werner Baer describes further the agricultural production policies of the 1930s: "Throughout the 1930s, the Vargas regime expanded state intervention with the goal of protecting and encouraging the growth of different sectors through the creation of *autarquias*. These autonomous public institutions were to negotiate with certain sectors, such as sugar, yerba mate, salt, pine lumber, fishing, merchant marine, and so forth. *Autarquias* collaborated with producers to regulate production and prices, to finance warehouse construction, and so forth. With time, these instruments of government control came to function as instruments to press for government benefits for specific sectors" (Baer, 390).

Direct government intervention in production, whether encouraging it or limiting it, came to be commonplace and increasingly widespread. The idea that a firm should assert itself in the free market, competing with others, went by the wayside. Any group of producers now had the right to expect and press for the protective intervention of the state, and gradually all began to do so. Before the Revolution of 1930, state intervention sheltered only coffee growing, an exception justified by the extraordinary importance of this activity to the country. With the interminable Depression—and revolution—intervention no longer had limits, and the federal government took up directing both the economy and the process of development.

This new orientation led to an explicit policy of fomenting import-substitution industrialization. As we have seen, Brazil had been industrializing in this way since the abolition of slavery, but up to this point, the process had depended essentially on market opportunities. With the crisis in the foreign markets, the federal government instituted exchange controls and limits on importation. Importing products with a domestic "equivalent" was made impossible. The domestic market was thus reserved for domestic industry. To prevent excess production, the importation of equipment for the textile and footwear industries was also prohibited until 1937.

With time, substitution of industrial and agricultural imports came to be the dominant strategy of industrialization. For this, financing for capital accumulation was needed, leading to the creation in 1937 of the Bank of Brazil's Fund for Agricultural and Industrial Capital (Carteira de Crédito Agrícola e Industrial, CREAI). CREAI offered middle- and long-term loans to agriculture and industry for the purposes of financing cultivation, acquiring livestock, and purchasing industrial and agricultural equipment. Until the founding of the National Economic Development Bank (Banco Nacional de Desenvolvimento Econômico, BNDE) in 1952, CREAI was the main source of financing for new industries, such as aluminum smelting, cellulose, and paper (Villela and Suzigan, 189–90).

Another area in which state intervention increased was labor relations. With the abolition of slavery, wage labor became the rule, although often in an archaic form, such as in the resident labor system in coffee areas (see chapter 2). The wages of the resident workers were paid in kind, as a share of the coffee harvested, land to live on, and the crops they could grow between the coffee rows.

When the workers bought supplies at the farm's store, wage exploitation mixed with usury, since they then lived in debt to the boss, thanks to his commercial monopoly.

In urban activities, however, wage labor mainly took a capitalist form: in exchange for a set day's work, the worker was paid in money. After abolition, as we have seen, wage labor in urban industry, trade, transportation, and services grew intensely. This growth fed the formation of working-class parties and unions with Socialist or anarchist ideologies first brought to Brazil by European immigrants.

Brazil had already felt the presence of a workers' movement at the time of the proclamation of the republic. This presence had raised great hopes among the Socialists who were active among the working class: "In January 1890, there appeared in Rio de Janeiro, the capital of the Republic, the first newspaper in Brazil that could be considered a labor organizing tool. It had a program of stated Socialist inspiration. . . . Suggestively called *A Voz do Povo* (The Voice of the People), it was heralded sympathetically by the official organ of the provisional government, *O País* (The Country). This reveals a climate favorable to activity on behalf of increased political participation" (Gomes, 38–39).

Two rival workers' parties competed in the Constituent Assembly elections. José Augusto Vinhaes headed the larger of the two, the Workers' Party Center (Centro do Partido Operário, CPO), run by important labor militants of the period. The CPO also represented employees of state shops, public service, and private factories. The party managed to elect Vinhaes as a representative to the assembly. His platform, with a few additions, would constitute the agenda for half a century of Brazilian labor struggles: "As far as substantive demands were concerned, the platforms were basically the same. The battle cries included issues of work schedule, protection of female and child workers, protections in old age and illness through savings or pension funds, and wage hikes. França e Silva's plan added better working, educational, and nutritional conditions for working families. Proposals also included establishing a court composed of workers and industrialists, whose goal would be to end conflicts and avoid strikes" (Gomes, 52).

Among the successful campaigns that the CPO conducted was the campaign for reform of the Penal Code, which had virtually outlawed any kind of work stoppage. In 1890, the CPO managed to limit the prohibition to strikes considered violent (Gomes, 56). Another significant accomplishment of Vinhaes was the formation of the Workers' Bank in the first half of 1890: "The bank was an institution where workers could deposit their savings and borrow money at modest interest for various undertakings. . . . Recall that this was the time of the Encilhamento.

The bank had a short and tumultuous lifespan (it failed in 1894), but, aside from the usual commercial transactions, among its goals were construction of convenient and inexpensive housing, the establishment of producer and consumer cooperatives, and the creation of a pension for the working class" (Gomes, 56–57).

During the First Republic, the very existence of a workers' movement was always precarious. Few workers' rights were protected by law. Working conditions were bad because of a constant labor surplus, fed by heavy immigration from Europe and Japan and by numerous former slaves, who were relegated to the worst-paid jobs. Conflicts between employees and their employers were frequent, short, and violent—begun out of desperation and ended with repression. In 1907, a landmark law regulating labor unions was passed, giving broad freedom of association to the trades and allowing trade unions to form without government authorization (Rodrigues, 512n). In spite of this legislation, union organizations did not manage to stabilize and grow because of the small number of members and the narrow margins of victory that could be achieved through direct action.

The Brazilian workers' movement was divided between Socialists and anarchists. The first group was inspired by European parties, especially the German, whose electoral victories had encouraged their partisans around the world. In Brazil, however, the electoral victories of the successive Socialist parties were few, either because not all workers were voters or because most of them were not inclined toward Socialism or its candidates. Moreover, representation was by district, which favored major parties and denied minority parties access to Congress.

Perhaps because of this lack of political success, after 1906, anarchism grew faster than all other ideological tendencies, and by the second decade of the twentieth century it was the dominant trend in all working-class organizations. The persuasion that played the most important role in the Brazilian labor movement was the anarchosyndicalists, who promoted the professional organization of workers with the goal of raising their awareness against capitalism. They repudiated any sort of political action, refusing to run in elections for the executive or legislature. They did not want to enter into a pact with the state, which they intended to abolish. Their political efforts were concentrated in education and propaganda, but they were unable to win permanent, effective improvements for the working class.

At the time of the Revolution of 1930, most of the proposals from 1890 had not been implemented. The provisional government did not delay in taking a position on labor relations. In November 1930, a few weeks after taking power, the government created the Ministry of Labor, Industry, and Commerce, which, by its very name, revealed the intention to intervene systematically in the relationships between urban companies and their employees. In March 1931, the government issued Decree no. 19770, which set guidelines for unions. It defined a union as a consultative organ in collaboration with government. It affirmed the principle of uniqueness, that is, that each class of workers should be represented by only one union. It was the union's task, along with the government and the ministry, to defend workers' interests, but, to exercise this function, it had to be recognized by the ministry. This decree made it clear that the provisional government intended to both protect and control labor unions. It offered them legal protection against police repression, which until then had affected all of the most combative unions. In compensation, it required that the unions apply for recognition from the Ministry of Labor, Industry, and Commerce. In this way, the exercise of union rights became subordinated to the ministry's policies, which could withhold or withdraw recognition from any union.

The new union policy drew strong criticism, and not only from the groups on the Left that competed for leadership of the working-class organizations. Socialists, anarchists, and Communists who had gained positions of power and influence in the unions made great efforts to preserve the independence of working-class organizations from the government. The Catholic Church, which had been engaged in creating denomination-based unions, felt hurt because Decree no. 19770, in addition to permitting only one union per class, also explicitly prohibited any religious affiliation of the unions. Business leaders raised their voices against the linkage of organizations representing both workers and management to the state (Gomes, 176). Since the unions had managed to get workers from the major trade groups to join, it was not easy for the ministry to make the unions submit spontaneously to its control. The government offensive had as its basis more enticement than repression, at least before 1934. During the term of Salgado Filho as labor minister (1932–34), almost all of the rights demanded in the platforms of 1890 were approved by decree: the eight-hour workday, protections for working women and minors, extension of retirement and pension benefits, and institutions to foster labor and mediate disputes such as the Bureaus of Reconciliation and Arbitration (Comissões e Juntas de Conciliação e Julgamento) and collective labor conventions.

Most of this legislation was developed with the participation of representatives of labor, management, and the ministry. The ministry's role was strengthened with powers to mediate between the opposing class interests: "Workers on the one hand and industrialists on the other act as pressure groups inside and outside of state institutions, each experiencing victories and defeats. Progressively and from the beginning in this process, the state positioned itself as an arbiter between employees and employers. The demands of the parties in conflict were brought within the apparatus of the state, the mediator of class relations. Direct negotiation between workers and managers was soon substituted by claims made before the state, which retained the decision-making power. Through this process the state came to incorporate both the working class and the managerial class" (Rodrigues, 516).

The application of new laws depended on oversight by the Ministry of Labor, Industry, and Commerce, which encountered strong resistance from employers: "Inspectors had broad punitive powers: they could fine business owners and investigate working conditions in their firms. At the same time that they were doing this, though, they could 'convince' the employer (even if by 'inspection blackmail') of the benefits of the laws and show that the Ministry wanted to give them full support within established guidelines of the unionization laws" (Gomes, 178).

In this way, the provisional government gradually won over the allegiance of some union leaders and was able to sponsor new unions that fit within the requirements of its legislation. Even so, the independent union resistance remained tenacious. Nevertheless, the government offensive pressed on: wherever the tactic of enticement did not win the day, it resorted to police violence and repression, pure and simple (see chapter 7). What finally managed to lay the leftist opposition low was the prospect of electing a bench of working-class representatives to the Constituent Assembly in 1933. They would be selected by the workers and business unions, naturally, on the condition that they were recognized by the ministry. The Communists and the Trotskyists (arising from the schism between the Union Opposition and the Brazilian Communist Party [Partido Comunista Brasileiro, PCB; see chapter 7) decided to join the official unions so they could fight within the system, instead of opposing them head-on. Only the anarchists remained untamed (Gomes, 180–81).

In this way, the labor movement defeated economic liberalism. In Brazil before 1930, the supporters of the movement had fought for legal regulation of workers' rights with the goal of extending to all wage earners protection against the predatory exploitation of the labor market. Great Britain had been passing this sort of legislation since the early nineteenth century, and the other industrializing countries followed suit. In the nineteenth century, however, the gains in labor legislation in no way implied the direct interference of the state in class struggle or, much less, in class-based organizations.

The corporatist policies that assigned administration of relations between employees and employers to the state began with European Fascist regimes. Notable was Mussolini's Carta del Lavoro, which is known to have inspired Brazilian labor law in the 1930s and 1940s. A little later, the New Deal in the United States instituted a similar process of assigning to the federal government the role of promoting elections in companies to determine what union would represent its workers. Since the New Deal was democratic, however, the corporatism that it established left control of the labor organizations to the members but made the state responsible for oversight, regulation, and arbitration of class conflicts.

The New Deal–era National Labor Relations Act, or Wagner Act, of 1935 established, among other provisions, the National Labor Relations Board (NLRB). The purpose of the NLRB was to regulate relations between unions and employers to prevent the latter, with their economic power, from blocking union organizing among their employees. The board was composed of three members with full power to administer and enforce the law. It had the power to subpoena witnesses, hold elections, and enforce its orders through federal courts. The NLRB was authorized to investigate matters of representation and debates over the right to recognize a union, and to certify unions as official representatives of groups of employees if these had registered a majority of employees in their NLRB-defined bargaining unit. When a union received such certification, the employer could not refuse to negotiate collectively (Phelps 1955, 150–51). Although far from being identical, Brazilian and U.S. laws shared the same spirit: to extend the protective mantle of the state to employees' right to organize.

What matters is that corporatism arose simultaneously in several countries in the period between the wars as a response to the failure of economic liberalism to maintain economic normality and to assure wage-earning citizens the right to collective labor bargaining. In Brazil, the state's concern with workers' rights was closely connected with its desire to keep workers away from the influence of the Left, which it saw as an enemy. After 1930, corporatism would become a structural feature of the state, taking on repressive connotations at times when the political regime was dictatorial and democratic connotations when the political regime was more open.

After the promulgation of the 1934 constitution, the restoration of democracy was increasingly threatened by rising ideological polarization. On the one hand was the authoritarian Right, of which the Brazilian Integralist Action (Ação Integralista Brasileira, AIB) was the most evident manifestation. The Integralists had trappings reminiscent of Italian Fascism but are better thought of as inspired by nationalism, economic nativism, and conservative Catholicism. On the other hand were Communists, who, thanks to former army officer Luiz Carlos Prestes's leadership, began to gain a mass following. Prestes, who had recently joined the PCB, had gained his military and political fame by leading other junior officers, the *tenentes* or lieutenants, with Communist leanings, in barracks revolts that shook the country in the 1920s. For the first time in Brazilian history the political scene was polarized between two opposing factions, neither of which was committed to democracy. Vargas manipulated this confrontation to stay in power. In late 1935, officers associated with the PCB attempted a barracks uprising at three army bases. The Vargas government learned of the plot and crushed it. This "Communist plot" was used as an excuse for a vast wave of persecution of most groups on the Left, culminating in a coup d'état against all political opposition factions: Vargas's proclamation of the Estado Novo (New State) in 1937.

During the Estado Novo regime (1937–45), the state took new, important steps toward involvement with economic development. Perhaps the most important step was the founding of an integrated steel mill, the National Steel Company (Companhia Siderúrgica Nacional, CSN). CSN was the state's first but not only foray into the creation of production firms. CSN took import-substitution industrialization to a new level. Up to that point, only light industries had been founded, viable on a modest scale of production that could be capitalized through accumulation of their own profits. CSN's plant in Volta Redonda, however, required heavy investment before it could produce and turn a profit.

The government's strategy was to seek foreign financing for CSN, which could only be state-run, given the excess supply of steel and almost all other commodities during the Great Depression. Germany under Hitler and the United States under Roosevelt competed for Brazil's allegiance by showing willingness to finance the company. At the same time, the world was marching toward World War II, which began 1 September 1939, when Nazi Germany and the Soviet Union invaded Poland. The war became global only with the Japanese attack on Pearl Harbor. In December 1941, Japan and the United States entered the war. Up to that point, the Brazilian government had tried to remain neutral, because it was divided between Axis and Allied partisans. Outside the government, however, there was strong pressure on Brazil to join the Allies since this world war was largely ideological, pitting democrats and Communists against Nazis and other Fascists. In 1942, Brazil allied itself with the United States against the Axis powers. This alignment helped reinforce the democratic tendencies in the military and in civil society, resulting in the redemocratization of the country the year that the war ended. As an immediate result, though, the United States financed the Volta Redonda plant, helping to create Brazil's industrial base.

Import-substitution industrialization depended on expansion of a domestic market to absorb its products. The existing railway system joined the hinterland of each region to its ports, which was logical at a time when economic growth was tied to world markets. Given, however, the contraction of international trade during the Great Depression and World War II and its slow recovery afterward, industry relied on domestic markets that found themselves segmented into regions precariously interconnected by coastal navigation.

Given these conditions, the physical unification of regional markets was the only way to give the new industries economies of scale through mass production. This unification was eventually accomplished, not through expansion of the railways but by highway construction. Advances in automobile technology had made the latter option much cheaper. A rail network entailed the construction of permanent tracks, including bridges over waterways, and acquisition of trains, which required plentiful capital before the finished railway could start to generate profit. At the same time, the old roadways were originally of packed earth, often opened only by the passage of vehicles. Highways were paved only once the traffic intensified, financed by taxing the new production that the roads made possible. The vehicle fleet was the result of investment by private transport companies. Competition among these companies tended to reduce costs, in contrast to the rail freight fares, controlled by the state but nevertheless kept high to cover the cost of unused space in the cars. The greater ability of trucking to adapt to demand was one of the reasons that it superseded rail transport in Brazil and in most other countries.

Between 1928 and 1952 the number of miles of railroad track grew only 16.5 percent, while the mileage of roads grew 304.8 percent. There is no doubt that, at this time, physical unification of the domestic market progressed rapidly, but at the cost of increased vehicle and fuel imports. The share of these items in the import total grew from 9 percent in 1925 to 13 percent in 1955. To deal with the difficulty of importing during the war, the government created the National Motor Factory (Fábrica Nacional de Motores, FNM). This factory was the first to manufacture—not just assemble—trucks in Brazil. By 1952, 35 percent of Brazil's trucks were made domestically (Singer, 219–24).

From this time on, import substitution was the order of the day. The weak growth in coffee and other exports fell far short of meeting the needs for importation of the industrial inputs that were in strong demand thanks to the accelerated growth of domestic industry. Six years after the end of the Estado Novo, Vargas returned to office as a democratically elected head of state. It was during this second Vargas administration (1951–54) that leaders decided to adopt a strategy of establishing a domestic automobile industry by attracting large manufacturers from around the world.

At first, this was a matter of stimulating import substitution by prohibiting the import of finished products. On 19 August 1952, the Bank of Brazil's Import-Export Fund (Carteira de Exportação e Importação, CEXIM) outlawed the importation of automobile parts that Brazil already produced. On 28 April 1953, the Bank of Brazil's Foreign Trade Fund (Carteira de Comércio Exterior, CACEX) blocked the import of assembled cars, since Ford and some other companies had already set up assembly plants in Brazil. After 1 November 1954, it was legal to import only unassembled automobiles not containing parts that Brazil could manufacture (Shapiro, 28). These measures led to the expansion of the parts industry, which at that point had a monopoly on the market. This still did not lead the U.S. Big Three — General Motors, Ford, and Chrysler — to begin manufacturing cars in the country.

In 1952, Vargas appointed a Subcommission on All-Terrain Vehicles, Tractors, Trucks, and Cars (Subcomissão de Jipes, Tratores, Caminhões e Automóveis) with Lúcio Meira as director. Ford invited Meira to visit the company in Dearborn, Michigan, to be instructed on the "senselessness of manufacturing trucks in a country with a limited market and with a deficient infrastructure" (Shapiro, 29). This was the dominant opinion not only at Ford but at the other multinational companies, including Volkswagen, which at that time produced cars only in Germany but had its eye on the Brazilian market — for export, of course, not for production.

Vargas did not complete his term. He committed suicide on 24 August 1954, under the threat of being overthrown by the armed forces. The air force had risen up because one of its majors, Rubens Vaz, had been accidentally killed in an assassination attempt against Vargas rival Carlos Lacerda. The suicide letter that the president left was both personal and political, and it had the effect of rallying the population in every city and leading the military to stand up for the constitutional regime. In the 1955 elections, a coalition of developmentalists and leftist forces brought Juscelino Kubitschek to power. Kubitschek would carry on

Vargas's work, including the establishment of an automobile industry. Kubitschek gave this project high priority in his Plan of Goals (Plano de Metas) because of the "strategic implications of the automotive industry that would have repercussions beyond just this sector. The hope was that the automotive industry would play the role of leading sector, given its capacity for attracting foreign capital and technology, and to give rise to an articulated production system. Holding back the development of the industrial base would compromise every other production sector" (Shapiro, 29).

Kubitschek formed the Automotive Industry Executive Group (Grupo Executivo para a Indústria Automotiva, GEIA) under Meira's leadership. GEIA was made up of representatives from all of the government agencies involved in the project. It was an important political innovation that centralized in one group all decision making related to this goal. This centralization prevented the individual agencies from overemphasizing their proposals from their particular viewpoints and from giving too much weight to their approvals by delaying decisions and imposing restrictions—all the usual ploys in the game of bureaucratic power: "In addition, this centralization in the executive branch meant, at least in theory, that GEIA's decisions would be removed from the political hubbub of Congress. In this way, these technocrats would enjoy a degree of autonomy never experienced in previous administrations. GEIA had the task of setting production and nationalization goals, and even of receiving individual investment proposals and monitoring their progress" (Shapiro, 32).

The concentration of power in GEIA proved both adequate and indispensable, since it had the Herculean chore of breaking the backs of some of the largest companies in the world, making them do what they did not want to do: establish truck and car manufacturing in Brazil. For this, the great weapon was standardization of foreign trade. Companies that contracted with the plan to create an industry that would produce domestically a minimum of 90 percent of the share of trucks and 95 percent of the share of cars and all-terrain vehicles in five years would have exchange rates at the preferred tax rate for importing parts and equipment, as well as credit from the BNDE. Those that did not join the plan would no longer be able to import into Brazil because they would not have the necessary exchange values. They would thus be excluded from the Brazilian market.

Under this pressure, the multinationals partially yielded. Of the proposals submitted to GEIA, eighteen were approved, but only eleven were carried out: "Of the eleven firms that started the process of domestic vehicle manufacture, three (Willys-Overland, Vemag, and the FNM) were controlled by Brazilian capital;

two (Mercedes-Benz and Simca) were joint ventures with 50 percent Brazilian capital and 50 percent foreign; and six (Ford, General Motors, International Harvester, Scania Vabis, Volkswagen, and Toyota) were controlled by or were wholly owned subsidiaries of foreign firms" (Shapiro, 24).

The multinationals met the Brazilian government's demands only in part because they submitted production plans only for utility vehicles. Ford, General Motors, Mercedes-Benz, and Scania Vabis proposed to build trucks; Volkswagen proposed to build vans; and Toyota proposed to build all-terrain vehicles. The darling of GEIA and especially of Kubitschek, however, was the private passenger car. It was much less important for the unification of the domestic market but very important in the eyes of middle- and upper-class consumers as a symbol of social status. Since the multinationals refused to meet GEIA's requirements for domestic production of passenger cars, this market was initially served by the companies with domestic capital: Vemag, Willys-Overland, FNM, and Simca. The only foreign company that submitted, against its will, a plan for cars was Volkswagen. With some delay, Volkswagen launched the Beetle (known as the Fusca in Brazil), which quickly came to dominate the domestic market.

Almost ten years later, experience showed that the Brazilian automobile plan was viable and, indeed, lucrative. The multinationals set about making up for lost time:

> In 1966, Chrysler, previously a minority stockholder of Simca of France, bought up 92 percent of its shares. It gained control of Simca in Brazil, which had been 50 percent domestically owned. Chrysler also acquired International Harvester's truck production facilities. Volkswagen took over Vemag, previously controlled by Brazilian capital, first by acquiring Auto Union, a minority stockholder, then by buying the rest of the shares. In 1967, Ford, through its purchase of a majority interest in Kaiser, gained control of Willys-Overland, another firm that had been Brazilian controlled. Alfa Romeo took over FNM, formerly a state-owned company. . . . As Meira had feared, only companies controlled by transnational capital remained. (Shapiro, 64)

There is no doubt that the development of the automotive industry provided opportunities for the metalworking and machinery sector, with the establishment of tractor, motorcycle, ship, and airplane manufacturing industries. The development of iron and steel smelting, the chemical industry, the manufacture of rubber and plastic products, and other industries required for the automotive parts industry in turn made possible other industries for transportation, machinery, appliances, and so forth.

The creation of the automotive industry in Brazil is an exemplary case of state-directed development that managed to impose its goals and deadlines on multinational companies in exchange for exclusive access to the domestic market. Analogous tactics were used by other countries on the global periphery to attract foreign capital for import-substitution industrialization.

The complete opening of the Brazilian automotive industry ten years later should not be seen as fatal. The example of South Korea, which was able to create domestic manufacturers of large-scale and international impact, shows that, with adequate industrial policies, a less-developed country can stimulate the rise of companies in any sector. In Korea's industrialization "compared with Latin America, there was a low rate of direct foreign investment. Instead, the tendency was for technology to enter through externalized modes and liabilities to be arranged through the international private banking system. That is, productive capital in heavy industry was mostly domestically owned. Majority ownership through direct foreign investment was limited to export activities for light manufactured goods and to unskilled metal and machine assembly. Joint ventures with foreign ownership never exceeding 50 percent prevailed in heavy industry" (Canuto, 105–6).

After 1970, economic development in Brazil once again turned outward, this time, however, as an exporter not only of primary products but of manufactured goods. This opportunity arose through the increased liberalization of international trade, which began in the so-called first world after World War II but reached the developing world only after 1980. The opening of borders to trade among western Europe, North America, and Japan happened gradually through a series of multilateral negotiations under the auspices of the General Agreement on Tariffs and Trade. The cumulative effect of liberalization after 1970 made it possible for the countries known then as newly industrialized countries (NICs) to export manufactured goods.

In the 1970s, Brazil was the largest of the NICs. In 1972 manufactured goods represented 36.1 percent of the value of Brazilian exports; in 1978, 47.4 percent; and in 1984, 66.3 percent (Fundação Getúlio Vargas). In a dozen years, Brazil shifted from an exporter of primary products, a sign of underdevelopment, to an exporter of manufactured goods, at that time the prerequisite for development.

One can better appreciate the speed of this change by considering the value of Brazil's exports: $1.44 billion in 1972, $6 billion in 1978, and $17.9 billion in 1984. In twelve years, the value of sales of Brazilian manufactured goods grew by 1,240 percent.

This change removed the main constraint on the development process after 1930, which was an insufficient import capacity, a consequence of slowed growth in export revenues. Until 1970, exports were limited mostly to coffee and some other agricultural and extractive products. With diversification, caused by the growth in the export of numerous manufactured products, revenue from foreign sales increased vigorously. Between 1972 and 1978, revenues went from $3.99 billion to $12.66 billion, more than tripling. In 1984 they reached $27 billion, more than double the 1978 amount. In these twelve years, revenues from Brazilian exports grew at an average annual rate of 17.3 percent. As we will see in the following section, this did not eliminate external strangulation of the economy, which worsened from 1982 on in the form of the foreign debt crisis. Even so, this strangulation changed in character from a trade matter to a financial matter, from a structural one to a circumstantial one.

The shift in Brazil's place in the international division of labor was due in large part to the multinational companies' interest in using semideveloped countries as platforms for their exports, profiting from their lower labor costs in comparison with those of the industrialized countries. This possibility did not exist before 1970 because of the trade barriers that protected domestic production in the developed countries and because multinationals had not developed a significant productive capacity in the so-called third world. Brazil's daring automotive industry policy begun in the 1950s was later imitated by other developing countries. Multinationals invested in these peripheral countries with the intent of producing for the countries' internal markets. This allowed the companies several decades later to transform some of these countries into platforms for export back to the "metropolis" and other "first world" countries.

From Development for Export to the Crisis of Globalization (1980–2000)

In the last two decades of the twentieth century, the world economic and political stage underwent a new and surprising change. The Keynesian paradigm was replaced by a new monetarist framework, which restored the old liberal beliefs that had been dominant up to 1930. The idea once again prevailed that markets stabilize at full employment and that people find themselves out of work only voluntarily because they do not accept the pay that the labor market offers.

According to Milton Friedman, the main theorist of the monetarist counter-revolution, when the government tries to reduce unemployment by expanding effective demand by increasing the supply of credit and forms of payment, it only deludes the economic actors by making them believe that they will receive the real salary that they seek. After several years, though, prices rise, and these actors realize that they have been victims of the "monetary illusion." That is, they did not realize that the cost of living was going to rise. Thus, when the workers perceive this reality, they become unemployed once again unless the central bank again injects money and credit into the economy, again fueling the illusion and its delayed reaction — inflation. Friedman does not explain how or why the workers come to be unemployed. Apparently, the workers abandon their jobs when they discover that the wages no longer have the purchasing power that they once did. No one has ever observed this in practice. When the cost of living rises, workers demand wage increases, and they have it in their power to strike to gain these raises. This does not result in unemployment, however.

According to Friedman, applying the policy of full employment achieves the desired effect only in the short term. It later leads to chronic, growing inflation that one day must be eliminated. When this occurs, the stabilization policies throw the economy into a recession whose length and depth will be in proportion to the depth of the inflationary outlook. At the end of this cycle, the economy recovers price stability, at the expense, however, of all prior growth in production and employment.

When Friedman proposed these ideas in the 1960s, very few took them seriously. Yet, in the following decade, two oil crises and the rise in international financial speculation produced a new type of condition, stagflation: the combination of economic stagnation and high, persistent inflation. Applying Keynesian policies did not bring about the desired effects; throwing the economy into recession did not eliminate inflation. Monetarism began to gain ground after this experience. With the election of Margaret Thatcher in the United Kingdom in 1979 and of Ronald Reagan in the United States the following year, the new economic doctrine found its vehicle in neoliberalism, which soon became the new orthodoxy.

Brazil delayed joining the new trend. When the first oil crisis struck in 1974, the government launched the alcohol fuels program Pró-álcool and other import-substitution programs to correct the balance of trade. While these programs were in force, private multinational banks offered loans in petrodollars at invitingly low interest rates. This led Brazil to expand its foreign debt, as did many other underdeveloped countries.

At the same time, the military regime began its slow but certain process of political opening. In 1978, the government did not repress a strike against and occupation of the Scania Vabis factory, as it had with all other strikes since 1964. This signaled a basic change: the government was allowing the return of free collective bargaining, including the right to strike. Fourteen years of pent-up demand and frustrated desires exploded in the following years in a vast wave of strikes that hit most labor classes and every state of the country. Many unions quickly awoke from their lethargy and set themselves at the forefront of mass movements of the day.

In 1974, as a result of the rise in the cost of petroleum and petroleum derivatives, along with other points of economic strangulation, inflation began to grow more quickly. After 1979, when the salary adjustments of the late 1970s were passed immediately on to prices, this inflationary process accelerated. The next year inflation hit three digits for the first time in Brazil's history. In 1980, Brazil's foreign accounts rolled back as a result of the policy of strict credit containment of the U.S. Federal Reserve under the direction of Paul Volcker. A large part of this debt had been contracted at variable interest rates, so when international interest rates increased sharply, Brazil's foreign debt service was thrust into the stratosphere.

In 1981, as a condition for new loans, the international banks that financed the deficit on Brazil's balance of payments account set policies of deep cuts on effective demand through reductions in fiscal spending and credit availability. The Brazilian economy immediately went into recession, and large firms, beginning with those in the automobile industry, suddenly laid off thousands of employees. Brazil was entering a new era: that of mass unemployment.

The euphoria of regaining union independence and the right to strike was short lived. The hundreds of thousands of laid-off workers who suddenly found themselves without prospects of new employment had a chilling effect, and strikes for wage increases stopped, in spite of the three-digit annual inflation. Instead, there were protests against layoffs and the threat of layoffs and strikes for employment stability.

In 1982, the increase in U.S. interest rates unleashed a flight of capital from Mexico. The Mexican government then declared itself incapable of servicing its foreign debt. This brought about a financial crisis that immediately struck most

Latin American countries and some in Asia and eastern Europe. International bankers that had been rolling over these countries' debts and providing them with new credit suspended any new financing, which left many "emerging markets" in default. The crisis undoubtedly would have led to the bankruptcy of many these international banks if not for the saving intervention of the International Monetary Fund, allied with the Federal Reserve, the World Bank, and the Bank of International Settlements (the banker to the central banks). These institutions granted emergency credit to the governments in default in exchange for recessive economic adjustments, mainly cuts in public spending and in the credit supply. After 1982, dozens of "overindebted" countries simultaneously went into recession, joining the developed countries already in recession because of Volcker's containment policies since 1980. This produced the longest, deepest international economic and financial crisis since World War II.

Brazil experienced extraordinarily intense stagflation. While production, employment, total per capita income (*massa salarial*), and consumption all fell, the cost of living continued to grow at three-digit rates. In 1983, the economy of the first world began to recover as a result of a change in the Federal Reserve's policy. It decided to loosen credit and means of payment, allowing a drop in interest rates and an expansion of consumption and, later, investment. This did not mean, however, a return to Keynesian policies. The priority continued to be fighting inflation without concern for the consequences for unemployment. Only Volcker, and with him the Federal Open Market Committee, thought that inflationary pressure in the United States had been overcome and that it was time to resume economic growth.

After 1984, the Brazilian economy began to grow again, but the huge inflation rates did not abate. In 1985, the military regime ended when José Sarney became the first civilian president since 1964. Sarney was actually the vice president, but after President Tancredo Neves died on the eve of what was to be his inauguration, Sarney fulfilled his term. Dealing with inflation became not just a priority but a national obsession. At the same time, neighboring countries, such as Argentina and Bolivia, suffered crises of hyperinflation. In 1986, the Brazilian government launched the Cruzado Plan, which froze wages and prices, and introduced a new currency, the cruzado, to replace the cruzeiro, which had been in use since 1942. For about six months, inflation fell, and there was a veritable spending spree, which led to production increases and redistribution of income. Unfortunately, inflation returned at an even higher level. In 1988 and 1989, inflation topped 1,000 percent per year.

Brazilian inflation at this time was not technically hyperinflation because prices did not explode and supply did not run the risk of collapse. Still, even though incomes were indexed, this huge inflation rate hurt the economy. The possibility of making economic calculations, even the most elementary, such as how to buy the cheapest supply and sell at a price high enough to earn a profit, were hindered by the lack of dependable information about price levels in the near future. The efficiency of market actors dropped noticeably, which slowed business. Operating in a situation where any price could rise every day, and no one knew by how much, was like driving on a highway in dense fog—all the vehicles on the road reduced their speed.

The great inflationary crisis partially paralyzed the Brazilian economy for about seven years, from 1987 to 1994. Another disruptive factor were the frequent "stabilization plans," which tried to both repeat the initial success of the Cruzado Plan and impede the subsequent return of inflation. Four of these— Bresser, Verão, Collor I, and Collor II—shook the economy by suddenly changing the rules of setting and adjusting prices and salaries and of setting the terms of financial contracts.

Under Fernando Collor, president from 1990 to 1992, Brazil became a giant laboratory of macroeconomic experiments. Some of these were extravagantly cruel, such as the plan known as Collor I, which froze access to liquid reserve accounts—that is, money that families and businesses had deposited in banks to spend in the near future. Thus the situation was dire for people, for example, who had births or scheduled medical procedures but found themselves without the ready cash to pay for them. The frozen funds would be returned only years later on a case-by-case basis, through a widely corrupt system run by the president's office. This finally provoked the broad-based popular movement of the Painted Faces (Caras Pintadas) that managed to convince Congress to impeach President Collor in 1992.

During his short term, Collor brought neoliberalism to Brazil. He gradually opened the domestic market to imports and started to privatize productive state companies. At the same time, the Metalworkers' Union of São Bernardo in the greater São Paulo area led the establishment of sector councils, which brought together representatives of companies, workers, and government, according to their production chains (the various productive branches responsible for a certain class of goods, for example the automotive, shipbuilding, apparel, or toy production chain). The councils coordinated efforts to increase Brazilian industrial productivity to confront competition from foreign imports. These operated for only a few years—1992–94—and were abandoned when President Fernando Henrique Cardoso took office in 1995. The most successful council was the automotive sector's, which managed to reach several agreements for reducing the prices of cars in exchange for the reduction of certain taxes on manufacturers' and retailers' profit margins. Car sales grew dramatically, which prevented further worker layoffs and allowed the industry to make gains in scale, thus strengthening the sector against competition from imported cars.

Most of the sector councils, however, were not able or did not have time to reach such agreements. Manufactured imports from countries with lower wages, most of them in Asia, took over large shares of the domestic market, forcing companies to decrease production and update their technologies. The two reactions resulted in massive workforce reductions, creating a structural crisis in agriculture and industry within the larger inflationary crisis.

The resignation of Collor in 1992 did not immediately relieve the economic crisis. Upon Collor's departure, his vice president, Itamar Franco, was sworn in. In 1993, Franco appointed Cardoso as his finance minister, signaling a shift in strategies to fight the crisis, though still within neoliberal approaches. In 1994, Franco and Cardoso launched the Real Plan, which was finally successful in beating inflation and stabilizing prices. This plan began by introducing an intermediate currency mechanism, the Real Unit of Value (Unidade Real de Valor, URV), which made all price, exchange, and salary adjustments uniform. The next step was the adoption of a new currency—the real—on 1 July 1994. During the inflationary crisis, the many currency name changes were concretely and psychologically motivated. The change from cruzeiro to cruzado in 1986, for example, signaled continuity in both value and name. The cruzado had been the name of a Portuguese coin. The real (meaning "royal"), too, had been a colonial, imperial, and early republican unit. The name was also a pun: as the URV indicated, the new real had "real" value. With the adoption of the real, the plan reduced import tariffs on numerous products, which allowed massive importation at low prices. This caused a price shock that forced domestic agricultural and industrial sectors to lower their prices.

In the second half of 1995 and the beginning of 1996, inflation fell because the costs of internationally traded products were lower than those of their Brazilian counterparts, in part because the real's value was high against the dollar's. In July 1994, the real had been set at a value equal to the dollar, but in the following weeks the dollar weakened and was worth only 0.83 reals. The Central Bank of Brazil took advantage of the influx of foreign capital into Brazil and raised the real's value, possibly avoiding any persisting inflationary pressure.

The Cardoso government achieved price stabilization at the expense of worsening the agricultural and industrial employment crisis, however. The price drop brought on by the flood of products imported mainly from Asia ruined a large number of businesses. Companies closed and millions lost their jobs, but in compensation, the purchasing power of many of the poor improved. This improvement was the result of the fall in inflation rates, which minimized the losses in real income of those who did not have bank accounts. Those with bank accounts had the benefit of daily adjustments in their balances for inflation; those without accounts had seen the value of their cash assets dwindle daily. Moreover, there was a real increase in the value of the minimum wage, which also benefited mainly the poor.

The contradictory effects of the Real Plan on poverty levels are synthesized by Sonia Rocha: "The income improvements that benefited everyone between 1993 and 1995 amounted to a much higher gain for those at the base of the income distribution pyramid, which caused a reduction of the incidence of poverty as measured by income from 44 percent to 34 percent" (Rocha, 15). This was the effect of the stabilization of the minimum wage. Rocha describes the consequences of the industrial and agricultural employment crisis, made worse by the recessions of 1997 and 1998, as follows: "The recent evolution in the metropolitan labor market has been especially unfavorable for the poorest. Understandably, the restructuring and modernization of production had the greatest impact on those with the least education—up to four years of school. Between the second half of 1994 and May 1999, 1.3 million jobs were lost among individuals at this level of education [in the metropolitan areas]. With the combined effect of job losses and the drop in average income, total income for workers with less than four years of education—representing one fourth of the workforce—dropped 11 percent in the last year" (Rocha, 150).

The effects of the overvalued real on economic activity were pernicious after the successive financial crises that struck Mexico in December 1994, Thailand in July 1997, South Korea in October 1997, Russia in September 1998, and finally Brazil in January 1999. All of these crises had repercussions in Brazil as a result of capital flight from the real. These could be reversed, except for the last, through strong increases in interest rates. The unwanted but not unexpected side effects

TABLE 3.2. *Unemployment Rates in Five Metropolitan Areas*

Metropolitan Area	December 1995	September 1996	Annual Average 1997	Annual Average 1998	September 1999	February 2000
Brasília	16.2	16.5	18.1	19.4	21.1	20.8
Belo Horizonte	11.1	12.8	13.4	15.9	17.8	17.2
Porto Alegre	10.9	12.9	13.5	15.9	19.6	16.7
Salvador	—	—	21.6	—	28.6	26.6
São Paulo	13.2	14.8	16.0	18.3	19.7	17.7

Source: State Data Analysis System Foundation (Fundação Sistema Estadual de Análise de Dados) and Interunion Department of Statistics and Socioeconomic Studies (Departamento Intersindical de Estatística e Estudos Socioeconômicos), *Pesqiusa de Emprego e Desemprego.*

were decreases in production and increases in unemployment. The effects of these crises on unemployment are shown in table 3.2.

In the five metropolitan areas in table 3.2, unemployment rose continuously from the first year of the Real Plan to 2000. Note, however, that unemployment was starting to drop in 2000. There is no doubt that price stabilization improved the situation of those at the lowest income levels, but the structural crisis in production of goods for trade eliminated millions of jobs in the formal sectors, most of them at midlevel salaries. This tossed millions of families into the base of the income distribution pyramid, constituting the "new poor." This new poverty was not limited to the unemployed, because many former wage earners reentered the job market as *terciarizados,* a generic term that covers various types of unstable employment: individually subcontracted employees, members of firms founded for this purpose, false cooperatives, and so forth. Such workers provide services without regular service contracts, and so their "contractors" are exempt from paying certain labor costs, including paid leave, social security, and the Retirement Fund (Fundo de Garantia de Tempo de Serviço, FGTS).

Survey data from the Monthly Employment Survey (Pesquisa Mensal de Emprego, PME) of the Brazilian Institute of Geography and Statistics (Instituto Brasileiro de Geografia e Estatística, IBGE) show the growth in precarious employment between 1991 and 1999 in the metropolitan areas of Belo Horizonte, Porto Alegre, Recife, Rio de Janeiro, Salvador, and São Paulo. The index of precarious labor, the overall percentage of those working outside the formal sector or self-employed, which was already high in 1991 at 40.91 percent, rose to 45.39 percent in 1994 and reached 49.92 percent in 1999 (Instituto de Pesquisa Econômica Aplicada).

Other data on Brazil come from the National Household Sample Survey (Pesquisa Nacional por Amostra de Domicílios, PNAD). In 1989, registered wage earners were 42.5 percent of the economically active population (população economicamente ativa, PEA) and the unemployed were 3 percent of the PEA. In 1996, the index of registered wage earners had dropped to 33 percent (Pochmann). Between 1989 and 1996 about 10 percent of the PEA lost regular jobs and about 4 percent joined the ranks of the unemployed. These percentages suggest that the new poverty caused by the opening of the markets not only to imports but to foreign capital was much more widespread than the "old poverty" that was eliminated by price stabilization and a minimum wage increase in 1995.

As a defensive reaction to this formidable deterioration in labor conditions for a significant portion of the working population, an economic solidarity movement arose in Brazil in the 1990s. This movement, which was a collective effort to create jobs, took on different forms. One of these was the struggle of workers and their unions to get companies that had failed or were about to fail to transfer their production facilities to their employees so that the latter could continue to operate the companies as cooperatives or under other modes of association. The ex-employees would use their "workers' credits"—FGTS, unpaid wages, unused leave—to acquire the net worth or productive capital of the failed company. They would organize the new company in accordance with international cooperative principles—equal participation in capital, in decision making (one person, one vote), and in the election of the governing body. Co-op members would decide how much the individuals' monthly withdrawal would be, how much of the surplus (the co-op's "profits") would go into co-op funds, and how much of this surplus would be distributed to the members and according to what criteria. Economic solidarity companies eliminate class distinctions because all members are at the same time both capitalists and workers.

Dozens of co-ops founded from formerly capitalist enterprises created the National Association of Worker-Managed Enterprises (Associação Nacional de Trabalhadores e Empresas de Autogestão, ANTEAG). ANTEAG's technical and legal assistance team provides courses in business and cooperative management. It also brings the cooperatives together, organizing them into business networks. The Landless Workers' Movement (Movimento dos Trabalhadores Rurais Sem Terra, MST) has undertaken a similar initiative. By mobilizing tens of thousands of families in camps all over the country, the MST has gotten the federal government to expropriate unproductive farms and settle landless agricultural workers there. This has occurred in spite of repression and bloody assaults against directors and supporters. In these settlements, the MST has organized different types of co-ops and engaged in technical training.

Aparecido Faria, the director of ANTEAG, describes the organization as follows:

[ANTEAG] is sixty-five companies with earnings of 320 million reals in 1999. . . . They include industries from the most varied sectors, transformed into productive cooperatives, organizing in the country a veritable movement of worker-managed businesses in response to unemployment and to economic globalization. . . . Its projects raised 20,000 positions and 80,000 indirect jobs from the ashes, at no cost to the public sector. . . . These companies do not receive government incentives. . . . Worker-managed companies pay the equivalent of R$91.5 in direct wages. In 1999 they paid R$26.83 in taxes. They are born of despair and the lack of alternatives with the growing number of workers laid off by companies in the process of closing or outsourcing. (Faria, 7)

Another component of the economic solidarity movement are the Technological Incubators for Popular Cooperatives (Incubadores Tecnológicas de Cooperativas Populares, ITCPs), organized in fourteen public and denominational universities. ITCPs work in shantytowns and low-income neighborhoods offering cooperative management courses and supporting groups that want to organize as work co-ops. In recent years some ITCPs have developed worker co-ops in electrical and telephone companies that have just been privatized and laid off their line maintenance crews in hopes of outsourcing this service to *terciarizados*. These co-ops are contracted by the companies from which they originated, guaranteeing their members working conditions and pay that are incomparably better than they would receive as *terciarizado* contract labor.

In December 1999, the United Workers' Congress (Central Única dos Trabalhadores, CUT), in partnership with the Unitrabalho Foundation, which brings together more than eighty Brazilian universities dedicated to putting their knowledge to work for labor, and with the Interunion Department of Statistics and Socioeconomic Studies (Departamento Intersindical de Estatística e Estudos Socioeconômicos, DIEESE), organized the Agency for Solidary Development (Agência de Desenvolvimento Solidário, ADS). One of the most important projects of the ADS was to organize a network of cooperative credit made up of a large number of credit unions. From this alliance came a powerful cooperative credit bank, able to finance the growing number of production, labor, and agricultural co-ops.

The co-ops formed during the economic solidarity movement are generally undercapitalized, and their managers have gained experience only gradually. Moreover, they have not managed to establish complementarity among themselves, and, therefore, the level of cooperation among them has been slight. Notwithstanding the difficulties, the co-op movement has a rapidly expanding presence. The great majority of the production co-ops have managed to resume in only a few months the pace of production and sales of their predecessor companies. Some are even replacing equipment and developing new products.

Economic solidarity is a response on the part of movements that seek a more democratic and egalitarian society and that were challenged by the damage to the backbone of the workers' movement—industrial workers—through outsourcing and unemployment. This solidarity movement is related to another reaction, of a different character, resulting from the same social crisis. This is the so-called third sector, made up of a large number of educational and welfare programs promoted by nongovernmental organizations, churches, associations, and so forth. Their financing is part public and part private, the latter coming from business foundations or directly from private companies.

Private welfare programs have always existed. They were once the domain of wealthy ladies and the Catholic Church. Today, growth in the quantity of assistance programs has resulted in changes in their quality. While the government has reduced government social spending, the demand for social services—schools, clinics, hospitals, child-care facilities, affordable housing, urban services for tenements and shantytowns—has increased. When this demand increases intensively as a result of social exclusion and impoverishment, civil society itself intervenes. This has already happened internationally, but it has only recently been significant in Brazil. Incidentally, private assistance, especially for at-risk students, frequently leads to the formation of production or labor co-ops.

Solidary economics and the "third sector" are not the same, but they give rise to parallel processes that converge at certain moments. The principles of cooperativism imply a deep critique of class-based society, while the third sector tries to make class-based society more just socially. Thus these strategic objectives differ in their concrete, day-to-day actions, though the two movements tend to support each other.

By Way of a Summary: A Century of Brazilian Economic History

During the First Republic, Brazil began to overcome its heritage of slave-based colonialism, which had survived about two generations after independence in 1822. In fact, the abolition of slavery and the proclamation of the republic were the revolutions that launched Brazil into the twentieth century. The nation began to industrialize, to become more urban, and to adapt scientific, cultural, and economic modernity to the Brazilian setting. Brazil began to make up for lost time by opening its doors to European and Japanese immigration and by forming "modern" classes—an industrial bourgeoisie and proletariat.

During this period, Brazil began to feel torn between the pull of the domestic market, reinforced by rapid population growth over a vast and supposedly wealthy area, and the attraction of the global market. Economic growth had been entirely focused on international trade, but during the economic crises and depressions, the economically dominant countries reduced their imports of coffee and other primary products or withdrew their capital. This contraction strengthened the temptation for Brazil to close its borders to the crises and to focus economic growth on the domestic market. This shift implied abandoning the gold standard and allowing the currency to devalue. The economy would thus "betray" the few foreign creditors that had not withdrawn their capital because their investments in the local currency would suffer a loss in value.

The struggles between the *papelistas* and the *metalistas* that began to run through Brazilian history in the middle of the nineteenth century set the agenda for the swings between these two poles of development. *Papelista* governments would lower the cost of credit and let the national currency lose value to save the coffee growers and other primary producers from bankruptcy. The *metalista* reaction would then defeat these governments once inflation mobilized the middle class. Once in power, the *metalistas* would "fix" the economy at the expense of breaking companies and increasing unemployment. This would set the stage for a new leap forward in production for the international market.

The Revolution of 1930 brought a fundamental change. The oligarchy committed to the gold standard was toppled from power, and the new rulers proved pragmatic and sensitive to the palpable needs of producers. Gradually, in the course of the 1930s and 1940s, a new technocratic and bureaucratic elite of developmentalists and interventionists was installed. When the Great Depression and World War II closed off the markets in the developed countries for a decade and a half, the domestic market consolidated and prevailed for half a century.

Under the direction of the state, which maintained some control over conflicts between the bourgeoisie and proletariat, development turned entirely inward. Even when the foreign markets reopened little by little at the end of the war, the main route for accumulation continued to be import-substitution industrialization. Brazil became a pioneer in 1932 when it broke with the rules of the gold standard and started to protect its domestic market. A high point came in 1950 when it used the great weight of its domestic market to force multinationals to establish modern industrial facilities in Brazil and begin automobile production.

Economic development in Brazil was not only pioneering, but it was among the most successful. Brazil was able to recover from historical backwardness in half a century. Between 1930 and 1980, the country enjoyed one of the fastest rates of economic growth in the world. Unfortunately, from 1980 on, the economy stagnated. The Keynesian revolution was exhausted, and the monetarist counterrevolution took its place. Nation-states, beginning with the United States, abandoned any pretense of controlling private capital flows, surrendering control over the world economic situation to the speculative play of large blocs of private multinational capital.

In the middle of that decade, though, Brazil found itself in the euphoria of redemocratization and in the process of drafting a new social democratic constitution. The constitution thus provided for strong redistribution of wealth. Then the foreign debt crisis of the 1980s struck Brazil, which had the largest foreign debt in the world. At the same time, the winds on the international scene were blowing in the direction of neoliberalism, price stabilization, and fiscal and monetary austerity—a late and imperfect reissue of the gold standard doctrine. The polarization between the demands of the domestic market, which required redistribution of income and acceleration of growth, and of the global market, which required recession and reduction in the size and cost of the state, led to an impasse in the form of a long and deep inflationary crisis.

The Brazilian economy stopped growing in the last two decades of the twentieth century. In 1994, the Real Plan succeeded in stabilizing prices, and the subsequent Cardoso government imposed the standard structural readjustment: opening the domestic market to goods and capital, privatizing profitable state companies, and opening much of the industrial sector and a significant portion of the financial sector to foreign investment and ownership. In the meanwhile, almost without a break from 1995 to 1999, the economy suffered a structural crisis in industry and agriculture, with mass unemployment and vulnerability to international financial crises.

TABLE 3.3. *Rates of Average Annual Growth in* GDP *in Select Countries* (%)

Country	1900–1930	1930–1980	1980–1994	1900–1994
Taiwan	2.9	6.1	6.5	5.1
Brazil	3.5	5.9	1.7	4.4
Mexico	1.3	5.6	1.9	3.7
Japan	2.8	5.3	3.4	4.2
Venezuela	5.8	5.3	1.4	4.8
South Korea	—	4.7	7.6	—
Turkey	—	4.7	4.5	—
Canada	3.9	4.3	2.5	3.9
USSR	1.7	3.9	−0.2	2.3
Italy	2.3	3.8	1.8	3.0
Germany	1.7	3.6	2.2	2.7
United States	3.0	3.4	2.5	3.2
China	1.3	2.7	6.8	2.8

Source: Maddison 1995, appendix, table B.

It is useful to compare the growth of the Brazilian economy throughout the twentieth century with that of other countries with rapidly expanding economies. Table 3.3 shows relevant data from countries that were the twentieth century's leaders of economic growth and is divided more or less according to the periods studied in this essay. In table 3.3, the countries are arranged in decreasing order of growth rates for the period 1930–80. This was the period of most accelerated growth for eight of the eleven countries for which we have data for all periods. Between 1930 and 1980, the fastest-growing economy was Taiwan's. Brazil's was close behind, followed closely by Mexico's. It is worth noting that in this half century of Keynesian policies, the countries with the fastest-growing economies were the "semiperipheral" countries of Latin American and Asia, with rates well above those of Europe and North America. Japan could be considered semiperipheral until the 1960s.

The Keynesian half century was preceded by thirty years of dominance of liberal economic ideas and followed by fourteen years (as far as these data go) of neoliberal domination. Between 1900 and 1930, the economy that grew the most was Venezuela's, probably because of petroleum exploration. Next in line were Canada, Brazil, the United States, Taiwan, and Japan. Countries that had revolutions with long periods of civil war—the USSR, China, and Mexico—showed the lowest rates of growth.

In the final period, 1980–94, growth slowed markedly in eight of the thirteen countries, including Brazil. Only three countries, all in Asia, managed accelerated growth in this period: South Korea, China, and Taiwan. Two countries had middling growth rates, Turkey and Japan. The rest presented growth rates below 3 percent. Brazil had one of the lowest growth rates, similar to Mexico's, Venezuela's, and Italy's. Of the three countries that grew the most in this period, China and Taiwan did not open their financial markets to foreign capital without some controls, and they did not make their currency convertible to the dollar. These were very likely the policy options that assured better performance of their economies.

There is no doubt that the Brazilian economic development between 1930 and 1980 was exceptional compared to that of the other "growth leaders." It was also above average prior to that period, during 1900–1930, yet it was much lower between 1980 and 1994. If we consider the entire span, 1900–94, the fastest growth was in Taiwan, followed by Venezuela, Brazil, Japan, Canada, and Mexico. Of the countries listed, the economies that grew the most in the twentieth century (at least through 1994 and for which we have data) were the three Latin American countries, including the largest two in the region, Brazil and Mexico; two East Asian countries (remembering that Taiwan was a Japanese possession until the end of World War II in 1945); and Canada.

Conclusion: What a Hundred Years of History Teaches

The evening knows what the morning never suspected.
— SWEDISH PROVERB

It is clear that the Brazilian economy developed markedly in the last century. This development was a result of the expansion of the domestic market, controlled by the state, financed by the BNDE and the Bank of Brazil (along with the World Bank and the Inter-American Development Bank, IDB), and brought about by an always unstable combination of links with the global capitalist economy and accumulation of domestic capital. The process was also conditioned by antagonisms: between the internationally minded entrepreneurial class and those dedicated to import-substitution industrialization; between financial capital (investments, pensions, and annuities) and capital invested in the production of merchandise; and among "big money," wage earners, and small autonomous producers.

Given the range of interests in play, it was inevitable that coalitions would form to struggle for hegemony. In the First Republic (1889–1930), the politically dominant coalition was the "internationalized" plutocracy of exporters, coffee growers, importers, and managers of foreign capital. The opposition groups were, on the one hand, the (few) industrialists who sought a consistent development policy and, on the other, the currents on the Left engaged in educating and organizing the working class.

The Great Depression of the 1930s destroyed the bases of plutocratic domination and made room for a new dominant coalition to emerge. One of the lessons of this revolution, which was unforeseen at least by foreigners, is that the ideological controversies were far removed from the viable alternatives, discovered as inevitable problems demanded pragmatic solutions. Import-substitution industrialization was led by an old guard politician from the powerful ranching state of Rio Grande do Sul surrounded by *tenentes* with leftist ideas and ideals forged in the barracks revolts of the 1920s and by others with Fascist leanings opposed to these same "lieutenants." The same can be said for the civilian intellectual advisers who built Vargas's peculiar social welfare state during the Estado Novo regime or Kubitschek's Plan of Goals.

This does not mean that ideologies were irrelevant. In the 1950s, there was a genuine effort to found a progressive nationalist plan on Marxist analyses. On another tangent, working-class social movements demanded agrarian reform as a forerunner of some future socialization of the means of production. These two currents flowed together into a movement that, between 1954 and 1964, prevented the military from returning power to the old plutocracy of internationalized financial capitalists. Even after the 1964 military coup, the successive authoritarian governments, influenced by the prior ideology, kept the economy on the road to development, in contrast to the choices tending toward economic liberalism made by the equally authoritarian military governments of Argentina, Chile, and Uruguay.

The supreme lesson from the history of recent years is that nothing is inexorable or irreversible. The developmentalist state and the social coalitions that created and sustained it began to be shaken by the intensification of social struggles in the first world—in the so-called center of the capitalist world—that turned wage earners (who had become prosperous, property-owning people) into shareholders in huge pension funds. These, therefore, became monetarist sympathizers opposed to any inflation. The new zeitgeist ended up penetrating into semiperipheral societies where the shareholding wage earners were few and the symbiosis of state and industry appeared unshakeable.

The turnaround after the Real Plan cannot be understood without bearing in mind the high degree of international integration of the Brazilian intellectual, business, and political elites as consumers of ideas and theories forged in the economic center. It is clear that these elites were ideologically recolonized and that this happened after Brazil had proven some decades before its political independence and its theoretical autonomy. Nevertheless, we cannot carry this insight too far. No doctrinal hegemony, including monetarism and neoliberalism, is supported without the rise of partisans invested in it — those whose vital interests are served and protected by the policies in force.

A significant portion of Brazil's capitalist class, already somewhat associated with major foreign multinational capital, resigned themselves to their new roles as investors and annuitants insofar as they had surrendered control over their companies to that capital. From then on, this segment became sympathetic to monetarism and opposed to any kind of inflation or any policy considered potentially inflationary. Another segment of this same class maintained an active role in their companies' management but became dependent on foreign financing because of persistently high interest rates and their continual adoption of new technologies available only from abroad. Of all dependencies, perhaps the hardest to overcome is technological dependency. Trade is always negotiable since it is not in the interest of one party to ruin the other. Financial dependency is basically a political choice, and so it is revocable. In an era such as ours of tempestuous technological transformation, however, it is impossible to ignore technological innovations.

The basic dilemma for a country like Brazil in such a moment is whether it intends to continue to be a perpetual client of the "advanced nations" or whether it intends to become one of those nations. If the preferred option is the latter, Brazil cannot hand over its future to the vicissitudes of the market, to the ever-fortuitous decisions about private capital. The big lesson of the twentieth century is that the nation must have a plan for itself and it must use the state to implement it. If Brazil wants to advance to the technological frontier, it must retake control of the main industries in which new problems and new solutions are defined. For most Brazilians, this dilemma is crucial, though they see it only from its threatening side: "Everything will go well as long as the international landscape does not get worse." Instead, they should come to conclude that Brazil is part of that international landscape and that large, partially developed countries like theirs can have considerable weight in determining the global future. Thus Brazil continues divided between the pull of the first world and the potential that geography and history have given it. Other countries are in a similar situation. It is up to Brazil to redefine its destiny and to find partners whose goals are compatible with the country's vision.

Notes

1. In 1886, São Paulo planters had formed the Immigration Promotion Society. In 1887 and 1888, there was an abrupt increase in the number of subsidized immigrants, reaching 92,086 in 1888 alone: "The costs of subsidization were easily absorbed by the rise in coffee prices and the increased income generated by the expansion of coffee output with the elastic supply of labor. Other factors contributing to this favorable climate for the use of foreign immigrants in the 1880s and 1890s in São Paulo were the economic stagnation in Italy, creating an available supply of immigrants at a relatively low supply price, and the decline in intercontinental maritime transport costs" (Merrick and Graham, 89 n. 13).

2. The financial boom in the London Stock Exchange in 1720, in which the investors in the stock of the South Sea Company let themselves be misled by the expected earnings from the company's trade with Spanish America. This trade depended on the approval of the Iberian metropolis, which had not been assured. After the speculative bubble burst, the episode became synonymous with pure speculation without any real economic basis.

3. The real was a monetary unit of Portuguese origin, and one mil-réis was 1,000 reals. The mil-réis was the monetary unit in place from colonization through 1942, and, of course, its legal bases, exchange rates, and purchasing power fluctuated throughout the period in which it was in use.

Bibliography

Arbix, Glauco, and Mauro Silbovicius, eds. De JK a FHC: A reinvenção dos carros. São Paulo: Scritta, 1997.

Baer, Werner. "O extenso setor público brasileiro." In Neuhaus 1980.

Calmon, Pedro. História social do Brasil. 3 vols. São Paulo, 1940.

Canuto, Otaviano. Brasil e Coréia do Sul: Os (des)caminhos da industrialização tardia. São Paulo: Nobel, 1994.

Dean, Warren. The Industrialization of São Paulo, 1880–1945. Latin American Monograph no. 17. Austin: Institute of Latin American Studies/University of Texas Press, 1969.

Faria, Aparecido. Prefácio. *Autogestão: Construindo uma nova cultura nas relações de trabalho.* São Paulo: ANTEAG, n.d.

Fausto, Boris, ed. *História geral da civilização brasileira.* Book 3: *O Brasil republicano.* Vol. 3, *Sociedade e política (1930–1964).* Vol. 4, *Cultura e economia (1930–1964).* São Paulo: Difusão Européia do Livro, 1981.

Fundação Getúlio Vargas. *Conjuntura Econômica,* May 1987.

Gomes, Angela de Castro. *A invenção do trabalhismo.* São Paulo: Vértice, 1988.

Ianni, Octavio. *Estado e capitalismo: Estrutura social e industrialização no Brasil.* Rio de Janeiro: Zahar, 1965.

Instituto de Pesquisa Econômica Aplicada. *Mercado de trabalho, conjuntura e análise.* Year 5, vol. 12 (February 2000).

Maddison, Angus. *La economia mundial 1820–1992: Análisis y estadísticas.* Paris: Organisation for Economic Co-operation and Development, 1995.

Merrick, Thomas W., and Douglas H. Graham. *Population and Economic Development in Brazil, 1800 to the Present.* Baltimore: Johns Hopkins University Press, 1979.

Neuhaus, Paulo. *História monetária do Brasil 1900–1945.* Rio de Janeiro: IBMEC, 1975.

————, ed. *Economia brasileira: Uma visão histórica.* Rio de Janeiro: Campus, 1980.

Pelaez, Carlos Manuel, and Wilson Suzigan. *História monetária do Brasil.* Brasília: Editora da Universidade de Brasília, 1976.

Phelps, Orme. *Introduction to Labor Economics.* 2nd ed. New York: McGraw-Hill, 1955.

Pochmann, Marcio. *O movimento de desestrruração do mercado do trabalho brasileiro nos anos 90: Uma análise regional.* Campinas: CESIT/IE/Universidade Estadual de Campinas, 1998.

Rocha, Sonia. *Pobreza e desigualdade no Brasil: O esgotamento dos efeitos redistributivos do Plano Real.* Rio de Janeiro: Instituto de Pesquisa Econômica Aplicada, 2000.

Rodrigues, Leôncio Martins. "Sindicalismo e classe operária (1930–1964)." In Fausto, book 3, vol. 3.

Schwarz, Roberto. *Misplaced Ideas: Essays on Brazilian Culture.* London: Verso, 1992.

Shapiro, Helen. "A primeira migração das montadoras: 1956–1968." In Arbix and Silbovicius.

Simonsen, Roberto C. *Evolução industrial do Brasil e outros estudos.* São Paulo: Nacional, 1973.

Singer, Paulo. "Interpretação do Brasil: Uma experiência histórica de desenvolvimento." In Fausto, book 3, vol. 4.

Vieira, Dorival Teixeira. "Evolução do sistema monetário brasileiro." *Boletim da Faculdade de Ciências Econômicas e Administrativas da USP* 24 (1962).

Villela, Annibal Villanova, and Wilson Suzigan. *Política do governo e crescimento da economia brasileira 1889–1945.* Rio de Janeiro: Instituto de Pesquisa Econômica Aplicada/ Instituto de Pesquisa e Estudos Sociais, 1973.

CELSO LAFER

Brazil and the World

This essay is an analysis of Brazil's international relations in the twentieth century. Such an analysis brings together a range of themes and problems. The organizing perspective of this survey, though, is that foreign policy is public policy whose purpose is translating domestic needs into possible foreign relations.

The Legacy of Rio Branco

For the history of Brazilian diplomacy, the nineteenth century stretched into the first decade of the twentieth century. This decade was the final phase of the career of José Maria da Silva Paranhos Jr., Baron of Rio Branco. Rio Branco's service as Brazil's minister of foreign relations from 1902 to 1912 crowned an exemplary diplomatic career. Rio Branco completed Brazil's primary task as a newly independent nation: consolidation of the national territory.[1] Setting international borders is always a key challenge in any country's foreign policy. The first problem on a new country's diplomatic agenda is establishing the difference between the "domestic" and "foreign" and, therefore, the specificity of foreign policy as public policy.

The detailed process of setting Brazil's borders, begun in the colonial and imperial periods, culminated in the republican era with Rio Branco's numerous efforts. In bequeathing to the nation the legal title to a continent-sized territory, Rio Branco brought to a positive close the activity of navigators, wilderness tamers, and diplomats since 1500, the year that Portugal laid claim to Brazil. These were the agents of history that, based in their Lusitanian heritage, managed to create "the body of the homeland."[2] Rio Branco managed to conclude this feat through peaceful means—through arbitration and negotiations that led to treaties. In the estimation of a recent ambassador to the United States, Rubens Ricúpero, the work of Rio Branco was a diplomatic undertaking with few parallels in the history of international relations, especially if one considers that Brazil has more neighbors than most countries and that, moreover, several other continent-size countries, including Russia, India, and China, still have not fully resolved their border problems.[3]

Setting the borders fixed Brazil's place in the world and allowed the release of the "deep forces" of economics and geography that would distinguish Brazilian foreign policy in the twentieth century.[4] It is the peculiarities arising from these "deep forces" that I will outline in this essay. These characteristics are expressed in Brazil's relationships with its neighbors, its posture in relation to the major powers, the affirmation of a "goal-oriented nationalism," focused on the development of the nation's territory, and the conduct of foreign policy in a Grotian mold, which, over time and space, has used diplomacy and law, without naivete, to deal with conflict and cooperation on the international level while addressing national interests.

The Best Policy for the Continent

By relieving Brazil of its border-drawing tasks, Rio Branco left the country free and at home in its South American setting — the site of Brazil's diplomatic first person, as José Ortega y Gasset would say. Once he had legally consolidated the map of Brazil, the next stage of Rio Branco's vision was to ensure peace and stimulate progress in South America.[5] In the twentieth century, Rio Branco's plan became a conduit for Brazilian foreign policy, which addressed the deep forces of economics and geography in diplomatically constructive ways. Indeed, a climate of peace in South America was an important condition for the development of Brazil's territory, and it was the predominant direction in Brazil's foreign policy after Rio Branco. This was why, in the 1930s, Brazil actively sought conciliatory solutions to the Leticia Conflict between Colombia and Peru and to the Chaco War between Bolivia and Paraguay. The role of Brazil in the 1990s as one of the guarantors of the 1942 Protocol of Rio de Janeiro that settled the Ecuador-Peru border dispute follows this same line.

This line of foreign policy that Rio Branco envisioned, directed toward peace and progress in South America, is representative of the classic concept of diplomacy: countries should try to make the best policy for their geography. In the course of the twentieth century, this principle was elaborated to foster development, the modern expression of the concept of progress. From this comes the driving idea that it is good to make not only the best foreign policies but also the best economy for one's geography. For example, Europe has been doing this since the 1950s through its integration process. This also explains the recent effort to transform Brazil's borders from classical frontier barriers to modern frontiers of cooperation. This line of Brazilian diplomatic policy toward its neighbors is rooted in the fact that South America is a physically contiguous whole that affords opportunities for economic cooperation. This cooperation maximizes the comparative advantages of the region in the global economy by adding value and reducing costs while stimulating trade and investment connections in a peaceful climate.

There are several landmarks in foreign policy aimed at strengthening regional cooperation, facilitated by Brazil's geographic and economic reach. These include the Latin American Free Trade Association (LAFTA) founded in 1960, followed in 1980 by the Latin American Integration Association; the River Plate Basin Treaty of 1969; the 1973 Itaipu Treaty with Paraguay to build the Itaipu hydroelectric dam; the 1979 accord among Argentina, Brazil, and Paraguay for use of the Itaipu and Corpus hydroelectric plants; and the Bolivia-Brazil gas pipeline opened in 1999.

Of course, the paradigm for this transformation of borders in South America is Mercosul (in Spanish Mercosur), the result of an effective strategic restructuring of relations between Argentina and Brazil. The most significant groundwork for Mercosul came after the end of the region's military regimes in the 1980s. Thanks to the initiatives of Presidents Raúl Alfonsín of Argentina and José Sarney of Brazil, the two countries reached a new level of understanding. The landmark for this new plateau was the 1988 Integration, Cooperation, and Development Treaty, which, in its broadest framework, the political one, undertook the consolidation of democratic values and respect for human rights. It accomplished this through confidence-building measures between the two partners meant to reduce strategic and military tensions, especially in the nuclear arena.

Mercosul proper was the achievement of Presidents Fernando Collor, Itamar Franco, and Fernando Henrique Cardoso on the Brazilian side and President Carlos Menem on the Argentine side. Established in 1991 by the Treaty of Asunción, Mercosul not only brought Paraguay and Uruguay into the integration process but also created an associative connection with Bolivia and Chile. Mercosul expresses a vision of open regionalism, works toward the compatibility of domestic and foreign agendas for modernization, and is a benchmark for countries that are integrating democratically. Notwithstanding the economic difficulties that the countries have been facing since the 1980s, Mercosul is a symbol of the new presence of South America in the post–Cold War world.

Just as the understanding between France and Germany built the foundation for the European Community, the understanding between Brazil and Argentina that is at the heart of Mercosul has an international security scope, especially in the nuclear arena. The confidence-building measures of the 1980s culminated in the 1990s in the creation of a formal mechanism for mutual inspections. These opened the two countries' nuclear facilities to international supervision and put the Treaty of Tlatelolco, which prohibits nuclear arms in Latin America, into full force. When Brazil ratified the Nuclear Non-proliferation Treaty in 1998, the international nonproliferation regime broadened its scope, since Argentina and Brazil were no longer "threshold states."

In summary, as a function of its geography, of its historical experience, and of the dominant diplomatic line of the twentieth century, the South American component of Brazil's international identity is one of the deep forces of economics and geography, and it is a positive force in Brazil's foreign policy at that. In a world that is simultaneously globalizing and regionalizing, Brazil's neighborhood fosters peace and development, in contrast to those of China, India, and Russia—also countries of a continental scale. Brazil charts its course into the future toward what Cardoso called the organization of the South American space.[6] In the new millennium, the specter of worry about the organization of this space lies in a feature of global security that has changed since the end of the Cold War. The threats of war and confrontation that can affect Brazil directly have been effectively reduced. In their place, though, diffuse risks of nameless violence have increased. In South America, these risks come from the potential weakness of state power among some of Brazil's neighbors. This weakness makes it difficult for some states to deal with centrifugal forces that lend themselves to upheavals by distinct groups, among these organized crime, drugs, and guerrilla warfare.

The Best Policy for the World Stage

As Brazil established the South American component of its international identity in the twentieth century, it did so through foreign policy activity based on a relative equality among states. Evidently, the farther South America was from the dynamics of the international system's political and economic center, the more this basis was affected by what Ambassador Ricúpero describes as "axes of asymmetrical relation." These are the interactions between Brazil (and other South American countries) and states that have appreciably different amounts of political and economic power.[7] At the beginning of the twentieth century, the "unwritten alliance" that Rio Branco forged with the United States took this asymmetry into account. From the Brazilian point of view, this alliance had two goals. On its axis of asymmetrical relations, it relieved Brazil of the political and economic burden of its previous relations with the European powers. The alliance also preserved the relative symmetry of relations with Brazil's neighbors, so as not to be contaminated by the asymmetrical axes. Rio Branco had always viewed Washington as "the main center of intrigues and petitions for intervention against Brazil by some of Brazil's neighbors, whether permanent rivals or momentarily adversaries."[8]

Preserving an autonomous space in establishing Brazil's vision of Pan-Americanism was a concern shared by both Rio Branco and Joaquim Nabuco, then ambassador to Washington, who presided over the Third Pan-American Conference in 1906. In the course of the twentieth century, this concern would mark Brazil's posture in both multilateralism and relations on the asymmetrical axis. For example, Brazil interpreted the Monroe Doctrine not as a unilateral declaration of the United States but rather as a part of international law in the Americas, applicable through the cooperative action of the principal republics. In other words, the multilateral interpretation of the Monroe Doctrine as a constituent part of Brazilian foreign policy doctrine entailed a controlling role over unilateral U.S. interference based on its premise of "manifest destiny."[9]

This political containment of the major powers was part of what came to be Brazil's vision of its role in twentieth-century international stratification. This vision did not arise clearly in the nineteenth century because, situated as it was on the geographic, political, and economic periphery of the Concert of Europe, Brazil had no way of proposing alternatives to an international political system that attributed power to manage the world order exclusively to a balance among the major powers. Although Brazil had no way of opposing this system of power exercised through the diplomatic logic of the Concert of Europe, it was not comfortable within it. This discomfort with the system eventually, after the legal consolidation of its territory discussed above, appeared as a deep force in Brazil's foreign policy.

This is the paradigmatic significance of senior statesman Rui Barbosa's actions as Brazil's ambassador to the Second Peace Conference in The Hague in 1907. This was Brazil's diplomatic debut in international forums. Representing republican Brazil, with the support of Rio Branco, and based on the principle of the legal equality of states, Barbosa claimed a role in developing and applying norms for governing the major international problems of the time. He thus questioned the logic of the major powers. This questioning of the world order gained conceptual clarity during the Paris Peace Conference of 1919. Brazil participated as a consequence of its role, albeit modest, in World War I. The discussion of the conference's rules led to the Treaty of Versailles and the pact creating the League of Nations. The debate over Article 1 posed a distinction between the warring nations with "general interests" (the United States, France, England, Italy, and Japan), who would participate in all of the sessions and commissions, and the other warring nations with "limited interests." The latter would participate only in sessions in which matters that affected them directly would be discussed. Martin Wright has judged this to be the best definition of "major power" because these countries believed that having "general interests" meant having interests that were as broad as the international system itself, which in the twentieth and twenty-first centuries has been global. This universality of interests and ambitions—to aspire to the whole world, "to the sum of human affairs" in Campanella's words—was illogical from Brazil's point of view. This was because the new inspirational principle of the League of Nations, based on Wilson's Fourteen Points, was opposed to the logic of the old Concert of Europe in that it affirmed the equality of nations before the law. Applying the rule of Article 1 would negate this concept, relegating those countries that were not major powers to the background, as satellites of the others, according to Brazil's delegate in Paris, Pandiá Calógeras. This would mean, in his estimation, allowing the more powerful nations to serve as tribunals for judging the interests of the less powerful ones. It was because of this assessment that Brazil took initiative along with the other countries with "limited interests" to force the major powers to accept the presence of less powerful nations in the various conference commissions.[10]

The affirmation that Brazil had "general interests" or, rather, that it had a view of the world and its operation, and that this view was important for protecting and guiding the specific interests of the country as made clear after World War I, became a constant of Brazil's international identity and another deep force in its foreign policy in the course of the twentieth century. The locus standi for this affirmation lies in the diplomatic competence with which Brazil has continuously conducted its international affairs as a midsize power of continental scale and regional relevance.

It is not easy to imagine what a "midsize power" is. In his 1589 book *The Reason of State*, Giovanni Botero pointed out that these powers have the characteristic of not being so weak that they are exposed to the violence that less powerful countries suffer. At the same time, they do not provoke the same envy that the major powers do as a result of their greatness. Moreover, because those in the middle participate in the two extremes, they have, in principle, the sensitivity to exercise the Aristotelian virtue of seeking the mean. The Aristotelian middle ground is a formula for justice and therefore can be a case for legitimacy, depending on the diplomatic circumstances. Such an approach is apt to achieve a general inclusiveness that is of interest to other global protagonists. Under these circumstances, midsize powers can and do act in the realm of politically viable diplomatic proposals, and in this arena they can become articulators of consensus.[11]

Brazil has shown a capacity for articulating consensus. It has frequently been a third-party mediator among the more and less powerful countries on the multilateral stage. The legal standing for this role—that is, of working toward the possibility of harmony—came from a detail that conferred on Brazil a unique identity in the international system. Brazil is a continent-size country, like the United States, Russia, China, and India. George F. Kennan, taking into account not only geographic and demographic data but also economic and political facts and the magnitude of their problems and challenges, considers these "monster countries."[12] At the same time, Brazil is not a monstrous country. In the first place, it does not have "an excess of power or an excess of cultural, economic, or political attraction," according to Ambassador Ramiro Saraiva Guerreiro. Thus it needs to build its international presence on the basis of confidence, expressed as coherence.[13] Even if Brazil is a midsize power because of its limited means, it is a continent-size one as well. This condition naturally confers on it a world-class quality. Brazil plays an international role because of its size, but not as a scary monster, because it behaves according to a Grotian reading of international reality. It does so because of its history and place in the world, both in symmetric and asymmetric relations. This group of factors gives Brazil the credibility of a "soft power," necessary for exercising the Aristotelian virtue of the middle ground. Contributing to this competence is a repertoire of comprehension of the world derived from an ample store of diplomatic relations that the Brazilian Ministry of Foreign Relations has cultivated over time. This comprehension also comes from the experience of economic development in the twentieth century, through which Brazil earned diversified markets in international trade and foreign investments from a range of sources in its domestic economy.[14] Brazil's mediating role in the sphere of international relations is not a given, however; it is a challenge in each diplomatic circumstance. Success or failure in these challenges depends on the relative intensity of tensions and controversies on the world scene at any given time.

Brazil has been playing the role of a "soft power" with the goal of assuring a position from which to defend its national interests. This function is a matter of a deep force of Brazilian foreign policy focused on the international stratification that arose in the course of the twentieth century, through the broadening of multilateralism as a result of the increasing activity of the United Nations after World War II. This broadening multilateralism has occurred in three areas: in the strategic and military arena, concerning the risks of war and the chances for peace; in the economic and financial arena, leading to norms of mutual cooperation directed toward the creation of international and regional legal frameworks for managing the interdependence of national economies; and in the area of values, which is related to discrepancies and affinities in conceptions of society.

In the course of the twentieth century, the latitude for mediating action adjusted to the varied and variable possibilities that both domestic and foreign circumstances offered. As Brazil enters the twenty-first century, the deep force of mediation is a positive one, both in the international sphere and in the sphere of domestic imperatives. In the international sphere, this is a function of the contribution that Brazil can make in reducing the precariousness of world order, which is being shaped by the centripetal logic of globalization and contested by the centrifugal logic of fragmentation characterized by an undeniable deficit of governability in the international system. In the sphere of domestic needs, the reason for Brazil's diplomatic actions came into sharp focus in the 1990s, with the end of the Cold War and the collapse of the Soviet Union. These events marked the end of what Eric Hobsbawm has called the "short twentieth century."[15] The twentieth century was also short for Brazil because, at the same time that world events offered Brazil the chance for positive outcomes from globalization, these events made even clearer that Brazil's specific interests were more than ever tied to the "general interests" in the dynamics of the new world order. This observation is based on evidence that I will point out in the next section.

Development and Goal-Oriented Nationalism

There are present dilemmas that are connected with putting into operation Brazil's "goal-oriented nationalism," another deep force of its foreign policy in the twentieth century. By addressing the issue of borders in the early twentieth century, Rio Branco made it possible for his successors to dedicate themselves to the line of diplomacy that has been and continues to be the distinguishing feature of Brazil's foreign policy, even given changes in domestic and foreign circumstances: development of Brazil's territory. The theme of development is a deep force in Brazilian foreign policy whose formulations were permeated by analyses of and reflections on national identity in the course of the twentieth century. These formulations were provoked in part by the issue of international stratification, that is, by perception of the Other that derived from power asymmetries among nations. At the same time, discussion about Brazilian development emphasized the contrast between the potential and the reality of a continent-size country like Brazil. This is the context in which one must examine the role of nationalism in the construction of Brazil's *international* identity. One thrust of this nationalism has been toward internal integration of Brazil's huge land area. It is not, therefore, an expansionist nationalism like some others. Instead, it is compatible with the conduct of diplomacy that characterized Brazil's relations with its neighbors and with the major powers in the twentieth century, described above.

The term "nationalism" carries multiple meanings. Summarizing a multifaceted debate, we can say that, on the one hand, there is a more naive trend of nationalism that patriotically exalts the potential of a new country. An early Brazilian example is Afonso Celso's 1900 book *Porque me ufano do meu país* (Why I Am Proud of My Country). On the other hand, there is a more profound trend of nationalism that entails a hard, realistic evaluation of the country's shortcomings. In Brazil, this evaluation has its roots in the classics of Brazilian social science of the 1930s by Gilberto Freyre, Sérgio Buarque de Holanda, and Caio Prado Jr. (see chapter 2) and their successors in the following decades, for example, Celso Furtado, Raimundo Faoro, and Florestan Fernandes. These scholars sought to interpret Brazil, and their work formed the basis of important academic production that, with differing methodological and political orientations, tried to explain the faults in the country's development. In this connection, the Revolution of 1930, a political, economic, and cultural watershed in twentieth-century Brazilian history, signaled a general change in perspective (see chapter 3). As a consequence, Brazilian nationalism deepened its critical understanding by posing the notion that Brazil was an underdeveloped country.[16]

The consequence of this process of growing awareness was that creating a national consciousness would require a plan that could systematically overcome the faults in development, one of which is social exclusion. From this came the driving idea of a nationalism devoted to national integration based on development. The result was a goal-oriented nationalism, which Hélio Jaguaribe described in the following terms: "Nationalism is not an imposition of our particularities, nor is it a simple expression of our national characteristics. On the contrary, it is a means to an end: development."[17]

The context that guided these reflections clearly fed Brazilian foreign policy and diplomatic activity beginning in the 1930s. According to Horácio Lafer, this policy and its activity had two main lines. The first was "to cultivate the autonomous space," that is, "to preserve the freedom to interpret the reality of the country and to find Brazilian solutions for Brazilian problems."[18] The second line was to identify the external resources in various international circumstances that could be mobilized to meet the domestic imperative of development.

In the Brazilian diplomatic logic of goal-oriented nationalism prior to the 1990s, these main lines meant developing ways of controlled integration into the world economy and mobilizing resources to deepen the process of import-substitution industrialization. This brought together the domestic market and state intervention to promote development. These lines also meant an effort to create conditions of sovereignty by putting moderate distance between Brazil and the poles of power with which Brazil had asymmetric international relations. This distance might be more or less depending on conditions afforded by the dynamics of global politics. This diplomatic behavior was made possible both by Brazil's continental scale and by the fact that Brazil was not on the front lines of tensions in the international system.

The effort to translate domestic necessities into foreign possibilities and thus to broaden the country's control over its destiny within the logic of goal-oriented nationalism took shape during the different phases of the first government of Getúlio Vargas (1930–45; see chapter 3). This period began amid the impact of the global economic crisis of 1929 on Brazil, which interrupted capital flows and caused the fall in the price of coffee, Brazil's primary export crop. The first problem was to obtain foreign exchange to service Brazil's foreign trade and financial obligations. In light of these needs, the Vargas government exploited gaps in the international system by pragmatically keeping an equal distance from the major powers. It sought short-term credit from England; it renegotiated international financial commitments; in 1935 it reached a bilateral trade agreement with the United States; and, at the same time, it maintained intense compensatory trade with Germany in spite of opposition from the United States. The circumstances were not only economically difficult but increasingly tense politically, marked by ideological struggles at home and abroad and by bellicose rivalry among the major powers that led to World War II. Under these challenging circumstances, Vargas wagered diplomatically with the potential strategic importance of the country to garner external resources for meeting internal needs.

Gerson Moura shows that the eruption of World War II led Brazil from pragmatic equidistance to an effective alignment with the United States in recognition of a fact: the weight of the United States in the inter-American context. Vargas was very aware of this, and it resulted in the care with which he cultivated his relationship with Franklin Roosevelt. At the same time, this alignment was negotiated in light of the diplomatic logic of goal-oriented nationalism. What lent weight to Brazil's position was what the country could offer to the war effort: essential raw materials and military bases in the Northeast, important for the war in Africa. This negotiation was expressed on two complementary levels: the strategic-military and the economic.

On the strategic and military level, the Vargas government's goal was to promote the country's development through a controlled entry into the world economy, which was compatible with what was occurring in the rest of the world. The example par excellence was the financing that Brazil got from the United States, after much negotiation, for the National Steel Company (Companhia Siderúrgica Nacional, CSN) and the establishment of the steel industry.

On the economic plane, the goal was to promote the reequipping of the armed forces and to get the proper support from the United States for the Vargas government's decision to participate in the war by sending the Brazilian Expeditionary Force to the European theater. This decision gave Brazil, in contrast to Argentina, for example, the legal standing and trustworthiness of a country truly allied with the winners, who were going to build the postwar world order.[19]

During the term of Eurico Dutra (1946–50), the rigid bipolarity of the Cold War and the United States' priorities in rebuilding Europe through the Marshall Plan made the legal standing of the Brazil-U.S. alignment one of the few compensations for the diplomatic logic of goal-oriented nationalism. For the same reasons, during his elected term (1951–54), Vargas had scant room to maneuver in the international arena since the Korean War limited the pragmatic diplomacy of the sort that he had used prior to World War II. This did not impede the progress, however, of Brazil's controlled entry into the world economy by moving forward with import substitution.

Fissures in the international system, revealed in the struggles over the Suez Canal in the 1950s, the 1955 African-Asian Conference in Bandung, Indonesia, and the 1956 Hungarian Revolution created a space for Brazilian foreign policy to exercise diplomatically its style of nationalism. This was the context for the Pan-American Operation (Operação Pan-Americana), the great initiative through which the diplomacy of President Juscelino Kubitschek (1956–61) articulated Brazil's domestic imperative for development within the scope of the inter-American system. Conditions for greater maneuverability within the international system along with domestic circumstances allowed the independent foreign policy of Presidents Jânio Quadros (1961) and João Goulart (1961–64) to broaden the scope of the Pan-American Operation to include the whole globe.

The installation of the military regime in 1964 temporarily reduced the autonomy that an independent foreign policy had recently afforded Brazil. This was because the military government, which was arrayed against the Left at home, reaffirmed Brazil's alignment with the United States in an international context increasingly marked by the East-West divide. Soon, however, the deep forces of goal-oriented nationalism flowered again, revealing a continuity in Brazil's international identity. This happened through developments in the domestic sphere and in light of the international system's activity that made room for the North-South divide in global life, for example in the rise of OPEC. In Brazil, the clearest affirmation of this flowering was the "responsible pragmatism" of President Ernesto Geisel (1974–78). This policy shift was a consequence of the 1973 oil shock, and it loosened the strict alignment with the United States to improve foreign trade options and lessen Brazil's dependence on foreign energy sources. Further evidence of the loosened alignment came with the 1975 accord with West Germany to help build nuclear power plants and Geisel's 1977 renunciation of the military alliance with the United States.

To synthesize, whenever an international system of defined polarization prevailed, for example East-West or North-South, and whenever the processes of import substitution based on the continental scale of the country were economically energetic, then Brazilian foreign policy sought autonomy through distance, within the logic of goal-oriented nationalism. This quest worked in a constructively flexible way through the Grotian conduct of diplomacy directed toward exploiting niches of opportunity offered by the competitive experience of bipolarity. According to Francisco Clementino de San Tiago Dantas, politician, diplomat, and champion of Brazil's "independent" foreign policy, the goal was for Brazil to develop itself in order to free itself—in the international sphere from the weight of the asymmetry of international stratification and in the domestic sphere from the weight of social exclusion, one of the shortcomings in the country's development.[20]

From the 1930s to the 1980s, Brazilian society changed significantly as a result of the whole of its public policy, including its foreign policy inspired by goal-oriented nationalism. Brazil urbanized, industrialized, experienced periods of authoritarianism, redemocratized, diversified its exports, and broadened its portfolio of diplomatic relations. In brief, it modernized and improved its international standing. Yet Brazil did not address the failing of social exclusion. Domestically, the 1980s were a decade of political success, with the transition from military regime to democracy. Economically, however, the country stagnated amid the foreign debt crisis, inflation, and the exhaustion of the import-substitution model.

This exhaustion became even more acute with international changes after the fall of the Berlin Wall. Under the impact of cost reductions in transportation and communication, thanks to advances in computer technology, the logic of globalization allowed the dilution of the financial and economic significance of borders. In a world of undefined polarities, this narrowing tests the efficiency and dynamism of the internalization of production chains through controlled insertion into the world economy. Aside from the dizzying acceleration of capital flows, the logic of globalization has envisioned the dismantling of production chains on a global scale. It has made outsourcing a routine business practice and has thus made foreign trade and domestic production of goods and services two sides of the same coin. For this reason, economic development managed by the state within a relatively distant and controlled insertion into the world economy, elaborated through the prior logic of goal-oriented nationalism, now became unworkable. The world that Brazil managed as an "external" phenomenon had become internalized, incorporating the effective repertoire of solutions assembled since the first Vargas government.

Again, from the point of view of Brazil's place in the world, the twentieth century was a "short century." It had as its starting point the results of Rio Branco's career at the end of the first decade of the 1900s. Once the legal borders of this continent-size country had been consolidated, Brazil could distinguish between the "foreign" and the "domestic." This released the deep forces of diplomacy based on goal-oriented nationalism. The endpoint was the consequences of the fall of the Berlin Wall and the collapse of the Soviet Union after 1989. These consequences, in anticipation of the fulfillment of the logic of globalization, narrowed the differences between the "foreign" and the "domestic."

Brazilian Foreign Policy in a Global World

Brazilian foreign policy, conceived as public policy, is directed toward development of the national territory, and this continues to be the paramount theme of its diplomatic activity. What are the consequences of the new global reality from the point of view of foreign policy? To what extent does the style of the conduct of foreign policy that has characterized Brazil in the twentieth century, associated with diplomatic activity in both the South American context and in relation to the major powers, offer answers to this question? These are the issues discussed in this last section.

The acceleration of time and the shortening of distances through the centripetal force of globalization that have diluted the differences between foreign and domestic have also intensified the questioning of the specific nature of a foreign policy as public policy within an international system that is predominantly international and intergovernmental. Because of this, scholars tend to define the field of international relations as one of complex networks of interactions, both governmental and nongovernmental, that structure the world's space and governance. From this arises the notion of global diplomacy, with a wide array of actors that includes transnational companies and nongovernmental organizations, media (in their role in forming public sensibilities and opinions), political parties, and labor unions.

At the same time, broadening the field of international relations and the scope of diplomacy does not eliminate the importance of states and nations in the dynamic of international life. On the contrary: not only do individuals continue to project their expectations, claims, and hopes onto the nations to which they belong, but the well-being of the vast majority of human beings continues to be closely linked to the performance of the countries in which they live. For these reasons, nations and the states that represent them have been and will continue to be indispensable public entities for mediation. They are domestic phenomena that mediate between political institutions and a population that shares within its territory an array of economic goods, technical and scientific knowledge, information, and culture. They are also phenomena of mediation with the world. This foreign mediation arises from a vision of collective identity, of a "we" that underscores our specific characteristics. Among these characteristics are geographic location, shared historical experience, linguistic and cultural codes, levels of development, and features of social stratification. This differentiation obeys a logic of identity that interacts with the logic of globalization within the international system. It is this interaction that shapes the world's pluralism. From it arises the reason for distinctions of strategic, political, and economic interests and of views that, in turn, give rise to the organizing perspective and the possible latitude of a country's insertion into the world.

Ortega y Gasset noted that perspective is one of the components of reality. Perspective does not distort reality; it organizes it. This general epistemological assessment is extremely appropriate for the analysis of foreign policy, which is naturally the expression of a country's point of view on the world and how it works. This point of view can have a dimension of continuity explicable as a result of the impact of certain persistent factors in a country's place in international life, as in the case of Brazil. These are the deep forces: the facts of South American geography and the importance of relations with numerous neighboring countries; territorial and linguistic unity; distance since independence in 1822 from the focal points of tension in the center of the international stage; and the circumstances of a continent-size country that has the issue of global stratification and the challenge of domestic development as priorities on its diplomatic agenda. These persistent factors contribute to explaining important features of Brazil's international identity.

The Ministry of Foreign Relations has contributed much to the construction of Brazil's international identity. It has succeeded in affirming itself, throughout the country's history, as a permanent national institution, able to represent Brazil's interests because it is endowed with authority and memory. In the twentieth century, in addition to peacefully establishing Brazil's continental-scale borders, Rio Branco was the ministry's great institution builder. Itamaraty, as the ministry is informally known, for the Itamaraty Palace it once occupied, to this day benefits in its authority from the aura of this great national figure. Rio Branco is also the inspiration for the style of diplomatic behavior that characterizes Brazil in light of its circumstances and history. This style is one of constructive moderation expressed in the capacity "to downplay the drama of the foreign policy agenda; that is, to reduce conflicts, crises, and difficulties in diplomatic currents," according to Gelson Fonseca Jr. This constructive moderation is permeated by a Grotian reading of international reality, identifying within it a positive ingredient of sociability that allows it to deal, though diplomacy and law, with conflict and cooperation and, in this way, reduce the force of "power politics." Brazil's agenda is sensibly guided by realism in its assessment of the determinants of power in international life. Based on the information absorbed from the facts of power, but without either paralyzing immobility or Machiavellian or Hobbesian impulses, Brazilian foreign policy tries to find new diplomatic and legal solutions as it channels themes related to Brazil's place in the world. Knowledge and memory of a Grotian diplomatic tradition confer on Brazilian foreign policy a coherence that derives from an amalgam of lines of continuity with lines of innovation in an "open work" geared to building the future.[21]

What is the meaning of this tradition, which acquired conceptual precision in the twentieth century, for the challenges facing the twenty-first century? What is the significance especially for a foreign policy conceived of as public policy directed to development of the national territory? Like Fonseca, I believe that, if in the twentieth century the country established the autonomy possible with reasonable success through a relative distancing from the world, then at the beginning of a new century this possible autonomy, which is necessary for development, can be maintained only through active participation in the elaboration of norms and agendas managing the world order. It is for this reason that the "open work" of continuity within change that characterizes Brazilian diplomacy requires that it deepen the lines of foreign policy begun in The Hague in 1907 in multilateral forums today. At the same time, Brazil must make a new push toward organizing the South American space to reinforce its standing and that of its partners within a world that is simultaneously globalizing and regionalizing.[22]

From the point of view of developing the national space and addressing poverty—the domestic imperatives of Brazil's foreign policy—the real challenge facing Brazil is in the negotiation of foreign trade and financial agendas. The goals of these negotiations include gaining access to markets and taming the online timing of capital flows, whose volatility has produced successive crises in the emerging market countries that struck Brazil directly and indirectly in the 1990s. In addition, a goal of negotiations must be to find space for the conduct of public policies, a space that has been reduced with the internalization of the world within the country as a result of globalization. In a country with Brazil's characteristics, development will not result automatically from just the right combination of fiscal, monetary, and exchange policies, even though these are the macroeconomic conditions of its sustainability. Development requires a broad array of public policies that are congruent and compatible with the broad macroeconomic balances that ensure currency stability, reduce inequality, and drive national development, giving economic agents, within their scope, the conditions for competitive equality before the law that allow them to face the challenge of globalization.

In conclusion, to repeat a musical metaphor I have used elsewhere, the challenge of Brazilian foreign policy in the early twenty-first century is to find ways to play the melody of the country's specific conditions in harmony with the world. It is not an easy challenge given the size of Brazil's domestic problems and the general cacophony resulting from the prevailing ruptures in the functioning of the system that characterizes the contemporary world. The challenge requires an effective reformulation of the way in which Brazil put its goal-oriented nationalism to work in the twentieth century. This is not easy for a country traditionally turned inward rather than outward. The historical experience of this continent-size country has accustomed it to autonomy through distance, and, for this very reason, it has not fully internalized the world. It is, however, a challenge for which the other components of the deep forces of Brazil's place in the world in the twentieth century—including its relations with its South American neighbors, its posture and legal standing in relation to the major powers, and its conduct of foreign policy within the Grotian mold—offer a meaningful basis for successful action.

Notes

1. Luis Felipe de Seixas Corrêa, "Política externa e identidade nacional brasileira," *Política Externa* 9, no. 1 (June–July–August 2000): 28.

2. Synésio Sampaio Góes Filho, *Navegantes, bandeirantes, diplomatas* (São Paulo: Martins Fontes, 1999); Demétrio Magnoli, *O corpo da pátria* (São Paulo: Editora da Universidade Estadual Paulista/Moderna, 1997).

3. Rubens Ricúpero, *Rio Branco: O Brasil no mundo* (Rio de Janeiro: Contraponto/Petrobrás, 2000), 33–34.

4. Pierre Renouvin and Jean-Baptiste Duroselle, *Introduction à l'histoire des relations internationales*, 4th ed. (Paris: Cocin, 1991), part 1.

5. Argentine diplomat and politician Ramón Cárcano spelled this out in Article 1 of the 1909 draft treaty among Argentina, Brazil, and Chile. Álvaro Lins, *Rio Branco*, 3rd ed. (São Paulo: Alfa-Omega, 1996), 432–89.

6. *O Presidente segundo o sociólogo: Entrevista de Fernando Henrique Cardoso a Roberto Pompeu de Toledo* (São Paulo: Companhia das Letras, 1998), 127.

7. Ricúpero, *Rio Branco*, 34–41.

8. J. Penn, "O Brasil, os Estados Unidos e o monroísmo," in *Estudos Históricos*, vol. 8,

Obras do Barão do Rio Branco (Rio de Janeiro: Ministério das Relações Exteriores, 1948), 151. See also Bradford E. Burns, *The Unwritten Alliance: Rio Branco and Brazilian-American Relations* (New York: Columbia University Press, 1966), chapter 8.

9. Lins, *Rio Branco*, 318, 322; João Frank da Costa, *Joaquim Nabuco e a política externa do Brasil* (Rio de Janeiro: Record, 1969), 109.

10. Martin Wight, Hedley Bull, and Carsten Holbrad, eds., *Power Politics* (New York: Holmes and Meir, 1979), 50; Hedley Bull, ed., *Systems of States* (Leicester: Leicester University Press, 1977), 136–41; Pandiá Calógeras, "Conferência de Paz: Diário," entries for 13, 18 January 1919, in *Calógeras na opinião dos seus contemporâneos*, ed. Roberto Simonsen, Antonio Gontijo de Carvalho, and Francisco Salles de Oliveira (São Paulo: Siqueira, 1934), 66, 689; Eugenio Vargas Garcia, *O Brasil e a Liga das Nações (1919–1926)* (Porto Alegre/Brasília: Editora da Universidade Federal do Rio Grande do Sul/Fundação Alexandre de Gusmão, 2000).

11. Giovanni Botero, *La razón del estado y otros escritos*, trans. Luciana de Stefano, ed. Manuel Garcia Pelayo (Caracas: Universidad Central de Venezuela, 1982), book 1.5, 96–97, book 2.5, 113; Gelson Fonseca Jr., *A legitimidade e outras questões internacionais* (São Paulo: Paz e Terra, 1998), 171–248.

12. George F. Kennan, *Around the Cragged Hill: A Personal and Political Philosophy* (New York: W. W. Norton, 1993), 143.

13. Ramiro Saraiva Guerreiro, lecture at the War College, Rio de Janeiro, 23 September 1982, *Resenha da Política Externa do Brasil* 34 (July–August–September 1982): 80–82.

14. Celso Lafer, "Brazilian International Identity and Foreign Policy: Past, Present, and Future," *Daedalus* 129, no. 2 (Spring 2000): 218–22.

15. Eric Hobsbawm, *The Age of Extremes* (New York: Pantheon Books, 1994).

16. Antonio Cândido, *Vários escritos*, 3rd ed. (São Paulo: Duas Cidades, 1995), 293–305; Antonio Cândido, *Teresina, etc.* (Rio de Janeiro: Paz e Terra, 1980), 135–52; Antonio Cândido, *A educação pela noite e outros ensaios* (São Paulo: Ática, 1987), 140–62, 181–98.

17. Hélio Jaguaribe, *Nacionalismo na atualidade brasileira* (Rio de Janeiro: Instituto Superior de Estudos Brasileiros, 1958), 52.

18. Horácio Lafer, speech at the inauguration of the minister of foreign relations, 4 August 1959, in *Gestão do Ministro Lafer na pasta das Relações Exteriores* (n.p.: Ministério das Relações Exteriores/Impresa Nacional, 1961), 83.

19. Gerson Moura, *Autonomia na dependência* (Rio de Janeiro: Nova Fronteira, 1980); Gerson Moura, *Sucessos e ilusões: Relações internacionais do Brasil durante e após a Segunda Guerra Mundial* (Rio de Janeiro: Fundação Getúlio Vargas, 1991); Marcelo de Paiva Abreu, *O Brasil e a economia mundial: 1930–1945* (Rio de Janeiro: Civilização Brasileira, 1999).

20. Francisco Clementino de San Tiago Dantas, "Política externa e desenvolvimento," *Revista Brasileira de Política Internacional*, year 8, no. 27 (September 1964): 524–25.

21. Fonseca, *A legitimidade e outras questões internacionais*, 356; Celso Lafer, *Política externa brasileira: Três momentos* (São Paulo: Fundação Konrad Adenauer Stiftung, 1993).

22. Fonseca, *A legitimidade e outras questões internacionais*, 353–54; Celso Lafer and Gelson Fonseca Jr., "Questões para a diplomacia no contexto internacional das polaridades indefinidas," analytic notes and some suggestions, in *Temas da política exterior II*, vol. 1, ed. Gelson Fonseca Jr. and Henrique Nabuco de Castro (Brasília/São Paulo: Fundação Alexandre de Gusmão/Paz e Terra, 1994), 49–77; Celso Lafer, "Brasil y el nuevo encenario mundial," *Archivos del Presente*, year 1, no. 3 (Summer 1995–96): 61–80; "Brasil: Dilemas e desafios da política externa," *Estudos Avançados* 14, no. 38 (January–April 2000): 260–67.

5

RENATO ORTIZ

Culture and Society

The topic of Brazilian culture over the span of a century is a broad one. I have chosen to limit the objects of this essay to the mass media and industries of culture. I hope to tailor the question of culture to these topics, broaching important themes from intellectual debates and from the development of Brazilian society.[1] My choice is not by chance: the media are constituents of modernity. They act as mediators among various parts of modern societies. In this sense, discussing Brazilian society using the media and industries of culture as a point of departure is to treat the problem of the emergence of modernity in Brazil and its constitution as a nation. The problem transcends the narrow details of the objects of study to address topics such as identity, national integration, and popular culture.

For the purpose of dividing the century into periods, I have chosen two milestones: 1930, the year of the Revolution, and 1964, the year of the military coup d'état. The utility of dates is relative, and this relativity is convincing only when associated with events that, from a more general point of view of history, are determining moments. These are dates that are recognized in Brazilian historiography as moments of political and economic significance. Such dates should not be seen as complete breaks, since the past always has implications beyond its limits. These milestones allow us, rather, to organize our thoughts and highlight certain patterns that shaped the periods in question.

1900–1930

At the beginning of the twentieth century, Brazil was an agrarian country. We could hardly call it a nation, that is, a modern society integrated within a coherent whole. The country had not yet had its industrial revolution. Traces of the slave-based society were not mere memories but elements alive in the present. The national territory, far from constituting a geographical and cultural unit, was better understood as an archipelago of social practices, interests, and powers (see chapters 1 and 2). This is the context in which one must place the means of cultural communication, in particular, the journalistic press, book publishing, and the cinema. The development of all of these sectors was fragmented and incipient. Strictly speaking, we cannot refer to a publishing "market." Of course, there had been a book trade since the nineteenth century, but it would be difficult to characterize it as a market activity, that is, as an autonomous practice within its own commercial circuit. For example, in the nineteenth century, booksellers such as the Garnier brothers depended on the sale not only of books but also of stationery and imported articles, such as umbrellas, walking canes, and cigars.

The data in this regard speak volumes. In 1920 in São Paulo, 209 titles and 900,000 copies of books and pamphlets were published. In the same decade in Rio de Janeiro, about 780 titles were edited per year, with total press runs of 2.2 million copies.[2] The average printing of a novel reached 1,000 copies. In 1918, a best seller like Monteiro Lobato's *Urupês*, a collection of short stories about rural poverty in the "old" coffee regions of São Paulo, sold 8,000 copies. In São Paulo between 1900 and 1920, there were published 92 novels, an annual average of fewer than 7 literature books per year, including short stories and novellas. We can better appreciate these numbers when compared to other data. Book production in Brazil at the beginning of the twentieth century was similar to that of France during the revolutionary period. In France, publishing activity grew from between 700 and 1,000 titles per year during the ancien régime to 7,658 in 1850 and 14,849 in 1889.[3] The Brazilian best sellers of the 1920s can hardly be compared to the books that sold the most in France during the romantic period — Eugène Sue's *Mysteries of Paris* (30,000 copies) and Daniel Defoe's *The Adventures of Robinson Crusoe* (50,000 copies). Brazilian book sales compared even less favorably with the French publishing industry at the end of the nineteenth century, which had been supported by the revolution in transportation (especially railroads), the redefinition of technological infrastructure, and the development of networks of bookstores. The same can be said in relation to the press. At the beginning of the twentieth century, the average press run for a daily newspaper in Rio de Janeiro did not exceed 3,000 copies, a number comparable to that in Paris at the beginning of the nineteenth century.

Limited production and distribution of books and newspapers is a characteristic feature of peripheral societies, and Brazil does not deviate from the rule. Paper had to be imported, machinery was outdated, and investment in the sector was small. Yet the limits at the time were not only technological and economic. The development of print media presupposes a prior effort: the creation of an ample literate public. In the last decades of the nineteenth century, the United States, England, and France had literacy rates of 90 percent. At the same time, Brazil's *illiteracy* rate limited the reading public: 84 percent in 1890 (and still as high as 75 percent in 1920). This meant that no written work of any type could be "popular," though literary critics speak, for example, of the "popularity" of the folletinesque novel, the plot-driven novels that were published in installments, in the Brazilian press. They are forgetting that, in a society whose heritage is based on colonialism and slavery, such popularity is an illusion. In fact, what marked verbal tradition was not literacy but orality, a feature that persists somewhat today, reinforced now not so much by the absence of schools but by the failure of the educational system and by the prominence of audiovisual media.

The weakness of print media had another implication. In nineteenth-century Europe, especially after the middle of the century, there was a growing movement toward autonomy in the sphere of the arts. Flaubert's principle of "art for art's sake" summarized a break between literature, now written for peers, and other social practices (politics, religion, journalism, science, and so forth). There was also a separation between restricted goods (consumable, in effect, only by a privileged cultural elite) and large-scale goods (directed to the "general public"), to use Pierre Bourdieu's terms.[4] The criticism of the folletinesque novel in the mid-nineteenth century, like the conflict between writers and journalists at the end of the same century, shows the antagonism between domains with different functions. The rules of art are opposed to the demands of the market.[5] The Brazilian case, however, is peculiar. Because of the limited development of technical means and the restriction of reading, the movement toward autonomy of the arts was never complete. In Brazil, the writer could not live off literature; he or she needed to practice other professions, for example, in teaching or in public service. In Brazil, the flourishing of literature is thus closely associated with the state bureaucracy.

Given these circumstances of literature, the relation between the spheres of restricted goods and large-scale goods tended to be somewhat blurred. For example, there was not a break between being a journalist and being an author. The poet Olavo Bilac (1865–1918) used to say that "the newspaper is a great boon to the Brazilian writer. It is really the only means for the writer to make himself read." In other words, the relations between the intellectual and his or her public began through the mass media. In the Brazilian case, as a consequence of insufficient institutionalization of the arts, an instrument primarily geared to the sphere of large-scale goods became a venue for the author's work and for legitimating the literary product. This interpenetration of worlds, mixing art and marketplace, was a characteristic of Brazil and of the whole of Latin America throughout the twentieth century. The symbioses between radio and literature, cinema and theater, and theater and television were constants.

At no time in the history of Brazilian society has there been a clear differentiation or opposition between "erudite" ("high") culture and "popular" ("low") culture. The movement among these domains is frequent and unbroken. Consider, for example, the importance of playwrights and other writers in creating a standard for *telenovelas*, serialized prime-time television dramas, especially in the late 1960s and early 1970s. In this way, in Brazil there has not been, as postmodern reasoning would suppose, a modern stage, in which the world of the arts dictates the norms of cultural production, that is later substituted by another, postmodern stage, in which, because of the mixture of arts with the culture industries, the former's authority is weakened. If we accept such reasoning, Latin American societies and, in particular, Brazil were always postmodern.

Brazilian society at the beginning of the twentieth century was therefore marked by the traditional-modern contradiction: its agrarian present contrasted with the ideal of a still absent modernity. The modernist movement in the arts dealt widely with this theme. Its participants celebrated the cinema, the airplane, electric trolleys, jazz bands, and industry questing after signs of modernity in Brazilian society in the 1920s. Modernism wanted a break with the traditional past. Various interpreters of the movement underscored this facet of rupture. Critic Alceu Amoroso Lima would say that the movement bore fruit in São Paulo because there artists experienced in their daily lives the components of modern life: "Motor, asphalt, radio, tumult, rumor, open-air life, great masses, the cinema carried into the realm of art, stamping them with their esthetics splintered reality, imagistic illusion, superposition and distortion of forms, primacy of technique over nature."[6] The description is vivid but unfocused. It hides the existence of a provincial São Paulo that was poorly adjusted to the ideal cultivated by the techniques and images of modernity. Poetic imagination must not cloud our judgment. The process of industrialization was slow in São Paulo in the 1920s, and the same can be said of all of Brazil. It is often forgotten that, in Brazil, modernism occurred without modernization. This means that there was a gap between the intentions of the aesthetic movement and the very society that sustained it. In this sense, modernity was not something current but rather an aspiration, a plan to be executed sometime in the future. It is not by chance that, already by the middle of the twentieth century, modernity was identified with the "national question." An example of this is Oswald de Andrade's "Manifesto da poesia pau-brasil" (Brazilwood Poetry Manifesto), which tried to envision a nation that in fact could be an alternative to Brazil's agrarian, traditional present.

1930–64

The Revolution of 1930 began a process of restructuring Brazil. From the economic point of view, it encouraged industrialization within a deliberate state policy. From the political point of view, it unified the nation. It is often forgotten that the separatist movements in the states of Rio Grande do Sul and São Paulo were testimony to the fragility of national unity, an unstable equilibrium that dominated during the First Republic (1889–1930). The Brazilian state did not have a monopoly on force since the army divided its responsibilities with the state militias, which represented local interests. The flag-burning ceremony after the triumph of the federal forces, commanded by Getúlio Vargas, was significant: the national flag was the only one that was to survive in the face of the symbolic destruction of the emblems representing each state. A progressive rationalization of the state apparatus also occurred, permitting it to coordinate and implement policies of a national character.

Two of these measures were important in the cultural sphere: the development of a language policy and the creation of a national school system. During the colonial and the imperial periods, at no time was Portuguese seriously threatened by other languages. The successive territorial challenges from the French and the Dutch were not successful, and the Treaty of Tordesillas guaranteed Portuguese rather than Spanish hegemony in Brazil, except in the border regions, where there were indeed mixture and conflict. The indigenous and African languages were confined to limited groups, however, and they declined in the face of Portuguese expansion. It was only with mass immigration that Portuguese found itself competing with other languages, this time written ones: there were newspapers published and music and theater performed in Italian, Japanese, and German. Vargas saw linguistic diversity as a sign of national fragmentation and prohibited the teaching of the immigrants' mother tongues to their children. Literacy programs, addressed within a systematic policy of expansion of elementary education under Vargas, were to be carried out only in Portuguese. As in many other countries, school and language thus become basic tools for constructing the "mental unity" of the nation, as French sociologist Marcel Mauss would say.[7]

This is the setting in which the media were established. Radio as a transmission technology had already been introduced into Brazil in 1922. During the 1920s it appeared in almost every country.[8] Nevertheless, until 1935, radio in Brazil was mainly organized on a noncommercial basis. Broadcasters formed societies and clubs whose programming was markedly literary and musical. There were few radio sets, and these were crystal. Listeners had to pay a fee to the government for use of the airwaves. This was an experimental phase: many amateurs built their own sound receivers, and radio broadcasting was under the aegis more of individual personalities than of business or governmental organizations. The technical problems were still considerable, and transmission suffered constant interruption. This situation began to change in the 1930s with the introduction of tube radios and legislation that allowed advertising on radio. Advertising was set initially at a limit of 10 percent of daily programming; in 1952 this limit would be raised to 20 percent. Radio stations could then count on a source of constant financing and build their programming on more permanent foundations. Therefore, there was a significant growth in the number of radio stations in the country, from 106 in 1944 to 300 in 1950. In addition, a radio culture flourished with the appearance of popular music shows, like auditorium programs, and radio dramas.

This was also the period in which cinema truly became a popular consumer good, first with the expansion of U.S. films. During the 1930s, Hollywood production was no longer shaped only by the domestic market, and studios began an aggressive policy of exportation. In the 1940s, the U.S. film industry captured once and for all the Latin American market.[9] Because the United States could not export films to Europe during the war, Latin America became an increasingly attractive market. Political motives were also present, since U.S. expansion around the globe occurred through the consolidation of its hegemony on the continent. The Good Neighbor Policy, a euphemism for imperialist intentions, thus included the cinema in its marriage of opening markets and political needs. In Brazil, this was when the outlines of a consolidated domestic industry appeared. Atlântida Studio was founded in 1941 and Vera Cruz in 1949. The cities of Rio de Janeiro and São Paulo became the centers of production of the musical comedies called *chanchadas*, dramas, and action films. To give an idea of this expansion in production, in São Paulo between 1935 and 1949, there were only six feature-length films made. Between 1951 and 1955, an average of twenty-seven films were made per year.[10]

The same happened with the markets for newspapers, magazines, and books, which broadened considerably. Paper imports grew, and after 1947, domestic companies such as Klabin began to manufacture it. In addition, between 1940 and 1960, the Brazilian population with more than four years of elementary education grew from 681,000 to 3.7 million in São Paulo and from 429,000 to 2.3 million in Rio de Janeiro. There was also clear expansion of the reading public as evidenced by the size of newspaper and magazine circulations. In 1948, Cruzeiro printed 300,000 copies a week; four years later, its weekly printing was 500,000. In 1952, Seleções Reader's Digest had a monthly run of 330,000 copies; in 1957 it reached 500,000. The expansion was not only quantitative. Magazines appeared targeting the female public. The fotonovelas of Grande Hotel (1951) and Capricho (1952) exploited the sorts of narratives used in radio dramas (rádionovelas), but in print with images. Similarly, children's and adolescents' literature broadened through comic books. Newspaper circulations also increased. In São Paul in 1949, A Gazeta and O Estado de São Paulo sold 76,000 and 70,000 copies, respectively. In Rio de Janeiro, O Globo and Diário da Noite sold 105,000 and 90,000 copies, respectively. In the same year, the circulation of all of the daily newspapers in São Paulo totaled 728,000 copies and those of Rio, 908,000. These were unsatisfactory numbers in comparison to those of the European and North American presses at the end of the nineteenth century, but they were substantially higher than newspaper circulations in Brazil prior to 1930.

In addition, print journalism underwent a profound restructuring.[11] Beginning in 1937, the profession of journalism was regulated, and some years later, schools were created specializing in professional training (for example, Cásper Líbero, São Paulo, 1947; Faculdade Nacional do Rio de Janeiro, 1948; Universidade Federal da Bahia, Salvador, 1949; Pontifícia Universidade Católica do Rio de Janeiro, 1951). As Brazilian journalism gradually moved from opinion to information, the very vehicle was reformulated. The number of pages covering daily events increased; articles, until then short and numerous, gave way to selected information; philosophical and literary debates, which had been numerous, declined and were moved to Sunday editions; and topics like fashion, restaurants, and shopping came to supplant information about cultural events. In addition, the divide between information and opinion sought to guarantee a kind of standardized, analytical writing at the expense of more personal editorializing.

The transformations under way, characteristic of urban industrial societies, had various implications. Remember that, up to that point, Brazil's heritage had radically devalued the popular cultures. The Brazilian elites' attitudes toward them were very negative because they represented society's "dark side," the barbarous element, which, separated as it was from the ideals of civilization, must necessarily be contained. There are various examples that confirm this negativity. In the literary realm, this was the theme of José de Alencar's 1857 novel *O Guarani* (The Guarani). The Legal Code of 1890 considered the art of healing a crime; magic and folk medicine practiced by curers were seen as factors in mental illness, and they appeared alongside alcoholism and syphilis as phenomena that promoted insanity and challenged the social order. The Afro-Brazilian religions were targets of the police practically everywhere in Brazil. In the city of Rio, the spirit of the belle époque was in conflict with the "ignorance" and "backwardness" of traditional festivals. Society, therefore, shunned popular festivals like the Punishing of Judas and the Bumba-meu-boi, folk practices that evoked medieval Iberian and African roots.

Ever since the proclamation of the republic in 1889, Brazil has intensely debated its national identity, but, to be sure, that identity was infected with racial prejudices. The mestizo was seen as a result of the crossbreeding of a superior race (the white) and two inferior ones (the Black and the Indian). It was not until the 1930s, a time when various intellectuals including Sérgio Buarque de Holanda and Caio Prado Jr. were revising the "portrait of Brazil," that sociologist Gilberto Freyre could define the Brazilian from a new perspective. Freyre's perspective embraced Brazil's racial and cultural formation and eliminated related ambiguities and doubts (see chapters 2 and 3). From then on, racial mixture was taken up as an ideal of national identity and became a positive fact. Thus to be Brazilian no longer meant being "indolent" or "lazy."

The urban industrial society that arose after the Revolution of 1930 managed to integrate some previously excluded segments of society. Florestan Fernandes once wrote that "the tragedy of Blacks between 1890 and 1930 was explained by their inability to adjust to the urban lifestyle."[12] By the 1930s, however, Blacks moved into the gaps in the society in formation, though not without obstacles and contradictions. It is important to stress, however, that room was made within this class-based society that popular phenomena sought to fill. This was when carnival, soccer, and samba ceased to be phenomena limited to certain social groups and were integrated into society as a whole. Soccer was professionalized and was no longer the pastime of an elite who met in private clubs. The *escolas de samba* (samba schools), the associations responsible for producing the music and pageantry of carnival, took samba to the streets, dethroning the old Luso-Brazilian *corso* parades. Samba was freed from its ethnic markers of "Blackness." The state played a crucial role in restoring value to these popular manifestations. Samba, soccer, and carnival were promoted as symbols of Brazilianness. After all, the definition of the Brazilian nation had already addressed the question of who formed its "people." The effort of the state in Brazilianizing certain (though not all) popular phenomena was great. Traditionally available cultural elements were reworked and took on new meanings. The Brazilian *ginga*, or "swing" in walk and dance, and its musicality both became national symbols, lending themselves even to export in the forms of Carmen Miranda's exoticism, the highly contested soccer championships, and the sensuality of the carnival samba schools.

The media had a central role in these changes in the meaning of popular culture. Because of their reach, they had the ability to distribute nationwide the new signs and symbols of identity. They were a venue within which many facets of popular phenomena could be expressed. The case of music is an example. The creation of Brazilian Popular Music (Música Popular Brasileira, MPB), which is distinct from other styles such as folk rhythms and songs, could hardly have occurred without the existence of radio. This was not just a matter of transmitting messages; radio was a site of experimentation, constructing popular formats, such as auditorium programs and radio dramas.

Cinema also had an important role in the development of a national consciousness. Atlântida's *chanchadas* were not simple comedies; they imparted a vision in which Brazil's carnivalesque spirit was centered on the image of the federal capital, Rio de Janeiro. Cultural practices, symbols, and identifications were incubated in these media. They were gradually learned and eventually shared among the various social classes and groups. The state was clear about the strategic importance of the media. In the 1930s, it was said the samba should "put on evening wear"; that is, it should be musically refurbished, better adapting its features to an urban and urbane public. For this reason, samba songs that celebrated the Rio de Janeiro brand of *malandragem* or roguishness came to be seen as encouraging indolence and laziness, because they appeared exactly at the moment that the state was promoting the work ethic compatible with Brazilian industrialization. The authorities intervened, censoring these songs and replacing them with others that stressed the value of hard work.[13]

In fact, the field of culture is a political space. This can be seen in various forms. One example comes from José Murilo de Carvalho's study of the construction of a national consciousness during the First Republic.[14] He observed that government authorities in Brazil had not succeeded in creating convincing myths and heroes that were truly national. Personalities such as Deodoro da Fonseca and the Duke of Caxias remained on the margins of popular imagination. Only Tiradentes, the eighteenth-century coconspirator in an anticolonial plot, succeeded in transcending the mythmakers' restricted circle. It was not, however, his qualities of citizenship, which, in principle, should guide the archetypes of civic heroes, that prevailed. Tiradentes is popularly seen as a prophet, a Christ figure, someone who has achieved a kind of sainthood in a religious mentality. Thus he is known as Brazil's Martyr for Liberty. The inability of Brazilian society to create national civic myths was due to a lack of a consciousness of citizenship.

We can add another dimension to Carvalho's interpretation. For cultural myths to be plausible, it is necessary for the creators of the mythology to succeed in inculcating it in a majority of the population. Since elementary schools practically did not exist during the First Republic, the effort of inculcating ideology was wasted; that is, it was confined to a limited group of the Brazilian elite. I would say that the problem was analogous during the Vargas government, except that Vargas had new tools at his disposal: the media. This opened a fertile field for the development and diffusion of ideas of Brazilianness. The problems related to civic consciousness remained, of course. In reaping the fruits of its integrating activity, the state conferred on all Brazilians a symbolic citizenship that in practice deprived most of the population of actual political citizenship. The playfulness and carnivalization of cultural phenomena, which were at the core of Brazilian identity, thus emerged as a substitute for human rights.

Given that the state intervened in the cultural sphere, it is necessary to understand the meaning and the implications of its activity. Various authors have pointed out the authoritarian character of the Vargas government, especially after the founding of the Estado Novo (New State) in 1937.[15] In 1939, Gustavo Capanema established the Press and Propaganda Department (Departamento de Impresa e Propaganda, DIP) and set for it the task of reaching all of the popular classes. The DIP was to be an instrument for broadcasting government propaganda as "mass culture." Formed in the mold of the Fascist state, the DIP sought to influence directly various cultural arenas, especially the media with the greatest reach, including radio and film. As the government intellectuals associated with the journal *Cultura Política* would say, the media should not be thought of as merely a means of entertainment but rather as political weapons under the control of the rationale of the state. At the same time, there was a gap between discourse and reality, intent and actualization. The goals that the authoritarian ideologues put forth hardly squared with the timidity of the Vargas government toward the media (not to mention toward censorship). Film was an example. The state refused to build a film industry and created only the National Educational Film Institute (Instituto Nacional do Cinema Educativo), whose impact on society was practically nil. Paradoxically, at the moment at which the institute garnered sufficient strength to outline a wide-ranging cultural policy, Brazil witnessed a growth in commercial radio. It is symptomatic that Rádio Nacional, founded by the government in 1940, did not resemble a vehicle for government propaganda; rather, it functioned along the lines of a private company. Its programs — popular music, radio theater, auditorium programs — did not differ from those presented by other broadcasters. While it is true that the state controlled Rádio Nacional through its government office, the percentage of programming dedicated to so-called cultural programs (meaning propaganda) did not exceed 4.5 percent. Thus most of the programming was geared to entertainment, and the principal source of income was not state funding but advertising.

The relation between the state and the mass media can be interpreted in various ways. From the economic point of view, one could say that the dream of an all-inclusive state ran up against financial motives. Building a national radio broadcasting network required capital and not just political will. Moreover, in spite of its centralizing tendency, the Vargas government had to accommodate to existing political forces, which included private capital, whose interests in the communications sector were substantial. For this reason, the model for the sector resembled that of the U.S. media. Brazil opted for privatization and commercialization of the mass communications sector, a pattern consolidated once and for all with the advent of television. Thus the media moved away from the ideal of public service exemplified by the BBC in Britain.

I previously considered the expansion in the sphere of large-scale goods in the period after 1930. I now take up this point with more nuance. In spite of the energy of postwar Brazilian society, it existed within very rigid limits. Economists call this phase "restricted industrialization," which means that the expansion of the cultural market was slowed by the impossibility of more general economic development. Various elements confirm this picture. Even if it is possible to speak of a book market, in contrast with the First Republic, there is no doubt that it was still weak and underdeveloped. One need only consider the market in São Paulo, the largest in the country: 1,642,000 copies in 1934, 2,116,000 in 1940, 5,650,000 in 1946, 5,980,000 in 1956. Clearly, there was growth, but in the decade 1946–56, it remained level. Between 1948 and 1953, the number of publishers in the entire country fell from 280 to 144, to a level below that of 1936.[16] Various elements contributed to the impossibility of real growth in the book market. Paper import subsidies applied only to newspapers and not books. Import taxes and the dollar exchange rate made it cheaper to import books than to print them in Brazil. Something similar occurred with the cinema. In spite of prior efforts, the domestic film industry failed when Vera Cruz went under in 1954 and Atlântida's *chanchada* production declined. The statistical data from 1955 show, moreover, that of all of the movie theaters in the country, more than half operated irregularly, not showing films daily and concentrating sessions on the weekends. Without a doubt, radio was the most popular of the media; nevertheless, its expansion was limited. In 1962 there were 4.7 million radio receivers in the country. In itself, this is a reasonable number. Given the population of the country, however, there were only 6.6 radio sets per 100 persons. This put Brazil in thirteenth place in Latin America. Juarez Brandão Lopes noted that in the 1940s and the 1950s, the golden age of radio, the communications network was rather weak throughout most of the country. This was because the broadcasters were local and concentrated in cities, mostly the larger ones, thus excluding much of the rural population form their range.[17]

The limitations of the time can be seen even better in the case of television. Even though it was established in the three largest cities in the 1950s — 1950 in São Paulo, 1951 in Rio de Janeiro, and 1955 in Belo Horizonte — throughout the decade, television maintained a structure that was not very compatible with a commercial rationale, and it had a restricted range. There was not a system of networks. The broadcasts were local, and the programs were recorded live, which made it impossible for broadcasters in different cities to exchange programs. Because of the limited purchasing power of a majority of the population and restrictions on the credit system, it was hard to market television sets. They were initially imported from the United States; only after 1959 did they begin to be produced in Brazil.

The precariousness of the television industry is clearly evident in the growth in the number of sets: 3,500 in 1951, 141,000 in 1955, and 434,000 in 1959 (the population of the country in 1960 was 71 million). Moreover, the habit of watching television was irregular, affecting the number of people that television reached. In São Paulo in 1954, the proportion of televisions turned off during the evening hours was from 50 percent to 90 percent, depending on the day of the week. In 1959 in Rio de Janeiro, only 7 percent of the upper class watched television, as opposed to 65 percent and 28 percent of the middle- and low-income classes, respectively. In 1958, only 8 percent of advertising spending went to television, compared to 22 percent to radio and 44 percent to newspapers, which shows that companies and advertising agencies preferred the "more traditional media" to promote their products. When TV Tupi went into business in São Paulo, an advertisement revealed the dilemmas of the day. In beseeching tones, it said, "Do you want television or not? To make television a reality in Brazil, a radio and newspaper consortium has invested million of cruzeiros. Now it is your turn. What will be your contribution to sustain such a grand undertaking? The progress of this marvel of electronic science in our country will depend on your support. To applaud and acclaim with admiration is praiseworthy, but it is not enough. Your support will only be effective when you acquire a television set."[18]

In other words, the consumer was to be convinced not by the quality of service offered but by a didactic discourse based on the need to modernize the country. It would be hard to apply to this case Adorno and Horkheimer's concept of cultural industry. Of course, each company tried to expand its commercial base. Even so, obstacles facing the development of Brazilian capitalism put limits on their growth.

1964–90

The transformations in Brazilian society after 1964 reorganized the cultural scene. The military coup had a double meaning. First, it meant repression, censorship, torture, and the dismantling of the opposition forces. Second, the military government was responsible for what several authors have labeled "authoritarian modernization."[19] The advent of a "second industrial revolution" consolidated a market for material goods and drove a national market for cultural goods, which expanded formidably after 1964. This was the period of consolidation of the great conglomerates that control the media (TV Globo and the publishing house Editora Abril). The data all point to unquestionable growth in this sector. Consider the magazine market, for example: between 1960 and 1985 its circulation grew from 104 million to 500 million. Once again, it was not only quantity that characterized this emerging market. More and more, the publishing sector diversified in response to specialized publics.

The case of Editora Abril is an example. Abril was founded in 1950 and began its production by buying the rights to *Donald Duck*. Between 1950 and 1959 the company edited only 7 titles. Between 1960 and 1969 this number rose to 27, and between 1970 and 1979 it reached 121 titles. In the 1950s, Abril supported itself by selling the *fotonovelas Capricho*, *Ilusão*, *Você*, and *Noturno* along with *Donald Duck* comics. In the 1960s and 1970s, fascicles emerged, each directed to a certain public: *Curso Intensivo de Madureza* (Intensive Course in Maturity) for youths, *Pensadores* (Thinkers) for university students, and *Conhecer* (Know) for the intellectually curious. Children's titles also multiplied, including the comics *Cebolinha*, *Luluzinha*, and *Piu-Piu*, as well as *Enciclopédia Disney*. In the 1950s, Abril addressed the women's market primarily with *fotonovelas*. In the 1960s and 1970s, however, Abril also began to issue specialized magazines: *Manequim* (Model), *Agulha de Ouro* (Golden Needle), *Forno e Fogão* (Oven and Stove), and, for home décor, *Cláudia*. The same occurred for the men's market: *Quatro Rodas* (Four Wheels), *O Carreteiro* (Trucker), *Moto* (Bike), *Playboy*, and *Esportes Náuticos* (Nautical Sports). Thus publishers sought to exploit the potential interests of readers from varied groups and social classes.

The market for phonographs and recordings, which had been in a vegetative state, took off in 1970, thanks to the ease that retail provided for purchasing domestic appliances and equipment — mainly through the introduction of credit to the working classes. Between 1967 and 1980, the sale of record players grew 83 percent. Another measure of the size of this market is the number of records sold, which between 1972 and 1979 grew from 25 million to 66 million. The LP, which was introduced to Brazil in 1948 but by the 1960s was still viewed as an expensive product, was now increasingly considered a consumer item for all classes. One can get an idea of the scale of the Brazilian cultural market from overall advertising investments, which grew from $3.9 million in 1992 to $10 million in 1996 — a considerable investment that made Brazil the seventh-largest advertising market and the sixth-largest phonographic market in the world.[20]

The changes that Brazil experienced in the second half of the twentieth century can be illustrated with the example of television. At this time the state had a role in promoting telecommunications policy. The ideology of national security, in particular through its idea of national integration, was launched through the creation of the Ministry of Telecommunications. Brazil then built a nationwide telecommunications infrastructure. Television and the telephone system thus received big pushes at this time. Through the granting of concessions by the authoritarian state, telecommunications was coupled with political control. The clearest example of cooperation between the policies of the authoritarian state and the development of television in Brazil is TV Globo, whose establishment was directly associated with the repressive policy of the military government.[21]

In 1970, significantly, during the World Cup, the nationwide network transmission was launched. In 1972, color television appeared. For the first time, different parts of the country could be joined, and programs were now able to incorporate the larger public into the consumer market. The numbers for the expansion of television are clear: 2.2 million sets in 1965, 4.3 million in 1970, 16 million in 1980, and 34 million in 1997. At the same time, the habit of watching television spread through all social classes.

It was not only the diffusion of television that changed. In the 1950s, the rationale of communications companies — radio, newspaper, television — was similar to what Fernando Henrique Cardoso observed of the captains of industry in his study of Brazilian entrepreneurs of the early twentieth century.[22] Their enterprises were characterized by family ties and a lack of clarity in set objectives — in sum, administration in which personal and political interests interfered structurally with management. Similarly, television's operation was far from being governed by the efficacy of technical or commercial calculus; the spirit of the modern manager was absent. The very incipient nature of Brazilian capitalism, aggravated by technical improvisation, justified this state of affairs: "Television was an adventure." The advent of a cultural market transformed the captains of industry's companies into a cultural industry. In this sense, TV Globo was a pioneer. When founded in 1965, it imported an administrative staff from the United States and sought to fit the standard of production to the demands of the market.[23]

The industrialization and commercialization of television can be seen in the growth of advertising investment. In 1970, television already accounted for 39.6 percent of these investments as compared to 21.9 percent for magazines, 21 percent for newspapers, and 13.2 percent for radio. In 1996, this distribution was 51 percent for television, 38 percent for newspapers, 8 percent for magazines, 4 percent for radio, and 1 percent for billboards. This meant that programming had to be adjusted to commercial standards, since advertisers were interested in reaching the largest consumer public possible. It was in this context that the *telenovela* became the locomotive of the television industry. Until the mid-1960s, a *telenovela* would air twice a week, and, since it was transmitted live, it could not be relayed on a national network. These programs were generally produced by foreign companies such as Colgate-Palmolive and Gessy-Lever (thus the term "soap opera" in English), renewing the scheme that had been successful in radio in the 1940s. After 1964, things changed. With the use of videotape, the *telenovela* could be produced daily. This entailed serialization, which required a high degree of industrialization. The success of the *telenovela* parallels the growth in television set sales. It redefined television programming, eliminating an entire prior tradition of television theater. In the 1970s, with the advent of the national broadcast networks, the *telenovela* would become the most important product in the Brazilian television industry.

The emergence and consolidation of culture industries have important consequences. Local and regional cultures were forced into a network that was organized from the top down. I do not mean to suggest that there was a process of homogenization in Brazil or that industrialization leads necessarily to the rise of a "one-dimensional person." At the same time, clearly, the changes were profound. In this context, the notion of "the popular" was redefined. It shifted from the traditional to the modern. The popular ceased to be seen as something tied to the traditional cultures of the "popular classes" (in the folkloric sense or not), and instead it became associated with products made and distributed by the cultural industries. And this shift had political implications. In the 1960s, various movements attributed to the (old) concept of "popular culture" a strictly political connotation. This content would be reinterpreted by the various currents in the Brazilian arena: it would be reformist for the intellectuals of the developmentalist Advanced Institute for Brazilian Studies (Instituto Superior de Estudos Brasileiros, ISEB), Marxist for the Popular Culture Centers (Centros Populares de Cultura, CPC), and Catholic for the Popular Culture Movement (Movimento de Cultura Popular, MCP). The category of "popular culture" suggests, then, something that transcends the present, driven by social forces toward a utopian political project that is opposed to the status quo. Paulo Freire's educational method, espoused in *The Pedagogy of the Oppressed*, is a good example. It was intended to create a popular education that would lead people on an alternative path. Similarly, when theater leaders (for example, Augusto Boal through his *Theatre of the Oppressed*) and filmmakers (for example, the Cinema Novo movement) tried to develop concepts of a "national-popular" theater or cinema, they were doing so from a perspective reminiscent of Sartre's "engaged" literature. Through popular culture, the popular classes were to be led to a critical consciousness that would be the first step in overcoming social problems. This sense, which emphasizes political issues, persists in some movements today, for example, the Christian Base Communities (Comunidades Eclesiais de Base, CEBs), in which prevails the ideology of liberation theology, with its "preferential option for the poor." At the same time, the hegemonic conception changed. The emergence of culture industries and a national market for "symbolic goods" (as opposed to material goods) redefined prior meanings. "Popular" now denotes what is most consumed. One can even establish a hierarchy of popularity among the various products that the market offers. A recording, a *telenovela*, or a play can each be more or less popular to the degree that it reaches a greater or smaller audience.

Another aspect concerns national identity. Brazilian intellectual tradition has always dealt with this problem in terms that clearly oppose the "native" to the "alien," the "domestic" to the "foreign." It is from this perspective that one can understand the "colonial situation" of Brazilian cultural phenomena. The theme of "cultural alienation" was central in the 1950s and 1960s, and the debate was corroborated by the strong presence of the foreign in the field of culture: Hollywood films were popular; *telenovelas* reproduced the standards and plots of those in Cuba and Mexico; *fotonovela* magazines were adapted from Italian originals; and, in the 1960s, U.S. series dominated television. The cultural landscape would be different some years later. Again, the example of television is paradigmatic. The comparison between *telenovelas* and U.S. series shows how this competition between foreign culture and national culture was reformulated. In 1963, only 2 percent of the programs aired in the state of São Paulo were *telenovelas*, while 25 percent were U.S. television series. In 1977, when the Brazilian *telenovela* had become a "national success"—that is, a daily serialized industrial product—22 percent of the viewing slots were filled with Brazilian *telenovelas*, compared to 17 percent with "canned programming" from abroad.[24]

The same Brazilian reformulation happened with the phonograph recording market. By 1997, 73 percent of the production was Brazilian music, even though the market had been exploited by the major transnational companies. *Fotonovelas* and radio dramas were also Brazilianized in content and form, articulating more specifically Brazilian narratives for the consumer public. In various cultural sectors—*telenovelas*, newspapers, television series, advertising, magazines—there was a sort of "import substitution," to use an economic metaphor, parallel to the expansion of Brazilian capitalism. Thus the quest for cultural Brazilianness finally materialized in the modern popular culture market, which in turn was even exported to the international market. This is the case with the *telenovela*, today an integral part of the world television market.

The transformation in the cultural sphere has repercussions, moreover, in the debate about modernity. When Brazilian modernists said that "in order to be modern, we must be national," they were shifting an idealized modernity to a future time. The same can be said of the developmentalists of the 1950s and 1960s. Their slogan, "There is no development without an ideology of development," asserted the primacy of ideas over reality. Ideology had to come before actualization; only then could "backwardness" be overcome in the future. This somewhat naive view of history led the Brazilian intelligentsia to overvalue the quest for a modern national identity without having a critical perspective on what it wanted to build. In the contest between the past and the future, the backward and the modern, the latter term, shifted in time, became the ontological bearer of various virtues — democracy, freedom, equality — that were never fulfilled. The changes changed the course of history. Late-developing capitalism is nonetheless capitalism. The multiplying signs of modernity — computers, television, polluting industries, jet airplanes, a nationwide network of roadways, and so forth — attest to the existence of a new reality. Unlike the past, when the modernists were writing, modernity no longer finds itself out of step with society, although this does not mean that it benefits society as a whole — on the contrary. The direction of the process of industrialization leaves no doubt, however: Brazil is a modern society. Modernity is a fact, not a quest or a utopia. To use Mannheim's old category, I would say that it has already become an ideology, that is, a vision of the world that tries to conform to the present. In this sense, the notion of modernity now demands that some adjust to its mandatory presence. "Backward," therefore, is what is out of step with the existing order — for example, the rural world of the landless.

Conclusion

The balance of an entire century, even if taken synthetically, appears consistent not only at the end of an era but also as the horizons open on a new one. The problem of the connections among popular culture, modernity, and nation could have been treated specifically within a framework of Brazilian society. At the same time, some other substantive changes were imposed on the topic we have been discussing. I am referring to the processes of globalization of societies and culture.[25] By way of a "nonconclusion," I raise a few questions that I believe will guide the debate in the coming decades.

The nation is the historical fruit of industrialization, a kind of social formation that has mobility as one of its main characteristics. It is a kind of social organization whose material base is industrialism. In this sense, national society, which is thus industrial, is radically different from the agrarian societies of the past, in which cultures, commercial exchanges, and political loyalties were confined to particular regions. The world of the ancien régime was made up of disparate units.

There was, for example, a peasant world, whose specificity was reflected in its culture, for example, in particular concepts of time and space. The Industrial Revolution, together with political revolutions, disrupted this scenario. By eliminating the old status groups, these revolutions fostered the mobility of the citizenry. The nation-modernity equation thus prevails, both in the "central" and "peripheral" countries. In the former countries, modernity has become synonymous with civilization, a central argument for the expansion of imperialism. Countries such as France, Britain, Germany, and the United States, in principle, have a civilizing mission, the ideological discourse justifying the expansion of their ambitions. Viewed through another prism, on the periphery, the nation-modernity equation is also valid. This is not an issue of asserting the rise of an incomplete capitalism. Rather, in the "third world," the nation is a utopia, a quest for modernity. Nationalist movements all over Latin America share this perspective.

I think that the nation-modernity relation has split. Historically, the nation could be fulfilled through modernity and vice versa. At the same time, modernity, ever since its beginning, held within it its own movement, a tendency that could hardly be contained within the limits of the national. With the progress of history, specifically, the transformations of the capitalist system, modernity became global. Under these circumstances, one can paraphrase the Brazilian modernists, that it is possible to be modern without necessarily being national. This has important, often drastic consequences for Latin American societies because traditional political debate was intimately connected to the issue of constructing modernity.

In the emerging context, the very idea of a "national project" is compromised. In fact, the nation-state has lost its monopoly on conferring meaning on collective action. This means that the debate on national identity is shifted, whether as a result of internal contradictions (for example, the emergence of "local" identities, such as the Black and Indian movements) or as a result of the global landscape. Brazilianness is cross-cut by internal and external currents that redefine the debate. Ironically, the presence of "Brazilian" modernity is not at all definitive. On the contrary, Brazil, like other countries, is far from "gaining its identity." Rather, it finds itself in crisis within globalization. That is, Brazil finds itself in a state of confrontation of identities marked, moreover, by the asymmetrical situation that the country occupies in the system of nations.

In this setting, once again, the notion of the popular was bound to change. Traditional culture in its many regional forms and commercial popular culture produced by the Brazilian culture industries are no longer the only points of reference. The global modernity has its own trappings: fast food, jeans, tennis shoes, pop music, movie stars, and so forth. We are confronted with these objects and images everywhere. This oneness of customs indicates that there is a globalized "civilizing" standard. Various social groups share even a collective consciousness. They are part of an international pop culture. In relation to those of the "national-popular," the national origins of this "international-popular" are secondary. "International-popular" culture, which is produced on a global scale, is closely connected with the consumer world, and it is transnational. It has weakened symbols of national identity. By the 1990s, Brazil found itself in a historically distinct situation from earlier periods, for example, from the beginning of the twentieth century, the 1930s, and the 1950s and 1960s. Brazil no longer needs to build a national modernity; rather, the very relation between nation and modernity has changed. The questions have shifted form the national level to the global, from the internal level to the external. Brazil is an integral part of a global society. That which supposedly had been so well defined as native now confronts at home the unequal forces of globalization of markets and cultures.

Notes

1. This is the strategy I used in *A moderna tradição brasileira* (São Paulo: Brasiliense, 1988).

2. Laurence Hallewell, *O livro no Brasil* (São Paulo: Editora da Universidade de São Paulo, 1985).

3. Martyn Lyons, *Le triomphe du livre* (Paris: Éditions du Cercle de la Librairie, 1987).

4. Pierre Bourdieu, *A economia das trocas simbólicas*, ed. Sergio Miceli (São Paulo: Perspectiva, 1975).

5. On the conflict between the *folhetim* (the literary section of a periodical) and literature, photography, and plastic arts, see Renato Ortiz, "Cultura e mercado," in *Cultura e modernidade: A França no século XIX* (São Paulo: Brasiliense, 1991).

6. Amoroso Lima quoted in Richard Morse, *From Community to Metropolis: A Biography of São Paulo, Brazil* (New York: Octagon, 1974), 265.

7. On language policy and nation building, see Pierre Bourdieu, *Ce que parler veut dire* (Paris: Fayard, 1982); Eugen Weber, *Peasants into Frenchmen: The Modernization of Rural France, 1870–1914* (Stanford, Calif.: Stanford University Press, 1976); Nanette Twine, "Standardizing Written Japanese: A Factor in Modernization," *Monumenta Nipponica* 43, no. 4 (1988).

8. Maria Bonavita Federico, *História da comunicação: Rádio e TV no Brasil* (Petrópolis: Vozes, 1982).

9. Thomas Guback, *La industria nacional del cine* (Madrid: Fundamentos, 1976); Gaiska Usabel, *The High Noon of American Films in Latin America* (Ann Arbor, Mich.: UMI Research Press, 1982).

10. Maria Rita Galvão, *Burguesia e cinema: O caso Vera Cruz* (Rio de Janeiro: Civilização Brasileira, 1981); Fernão Ramos, ed., *História do cinema brasileiro* (São Paulo: Art, 1987).

11. André de Seguin des Hons, *Le Brésil: Presse et histoire 1930–1985* (Paris: L'Harmattan, 1985).

12. Florestan Fernandes, *A integração do negro na sociedade de classes* (São Paulo: Ática, 1978), 168. See Florestan Fernandes, "Racial Heteronomy in a Class Society 1900–1930," in *The Negro in Brazilian Society* (New York: Atheneum, 1971), 131–86.

13. Ruben Oliven, *Violência e cultura no Brasil* (Petrópolis: Vozes, 1988).

14. José Murilo de Carvalho, *A formação das almas: O imaginário da República no Brasil* (São Paulo: Companhia das Letras, 1990).

15. Simon Schwartzman, Helena Maria Bousquet Bomeny, and Vanda Maria Ribeiro Costa, *Tempos de Capanema* (Rio de Janeiro: Paz e Terra, 1984); Lúcia Lippi Oliveira, Mônica Pimenta Velloso, and Angela Maria Castro Gomes, *Estado Novo: Ideologia e poder* (Rio de Janeiro: Zahar, 1982).

16. Olímpio de Souza Andrade, *O livro brasileiro: 1920–1971* (Rio de Janeiro: Paralelo, 1974).

17. Juarez Rubens Brandão Lopes, *Desenvolvimento e mudança social: Formação da sociedade urbano-industrial no Brasil* (São Paulo: Companhia Editora Nacional, 1976).

18. Quoted in Iminá Simões, *TV Tupi* (Rio de Janeiro: Funarte, n.d.).

19. See, for example, Octávio Ianni, *Estado e planejamento no Brasil* (Rio de Janeiro: Civilização Brasileira, 1979).

20. Eduardo Vicente, "A indústria fonográfica brasileira nos anos 90," *Arte e Cultura da América Latina* 6, no. 2 (1999).

21. M. R. Kehl, *Reflexões para uma história da TV Globo* (Rio de Janeiro: Funarte, 1982).

22. Fernando Henrique Cardoso, *Empresário industrial e desenvolvimento econômico no Brasil* (São Paulo: Difusão Européia do Livro, 1972).

23. J. M. O. Ramos, "Un bâtisseur d'empire: O doutor Roberto Marinho," in *L'Amérique Latine et ses télévisions*, ed. G. Scheneir-Madanes (Paris: Anthropos, 1995); R. Ortiz, J. M. O. Ramos, and S. Borelli, *Telenovelos: História e produção* (São Paulo: Brasiliense, 1989).

24. J. Straubhaar, "The Development of the Telenovela as the Pre-eminent Form of Popular Culture in Brazil," *Studies in Latin American Popular Culture* 1 (1982): 144.

25. Octávio Ianni, *Teoria da globalização* (Rio de Janeiro: Civilização Brasileira, 1995); Renato Ortiz, *Mundialização e cultura* (São Paulo: Brasiliense, 1994).

6

LUIZ CARLOS BRESSER PEREIRA

From the Patrimonial State
to the Managerial State

At the beginning of the twentieth century, Brazil was an oligarchic patrimonial state in the midst of an agricultural mercantile economy and of a class-based society that had barely emerged from slavery. A hundred years later, it is a democratic state, somewhere between bureaucratic and managerial, presiding over a globalized capitalist economy and an emerging postindustrial society that is no longer essentially class based but rather is stratified. The transition from patrimonial state to managerial state or, using a different criterion of classification, from an authoritarian state to a democratic one was, therefore, immense and full of contradictions. Politics ceased being only for and by elites, and Brazil became a democracy of civil society, in which public opinion has a growing importance, even though elitist traces and a low degree of representation of the governed persist. The economy underwent an intense process of industrialization. Even so, Brazil cannot be called developed since the wealthy countries have grown at higher per capita rates, thus increasing their economic and technological distance from Brazil. Society is no longer seigniorial, with masters and slaves, but it has not yet become a classical capitalist society, with bourgeois and workers. It actually has gone beyond that and assumed increasing characteristics of a postindustrial society insofar as the small state bureaucratic status group has given way to a large public and private technobureaucratic middle class, whose highest status group has come to share not only power but economic surplus with the upper class. This happened mainly because the new professional middle class was defined by its control over the new strategic factor in production: technical and organizational know-how. The capitalist bourgeoisie and the organized proletariat broadened their bases and diversified. A huge stratum of poor, if not destitute, workers, however, continued to be imperfectly absorbed into the capitalist system and excluded from the benefits of economic development. In the first eighty years of the twentieth century, this development advanced with enormous speed even though it passed through cyclical crises. The last twenty years of the century, however, were marked by a fiscal crisis of the state and were a time of near stagnation of per capita income.

The country's accelerated modernization took place mainly between 1850, when coffee became dominant in Brazil, and 1980, when industrial development stalled and the public fiscal crisis began. Nevertheless, though often in a pernicious form, modernization continued after 1980, such that today the country is radically different from the Brazil of a century or a century and a half ago. It has a wealthier economy, a more diversified society, a more democratic state, and a public administration that is less patrimonial and more managerial. Still, injustice persists alongside modernization, and development has not led to convergence with the wealthy nations. The transition has been profound but uncertain. This is not only because the extraordinary acceleration of technical progress has made the future more difficult to predict but also because the economic failures of the last twenty years of the century have led Brazilians to be less confident of the future.

To summarize: On the political level, Brazil has changed from an oligarchic state to a democratic state of elites. On the administrative level, it has gone from a patrimonial state to a managerial one. On the social level, it has moved from a seigniorial society to a postindustrial one. In Europe, the modernizing authoritarian state, the bureaucratic state, and capitalist society all had long lives on these three levels. In contrast, in Brazil, the transitions were rapid, as one would expect of a country that skips stages but remains underdeveloped, that modernizes but remains backward because of its dual and unjust nature.

As Brazil transitioned from an oligarchic political regime to a democratic regime, it experienced the modernizing authoritarian regimes of Getúlio Vargas and later of Castelo Branco. In the course of this trajectory, Brazilians critiqued the patrimonial state administration of the oligarchic regime, began to replace it with a bureaucratic public administration, and then ended the century in full transition to a managerial public administration. In this essay I will deal specifically with the change on the administrative level of the patrimonial state to the managerial, but I will do this from a broad perspective in which the other levels are also considered. The chapter is divided into five sections. In the first, I examine the oligarchic patrimonial state that characterized the empire (1822–89) and the First Republic (1889–1930). This serves as a benchmark for change. The bureaucratic-authoritarian state that emerged in the first Vargas government and the bureaucratic reform of 1936 are the topics of the second section. In the third, I treat the developmentalist reform of Castelo Branco, in which managerial features were clearly present. In the fourth section, I examine the bureaucratic regression that, paradoxically, came with the transition to democracy in 1985. Finally, I analyze the managerial reform of 1995.

To characterize Brazilian society, I will use three terms: "seigniorial-mercantile" describes society until 1930; after this, it is predominantly "industrial-capitalist," although late in this period one can already see signs of the "postindustrial." To define the Brazilian state on the political level, I employ three expressions: politics are "oligarchic" until 1930, "capitalist-authoritarian" in the periods 1930–45 and 1964–85, and "democratic" between 1946 and 1964 and after 1985. The first form that democracy assumed, in 1946, was that of elites, and in 1985, it assumed this form again, but there are indications that Brazilian democracy is beginning to transition to one of civil society, in which public opinion abandons alliances of class and takes on a determining role in the political process. On the administrative level of the state, again three terms are used: public administration is "patrimonial" (or "mercantile-patrimonial") until 1930, "bureaucratic" (or "industrial-bureaucratic") between 1930 and 1995, and "managerial" (or "postindustrial-managerial") after 1995. The simple labels indicate types of administrations. The compound terms add the notion of the dominant class or relation of production.

The third phase and its respective names are admittedly imprecise. The managerial reform of the state has only recently begun. The social formation continues to be capitalist but is increasingly postindustrial, given the existence of an enormous professional and technobureaucratic middle class. In any class, we have in these three phases corresponding class alliances. In the first, there is the alliance of the landowning and patrimonial status groups with the rural and urban mercantile bourgeoisie. In the second, there is an alliance of the industrial bourgeoisie with the new professional middle class. In the third, there is the progressive substitution of classes with social levels or strata whose power and income derive from technical or organizational skills. Table 6.1 summarizes these phases and terms, which are, naturally, a heroic oversimplification but will help in understanding the Brazilian state and its administration.

TABLE 6.1. *Historical Forms of State and Society in Brazil*

	1821–1930	1930–	Beginning?
Society	Seigniorial-mercantile	Industrial-capitalist	Postindustrial (?)
State (politics)	Oligarchic	Capitalist-authoritarian	Democratic (1985)
Estate (administration)	Patrimonial	Bureaucratic	Managerial (1995)

The Oligarchic Patrimonial State

The Brazilian state in 1900 was still oligarchic, in which a small elite of *senhores da terra* (planters) and of politicians allied with the landed class generally dominated the country. No one better describes this state than Raimundo Faoro in *Os donos do poder* (The Power Holders, 1957, 1975), using the Weberian concept of patrimonial bureaucracy. For Faoro, the political power of the state was concentrated in an aristocratic bureaucratic status group of jurists, educated men, and the military, whose power and income came from the state itself. As opposed to the other authors who have studied Brazilian social formation of the empire and First Republic, for Faoro, the political regime was not dominated by an oligarchy of landowners. In the classic analysis, these oligarchs were, in the first phase, the *senhores de engenho*, the sugar mill owners of the coast, and the *coronéis de gado*, the cattle barons of the backlands, both of the Northeast. In the second phase, the oligarchs were the early coffee planters of the Paraíba Valley in the Southeast. Finally, there were the later coffee planters in the west of the state of São Paulo. These oligarchies, together with the mercantile bourgeoisie, constituted the dominant classes. Faoro does not deny these classes, but he understands that the patrimonial status group, as a ruling political group, reproduced in Brazil the system established in Portugal in the fourteenth century by King John I, the Master of Avis. That is, it was a status group, originally aristocratic, formed of a decadent nobility that, upon losing its income from land, became increasingly bureaucratic without losing its aristocratic character. This status group was no longer seigniorial because it did not receive its income from land; rather, it was patrimonial because it derived its patrimony from the state, which, in part, was merged with the patrimony of each one of its members. The state collected taxes from the constituent classes, especially from the mercantile bourgeoisie, which were used to support the dominant class status group and the large body of mid-level civil servants connected to it through all sorts of ties.

Faoro is well aware that his thesis conflicts as much with the Marxist perspective as with the liberal. He does not hesitate to oppose both: "The critique from liberal sources, paradoxically, aligns with the Marxist critique. Old capitalism, identified by simplification with feudalism or with precapitalism, will be devoured by industrial capitalism." Continuing, Faoro argues, "Brazilian historical reality demonstrates the secular persistence of patrimonial structures, gallantly, inviolately resisting the repetition, in progressive phrases, of capitalist experiences. It adopts from capitalism the technique, the machinery, the companies, without accepting its soul anxious to transmigrate."[1] This analysis illuminates well the imperial period in Brazil, and it is enlightening even for the First Republic. Now it is very clear what the dominant role during the empire was of a bureaucratic status group of patrician origin, very similar to that which dominated Portugal, connected to the rural aristocracy through family ties. At the same time that the planters, the large-scale merchants, and the slave traders were concerned with the economy, this bureaucratic class dominated the state and politics with relative autonomy. I would add that this bureaucratic class was a new middle class in formation, though at that moment it was more of a status group of politicians and patrimonial bureaucrats appropriating from the economic surplus within the state, not directly through economic activity. The most important feature at that moment, however, was still the mark of Portuguese colonialism. For the subtitle of his classic *A América Latina*, Manoel Bomfim chose the expression *Males de origem* (Ills of Origin) to foreground Brazil's underdevelopment—or rather, in his words, its "general backwardness"—which, like the backwardness of the rest of the Latin American countries, was intrinsically linked to the decadence of their two colonizing nations, Portugal and Spain.[2]

There is a traditional idea that the function of the state in this era was to guarantee employment for the lower middle class connected by ties of family or dependency to rural landowners. There is no doubt about this role of the state. In the afterword to *Um estadista do Império*, for example, Evaldo Cabral de Mello points out that "the state itself cannot be understood without reference to the function of absorbing members of the slavocratic order through public employment." Mello cites the anthologized text of abolitionist statesman and writer Joaquim Nabuco in which he states that agriculture, aside from supporting those that make high-interest loans to them, yields leftovers, which the state "distributes . . . among its army of public servants, which in turn, support numerous dependents of all classes."[3] If, however, we are left only with this idea, then, for the empire, the classic concept of classes and their succession in history that Ricardo and Marx bequeathed to us remains valid.

The picture changes, however, if we consider that, during the empire, following a centuries-old Portuguese tradition, a patrimonialist governing elite had formed that lived off income from the state and not from the land and itself held considerable autonomy and immense political power. In the same essay, Mello recalls, with Nabuco to support him, that many statesmen of the empire were poor and so married daughters of wealthy landowners or made a living as public servants or judges. José Murilo de Carvalho, in his noteworthy analysis of the origins of the imperial ministers, points out that the great majority of them had degrees in letters or law and that, though they might be tied to landowning families, they were above all else patrimonialist bureaucrats, lawyers and men of letters supported by the state. Because of their status group origins or relation to the rural aristocracy, they would study first at the university in Coimbra, Portugal, and afterward at the law school in Olinda or São Paulo in Brazil. Based on this expertise, they would come to occupy high positions in the empire. According to Carvalho, "What happened with the Brazilian bureaucracy also happened in part with the political elite since the latter, to a large extent, were melded with the upper echelons of the former."[4] The historian notes that, at the same time, this did not mean that the imperial elite was, as Nestor Duarte says, "simply the representative of the rural landowners," or as Faoro says, "a solidly established status group that, by means of the state, became the arbiter of the nation and proprietor of the national sovereignty." Perhaps Carvalho made this qualification given the radical nature of Faoro's position, but his historical research leans more in Faoro's direction than in Duarte's, the latter representing here Marxist and liberal conventional wisdom. The Brazilian elite was basically formed of jurists, and these were, as a rule, judges and other public employees, as is characteristic of patrimonialism. This is different from England, where the jurists were increasingly lawyers, serving the nascent bourgeoisie. These judges displayed an extraordinary homogeneity, which education in the law schools had imparted. It was a conservative homogeneity, inherited from the backward conservatism of Coimbra. On the other hand, "the capacity of this elite to try conflicts among dominant groups within constitutional norms accepted by all constitutes the fulcrum of the imperial system's stability."[5]

Carvalho is right, however, in pointing out that the Brazilian patrimonial elite of the empire lacked the power to govern alone. In fact, there was an alliance between the patrimonial status group and the mercantile bourgeoisie of landowners and merchants. In the course of the nineteenth century, this bourgeoisie shifted from an oligarchy mainly of northeastern sugar planters to São Paulo coffee planters. Thus Brazil had a patrimonial-mercantile state that lasted from the empire to the First Republic. The power of the patrimonial status group was indeed great, as Faoro argues, but it was not the only power.

Eve though the imperial patrimonial elite had its origins mainly in the land-owning families, it gradually gained autonomy in its own reproduction. What characterized it was its formal juridical knowledge, transformed into a tool of the trade and an instrument of power. The absolute majority of ministers, counselors, provincial presidents, and legislative deputies were law graduates. There were also those with military, religious, and medical backgrounds. Engineers and businessmen were few. All were bureaucrats because their income essentially came from the state, and patrimonialists because the criteria of their choices were not legal-rational and because they built a complex system of dependents and clients around them supported by the state, blurring private and state patrimony. Sérgio Buarque de Holanda, the author of *Raízes do Brasil* (Roots of Brazil), was the first to use the concept of patrimonialism to characterize the Brazilian political elites. He distinguished the "patrimonial public employee from the pure bureaucrat" and observed that "it was not easy for the holders of public positions and responsibilities formed by the environment of the patriarchal family to understand the basic distinction between the private and the public domains."

This was the educated, conservative political elite that ruled in an authoritarian or oligarchic way. There was no democracy. Elections were farces. The social and educational distance between the political elite and the rest of the population was immense. Finally, in the midst of this elite, there was a stratum of public employees, holders more of sinecures than functions, given that the role of the patrimonial state was to guarantee them employment and survival. As Buarque de Holanda observes, "In Brazil, only exceptionally have we had an administrative system and a corps of public servants purely dedicated to objective interests and founded on these interests."[6] In the face of these, the testimony of early republican thinkers such as Tobias Barreto, Sílvio Romero, and Nabuco always ran in the same direction. Public employment, though it did not guarantee complete stability given the practice of "massacres" when ministers of one party replaced those of another, it was the only route possible for a vast unemployed middle class. From it were recruited the political elite.

One can imagine that administrative criteria were personal, and concern with the efficiency of the machinery of the state was nil. Carvalho emphasizes that the "unemployed middle class" to which Barreto and Romero referred, made up mainly of liberal professionals, especially those with law degrees, and mostly mestizos, had a vocation for the public employment. It was not "the vocation of all, as Nabuco exaggerated, but it was that of urban minorities, especially of their most educated and assertive elements." Gaining access, therefore, was not easy, especially to the navy and the judiciary, which maintained their aristocratic character. Entry into the clergy and the army was less difficult.[7]

When the class-based bureaucracy of aristocratic character began to be infiltrated by external elements of lower social origin, as with the clergy and, in the apparatus of the state properly speaking, with the army, it was clear that one could no longer refer to it as a patrimonial status group, as Faoro meant it. It was rather a bureaucratic state administration, a capitalist bureaucratic-authoritarianism, that emerged, mainly through the military and the revolutions that it promoted in the name of an abstract "reason," whose classic capitalist and bureaucratic roots were evident.

The Bureaucratic-Authoritarian State

The First Republic was a period of transition. It began with the proclamation of the republic in 1889, the first military coup in Brazilian history. It was meant to be a middle-class revolution, as would be the other three military revolutions in Brazil — the Revolution of 1930, the overthrow of Vargas and restoration of democracy in 1945, and the bureaucratic-authoritarian coup of 1964, all of which are discussed below. This military regime had a brief lifespan, during the Deodoro da Fonseca and Floriano Peixoto governments. With the election in 1894 of Prudente de Morais, the coffee oligarchy returned to power, reestablishing the alliance of imperial times between the aristocratic bureaucratic status group and the coffee-dominated oligarchy. A transition, however, was in progress, and it implied a substantive change: the effective presence henceforth of the army in the power alliance. This was a new phenomenon, because these military men, in contrast to those of the navy, could not be legitimately included in the imperial aristocratic bureaucratic status group. The representatives of the modern techno-bureaucratic middle class, which, in the twentieth century, would expand and diversify enormously, thus appeared for the first time in Brazilian history, through the intermediary of the army.

The military coup did not have a real base in society, so it did not truly involve the population. As Carvalho points out, the observers of the time denied the existence of a "people" or of a civil society in the country: "According to Aristides Lobo, the population witnessed the proclamation of the Republic like beasts;

there was not a Brazilian citizenry, according to foreign observers such as the well-informed Louis Couty." Carvalho then asks if this is "a prejudiced view on the part of members of the elite, albeit a progressive elite? More than that. . . . Once the initial enthusiasm over the proclamation of the Republic had passed, in the realm of ideas, not even the elite could manage to come to a certain agreement on the definition of what should be the relation between the citizen and the state. In the realm of political action, the attempts to mobilize and organize the population in accordance with the known standards of liberal systems failed systematically."[8]

The regime remained oligarchic, and the elections, fraudulent. The electorate rose from 1 percent to 2 percent with the coming of the republic. The economic and power structures did not change. Renato Lessa observes that "it is difficult to think of the political change effected at the end of the nineteenth century as the needed manifestation of the structural changes in society."[9] On the contrary, with the establishment of the federation by the 1891 constitution and the resulting political decentralization of a national government that had been highly centralized during the empire, the power of the state governors and local oligarchs increased rather than decreased. A "politics of the state houses" arose, which would define the course of the country's politics until 1930. Nevertheless, the increase in power of the state governors was contradictory: they had more power in relation to the federal union, but they had less power in relation to the local bosses, on whom they came to depend.[10]

These problems were at the root of the growing dissatisfaction in the military, which was demanding the order and the progress announced in the motto of the republican flag, and of the indignation of liberals calling for democracy. The result was the unstable political alliance of 1930, which led not to the liberal state of which the latter group dreamed but rather to the bureaucratic-authoritarian state of the first Vargas government. The electoral campaign of 1919 (in which Rui Barbosa garnered substantial urban popular support in a protest vote against the political machinery), the revolts of mid-echelon military officers in 1922 and 1924, and the march of the Prestes Column in 1935–37 were all harbingers of the change coming in 1930. The revolutionary movement that would lead to the Revolution of 1930 and the first Vargas government was intrinsically contradictory. In its largely civil component, it was liberal: it protested against the farcical elections and proposed to broaden the electorate and to institute the secret ballot. It demanded amnesty for those convicted for political reasons. It sought to end the power of the local oligarchies (*coronéis* and *jagunços*, the bosses and their thugs) and the regional oligarchies (the provincial presidents and, later, state governors). It was also a conservative movement insofar as many participants were themselves members of the state oligarchies, especially in Rio Grande do Sul, Minas Gerais, and Paraíba. As Alexandre Barbosa Lima Sobrinho has observed, "Almost all were captured from the field of reactionaries; they not only needed to silence their own ideas but propagate those, like amnesty and secret ballot, that just the day before they had fought intransigently."[11] Finally, at the same time, the alliance had a military component that was *tenentista*, bureaucratic, and authoritarian. This group's greatest objective was to centralize national power, placing under its control the state and local bosses (see chapters 3 and 8).

When all was said and done, the third face of the revolutionary movement would predominate during the fifteen years that Vargas stayed in power—the last eight of which were within the framework of a strictly authoritarian regime. These fifteen years, however, were powerfully transformative. A cold statesman when it came to the use of power but a passionate one when it came to his mission to change the country, Vargas led the transition with extraordinary political and administrative competence. He established the power of the union over the federated states and the local oligarchies, and he pressed forward with the process of industrialization. He is called a populist because he perceived that the popular classes were finally emerging, and for them he had a social discourse and practice. Like Perón, Vargas was a political populist, but he had none of Perón's economic populism, that is, a populism that was irresponsible with the public budget and economic restrictions.[12] The First Republic had been oligarchic and tending toward decentralization. Even though it preserved elements of the old aristocracy, the new government founded after the Revolution of 1930 was, more than anything, a bureaucratic-authoritarian state within a society in which industrial capitalism had finally become dominant. Vargas, who was from a southern cattle-ranching family, was part of the "import-substituting oligarchy," to use Ignacio Rangel's expression. Yet the two classes over which he would preside were new: the industrial bourgeoisie and the technobureaucratic middle class. Both had their origins in old classes or status groups—the industrial bourgeoisie in the mercantile bourgeoisie, and the modern bureaucracy in the patrimonial bureaucracy. In contrast with its antecedent, the new bureaucracy did not have an aristocratic character, nor was it circumscribed by the state, in terms of Faoro's interpretation. In addition to the classic political and administrative task, the new bureaucracy came to have an essential economic function: coordination of the large firms that produced goods and services, both public and private.

The attention of Brazilian analysts has always been focused on the state aspect of the bureaucracy, which indeed had an undeniable political power. Nevertheless, we will understand the nature of the capitalist society and of the bureaucratic state that was forming in the 1930s only if we also consider the emergence of a new middle class of midlevel administrators and liberal professionals of all sorts, not just the traditional lawyers and doctors.[13] During the 1930s, Vargas carried out a civil service reform in the public sector, which in France, England, and Germany had happened in the second half of the nineteenth century, and in the United States, in the first decade of the twentieth. At the same time, in the private sector, the rise of large private and public enterprises promoted the rise of a productive, modern bureaucracy.

My attention in this essay, however, is focused on the state bureaucracy. Brazilian civil service reform had as a precursor the reform implemented by Ambassador Maurício Nabuco in the Ministry of Foreign Relations in the late 1920s. It began in earnest in 1936 under the leadership of Vargas and his deputy in this matter, Luiz Simões Lopes.[14] In this same year, Law no. 284 created the Federal Council of Civil Public Service (Conselho Federal da Serviço Público Civil), which instituted the first overall plan for classification of personnel positions and introduced a merit system. The Federal Council of Civil Public Service was consolidated by its absorption two years later into the Administrative Department of Public Service (Departamento Administrativo do Serviço Público, DASP). Created by Decree-Law no. 579, DASP was essentially a central organization for personnel, materiel, budget, organization, and methods. It became not only the bureaucracy's administrative organization but also the formulator of new ways of thinking about and organizing public administration. The creation of DASP within the framework of Vargas's Estado Novo (New State, 1937–45) occurred at a moment when Brazilian authoritarianism returned with force, this time to implement a modernizing revolution in the country, to industrialize it, and to place value on technical competence. Maria Celina D'Araújo observes that "the Estado Novo exalted the technical at the expense of the political, which was the dirty side of 'private interests.'"[15] On the administrative level, it was thus the affirmation of the centralizing and hierarchical principles of classic bureaucracy.

Beatriz Marques de Souza Wahrlich, whose book *A reforma administrativa da era de Vargas* (The Administrative Reform of the Vargas Era) is a fundamental work for the analysis of bureaucratic reform in Brazil, thus summarizes the main accomplishments of DASP: entry into the civil service through competitive selection, overall uniform classification criteria for positions, organization of personnel services and of their systematic training, standardization of state purchasing, and overall rationalization of methods.[16] In addition, DASP cooperated in the establishment of a series of regulatory agencies (councils, commissions, and institutes) in the social and economic arenas. Thereafter, between 1930 and 1950, a small number of state enterprises were created that constituted the nucleus of industrial development for import substitution.

This was already a different world from the patrimonialist one described by Faoro, who, by freezing society and state in this formation, asserts that the Vargas government was still an expression of the patrimonial state. Faoro is clear in this respect: "From King John I to Getúlio Vargas, in a course of six centuries, a sociopolitical structure resisted all transformations."[17] By insisting on this thesis, Faoro overlooks the basic difference between patrimonialism and legal-rational bureaucracy, which Weber highlights. Faoro does not consider the essentially traditional character of the patrimonial state as opposed to the modern character of industrial capitalism and legal-rational bureaucracy. This is an error that Buarque de Holanda does not commit, for example, when he asserts, "Patrimonial functionalism can, with the progressive division of functions and with rationalization, acquire bureaucratic traits. In essence, however, the more one characterizes the two types—patrimonialism and bureaucracy, the more different they are."[18]

Whereas the patrimonial state had a long life within seigniorial-mercantile society, the bureaucratic state within industrial-capitalist society was short lived. It was brief because industrialization arrived late and soon began to be replaced by a knowledge- and service-based postindustrial society. It was also brief because the bureaucratic reform of 1936 began late and was overtaken by the 1995 managerial reform, which globalization imposed and which democracy made possible.

The Developmentalist Reform of 1967

The bureaucratic reform had barely begun when, in 1938, with the creation of the first *autarquia* or semiautonomous government agency, the first signs of managerial public administration appeared. There arose then the idea that public services in "indirect administration" should be decentralized and not obey all of the bureaucratic requirements of the "direct" or central administration. In the meanwhile, the route to reforming DASP itself continued to be the establishment of a classical bureaucracy, with the French and U.S. reforms as models. In the 1960s, Lawrence S. Graham observed that "the attempt to reform the Brazilian Civil

Service by use of an American-style personnel policy has led to the creation of an administrative system characterized by a high degree of formalism." He added, however, that this was a formalism "in which there is a considerable discrepancy between norms and reality."[19]

The 1936 reform was imposed from the top down. It did not address the real, contradictory needs of Brazilian society and politics. The state lacked a professional bureaucracy but made concessions to the old patrimonialism, which, in the nascent democracy, took on the form of clientelism. On the other hand, the bureaucratic elite, which had assumed the role of political leadership in the transition to industrial capitalism, should have been professionalized but freed from the ties of bureaucratic formalism.

It is not surprising, therefore, that soon after the collapse of Vargas's authoritarian regime, the old patrimonial elements and the new clientelistic ones made themselves felt in a powerful way. Vargas was deposed in October 1945, removing from the bureaucratic reform of 1936 the backing that the authoritarian regime might have conferred on it. In the new, democratic government, DASP lost a large number of its functions. In the five years that followed, administrative reform would be conducted through perfunctory and trivial government actions, while clientelistic practices got new life within the state.

After this five-year gap, when elections returned Vargas to power (1951–54), Wahrlich detected new attempts to resume the initial push, attempts that would span from 1951 to 1963.[20] The efforts in the direction of establishing a bureaucratic public administration would not yet have an effect on administration. It became clear that it was not only the backward forces of patrimonialism and clientelism that were in play against the attempts to proceed with the bureaucratic reform of 1936. The forces committed to economic development—which were already present in the Vargas government, would continue in the Juscelino Kubitschek government (1956–60), and would be reorganized in the military government (1964–84)—were also opposed to reform to the extent that bureaucratic formalism turned out to be incompatible with the needs of the country.

The belief in the early 1960s that the use of rigid principles of bureaucratic public administration was a roadblock to the country's development really had its roots in the previous decade. In the 1950s, however, the accelerated economic development that was occurring allowed ad hoc solutions to be found to get around the problem. This was the case, for example, of the sectoral executive groups of the Kubitschek government. The problem would return in the 1960s with the economic crisis. The prominent sociologist Alberto Guerreiro Ramos expressed his dissatisfaction with the bureaucratic model in place: "An obsolete model of organization and bureaucracy shapes the dominant administrative practice. Consciously or unconsciously subject to deeply rooted interests, many administrators are trying to solve today's problems with yesterday's solutions."[21]

Studies of a more efficient reform were conducted in 1963, when President João Goulart named Federal Deputy Amaral Peixoto to become special minister for administrative reform. Decree-Law no. 51705 of 14 February created the Amaral Peixoto Commission (Comissão Amaral Peixoto), with the charge of "reforming the federal civil service." Amaral Peixoto's task was to direct various study groups charged with formulating reform plans. At the end of the year, the commission presented four important plans, with a view to broad, general restructuring of government activities. Only after the coup of 1964, though, did this reform come about.

Nineteen years before, in 1945, the military had returned democracy to Brazil and, with it, decentralization of political and administrative power. For the first time in the country's history, Brazilians enjoyed a government that reasonably deserved to be called a democracy. A democracy of elites, to be sure, but a government in which the electorate was defined in broad terms, elections were free, and the will of the people began to be manifest. Only those who could not read and write were not able to vote. However, the collapse of the populist pact established by Vargas and political radicalization on the heels of the economic crisis of the early 1960s would lead to the end of the young democracy.

In 1964, the military intervened for the fourth time in the country's history, and, for nearly twenty years, Brazil had a bureaucratic-capitalist, modernizing authoritarian regime. This heralded a grand alliance of the modern civil and military bureaucracy; the bureaucratic middle classes of the private sector, which, in this period, had grown and diversified; and the Brazilian bourgeoisie, which was no longer only mercantile or industrial but a complex, diversified capitalist class.

Once again in power, the military, with the active participation of civilian sectors, advanced the administrative reform of 1967, consolidated in Decree-Law no. 200. This was a pioneering reform that prefigured the managerial reforms that would occur in some countries of the developed world beginning in the 1980s and in Brazil beginning in 1995. Recognizing that the rigid bureaucratic structures were almost as big an obstacle to development as the patrimonialist and populist distortions, the reformers tried to replace bureaucratic public administration with an "administration for development." They clearly distinguished between direct and indirect administration. They guaranteed the *autarquias*, which were the foundations of this second sector, and the state enterprises a much greater managerial autonomy than they had previously had. They made the merit system stronger and more flexible, and, finally, they made the system of state purchasing less bureaucratic.

On the other hand, power that since 1945 had devolved to the states of the federation returned to the hands of the federal government. There was thus a dual action of the Brazilian state: administrative reform led to a dilution of power through administrative decentralization and greater decision-making autonomy in the agencies while, on the political level of the federation, power was once again centralized in the federal government (see chapter 8).

The most remarkable aspect of the developmentalist reform of 1967 was the decentralization of indirect administration, particularly of the foundations of private rights, created by the state, the public enterprises, the mixed enterprises, and the *autarquias* that had existed since 1938. By means of the foundations, which anticipated the social organizations created by the managerial reform of 1995, the state gave much administrative autonomy to social and scholarly services, which were now able to contract employees subject to the Consolidation of Labor Laws (Consolidação das Leis do Trabalho, CLT), Vargas's labor law reform. The autonomy given to mixed enterprises made possible a broad industrialization plan, with a basis in the large infrastructural and public service state companies. These had begun in the 1940s with the founding of the National Steel Company (Companhia Siderúrgica Nacional, CSN) and had accelerated in the 1950s with the creation of Petrobras, Eletrobrás, Telebrás, and the National Economic Development Bank (Banco Nacional de Desenvolvimento Econômico, BNDE). On the other hand, new regulatory agencies were developed, like the Central Bank of Brazil. These regulated, also with autonomy, economic activities, always with the criterion of promoting industrial development. During the military regime, some of these agencies and companies, which Luciano Martins has studied in depth, became successful examples of bureaucratic insulation.[22]

The Ministry of Planning and General Coordination came to have potentially the greatest authority of any ministry. This was because this organization played the role of central agency in matters of planning and internal accounting and auditing. The latter function had formerly been the responsibility of the Ministry of Finance. Later, the Ministry of Planning took over the control system of state enterprises, *autarquias*, and foundations, so that its power overlapped with the sectoral control exercised up to that point solely by the various other ministries.

From the issue of Decree-Law no. 200 in 1967 until 1979, developmentalist reform was conducted mainly by the Subsecretariat of Modernization and Administrative Reform (Subsecretaria de Modernização e Reforma Administrativa, SEMOR) in the Planning Ministry. During the 1970s, one of SEMOR's functions was to promote periodic reviews of existing organizational structures and projects routed by other public agencies, with a view to instituting new agencies and programs, at the same time that it devoted special attention to developing human resources for the planning system. In the meanwhile, DASP, now limited to personnel administration, remained bound by the principles of the bureaucratic reform of 1936, which, at the same time, it could not manage to advance. The concept of a public service "career" was limited to the lower echelons, while the senior administrative positions came to be filled by presidential appointment, with recruitment especially through the state enterprises, in accordance with the developmentalist philosophy of the day.

After 1979, Hélio Beltrão, who had already participated actively in the developmentalist reform of 1967, returned to the scene, this time as the head of the Ministry of Debureaucratization under President João Figueriedo (1979–85). Between 1979 and 1983, Beltrão was the herald of new ideas, criticizing more than once the centralization of power, the formalism of the administrative process, and the mistrust that was behind the excess of bureaucratic rules. He proposed, instead, a public administration more responsive to the citizenry. He himself defined his National Debureaucratization Program as a political proposal that had as its goal, through public administration, "removing the user from the colonial condition of subject and vesting him in that of citizen, the intended recipient of all activity of the state."[23]

In summary, Decree-Law no. 200 was an attempt to overcome bureaucratic rigidity. It can be considered the first instance of managerial administration in Brazil. At the same time, the reform had two unexpected and undesirable consequences. By allowing employees to be contracted without going through a public competitive selection, it facilitated the continuation of clientelistic practices. Also, by not concerning itself with changes in the realm of central or direct administration, which was seen pejoratively as "bureaucratic" or rigid, the reform failed to hold competitive selections and develop the careers of upper-level administrators. The strategic core of the state was, in fact, unduly weakened by the military's opportunistic or ad hoc strategies of contracting upper-level administrators from the state companies. In this way, the administrative reform envisioned in Decree-Law no. 200 was especially prejudiced by its pragmatism.

It lacked essential elements that would have made it a true managerial reform of the Brazilian government, such as a clear distinction between exclusive activities and nonexclusive activities of the state, systematic use of strategic planning in each organization, and control through management contracts and administered competition. It also lacked a clear recognition of the importance of strengthening the strategic core of the state.

It is true that a high-quality public bureaucracy emerged that was well trained and well paid and that had a fundamental role in the execution of industrial development plans of the time. This bureaucratic elite, contracted mainly by state companies, followed informal, very flexible careers, which Ben Ross Schneider has studied.[24] The new public administrators were mainly engineers and economists, who had nothing to do with the bureaucratic system of rigid careers envisioned in the bureaucratic reform of 1938. The results that they achieved in their *autarquias*, foundations, and public and mixed enterprises were substantial. The state careers, then, were largely abandoned, with the exception of those in the judiciary, the diplomatic corps, and the military. The public selective competitions became less frequent, and salaries declined. Thus a serious lack of qualified personnel for exclusive functions of the state arose.

The Bureaucratic Regression

In 1977, President Ernesto Geisel (1974–79), whose government was following an official course of *distensão*, or internal political détente, launched a series of restrictive political measures that came to be known as the "April Package." In 1985, after a long and difficult transition that began with civil society's reaction to the April Package, Brazil returned to democratic rule. With democracy, federal power was once again decentralized, returning to the states and this time also to the municipalities. State governors recovered the power that they had had in the First Republic and in the Third Republic (the democratic period of 1945–64). At the same time, mayors also came to the fore as relevant political actors. Fernando Abrucio attributes the new power of the governors, whom he calls "Barons of the Republic," to opposition gains in the 1982 elections for state houses (the first such elections held since 1964) and to the federal financial crisis of the 1980s attributable more broadly to the financial crisis in the nationalist-developmentalist model directed by the federal government.[25] The crisis, both fiscal and political, in the capitalist bureaucratic-authoritarian state inaugurated in 1964 was no doubt at the root of political decentralization. In the past, decentralization had been a result of the strength of local oligarchies. This time, however, it was the result of the demands of the new civil society that was emerging all over the country.

The democratic transition was a huge victory, but it had its price. On the administrative and political levels, even though it was necessary and inevitable, it went too far in allowing states and municipalities to incur debts during the financial crisis and, at the same time, keeping the union as the party ultimately responsible for these debts. Autonomy can be granted only along with corresponding fiscal responsibility.

On the economic level, democratization was accompanied, as it had been in 1945, by a populist cycle. The two parties that managed the transition were democratic but populist. They did not have, as Brazilian society as a whole did not have, a notion of the gravity of the fiscal crisis, much less of the governmental crisis that the country had been suffering ever since the external debt crisis had been unleashed. There was still a sort of populist democratic euphoria, an idea that it would be possible to return to the golden years of democracy and development that Brazil had enjoyed in the 1950s.

In the first two years of the new democratic regime, the fiscal crisis and the need to review the form of state intervention in the economy were ignored. The return to democracy made the resumption of development and the implementation of social justice simply matters of will. Vargas had never thought in this way. He was populist on the political level but not on the economic. Economic populism combined with political populism, of which, between 1955 and 1964, Presidents Kubitschek and Goulart were the best examples, returned in full force in 1985. The democratic transition had occurred thanks to an alliance very similar to that which had prevailed in the populist pact of 1930–60: an alliance of the bourgeoisie (more specifically, industrialists), democratic groups, and groups from the bureaucratic middle-class Left. The dominant ideology, in addition to nationalist and developmentalist, protectionist and statist, tried to be Keynesian. Development and income distribution would be magically combined through public debt.

The populist cycle reached its extreme in 1986 in the Cruzado Plan. The populist illusions appeared to be confirmed when the plan, which had been competently conceived on the basis of the theory of inflation inertia, was corrupted in a grossly populist way and produced a false prosperity for a year. After its collapse there was an attempt at fiscal adjustment begun during my brief tenure at the Ministry of Finance in 1987. It, however, did not have the necessary support of

Brazilian society, which witnessed with perplexity the crisis in the regime that they had so desired. Instead of adjustment and reform, in 1988–89, under the aegis of a populist political coalition in Congress—the Centrão, or "Big Center"—the country plunged into an out-of-control economic policy, which, given the existing fiscal crisis, led to quasi hyperinflation in early 1990.

Contradictorily, while the country was decentralizing on the political level and embarking on irresponsible populist policies on the economic level, by way of the 1988 constitution, it returned to administrative centralization, drastically limiting the autonomy of state companies and agencies and returning to the ideas of the bureaucratic reform of 1936. The section on public administration in the 1988 constitution was a result of the political coalition that controlled the government of President José Sarney (1985–90). This was a democratic coalition, ostensibly of the Left but, in fact, populist and nationalist-developmentalist. The interventionist, social democratic strategy that since 1930 had been successful in promoting economic development and social welfare went into crisis in the first world in the 1970s. Nevertheless, in Brazil, this strategy continued to be potent in its bureaucratic, underdeveloped version. Only at the end of the 1980s would it too enter a crisis. The influence of this strategy, therefore, dominated the 1988 constitution.

On the other hand, the articles having to do with public administration in the 1988 constitution were also the result of a deliberate effort by bureaucratic groups that, either as members themselves of the Constituent Assembly or as members of pressure groups, believed that they should complete the 1936 reform. Even though many of these members were beneficiaries of the wave of clientelism that had come with democracy, they did not hesitate to influence the constitution to adopt classic bureaucratic principles. Public administration went back to being hierarchical and rigid, and the distinction between direct and indirect administration practically disappeared. The legal system regulating public servants came to be uniform for the entire union and at every level of the federation. The new orientation of public administration that had been implemented since 1967 was more than overlooked; it was destroyed, as the bureaucracy established privileges for itself, such as retirement with full benefits without regard to length of time of service or value of contributions, and job security gained almost automatically after the public selection competition. Even so, the 1988 constitution had one great merit: it required a public selection competition for entrance into public service, substantially reducing the amount of patronage employment that had always characterized the patrimonial state and the early managerial experience.

The bureaucratic regression of 1988 resulted from the mistaken belief that the decrease in centralization and rigidity in public administration that Decree-Law no. 200 would have promoted was at the root of the state crisis, when in fact it derived, more than anything, from the fiscal crisis brought on by the developmentalist strategy. Although some abuses had been committed in its name, the 1967 reform had constituted a pioneering advance in the history of Brazilian public administration. The retreat also came from resentment on the part of the old bureaucracy in direct administrative positions about how they had been treated during the military regime, frequently pushed aside in favor of administrators from state firms. It was, moreover, the consequence of their loss, along with that of their traditional allies, the industrial bourgeoisie, of a common national project. This project, of industrial development via import substitution, had been exhausted, and nothing had come along to take its place. The only new idea, which occurred to some in the Ministry of Finance and the Central Bank of Brazil, was the correct, if negative, one that it was necessary to proceed with fiscal adjustment and reduction of the size of the state. When a social group loses its national goals and, moreover, feels itself threatened, it is natural that it would resort to a policy of "every man for himself." Finally, the retreat to bureaucracy resulted from the fact that the industrial bourgeoisie joined without qualification the campaign to privatize the state companies that had been a part of the Right's agenda in the entire transition to democracy. This campaign led the Constituent Assembly to increase bureaucratic controls over state companies, which had gained much autonomy thanks to Decree-Law no. 200.

The bureaucratic regression happened on the eve of the definitive crisis of nationalist developmentalism, which had been financed during the 1970s by foreign debt. The external debt crisis of the 1980s thus led to a crisis in the developmentalist model. In the meanwhile, the Brazilian elites, and especially the bureaucratic-industrial alliance that had been promoting development since the 1930s, refused to acknowledge the crisis, and for ten years they tried to prop up the old model. The 1988 constitution is full of contradictions exactly because it is the result of this unfeasible attempt, which would result in quasi hyperinflation in 1990. With the democratic opening, it would be natural for the state bureaucracy to draw back politically. At the same time, there was now room for its traditional ally, the industrial bourgeoisie. Nevertheless, even though it had had a decisive role in the democratic opening, the industrial bourgeoisie failed to assume political leadership of the country. Instead of seeing that it was time to open the economy to make it more competitive and to reform the state to rebuild it, the bourgeoisie insisted on opposing the opening of trade and in defending a vague industrial policy, thus weakening itself politically. This strategy made no sense for the nation, given the crisis of the state and the size of the external debt into which the country had plunged. The discourse had lost it way, opening the door wide for the headlong rush into neoliberal and globalist ideas after the quasi hyperinflation of 1990.[26]

The bureaucratic regression of 1988 was accompanied by organizational changes in the federal state apparatus. DASP was abolished in 1986, giving way to the Office of Public Administration in the Office of the President of the Republic (Secretaria de Administração Pública da Presidência da República, SEDAP), which, in January 1989, would be incorporated into the President's Office of Planning (Secretaria do Planejamento da Presidência da República). In March 1989, DASP was reborn with the creation of the President's Office of Federal Administration (Secretaria de Administração Federal da Presidência da República, SAF), which was moved to the Labor Ministry in April 1992 and then back to the Office of the President in January 1993.

In this process of reorganization under the aegis of the return to bureaucracy, the government's training organization, the Public Service Training Center Foundation (Fundação Centro de Formação do Servidor Público, FUNCEP), was transformed into the National School of Public Administration (Escola Nacional de Administração Pública, ENAP), modeled on the National School of Administration (École Nacionale d'Administration, ENA) of France. On the other hand, the career of public manager (a specialist in public policy and government administration) was created. This was an upper-level administrative career, one that was obviously lacking in Brazil. However, the public manager had a rigorously bureaucratic orientation geared toward a critique of the patrimonialist past, instead of directed to the future, to modernity in a rapidly changing world, which was globalizing and becoming more competitive every day.

In summary, the bureaucratic regression between 1985 and 1989 was a reaction to the clientelism that dominated the country in those years, but it was also an affirmation of the corporatist and patrimonialist privileges incompatible with the bureaucratic ethos. In addition, it was a consequence of the defensive attitude of the senior bureaucracy, which, feeling besieged and unjustly accused, defended itself in an irrational way. The result was a decline in the prestige of Brazilian public administration, notwithstanding that the service was largely made up of competent, honest professionals endowed with public spirit.[27]

With the end of authoritarianism and the failure of the industrial bourgeoisie to lead the country politically, the industrial-capitalist society and the industrial-bureaucratic state disappeared. In their places, the contours of what we have today began to emerge: an ill-defined postindustrial society, in which the bourgeois and bureaucratic elites, public and private, have grown and diversified internally; the same happening with the working class; and a managerial state in formation, from the time that the managerial reform of 1995 resumed the ideas of a reconstituted state, efficient and democratic. With the extraordinary increase in the new bureaucratic or technobureaucratic middle class working for large organizations or as service professionals, society ceased to be essentially one of classes and began to be increasingly one of social layers, defined less by the type of property people had or their relation to production and more by level of education, social prestige, and occupation of positions in large public and private organizations. At the same time, the problem of international competition among nations became increasingly intense, obliging public and private organizations to be more efficient. The path was clear for managerial reform of public administration that could rebuild the state within a democratic framework, but it needed a state that was strong enough not to submit to the globalist ideology.

It was after the episode of near hyperinflation of early 1990 and the end of the Sarney government that Brazilian society opened its eyes to the crisis. As a consequence, economic reforms and fiscal adjustment gained momentum during the term of Fernando Collor (1990–92). It was this contradictory, if not schizophrenic, government that would take the decisive steps in the direction of needed market-oriented reforms. In the arena of the state and specifically of public administration, the Collor government's attempts at reform were mistaken in confusing state reform with cutting public employees, reducing real salaries, and reducing the size of the state—all characteristics of the neoliberal Right that was then coming into power.

At the beginning of the Itamar Franco government (1992–94), Brazilian society began to understand the crisis in public administration. There was still, however, much perplexity and confusion. Bureaucratic ideology, which had been dominant in Brasília since the transition to democracy, would remain in place throughout this government.

Managerial Reform

In 1995, Fernando Henrique Cardoso became president of Brazil. The crisis of the industrial-bureaucratic state or, rather, the developmentalist-bureaucratic state was a fact. Even so, there was no proposal to replace this model other than globalist ideas, according to which globalization entailed the loss of relevance of the role of nation-states without any alternative other than nations' submitting to the rules of the global market. I had been criticizing this vision since the 1980s. The large crisis that the country had been confronting since 1980 was a crisis of the state, but it was a cyclic crisis resulting from the distortions that the state had undergone in the previous fifty years. The solution, therefore, was not to replace the state with the market but to reform and rebuild the state so that it could be an effective agent of market regulation and of training businesses in the international competitive process.

When the new president transformed the SAF into the Ministry of Federal Administration and State Reform (Ministério da Administração Federal e Reforma do Estado, MARE) and nominated me as its minister, I did not delay in setting the guidelines and goals of my task. I then began the managerial reform in 1995. I was not the one who had requested the change in status and name of the ministry, but this change had made sense to the president: in this way, he issued a challenge to the new minister and to the team that the new minister would assemble to confront reform of public administration from the perspective of broad state reform.

I already had several ideas about the new public administration, which I would later come to call "managerial," that were gained from reading *Reinventing Government* by David Osborne and Ted Gaebler, but I needed to learn more. The countries of the Organization for Economic Cooperation and Development (OECD), especially the United Kingdom, had undertaken the second great administrative reform in the history of capitalism, after the bureaucratic reform of the nineteenth century. The new ideas of managerial reform were in full flower. In the United Kingdom a new discipline was emerging, "new public management," which, although influenced by neoliberal ideas, could not really be confused with ideas of the Right: many social democratic countries of Europe were involved in the reform process and were implementing new administrative processes. Brazil had the opportunity to participate in this great reform movement and to become the first developing country to carry it out. For this reason, I went to England right at the beginning of the term and became acquainted with the literature developing mainly in that country on the topic of new public management.

The result in the first semester of 1995 was elaborating *Plano diretor da reforma do aparelho do Estado* (Blueprint for Reform of the State Apparatus) and the constitutional amendment for administrative reform, which had as a basis the recent experiences in countries of the OECD, especially the United Kingdom. When these ideas were initially presented, in January 1995, the resistance was great. I tried to confront this resistance as directly and openly as possible, using the media as a means of communication. The topic was novel and complex for the public, and the press had trouble presenting a complete and faithful view of the debate. Nevertheless, the press served as a powerful tool for the discussion of ideas. My main strategy was to attack the bureaucratic public administration at the same time that I defended state careers and the fortifying of their managerial capacity. In this way, I confused my critics, who asserted that I was acting against public administrators or bureaucrats when instead I was trying to strengthen them and make them more autonomous and responsible. In a short while, a topic that had not been on the public agenda took on the character of a broad national debate. Political and intellectual support soon followed, and, finally, when the constitutional reform was promulgated in April 1998, a near consensus had formed on its importance for the country, now strongly supported by the public, by the shapers of public opinion, and, most especially, by public administrators.

Plano diretor was the foundational document of the reform, whose principles continue to guide the reform activity of the government. Through it, the government sought to define institutions and establish guidelines for implementation of managerial public administration in the country. One should, therefore, not confuse the managerial reform of 1995 with the constitutional amendment of 1995 christened "administrative reform." The constitutional reform was a basic part of the managerial reform of 1995, since it changed fundamental normative institutions. Many institutional changes, however, did not involve changes to the constitution. For example, the formal creation in 1997 of the two new basic organizational institutions (the "executive agencies," state institutions that carried out exclusively state activities, and the "social organizations," hybrid institutions between state and society that carried out social and competitive services) did not depend on changes to the constitution. There were also major changes in the form of remuneration for positions of trust and in the ways of recruiting, selecting, and paying those in government careers. By means of the constitutional amendment, the legal system regulating public service ceased being uniform (equal for public servants at national, state, and municipal levels). As a consequence, in 1999, a law was passed that set, alongside the statutory regime, a legal system similar to the one that regulated labor in private enterprises. Even before the amendment was passed, however, major alterations had been introduced between 1976 and 1978 in the rules that governed statutory position management.

The managerial reform of 1995 had three facets: an institutional one, a cultural one, and a management one.[28] In the work that my team and I carried out in MARE, we gave priority to institutional change, since real reform is more this than anything else. However, it was possible to approve the new institutions only after a national debate, in which the bureaucratic culture dominant until then was submitted to a systematic critique at the same time that the new institutions were being defined. In particular, this meant breaking the complete stability that civil servants had enjoyed in the 1988 constitution and transforming the social and scientific services that the state provided into social organizations, that is, into nonstate public organizations financed by the state budget but supervised by means of management contracts.

The 1995 managerial reform was based on a reform model that my team and I developed in the first months of Cardoso's first term (1995–98). I was not interested in debating with neoliberals the degree of state intervention in the economy, and I believe that today we have reached a reasonable consensus about the lack of viability of the minimal state and the need for corrective and stimulating state regulatory activity. Instead of insisting on this issue, I first asked myself which were the exclusive activities of the state, those involving state power; second, which of the activities for which this exclusivity no longer existed did society and the state consider it necessary to finance (especially social and scholarly activities); and, finally, which were the entrepreneurial activities of production of goods and services for the marketplace? To these three questions, I added one more: what were the relevant forms of property or organization in contemporary capitalism? That is, were there only the categories of private and public, or was there a third in between these, which would assume increasing importance in contemporary societies: that of public nonstate property?

From these questions and from the bureaucratic/managerial administrative dichotomy, it was possible for me to build the model for reform. Modern states involve three sectors: the sector of exclusively state activities, within which are the strategic core and the executive or regulatory agencies; the sector of social and scholarly activities, which are not exclusively the state's but, given the externalities and the human rights involved, justify, indeed, require strong state financing; and, finally, the sector that produces goods and services for the marketplace.

In light of these three sectors, there are three additional questions: what type of administration, what type of property, and what type of organizational institution should prevail in each sector? The answer to the first question is simple: managerial public administration should be adopted. On the level of exclusively state activities, however, it is essential to reinforce the strategic core, filling it with highly competent, well-trained, and well-paid public servants.

The question of property is essential in the managerial reform model. In the strategic core and in the other exclusively state activities, property should be, by definition, state property. In the production of goods and services, there is today, in contrast, a growing consensus that property must be private, especially in cases in which the market controls the commercial companies. In the domain of social and scholarly services, the property should be public nonstate property. Social activities, mainly in the areas of health, basic education, and guarantees of minimum wage, and the performance of scholarly research involve certain externalities and concern basic human rights. They are, therefore, activities that the market cannot adequately guarantee through price and profit. Thus they should not be private. On the other hand, if they do not imply the exercise of state power, then there is no reason for them to be controlled by the state and to be submitted to controls inherent in the state bureaucracy, which can be contrary to administrative efficiency and which managerial reform can reduce but not eliminate. Thus, if they should be neither private nor state, the alternative is to adopt the category of nonstate public property, that is, to use organizations under private law, but with public, not-for-profit purposes. This is "public" property in the sense that it must be dedicated to the public interest, of all and for all, without the goal of profit. It is "nonstate" because it is not part of the state apparatus. Nonstate public organizations can be largely or, in some cases, entirely financed by the state. For example, a community basic education school should be free and entirely financed by the public sector, as already occurs in many countries. This form of property guarantees social and scholarly services that are more efficient than those executed directly by the state and more trustworthy than those provided by private companies motivated by profit rather than public interest. It is more efficient than state institutions because it can dispense with rigid bureaucratic controls insofar as the activities involved are generally competitive activities that can be controlled with relative ease by results. It is more trustworthy than the private companies because in areas as delicate as education and health, the profit motive is very dangerous.

Three organizational institutions emerged from the reform, itself a group of new institutions: the "regulatory agencies," the "executive agencies," and the "social organizations." In the area of exclusively state activities, the regulatory agencies are entities with the autonomy to regulate entrepreneurial sectors that operate in insufficiently competitive markets. Executive agencies are mainly concerned with the execution of laws. In both cases, but mainly in the regulatory agencies, the law leaves room for discretionary regulatory action, since it is neither possible nor desirable to regulate everything by means of laws and decrees. In the area of social and scientific services or rather in the activities that the state carries out but that are not exclusive to it, the idea was to transform the existing state foundations into social organizations. While the executive agencies would be fully integrated into the state, the social organizations would be included in the nonstate public sector. Social organizations are nonstate organizations that are authorized by Congress to receive budget allocations; thus their income is derived partially or wholly from the national treasury.

The management contract is the instrument that the strategic core uses to control the exclusively state activities, executed by the agencies, and the nonexclusive activities, carried out by the social organizations. In the agencies, the minister names an executive director and signs the management contract with him or her. In the social organizations, the executive director is chosen by the administrative board, yet the minister is responsible for signing the management contract and overseeing the results. The management contracts must plan for the personnel, material, and financial resources that the agencies or social organizations will need, and they must clearly set, quantitatively and qualitatively, the goals and performance indicators to be achieved, as agreed to by the parties.

Conclusion

From the end of 1997, it became clear that the managerial form was successful on the cultural and institutional levels.[29] The idea of a managerial public administration's replacing a bureaucratic model had become victorious, and the main institutions needed to implement it had been approved or were in the final approval process in Congress. At the same time, it was also clear to me that MARE did not have enough power for the second stage of the reform: its implementation. It would have sufficient power only if it were a special secretariat of the Office of the President and depended on the president's direct interest. Since this alternative was not realistic, beginning in early 1998, I turned to promoting within the government the integration of MARE into the Planning Ministry, with the argument that within the ministry that controls the federal budget there would be enough power to implement the reform. My proposal matched the Presidential Staff Office's (Casa Civil's) view of the problem and so was accepted as part of the ministerial reform launched in January 1999 by the second Cardoso administration (1999–2002). MARE was merged with the Ministry of Planning, and the new ministry was named the Ministry of Planning, Budget, and Management.[30]

This new ministry, which was charged with implementing the managerial reform, did not, however, give sufficient attention to the mission, except in the actions related to the proposals of the Multiyear Plan (Plano Plurianual, PPA). The budget was not directly related to the quality management program. The transformation of the state organizations into executive agencies or, in some cases, social organizations did not gain momentum. The annual public competitions for state positions were discontinued in the name of fiscal economy. Nevertheless, the managerial concepts remained alive, especially among the younger public managers.

On the other hand, in the states and municipalities, the ideas and institutions of managerial reform are being implemented with more and more consistency. For instance, I recently received a copy from the government of the state of Pernambuco a copy of its *Plano diretor da reforma do Estado* (Blueprint for State Reform). This plan, which was approved and published by the State Reform Steering Commission (Commissão Diretora da Reforma do Estado), faithfully follows the 1995 managerial reform, with a distinction between exclusive and nonexclusive state activities.

On a broader level, the ideas of the 1995 managerial reform have gone beyond the national borders. These ideas have spread thanks to the Latin American Centre for Development Administration (Centro Latinoamericano de Administración para el Desarrollo, CLAD). With headquarters in Caracas, CLAD convenes the governments of twenty-four Latin American and Caribbean nations and those of the two Iberian nations. Its administrative council is made up of the ministers of administration or their equivalent from each country. This council has approved the document *A New Public Management for Latin America*, developed by CLAD's scientific council.[31]

The implementation in Brazil of the 1995 managerial reform will take many years. It will experience advances and setbacks. It will face the natural resistance to change and the corporatism of the old bureaucrats, the electoral interests of politicians, and the interests of capitalists in obtaining benefits from the state. The patrimonial state was, by definition, a state held in thrall by class interests. The industrial-bureaucratic state and the managerial state are transitions from a politics of elites to a modern democracy. This means a democracy in which civil society and public opinion are increasingly important and one that defends republican rights — that is, the right that each citizen has to demand that the public patrimony be used in a public way. These relations are increasingly possible and, indeed, necessary.[32]

Without a doubt, injustice and privilege are still widely dominant in Brazil. Without a doubt, violations of social rights still coexist with violations of civil rights, especially those of the poorest. Even so, there has been progress in all areas. In the area that this chapter has analyzed, that of administration and the state, republican rights, which were ignored during the patrimonial state, became a central concern of both society and the state. Brazilian citizens increasingly hold it to be self evident that the public patrimony can and must be used for public purposes. For this reason, the cries against privatization, against the takeover of the state by capitalists or bureaucrats, against corruption and nepotism should not be viewed pessimistically, as a decline in the public realm. Rather they should be seen as a healthy sign that Brazilians are fighting patrimonialism and that a democratic, managerial Brazilian state is in formation.

Notes

The author is grateful to Denis Rosenfield, Evelyn Levy, and Sérgio Azevedo for their comments.

1. Faoro, *Os donos do poder*, 734–36.

2. Bomfim, *A América Latina*, 54.

3. Mello, "Posfácio," 1325. In these texts, both Nabuco and Mello seek to show the functional relation between slavery and the state, the slave-based plantation supporting the patrimonial state.

4. Carvalho, *A construção da ordem*, 38. This book is based on his doctoral dissertation, defended at Stanford University in 1975.

5. *Ibid.*, 39.

6. Buarque de Holanda, *Raízes do Brasil*, 105–6.

7. Carvalho, *A construção da ordem*, 130.

8. Carvalho, *Os bestializados*, 140–41.

9. Lessa, *A invenção republicana*, 74.

10. I owe this observation to Márcio Moreira Alves.

11. Barbosa Lima Sobrinho, *A verdade sobre a Revolução de Outubro*, 102.

12. On the concept of economic populism, see the essays in my *Populismo econômico*.

13. I analyzed this phenomenon in my first academic work, "The Rise of Middle Class and Middle Management in Brazil" (1962), which became chapter 3 of *Desenvolvimento e crise no Brasil* (1st ed. 1968, 2nd ed. 1970, 3rd ed. 1972, 4th ed. 1984), published in English as *Development and Crisis in Brazil, 1930–1983*.

14. Luiz Simões Lopes would continue his work on rationalizing the state apparatus with the creation in 1944 of the Getúlio Vargas Foundation (Fundação Getúlio Vargas), which, through the Brazilian School of Public Administration (Escola Brasileira de Administração Pública, EBAP), would become the major center for studies of public administration in the country. In the 1960s, he would promote the creation of public administration programs at the Getúlio Vargas Foundation's São Paulo School of Business Administration (Escola de Administração de Empresas de São Paulo), founded in 1954. I have taught courses in administration and economics in this school since 1959.

15. D'Araújo, O Estado Novo, 31.

16. Wahrlich (1915–94) was one of the founders of EBAP. Because of the quality of her studies, research, and teaching, she has become known as the patron saint of public administration in Brazil. She was the principal theorist of the developmentalist reforms of the 1960s and 1970s (see Wahrlich, A reforma administrativa da era de Vargas, "A reforma administrativa no Brasil," and "Uma reforma de administração de pessoal vinculada ao processo de desenvolvimento nacional").

17. Faoro, Os donos do poder, 733–36.

18. Buarque de Holanda, Raízes do Brasil, 106.

19. Graham, Civil Service Reform in Brazil, 6. Graham's book was the first general study of the Brazilian bureaucratic reform.

20. Wahrlich, "Uma reforma de administração de pessoal vinculada ao processo de desenvolvimento nacional."

21. Guerreiro Ramos, "A nova ignorância e o futuro da administração pública na América Latina," 19.

22. See Martins, Estado capitalista e burocracia no Brasil pós-64, Pouvoir et développement economique, and Reforma da administração pública e cultura política no Brasil. Also important are Evans, The Alliance of Multinational, State, and Local Capital in Brazil; Nunes, A gramática política do Brasil and "Bureaucratic Isolation and Clientelism in Contemporary Brazil"; and Schneider, Bureaucracy and Industrial Policy in Brazil. The last two were written at the University of California–Berkeley in the 1980s.

23. Beltrão, Descentralização e liberdade, 11.

24. Schneider, Bureaucracy and Industrial Policy in Brazil. It is curious, however, that Schneider—who, in his study, adopts a line similar to that of Evans's work on the petrochemical industry and the alliance that was then established among the state bureaucracy, the domestic business community, and multinational firms—does not mention (as Evans does not mention) that this successful developmentalist managerial bureaucracy had little in common with "Weberian bureaucracy."

25. Abrucio, Os barões da Federação.

26. By "globalist ideas," I mean the ideology born out of globalization that affirms the

loss of autonomy and relevance of the state in the modern world, in which will prevail not only a global market but a global society.

27. On the competence and public spirit of senior Brazilian administrators, see Schneider, *Burocracia pública e política industrial no Brasil*; Gouvéa, *Burocracia e elites dominates do país*; and Hochman, "Os cardeais da previdência social." I wrote the prefaces of the first two before I even imagined that I would soon become the minister of federal administration and state reform.

28. Formulation of the reform came about through work on the *Plano diretor* at the same time that I was writing several works synthesized in the book *Reforma do Estado para a cidadania*. Regarding the managerial reform of 1995, see Petrucci and Schwarz, *Administration pública gerencial*, and Gill, *Some Determinants of Sustainable Public Administration Reform* (prepared for the seminar sponsored by the British Council, "Public Reform in Brazil and the British Technical Cooperation," London, 23 November 1998).

29. On the political process of passing the reform, see Melo, "A política de reforma do Estado no Brasil," and Bresser Pereira, "Reflexões sobre a reforma gerencial brasileira de 1995."

30. When merging the two ministries, the president informed me that he understood my mission in federal administration to be complete and invited me to take over the Ministry of Science and Technology. I remained in that position from January to July 1999, after which I returned to my academic activities.

31. Centro Latinoamericano de Administración para el Desarrollo, *A New Public Management for Latin America*. Also available in Portuguese and Spanish from CLAD.

32. On republican rights, which constitute the theoretical basis for the 1995 managerial reform, see Bresser Pereira, "Cidadania e *Res Publica*."

Bibliography

Abrucio, Fernando. *Os barões da Federação*. São Paulo: Hucitec, 1998.

Barbosa Lima Sobrinho, Alexandre. *A verdade sobre a Revolução de Outubro*. São Paulo: Edições Unitas, 1933.

Beltrão, Hélio. *Descentralização e liberdade*. Rio de Janeiro: Record, 1984.

Bomfim, Manoel. *A América Latina: Males de origem*. Rio de Janeiro: Topbooks, 1993.

Bresser Pereira, Luiz Carlos. *Desenvolvimento e crise no Brasil: 1930–1983*. 4th ed. São Paulo: Brasiliense, 1984.

———. *Development and Crisis in Brazil, 1930–1983*. Boulder, Colo.: Westview, 1984.

———, ed. *Populismo econômico*. São Paulo: Nobel, 1991.

———. "Cidadania e *Res Publica*: A emergência dos direitos republicanos." *Revista de Filosofia Política*, Nova Série 1 (1997).

————. *Reforma do Estado para a cidadania*. São Paulo: Editora 34, 1998.

————. "Reflexões sobre a reforma gerencial brasileira de 1995." *Revista do Serviço Público* 50, no. 4 (2000).

Buarque de Holanda, Sérgio. *Raízes do Brasil*. 1st ed. Rio de Janeiro: José Olympio, 1936. 5th ed., with definitive text. Rio de Janeiro: José Olympio, 1969.

Carvalho, José Murilo de. *A construção da ordem*. Brasília: Editora da Universidade de Brasília, 1980.

————. *Os bestializados: O Rio de Janeiro e a República que não foi*. 3rd ed. São Paulo: Companhias das Letras, 1998.

Centro Latinoamericano de Administración para el Desarrollo. *A New Public Management for Latin America*. Caracas: CLAD, 1998.

D'Araújo, Maria Celina. *O Estado Novo*. Rio de Janeiro: Zahar, 2000.

Evans, Peter. *The Alliance of Multinational, State, and Local Capital in Brazil*. Princeton, N.J.: Princeton University Press, 1979.

Faoro, Raimundo. *Os donos do poder: Formação do patronato político brasileiro.* 2nd ed. Porto Alegre/São Paulo: Globo/Editora da Universidade de São Paulo, 1975.

Gill, Indermit S. *Some Determinants of Sustainable Public Administration Reform; or, Why I Am Optimistic about Administrative Reforms in Brazil*. Brasília: Escritório do Banco Mundial em Brasília, 1998.

Gouvéa, Gilda Portugal. *Burocracia e elites dominates do país*. São Paulo: Paulicéia, 1994.

Governo do Estado de Pernambuco. *Plano diretor da reforma do Estado*. Recife: Commissão Diretora de Reforma do Estado, 2000.

Graham, Lawrence S. *Civil Service Reform in Brazil*. Austin: University of Texas Press, 1968.

Guerreiro Ramos, Alberto. "A nova ignorância e o futuro da administração pública na América Latina." *Revista de Administração Pública* 4, no. 2 (July 1970).

Hochman, Gilberto. "Os cardeais da previdência social: Gênese e consolidaçãode uma elite burocrática." *Dados* 35, no. 3 (1992).

Lessa, Renato. *A invenção republicana*. Rio de Janeiro: Topbooks, 1999.

Martins, Luciano. *Pouvoir et développement economique*. Paris: Editions Anthropos, 1976.

————. *Estado capitalista e burocracia no Brasil pós-64*. Rio de Janeiro: Paz e Terra, 1985.

————. *Reforma da administração pública e cultura política no Brasil: Uma visão geral*. Cadernos ENAP no. 8. Brasília: Escola Nacional de Administração Pública, 1995.

Mello, Evaldo Cabral de. "Posfácio." In Nabuco, *Um estadista do Império*.

Melo, Marcus André. "A política de reforma do Estado no Brasil: *Issue areas* e processo decisório da reforma prevedenciária, administrativa e tributária." Paper presented at the seminar "The Political Economy of Administrative Reform in Developing Countries," CIDE/Northwestern University, Mexico City, 5–6 June 1998.

Ministério da Administração Federal e Reforma do Estado. *Plano diretor da reforma do aparelho do Estado.* Brasília: Impresna Nacional, 1995.

Nabuco, Joaquim. *Um estadista do Império.* 5th ed. Rio de Janeiro: Topbooks, 1998.

Nunes, Edson de Oliveira. "Bureaucratic Isolation and Clientelism in Contemporary Brazil: Uneven State Building and the Taming of Modernity." Ph.D. diss., University of California–Berkeley, 1984.

———. *A gramática política do Brasil.* Rio de Janeiro: Zahar; Brasília: Escola Nacional de Administração, 1997.

Osborne, David, and Ted Gaebler. *Reinventing Government.* Reading, Mass.: Addison-Wesley, 1992.

Petrucci, Vera, and Letícia Schwarz, eds. *Administration pública gerencial: A reforma de 1995.* Brasília: Editora da Universidade de Brasília, 1998.

Schneider, Ben Ross. *Bureaucracy and Industrial Policy in Brazil.* Pittsburgh: Pittsburgh University Press, 1991.

———. *Burocracia pública e política industrial no Brasil.* São Paulo: Sumaré, 1994.

Wahrlich, Beatriz Marques de Souza. "A reforma administrativa no Brasil: Experiência anterior, situação atual e perspectivas; Uma apreciação geral." *Revista de Administração Pública* 4, no. 1 (January 1970).

———. *A reforma administrativa da era de Vargas.* Rio de Janeiro: Fundação Getúlio Vargas, 1983.

———. "Uma reforma de administração de pessoal vinculada ao processo de desenvolvimento nacional." *Revista de Administração Pública* 18, no. 1 (January 1984).

PAULO SÉRGIO PINHEIRO

Political Transition and the (Un)rule of Law in the Republic

IN MEMORIAM *Raul Amaro Nin Ferreira*[1]

*Our century has come up with too few improvements in the
way it manages to govern, but it has marvelously advanced,
while coarsening, the techniques for controlling the governed.*

— MURRAY KEMPTON[2]

A French diplomat, Charles Wiener, who served in Rio de Janeiro in the nineteenth century, returned to Brazil in 1911. He recalled, "At that time, thirty-five years ago, there was still slavery in Brazil. One *bought* workers, laborers, artisans, domestic servants, as one would buy a horse, a sheep, a cow, or a dog. In 1875, I witnessed the sale of people of color. This occurred in a sort of open shop in downtown Rio."[3] Only fourteen years separated these scenes from the proclamation of the republic. A century later, the American writer Elizabeth Hardwick, on a visit to Brazil, noted that "the centuries seem to inhabit each moment; the diamonds at Minas, the slave ships, Dom Pedro in his summer palace at Petrópolis, the liberal tradition, the terrorists, the police, Vargas, Kubitschek, the Jesuits. All exist in a continuous present—a consciousness overcrowded and given to fatigue."[4]

The legacy of African slavery was quite visible in the capital of the republic on the eve of World War I in 1914: "It cannot be denied that the long practice of slavery and its sudden final abolition have left a definite mark on Rio society. Hosts of Negro freedmen forsook the back country plantations for the capital, and to-day the great number of ex-slaves and their descendants, full blood Africans or half-castes is a distinctive feature of the city's life." One senses a vision imbued with exoticism: "To Europeans familiar with cities like Cairo and Constantinople, this fact, however, adds a pleasant picturesqueness to the streets, and differentiates Rio de Janeiro from its southern and more prosaic Argentine rival, Buenos Aires, where the negro is practically non-existent."[5] This lovable touch did not mean that the Brazilians had renounced their discriminatory treatment of the former slaves: "The Brazilian behaves to his negro fellow citizens much as an English government official in Egypt behaves to his Syrian and Armenian fellow workers, although sufficiently imperious and aristocratic not to treat negro workmen and servants as his equals."[6]

The past was not dead; indeed, in 1922, a century after independence, it was if the past were not really past: "Class distinction still reigns in Brazil to a certain degree as may be expected in a land where slavery existed until twenty-eight years ago, and which twenty-seven years ago still had an Emperor and a Court with a retinue of nobles."[7] In spite of the proclamation of the republic, no major transformations in the social structure or in the groups in power had occurred. The continuity from the empire to the First Republic followed a pattern borne out in the history of Brazil. In such transitions, the political elites tend to change little. Because of this deep continuity, it is hard to establish a distinction between the political cadres of the First Republic (1889–1930) and the dignitaries of the empire, just as later it would be difficult to tell the difference between the personnel of the military dictatorship and the ruling class of the New Republic inaugurated in 1985. One of the most persistent features of the elites of the First Republic was that, "as a class, they remain generally oblivious to the great bulk of poor and ignorant population around them, half savage in certain regions."[8]

It had been hoped that, with the end of the Orleans and Braganza dynasty's rule, a new political system would be born with the republic. This hope was renewed during the political transitions that followed the end of the empire. After the Vargas dictatorship and also after the military dictatorship, it was expected that the return to democratic government would ensure that the protection of civil rights won for political dissidents would be extended to all citizens. It was a beautiful dream. The authoritarian practices of past governments were little affected by changes in political regimes or elections. The arbitrary actions of agents of state repression against the most vulnerable groups of the population were practically unchanged. Under democratic governments, an authoritarian system has prevailed, embedded especially in the institutions of control of violence and crime, such as the police and the judiciary. In spite of the undeniable changes that Brazil experienced in the twentieth century—including an obvious increase in social complexity, a strengthening of civil society, and a formidable transformation of the economy—there survives a "socially implanted authoritarianism" that the end of each exceptional regime does not eliminate. Each new non-authoritarian political phase is marked by the cumulative remainders of slavery, concentration of land and income, social and racial inequality, microdespotisms (to use Guillermo O'Donnell's expression), and a complex system of hierarchies, as revealed by Roberto DaMatta.[9]

By pointing out the legacy of the past in the evolution of the republic, I do not mean to affirm that the past continues automatically into the future, by some economic, psychological, or social determinism. This is because of the simple fact that, as Michel Debrun observes, "In the same society, the force coming from each past runs into the forces originating from other pasts. This is because the various trends—except when they are crystallized, and then they are not trends but habits, routines—always include a component of weakness."[10] That there are legacies and continuities does not prevent new and unexpected configurations from emerging in each political moment. Such configurations are formed of elements from society's various pasts, always altered, like images in a kaleidoscope, composed of the interdependencies among groups and actors.[11]

The obstacles to consolidation of the republic and to effective democracy have persisted because, in all transitions, the old opposition parties, in fear of real ruptures in the balance of power, with popular mobilization have formed coalitions with defectors from the ruling parties. In all of the republic's transitions, such conciliation has been a constant, as Debrun lucidly observes in his treatment of this "archetype" of Brazilian political thought and action.[12] We must be clear that an archetype is not determined by its content but rather by its form, because it can be present in distinct contexts. As Carl Jung states, "The archetype itself is empty and purely formal, nothing but a *facultas praeformandi*, a possibility of representation, which is given *a priori*."[13] Debrun argues that "conciliation" developed not to avoid conflicts among contenders of equal strength "but, to the contrary, to formalize and regulate the relation among unequal actors, some now dominant and some now subordinate, and to allow the former to exploit the latter for their benefit as junior partners. Transitions almost always serve to reinforce those who already have power."[14] Each transition takes on again the form of the archetype of conciliation, and each era confers on it different contents.

Hegemonies masquerading as popular consensus do not have the political means to confront the authoritarian legacy. This legacy has been repeatedly underestimated, and, consequently, the ability of political oppositions that emerged during the resistance to authoritarian governments and during political transitions to promote democracy has been overestimated. This is because these oppositions came to power without settling accounts with the past. By the very internal logic of resistance and protest under the seamless tunic of change, democratic political forces—the parties and elites that led the political transitions in government—abdicated their responsibility to remove the "authoritarian rubble" and to reform the institutions inherited from the dictatorships. The superficial rearrangement that allows the transition also leaves the institutions that control violence, such as the police and the judiciary, nearly untouched.

During the republic's transitions, the ruling classes seemed to suffer from "transformism," the capacity of political parties or leaders to assume suddenly positions or alternatives radically different from those that brought them to power, for example the reconstitution of a progressive party as a conservative party.[15] Radical reformism ceases to exist the instant that these parties shift from opposition to government. After the transition, it is difficult to find residues of the street agitations, the insurrections, and the rallies of dissidents in the programs of the new government party. The nature of groups that appeared extremist in opposition to the political "exceptional regimes," that is, dictatorships, alters upon coming to power. These symptoms can be seen since the civic preaching of the First Republic, which was affected by its fragile legitimacy, by limited suffrage, and by precarious respect for liberal formalities. The First Republic was condemned to be a mere stage curtain for the drama of negotiations among extremely restricted elites. While visiting São Paulo in 1924, Rudyard Kipling rightly remarked that Brazilian politics was a quite dangerous game during the First Republic, limited to the elites.[16] Because of the unwillingness of the ruling classes in a democracy to transform the order bequeathed by preceding authoritarian regimes, the unreformed institutions are inadequate to control or overcome the forms of incivility present in Brazilian society, which are always worse after the exceptional regimes. Indeed, the succession of each authoritarian period, untouched by the governments that arise in the periods of democratic transitions, reactivates and deepens the authoritarian legacy.

Of course, we are aware that "*all known forms of civil society are plagued by endogenous sources of incivility* so much so . . . that incivility is a chronic feature of civil society."[17] What is remarkable in Brazil is that the forms of excessive use of force on the part of the state, which were equivalent in the first two decades of the century to those in the great industrial economies at least until the Russian

Revolution, tended to survive much longer, despite some progress in political democracy. It continues to be an enigma why, in Brazil, there were high rates of illegal state violence against minorities that, at least in the First Republic, did not seem to present a serious risk to the hegemony of the dominant classes. Very high rates of overt, illegal physical violence by the state persisted even after the ruling classes and governments after 1930 discovered the advantages of the "symbolic violence" of ideological manipulation over physical violence. The corporatist labor legislation that was passed in the 1930s, called "the most advanced in the world" at the time, did not entail the renunciation of overt physical violence for controlling the popular classes. This violence eternally fell on the poor and indigent populations of Brazil. The great majority of those punished or imprisoned, with the exception of those who committed heinous crimes, were the powerless, the nonelites. In Brazil and, for that matter, in all of Latin America, social discrimination weighs heavily in the application of penal law, as Jean-Paul Brodeur has shown.[18]

There is a dramatic distance between this reality and the declaration of rights de rigueur in all of the democratic and dictatorial constitutions. Article 72 of the first republican constitution of 1891 contained a long, solemn list of rights and guarantees, not very different from those inscribed in the imperial constitution of 1824, and no fewer than those in the constitutions of 1937, 1943, 1946, 1967, and in the first amendment to the constitution of 1969. It was only surpassed by the 1988 constitution. In spite of this Brazilian "bill of rights," these rights always fell away, and most perpetrators were not charged with or punished for their crimes by the judicial system.

This essay examines the unwillingness of the nondictatorial republican governments to establish the rule of law for a majority of the Brazilian population. It also deals with the struggles of civil society organizations, their profiles and their transformations, in the context of a state of limited rule of law. The state, governments, and ruling classes have not ensured the basic conditions for rendering rights effective for the majority of the population: the poor and vulnerable. In a vicious cycle, the "verticalities of Brazilian inequalities" favor agreed-on conciliation and transition, without ruptures with the past, and, in turn, conciliation and transition contribute to these verticalities.[19]

This essay will also reveal the excessive use of force by the governments under democratic constitutionalism, a term applicable only to the short interregnum of 1934–35, the constitutional regime starting in 1946, and the constitutional regime starting in 1988. Of course, these historical moments were substantially distinct phenomena, with forms of excessive repression of crime and generalized repression of popular classes in rather different contexts. During the twentieth century, moreover, there were great changes in the composition of the dominant and popular classes in their motivations, projects, and practices. During the First Republic, there was a nascent industrial working class, made up of foreign immigrant labor. Between 1930 and 1937, in a context of rising Fascism, and after 1946, in the context of the Cold War, the government feared the "red peril" and wrestled against the Communists and their allies. Under the so-called populist democracy of the Third Republic, repression of the workers' movement was sustained until 1951, when Getúlio Vargas took office for a second time, elected in good part thanks to workers' votes. Even so, the government kept up its intervention in the unions for some time, but this diminished gradually, making strikes possible once again.[20] In the following populist administrations, political repression loosened or tightened depending on the political circumstances. For example, during the crisis that followed President Jânio Quadros's resignation on 25 August 1961, the political police took advantage of the situation and resumed persecution of Communists.[21] After 1985, the state found itself facing civil society movements on a much greater scale than at any moment in the past. It also faced epidemic violence. While the use of "political" violence was interrupted, the excessive use of force by the police against suspects of common crimes seems to have been uninterrupted. Comparison of some common traits in these diverse phases perhaps can explain the formidable changes and the enormous obstacles present in the formation of a rule of law in the twentieth century.

Even though the basic rights of the citizen are well defined by most of Brazil's democratic constitutions, the exercise of full citizenship has always been limited for a majority of the population. How could it have been otherwise? Ever since antiquity, a state's constitution has been rooted in the social system.[22] Far from the ideals present in its constitutions, judicial procedures and the workings of the law reflect the cruel realities of Brazilian society and never manage to moderate the vast differences between the rich and the poor.[23] The legal system is a tool and a reflection of society and, therefore, of social inequalities. The law is not situated outside and above society and social facts, as though it had its own essence, autonomous logic, or independent existence. The state cannot be different from its own society. Is it not within it that the interests and classes in conflict face off? Forms of governing depend on the particular structure of a society. Therefore, a government cannot function democratically in a country where, during various constitutional periods, women and illiterates do not have the vote, rural workers and domestic servants are not covered by social rights, a structural racism predominates, and the organs of the state never renounce the use of excessive force.

No regime can be effectively democratic if the less-favored social strata do not have access to rights or to instruments of effective control of the elites. Aside from the minimal requirements of a democratic constitutionalism—freedom of assembly, freedom of expression, universal suffrage, fair and regular elections, separation of powers—democracy requires fulfillment of a wider array of demands. These are the rule of law, due process or the right to a fair trial, and respect for the physical integrity of its citizens. These last demands, independent of the political regime in power, were addressed by the republic in only a limited way.

After each political transition, the new democratic regime has not fulfilled the great aspirations for freedom and rights that characterized the movements of resistance to authoritarianism that preceded it. The criminalization of dissidence and of popular movements in nondictatorial periods has been a constant in Brazil, although not unique to it. Examples include the myth of the immigrant worker as revolutionary, including the anarcho-syndicalists of 1900–1920, studied by Michael M. Hall; the Communists in 1930 and 1945; the rural and urban unions in the 1960s; and the Landless Workers' Movement (Movimento dos Trabalhadores Rurais Sem Terra, MST) of the 1990s. Every popular, worker, or peasant mobilization, every example of "defensive violence," in Herbert Marcuse's terms, tends to be blocked by state agents resorting to illegal violence that is much broader than the practice of disrespect of legality that is built into the state. For example, the Peasant Leagues (Ligas Camponesas) in the Northeast led by Francisco Julião were well repressed before the 1964 military coup (see chapter 2).

This essay examines four periods, defined by the republican constitution of 1891 and the three democratic constitutions of the twentieth century. The four transitions and their subsequent periods are the proclamation of the republic in 1889, followed by the 1891 constitution that launched the First Republic; on the heels of the Revolution of 1930, the constitution of 1934, which opened the Second Republic, the shortest democratic interregnum in Brazilian history, which was ended by the Estado Novo (New State) in 1937; the transition at the end of the Estado Novo leading to the promulgation and ratification of the 1946 constitution of the Third Republic, which lasted until the 1964 military coup; and finally, the end of the military dictatorship and return to civilian rule in 1985 and the "citizens'" constitution of 1988. Admittedly, the essay treats these periods un-evenly because of the current state of historical research on the various phases.

In theory, the democratic constitutions should spell out the conditions for the exercise of physical violence by the state and guarantee citizens' rights in the face of excessive use of force. In fact, the implementation of these guarantees has been quite precarious. Nothing shows the chronic limitations of the democratic state in Brazil between 1946 and 1964 and after 1988 than the democratic states at the center of analysis: a state is what makes a government.[24]

The "Parallel Exceptional Regime" and the Constitutional Regime

During the First Republic, privileged groups were favored by the federal struc-ture. This took the form of a "politics of the governors," in which the local ruling parties were not contested and could always count on a harmless federal gov-ernment in the face of arbitrary regional and local power (see chapter 8). In this period, widespread areas of the countryside were abandoned to the rule of the local bosses or *coronéis* because the state and federal governments looked the other way at their abuses in a perverse sort of delegation of power. In this regard, a respected French geographer, also an anarchist, Élysée Reclus, made a clairvoyant assertion over a hundred years ago: "Here is the greatest issue for the near future of Brazil: the workers demand land, in certain places, they seize it and cultivate it by force, and the landowners refuse to let them have it or seek to retake it."[25]

In this period, marked by rigidity of the political system and its refusal to allow an extension of citizenship within the liberal framework,[26] what stands out is the combination of a liberal constitution and a de facto or de jure exceptional regime. What we have here is what could be called a "parallel exceptional state," parallel, that is, to the existing constitutional legality. This would be a political regime in which the illegality to which the popular classes are generally submitted is much broader than the latitude granted by public opinion that is always present in the state's exercise of its monopoly on physical violence. This parallel regime never had its rule suspended in the course of the country's political evolution, at least as regards the conditions of existence of the most vulnerable groups. It was simply extended to groups close to the elites during the states of siege in the First Re-public, the Estado Novo dictatorship of 1937–45, and the military dictatorship of

1964–85. At certain nondictatorial moments, this parallel regime was legalized by the laws repressing anarchism or by the 1935 National Security Law (Lei de Segurança Nacional), which preceded the Estado Novo.

In the first three decades of the First Republic, some elements attested to the profound continuity with the previous regime. In 1907, an immense hierarchy persisted, with "a clear line that divided the upper class, the aristocracy, from the lower classes of workers." Even though democratic ideas held a fascination for the population, "the monarchy had ended so recently that, in their minds, a blood aristocracy prevailed. In reality this aristocracy was one of land and money."[27] Many members of the elites who had not participated actively in politics before were acknowledged to be part of this aristocracy, since "they continued in that role after the inauguration of the republican regime, and their descendents are in this position today." The bases of power, such as the large landowners, legacies of slavery, and the maintenance of important government positions, "came together to create a sort of feudal society that transmitted social and political preeminence even without the help of hereditary titles. . . . The families that had enjoyed these prerogatives preserved not only the pride of their ancestry but also a considerable measure of social deference from the rest of the population." Indeed, a homologous combination exists today: plantation-owning "electronic *coronéis*" with positions of power in the federal and state governments. In spite of the abolition of the titles of nobility, which, in fact, were only hereditary in the circle of the imperial family, social and political privileges survived into the republic, since "much of the patrimony that they still retained, with the development of the country, proved to be an even greater source of wealth than before." These conditions allowed "this class still to occupy an incontestable supremacy in Brazilian politics."[28]

The marks of slavery were indelible. Reclus stressed, "Say what one will, Blacks, the children of slaves, are who do most of the agricultural work in the regions where the Italian, German, and other immigrants have not yet come to help." Accustomed to the "frugality" of the Africans and unaccustomed to the more demanding European workers, the large landowners machinated to preserve old forms of exploitation: "Desirous of continuing the old practices of slavery under a new guise, they managed to get the Legislature to vote for the introduction of Chinese coolies onto their farms."[29] During the First Republic, basic rights—that is, the right to assembly, the right of freedom of movement, and the right of freedom of expression—were systematically flouted.

Repression of the workers' movement in Brazil in the first three decades of the republic was far from an isolated case in the world. Consider the Colossus of the North, as then foreign minister Baron of Rio Branco called the United States, in the period between the end of the nineteenth century and 1914: the workers' press in São Paulo noted in 1900 that "the United States has had the bloodiest and most violent labor history of any other industrial nation in the world."[30] Of course, the repression in tsarist Russia was worse, as the same press never tired of pointing out, but Brazilians noticed the level of industrial violence and paramilitary repression. One must also take into consideration that in the industrialized countries, industrial workers were the minority. In Brazil, they were located in a few centers, with immigrant militants leading the movement, in the middle of a sea of rural workers and former slaves.

In Brazil, as in Russia and the United States, violence was always initiated by bosses or government authorities, and the persons affected were almost always workers. In Brazil the expulsion of militant foreign workers as well as overall repression served to break the back of the workers' movement. Observers of the time emphasized the generalized and gratuitous nature of the police violence, its disregard for legal norms, and the high incidence of physical attacks. According to the São Paulo workers' newspaper *Fanfulla*, "Since [the police] have neither the skill nor the courage to apprehend real thieves, they arrest the first peaceful citizen whose appearance they do not like and throw him in jail for several days."[31] Police inspections in poor and working-class neighborhoods were common: "In the cafés, taverns, bars, shops, one, two, or three policemen enter suddenly, uniformed or not, and—with no legal warrant—inspect people as if, instead of free Brazil, we were in Holy Russia."[32] The police precinct of Barão de Iguape, in a working-class district of São Paulo, had the notoriety of being a place where the police "strike with the most enthusiasm, where they arrest people out of pure whim."[33] Quantitative data analyzed by Boris Fausto suggest a generalized policy of repression. For example, the per capita rate of imprisonment in São Paulo between 1892 and 1904 was approximately double that of London. Various other data suggest that only slightly more than 10 percent of the people arrested in this period were ever formally charged with a crime.[34]

Apparently, the number of Civil Police agents in Rio, the capital city, even in absolute terms, was low. An analysis of the Civil Police force in the Federal District for 1911 shows that, for a population of 1 million inhabitants, there were 1,400 policemen, or 1 for every 714 inhabitants. In comparison, London, with a population of 7 million, had 21,000 policemen, or 1 for every 333 inhabitants. New York, with 5 million inhabitants, had 10,208 policemen, or 1 for every 489 inhabitants.[35] If we add the Federal District's Civil Police numbers to those for the Military Police, which at the time was subordinate to the army, they quadruple: 177 officers and 3,659 men,[36] giving the impression that the police were omnipresent.[37] The target of some reforms in the second decade of the twentieth century, "this corps did not enjoy great favor among the population, who, no doubt, remembered past abuses; according to their origin. It is difficult to get from these agents a perfect distinction between reason and the absence thereof; it is a grace that the force especially lacks."[38]

The repression of popular revolts in the first decade of the twentieth century, of labor strikes in the second, and during the prolonged states of siege that followed the midlevel officer "lieutenant" or *tenente* revolts of the 1920s clearly revealed the routine, arbitrary practices of agents of the state. As journalist and distinguished author of fiction Afonso Henriques de Lima Barreto noted in his diary during the Vaccine Revolt of 1904, a popular protest against compulsory vaccination that had its roots in the urban poor's mistrust of the government, "The police seized people left and right that they found in the street. They brought them to the precinct stations and afterwards gathered them at the central police station. There they violently and humiliatingly pulled down the waistbands of their pants and pushed them onto a large patio. Gathered as they were by the dozens, they were sent to Snake Island [Ilha das Cobras], where they were clumsily beaten. . . . Thirty years later, the place is the same. All of the violence of the government is exposed on Snake Island. Innocent bums are brought together there, beaten, and sent to Acre in the far Amazon."[39]

From that time to the end of the term of President Arthur Bernardes (1922–26), the government banished to colonies in the North, without trial or prison sentence, hundreds of "undesirables," a category that included workers, the unemployed, and rebellious soldiers. It was a virtual death sentence. It is notable that public opinion of the time tolerated the removal of hundreds of these internal exiles, which has something in common with the complacency of governments and elites in the face of current scenes on television of prisoners piling up in police custody or children and youths systematically tortured in São Paulo.

The "Brazilian exception," the enigma that historical research has not untangled, is not the high level of repression of the labor movement in the first decades of the republic but its persistence in later periods at the same time that this violence had fallen out of use in the North. In the United States, overt violence against the labor movement declined after the 1940s, even though racial violence and discrimination continued, such as lynchings (which dropped off in the 1950s) and segregation (which became illegal after 1963, when civil rights legislation was passed under Lyndon Johnson). In the First Republic, the elites were terrified by the Bolshevik Revolution of 1917. Seeing in any sort of protest the phantom of revolution, rulers vacillated between minimal reforms and brutal repression. Internal conflict was almost always resolved through military force because of the instinctive fear that autonomous power structures could emerge in civil society. Throughout the First Republic, the government made uncontrolled use of imprisonment and even military repression of workers. An example was the dispatch in 1908 of torpedo boat destroyers to the coast of Santos, the main port for São Paulo, when dockworkers were striking for an eight-hour workday. During the 1924 revolt, the government did not hesitate to bomb industrial districts of São Paulo after airdropping leaflets calling on the population to flee from the bombardment. This caused an unaccustomed visitor, the historian Alan K. Manchester, to record that "the bombardment of the city by the Federal forces turned the eight hundred thousand inhabitants almost unanimously in favor of the rebels. . . . In the industrial Moöca zone, ditches were dug, bodies thrown in with an arm and hand left sticking up to mark the spot of such groups for later more decent burial. Similar tombstones were numerous in the industrial parts of the city."[40] Another witness, the French poet Blaise Cendrars, noted, "Airplanes directed the operation, dropping bombs that fell everywhere and exploded randomly. This absurdity lasted twenty-nine days. At night, incendiary shelling from howitzers set fires in the working-class neighborhoods of Luz and Mooca, causing the Shell reserve tanks and the coffee warehouses to explode."[41] This insane, criminal bombardment shows how far the dominant classes of the First Republic could go in their disregard for the defenseless civilian population.

The military coup that deposed President Washington Luís on 24 October 1930 cleared the way for the provisional government headed by Vargas. This government was founded on the dissident factions of the ruling parties in the state of Minas Gerais and Rio Grande do Sul and on the leadership of the *tenentista* revolts of the 1920s. The 1891 constitution was suspended. In the first three years of the provisional government, without laws or other encumbrances, Vargas ruled with his ministers, legislated with them, and passed judgment in a court without codes using nouns and adjectives, without a constitution, without anything other than the free will of the ministers, legislators, and judges, as constitutional scholar Karl Loewenstein reported on a visit to Brazil in 1941.[42] Note that the pattern of state use of excessive force had not changed. The violence inflicted on the popular classes by police in the streets, in the precinct stations, and in the prisons was no different than before. "At no time in Brazil was the labor movement subject to so much violence as after 24 October 1930," summarized Astrojildo Pereira, former secretary-general and cofounder of the Brazilian Communist Party (Partido Comunista Brasileiro, PCB), who also knew well the repression of the First Republic.[43] Under the guise of expelling resident foreigners, some militant workers were exiled by force to Europe. In June 1931, Otávio Brandão, an intellectual and a Communist leader, was taken from a prison in Rio and deported, with his wife, poet Laura Brandão, and three children, to Bremen, Germany. Later, on 4 April 1935, the National Security Law was passed to confront demonstrations by the National Liberation Alliance (Aliança Nacional Libertadora, ANL), a leftist front under the influence of the Communists. Three months later, based on this law, Decree no. 229 of 11 July 1935 closed down the ANL.[44]

The period of 1930–34 has been treated with great leniency by many historians, but, in fact, this was an exceptional regime, a dictatorship unlike any seen before. Instead of considering this a provisional interregnum for the constitutional democracy that would come in 1934, another periodization is possible: the government of 1930–34 was already a dictatorship, interrupted by a brief period of a little more than a year, that would be resumed by the coup d'état of 1937. The provisional Vargas government "in a nutshell contained all of the trimmings of the . . . constitution of 1937, which inaugurated the New State," according to Loewenstein.[45]

From the Cradle of the Coup to the Phantom Constitution

It was a particularly scorching day in Rio de Janeiro when a collection of American and Brazilian businessmen filed into the "resplendent" white building of the Jockey Club on Rio Branco Avenue. The purpose of the gathering was a luncheon at which the president of the Pan-American Union was scheduled to speak. The atmosphere was feverish with the news that, earlier that morning, President Vargas had declared a state of war. Someone asked one of the businessmen about this, and he responded with a shrug of his shoulders:

> "There have been communistic disturbances again; this decree is merely a precaution. Now the President is empowered to act as he sees fit."
>
> "Real communism?"
>
> "Well, opposition to the government, at least. From troublemakers. Re-

member, South America has a tradition for revolutions. You saw the regiment garrison that had been bombarded? Done by a group of young army officers with too liberal leanings."[46]

After the 1934 interregnum, Legislative Decree no. 6 of 18 December 1935 authorized the suspension of constitutional guarantees, in order to combat Communism. Since the government was happy neither with the powers deriving from a state of siege nor the definition of a state of war provided for in the constitution of 1934, the legislators approved three amendments to the constitution that extended the concept of "state of war" to cover circumstances that were not those of war. "In a memorable session, the House of Deputies approved three amendments of the Constitution. The first passed 210 to 59, the others by an even smaller margin," noted President Vargas in his diary.[47] The first amendment allowed the Chamber of Deputies, with the approval of the Senate, to declare a state of war in any part of the nation in the case of "serious internal commotion" of political and social institutions. With these amendments, Vargas acquired near-dictatorial powers through legal authorization. However, as Loewenstein remarked, it "served in Brazil, as everywhere else when the government is planning to slip out from parliamentary control, as the vehicle for overthrowing constitutional government."[48]

During the crackdown after the 1935 revolt, 7,056 persons were detained in the Federal District, including those transferred by military authorities from other states. The prisons received journalists, doctors, and students, reflecting the composition of the ANL movement. The house of detention in Rio was so full that it was necessary to transform a Lloyd Brasileiro ship, the *Pedro I*, into a prison. The ship, which had been seized from the Germans in World War I, was anchored at the Glória docks, with a destroyer next to it, manned by a Military Police detachment. Numerous allegations of torture and persecutions were directed to the Chamber of Deputies. On 21 March 1936, the president, using Congress's 1935 authorization, signed a decree declaring "a state of war for ninety days: new studies and investigations had revealed a renewal of subversive activities, justifying the forceful measures of repression."

Another decree passed by a standing Senate committee, which at this time was in recess, eliminated several more guarantees that remained in force during a state of war, such as immunity for members of Congress. Several members of Congress were arrested, accused of links with Communism. The crackdown unleashed under the pretext of suppressing Communism resumed the old practices of the First Republic in regard to the poor, especially in the capital. The arrests, as during the Bernardes government, were based on simple profiling—probable expectation based on a threat reconstructed from previously perpetrated crimes— rather than the actual commission of a crime. From 1889 through at least the 1930s, the state always made use of repression as "social prophylaxis" against the poor and working class, even during periods of constitutional legality. On 10 May 1936, a young student, Carlos Marighela, was imprisoned; he was tortured for twenty-two days. Marighela would later become a high-profile Communist leader and eventually a proponent of and participant in the armed struggle against the military dictatorship of 1964. He was murdered by the police of the military dictatorship in 1969.

Confronted with the task of trying prisoners taken after the 1935 revolt, on 11 September 1936, the government created a special court, the National Security Court (Tribunal de Segurança Nacional, TSN), for trials of political "crimes." This tribunal functioned as an organ of the Military Justice Department, as a court of first instance, until December 1937. After the 1964 coup, it was elevated to the category of exceptional court, charged with protecting the regime by dealing with its enemies.[49] The democratic interregnum begun by the 1934 constitution had ended the "dictatorship," a term used by Vargas himself in his diary.[50] The interregnum itself ended after twenty months under the pretext of lessening the dangers awakened by the 1935 revolt. The period 1935–37 was the cradle of the coup d'état and the authoritarian constitution of 1937.

In early November 1937, presidential candidate Armando de Salles Oliveira, from São Paulo, sent a letter "to the military chiefs of Brazil," alerting them of the coup that was in preparation and calling on them to block it. Vargas noted in his diary, "In light of this, it was necessary to move quickly, taking advantage of surprise. I had the chief of police and the minister of justice summoned immediately. With the latter, the minister of war planned all of the measures. On the next day, the 11th [in fact, 10 November], in the morning, the two houses of Congress found themselves guarded by the police [the state assemblies and municipal chambers had also been dissolved]. At 10:00 am, the ministry met and we signed the constitution. . . . In the afternoon, I went to the Catete Palace [the presidential residence] . . . and worked until 8:00 at night, when I delivered the 'Manifesto to the Nation' on the radio."[51]

In this manifesto, the now dictator announced that the new constitution and other institutional measures of the new regime were in force. The 1937 constitution was a "phantom constitution," according to Loewenstein, existing only on paper, void of real life.[52] Article 80 of the transitory and final provisions announced the true constitution, the personal power of the dictator: "Until the National Parliament [Congress] meets again, the president of the republic shall have the power to expedite decree-laws in all matters of the Union's legislative competence." Congress never met during the Estado Novo. Once the legal obstacles of the rule of law were removed, the personal dictatorship successfully imposed its control over the popular classes.[53]

Undeniably, some concrete benefits came to some labor sectors through the Estado Novo's social and labor legislation. This set of laws, in conjunction with the repressive apparatus, was used by the wide variety of political regimes that followed the Estado Novo. The paternalistic tone, which is not lacking in arbitrary power, of the various governments after 1946 derives exactly from the plausibility of these social policies.[54] Perhaps this is one of the keys to understanding the continuity of procedures with their Dr. Jekyll and Mr. Hyde — or, to use an image from the era, Carmen Miranda and Felinto Müller — ambivalence toward the poor and working class.[55]

The social and labor legislation was an extraordinary mask for the overt physical violence against the working class. It was imposed on the industrial bourgeoisie in spite of their resistance to effective implementation, yet it served as an important prop for bourgeois domination. The Estado Novo constructed a centralized state apparatus in the service of the industrial sectors that would service the exceptional regime. This labor legislation eliminated union leaderships, at least until the Dutra government (1945–50), and it repressed independent expression of vast sectors of civil society. In the meanwhile it constructed the semblance of a state that rose above the class association, and this continued to be an indispensable myth during the period of developmentalist populism after 1950.

It is no matter that, during certain periods that followed, the state defined itself as democratic; what matters are the practices of government institutions, because there is no significant difference between state and government. In any regime, citizens establish a direct equation between the two. As Harold Laski pointed out, the citizen knows the nature of the state through the actions of the government.[56] In Brazil, there was a century of split personality between a democratic state and a government of policies marked by arbitrary power.

From the Fall of the Dictatorship to the "Social Oasis" of the Populist Governments

"Overnight, the dictatorship finally fell," wrote historian Caio Prado Jr. in his diary on 30 October 1945.[57] A military coup had apparently ended the Estado Novo. At the same time, president-elect General Eurico Gaspar Dutra, who had loyally served as Vargas's minister of war, would play a role of profound continuity with the dictatorship that had just ended, especially in the interregnum of October 1945 to September 1946, when the "exceptional" laws of the preceding regime went into force. This legislation would be vigorously applied by the government faced with intense popular participation and actions of the working class. The waves of industrial strikes and protests at this time would be equaled in breadth and intensity only in the great phase of confrontation that preceded the 1964 coup.[58] If the previous regime could be called "authoritarian" as far as the form of government and the type and technique of power in defining policies were concerned, many of these characteristics certainly continued until the 1946 constitution, and even beyond.[59]

In spite of the 1946 constitution, the new regime declined to create conditions for the emergence of a sufficiently autonomous union movement or to foment viable social reform that would improve the living conditions of the poor majority. It did not even aim to consolidate a system for guaranteeing liberties or promoting a genuinely representative democracy. The various agendas of the groups that asserted a sudden commitment to democratic policy were diverse and mutually contradictory, as Peter Flynn has noted. One could not expect that the corporatist structures and institutions, such as labor legislation and the repressive apparatus built up over fifteen years, could be dismantled overnight by members of the very groups that had set them up earlier. As in all political transitions in Brazil, authoritarians became liberators or democrats of a formal transition engaged in an "irreversible dynamic."[60]

Continuity of the corporatist union legislation was opportune for the government faced with a wave of strikes since it left intact the state's control over the unions. The Labor Ministry took various repressive measures: it suspended or intervened in union elections and shut down the Unifying Movement of Workers (Movimento Unificador dos Trabalhadores, MUT), which led to the creation of the Confederation of Brazilian Workers (Confederação dos Trabalhadores do Brasil, CTB), closed, in turn, in the following year. As in the Estado Novo, these measures were complemented by police repression. The police in the capital violently cracked down on demonstrations, charging the participants with violations of the dictatorship's National Security Law, which continued in force with the approval of the new government's minister of justice, Carlos Luz. Later, as president of the Chamber of Deputies, Luz would preside over the frustrated 1956 coup against the inauguration of president-elect Juscelino Kubitschek.

At the meeting of the Constituent Assembly, there were frequent accusations of repression from parliamentarians of various parties. Work on the constitution was interspersed with waves of repression during each vote. In March 1946, police closed down several headquarters of the PCB, which were reopened soon thereafter because the party was legal. On 23 May, days before sending the draft to the plenary session scheduled for 27 May, a rally organized by the PCB to commemorate one year of legality was broken up by force. In June, when the constituents were discussing the draft, police closed down the PCB headquarters in several cities. The next month, various political and social conflicts were put down in Rio, in Santos, and in other cities in the states of Rio de Janeiro, São Paulo, Minas Gerais, Bahia, Rio Grande do Sul, and Piauí. On 15 August, the minister of justice ordered the seizing of that day's edition of the *Tribuna Popular*, the main Communist newspaper in Rio de Janeiro, and banned its circulation for fifteen days. On 23 August, rallies were prohibited in the country. It was difficult to discern when the Estado Novo had ended and when the government of the democratic transition had begun.[61]

If the "dictatorial rubble" of the Estado Novo allowed the Dutra government to make use of a wide range of excessive force after the ratification of the 1946 constitution, the new regime did not block the ongoing violence outside the constitutional order, of which the Communists took fleeting advantage to protest. The police cracked down with street clashes and beatings,[62] and they did not hesitate in opening fire on legal Communist demonstrations in the capital city. The police in Belo Horizonte even banned lectures by the Marxist intellectual Roger Garaudy, at that time connected with the French Communist Party.

In February 1948, there were numerous press reports of accusations of torture of political activists. Gregório Bezerra, a prominent Communist leader, was accused of involvement with an attack on an army barracks in the state of Paraíba and was beaten. On 3 February, a telegram from the mayor and municipal council of Petrópolis denounced violence committed against railway workers and the detention of strikers. On 4 February, a telegram to the minister of justice from the municipality of Rio Verde, in the state of Goiás, related "lamentable events occurring in this municipality, which finds itself under a veritable reign of terror caused by elements of the police that roam about the region, invading houses, breaking into boxes with the goal of seizing harmless weapons from farmers, and committing illegal, unjust arrests and beatings."[63]

In the post-1945 transition there were substantial changes in the behavior of rural workers. The classic interpretation holds that those workers who migrated in large numbers to the cities between the 1940s and the 1960s massively supported the populist leadership because of their precarious political formation. In reality, what happened with them was a rather more complex phenomenon than a simple transfer of the political base of *coronelismo* to a potential base for populism. Because of these very changes in their circumstances, for the first time, these workers were being offered the opportunity to rise up, through the vote, against the political domination of the rural bosses. Political participation was freer than ever before in 1945, and the political parties began to compete for the rural vote. Two changes that Vargas wrought in preparation for the 1945 transition contributed to this increase in electoral participation and had a profound impact among both rural and urban workers: the legalization of the PCB and the changes in electoral legislation that facilitated voter registration. In the elections for state governors on 19 January 1947, it became clear that the larger rural landholders were losing control of the rural vote.[64]

To understand the vigor of the Dutra government's repression of popular movements, one must remember that, in the process of incorporating workers into the official unions, there was an undeniable increase in political participation. In 1881, imperial electoral reform struck illiterates from the electoral rolls. In 1887, the number of voters in Brazil was about 220,000, or about 1.5 percent of the population. This caused a statistician to record candidly in one of the imperial government's publications that "it is one of the least numerous electorates in the world."[65] It was indeed very small, even though the picture of electoral participation in the democracies of Europe in the same period was not any brighter. After Brazil's first truly competitive presidential election in 1910, the proportion of voters grew to 5 percent. In 1945, more than 6 million voted, a 400 percent increase over 1933–34. There was, then, a constant growth in the electorate, which implies, as Gláucio Ary Dillon Soares recognizes, "a continuous extension of citizenship to less privileged social groups and classes."[66] There was further growth, to about 17 million voters, in 1966—a more than tenfold increase in the 1934 number of fewer than 1.5 million. After 1946, growing electoral participation brought greater power to the mass parties, leading new social classes to break into politics and support different parties.

The increased electoral participation of the nonelites would suffer a serious blow, however, causing damage to the electoral system that would be felt for four decades. The results of the elections of 1945 and 1947 did not please either the PCB or the Social Democratic Party (Partido Social Democrático, PSD) in the government, even though the former had managed some gains at the expense of other parties. The increasing popularity and the electoral success of the PCB led the government to deem it illegal.[67] In the same way that the constitutional amendments of 1935 opened the door to the authoritarian regime of 1937, the ban on the PCB soon after the 1946 constitution chipped away at the rule of law, throwing the mobilization of various currents of civil society into the extralegal arena. After the elections of January 1947, on 7 May 1948, the Dutra government got legal authorization from Congress to suppress the registration of the PCB, which was very strong in Rio and whose vote in São Paulo was larger than that of the National Democratic Union (União Democrática Nacional, UDN), Dutra's main opposition party. Consequently, Luiz Carlos Prestes was barred from fulfilling his Senate term, along with fourteen federal deputies and forty-six deputies in fifteen state assemblies and hundreds of municipal council members, weakening the credibility of the electoral system. The capacity of the political system to express popular claims was affected, thus lessening the break with the previous regime.[68] Obviously, the banning of the PCB cannot be explained solely by Brazilian political history since it corresponds to the headlong race of the United States and the entire American continent into the Cold War, in which confrontation with the Soviet Union and with Communist parties would be part of the obligatory alignment of old allies such as Brazil. Together with other processes at work in the postwar era in Brazil and the international community, outlawing the registration of the PCB pushed the country even further toward what would come to be described as "populist" politics. This loss of a channel for political representation of the working class would have irreparable consequences for the political system.[69] If there was ever a moment in which the PCB represented the working class, that moment was 1945–48.

If there was a pattern in the political evolution of Brazil in the twentieth century, it was the persistence with which the dominant classes scoffed at the chances for political representation of the popular classes. Blocking illiterates from voting on the 1946 constitution crippled the political representation of practically half of the electorate. The damage was greater if we consider the growth in the Brazilian population. According to the 1950 census, Brazil had 51,722,000 inhabitants. Of these, 1,256,307 were industrial workers and about 500,000 were bureaucrats. In the 1950s, the concentration of the population in urban centers, where social conflicts were more clearly exposed, increased. The main demands were for better salaries and lower cost of living. These desires were translated into strikes and public protests in the major cities.

After 1949, in their fight against the "defrauding of rights," the style and form of workers' actions changed, particularly among workers most involved in protest struggles. One began to notice activity through the "legal" channels of the moment, whether these were laws decreed or consolidated during the Estado Novo, new laws, or even older laws newly voted on and "naturalized" by the democratic administration that emerged from the New State. The assertions about the passivity of the labor movement during the populist governments, especially in the 1950s, belie the struggles for enforcement of and respect for the Vargas-era Consolidation of Labor Laws (Consolidação das Leis do Trabalho, CLT), which employers had dodged during the symbolic oversight of the Ministry of Labor. In addition to the beneficent role played by the unions "of insertion into the labor market and formation of a collective identity, the role of protest was also quite apparent: the struggle to recover, implement, and broaden rights as an exercise of and expansion of the boundaries of citizenship."[70]

The crises that drove Vargas to suicide on 24 August 1954 and later led to the overthrow of the constitutional president João Goulart on 31 March 1964 were preceded by social conflicts. In the major cities, there was a militant trade unionism, with workers fighting for better living conditions. This is not the place for a list of all of the demonstrations by civil society in the period. I will simply point out some events that showed independent manifestations of civil society in the supposed political activist void of the populist governments. In the 1950s, alongside the union struggles, there were innumerable protests demanding better salaries and living conditions in many cities of the country. In 1950, the Black movement held the First Black Brazilian Congress (Primeiro Congresso do Negro Brasileiro) and founded the National Congress of Black Women (Congresso Nacional das Mulheres Negras). From the mid-1950s to 1964, the neighborhood association movement grew, formed in large part by migrants who had arrived in the cities in search of employment.

One of the movements that had the greatest impact was the "strike of the 300,000" that began in São Paulo city in March 1953. A textile workers' protest movement had been classified as "social agitation" by the Regional Labor Office. As a consequence, negotiations were suspended, and the Textile Workers' Union (Sindicato dos Trabalhadores da Indústria Têxtil) started preparations for the strike. In addition to the textile workers, workers in other classes got involved: metalwork, woodwork, graphic industries, glass, civil construction, utilities, and public works. Demonstrations took over downtown São Paulo but were put down by the police. In the name of "maintenance of public order," "right to work," and "protection of private property," both Civil and Military Police clashed with workers, resulting in hundreds wounded and imprisoned. After a month, the strike ended, and the labor courts proposed a 32 percent adjustment instead of the 60 percent demanded, along with guarantees that the imprisoned leaders would be freed.

Police repression did not spare the demonstrations that followed the news of Vargas's suicide either, provoking violent popular uprisings in Rio in spite of the crackdown. The pattern of police actions was identical to that of prior decades. Agents of the Division of Political and Social Police (Divisão de Polícia Política e Social) under President Café Filho (1954–55) attacked the workers' movement. Labor organizations for workers in the hotel, shipping, metallurgy, furniture, textile, urban transport, sugar, and wheat industries had their offices invaded at night. About fifty trade unionists from these organizations, including presidents, treasurers, and militants, were arrested.[71]

It is a myth that the class struggle was suspended during the Kubitschek government (1956–60), which has been seen as an "oasis" of social peace.[72] On 15 October 1957, the "strike of the 400,000" against cost of living began and in the state of São Paulo lasted for ten days. This strike affected employees in the textile, metalworking, and graphic sectors and spread to other sectors. Far from being an "upper-echelon unionism out of touch with its bases,"[73] this was a strike by a union movement that sought to address the needs of workers. Police repression was felt after the third day of the strike, but the movement continued, with many demonstrations of solidarity from other social organizations and movements.

At the same time, there were various protests in the countryside. In 1954 Julião's Peasant Leagues, which arose among sugar workers in the state of Pernambuco, began to have an impact on Brazilian political life and were severely repressed (see chapter 2). In 1955, there were agrarian conflicts in the region of Formoso, in the state of Goiás, when migrants from other regions settled and organized themselves into councils to resist eviction. That same year, a rural tenants' movement burst forth in Santa Fé do Sul, in Rio Grande do Sul. The Formoso and Santa Fé movements each lasted a decade.

As Andrei Koerner points out, in the governments after 1946, "the previous pattern of activity in the area of criminal justice, in which the judiciary completed rather than managed the illegal practices of the police for controlling urban groups not yet incorporated into regulated citizenry," was accompanied, as it was before and after, by limited access to the courts.[74] A study of court cases in São Paulo in the 1950s shows continuity in the police and criminal procedures in controlling popular organizations and in criminalizing poor and Black people. Paulo Fontes has called my attention to the numerous cases against both patients and practitioners of abortion, with widespread use of violence.[75]

Depending on the administration, political repression rose or fell, but the debate about criminality and the ways of fighting it became clearer. The need also arose to control migrant populations that began to swell the city peripheries and suburbs and, in the case of Rio de Janeiro, the hillside favelas. The so-called Sertão Carioca (Rio Hinterland) in the West Zone of the municipality Rio de Janeiro—the districts of Campo Grande, Santa Cruz, and Guaratiba—had the largest concentration of voters: about 100,000.[76] São Paulo also had a large electorate. From their origins in 1946, the slums of São Paulo were stigmatized, with the help of police repression, as the home of hoods and bums (and, therefore, Blacks). They were in fact inhabited mostly by wage earners from São Paulo, spilling out of the inner city.[77]

The proposal to remove the urban favela dwellers to as-yet-uncreated distant industrial zones of Rio dates from the term of Carlos Lacerda (1960–65), governor of the state of Guanabara.[78] Amid these lofty "interests of the city" were matters of urban land use, since the favelas were often on valuable real estate in the South Zone of Rio, and the desire was to move these mostly Black and poor populations far away from mostly white affluent and middle-class neighborhoods. Several favelas were moved, over the strong resistance of their residents, to housing blocks far from the city, with precarious, only partially implemented transportation. Favela dwellers were stigmatized as criminals, but the South Zone of Rio offered them nearby opportunities for unskilled employment as maids, doormen, custodians, vendors, and masons.[79]

In the state of Guanabara there was also an incident of beggars being thrown into a river. Lacerda himself recalled the case: "Once I read in *Última Hora* that there appeared floating in the Guarda River near the Guandu River on the border with the old state of Rio, the body of a man who had been tied up, with bullet holes in the back of his neck, and that another had survived and gone to the police station in Santa Cruz or Campo Grande—I do not know where—and reported that the police had taken him there and thrown him into the river." When pressed by the governor, the secretary of security had explained that, "since a lot of beggars come to Rio, sometimes they do a cleanup like this in the city and return the beggars to their place of origin."[80] An inquest revealed that an employee in the Service for the Recuperation of Beggars (Serviço de Recuperação de Mendigos) had formed "a little 'death squad,' and with other aides had seized the beggar and gone to the Guarda River; arriving there, they tied him up, shot him, threw the body in the water, and left."

Both the removal of favela dwellers and the "cleanup" of the city by murdering beggars were practices that have as a common denominator the motivation of social prophylaxis so evident in the First Republic. The case of the beggars offers a glimpse of the formation of the first death squads by public employees, which were organized for political repression during the military dictatorship. One can see, therefore, a two-way exchange of practices of excessive use of force between democratic and dictatorial regimes.

In the 1950s and the 1960s, an entire police network that had infiltrated companies and the union movement continued to operate. Communication with personnel departments, often administered by retired policemen or military men, came to be truly friendly. Under populist governments, a solid business-police alliance was maintained, going back to 1924 in São Paulo, when the Department of Social and Political Order (Departamento de Ordem Política e Social, DOPS) was established. DOPS maintained permanent contact with companies, which sent lists of workers to check whether or not they were Communists. The police exercised control in the workplace as if the dictatorship had not ended. Cases of suspicion of theft in the factories continued to be investigated by DOPS, which was also charged with enforcing respect for price controls by small businessmen and vendors.

This period saw the rise of a police blotter press whose aim was to cover common crime and its repression, such as the newspapers *A Hora* and *O Dia*.[81] *Luta Democrática* was founded in 1954 by Tenório Cavalcanti, a populist deputy from the poor Rio suburb of Duque de Caxias. These newspapers adopted popular language and resorted to sensationalist appeals, such as ambiguous headlines, and they were well received by the popular classes. Cavalcanti himself was notorious for his violent political career. He cultivated his image as a vigilante, wrapped in a black cloak, which hid his machine gun, "Lurdinha," from which he was never apart.[82]

In later periods, the pattern of repression of the Estado Novo and the Dutra government only softened. It was not interrupted for the simple reason that the practices of law enforcement institutions remained fundamentally unaltered; the patterns were only modified. The Communists continued to be outlawed through the transition to dictatorship in 1964, submitted to different sorts of repression in each period. The federal and state governments preferred to infiltrate workers' organizations and try to develop a more qualified repression. After the 1945 transition, the intensity of illegal state repression was disguised in the attempt to reach groups of the powerless, just as after 1985, when only whites, students, and intellectuals were no longer the preferred targets of arbitrary violence. None of the innovations by dictatorships in the excessive use of force seem to have ceased in the democratic periods, for example, the illegal imprisonments, torture, and summary executions that continued to be used against the popular classes. There is promising research, still in the early stages, that shows that the populist governments did not renounce illegal practices in this period. During democratic regimes, the targets simply ceased being members of the white elites or the opposition. Thus, even during democratic eras, judicial procedures and police investigations were officially inquisitorial, making the systematic recourse to torture seem to be a "legitimate," albeit unofficial, means of obtaining confessions from common prisoners.[83]

"If Only Everyone Were like Tancredo!" From the Dictatorship of the Old *Tenentes* Emerges the New Republic, Again

On 30 March 1964, President Goulart appeared at a gathering of sergeants at the headquarters of the Automobile Club of Brazil in Rio de Janeiro. The president gave an improvised speech, broadcast on television, that emphasized the intermediary position of the sergeants between the armed forces and the people. He also denounced the defamatory campaigns and other difficulties created by his adversaries. This perceived interference in military discipline was the evidence that the civil and military conspirators needed of the president's "law breaking" to move up the coup to the next day. On the morning of 31 March, General Amaury Kruel, commander of the Second Army, in São Paulo, who had been vacillating in joining in the overthrow, proposed to the president closing the radical General Workers' Command (Comando Geral dos Trabalhadores, CGT) and the leftist National Student Union (União Nacional dos Estudantes, UNE), intervening in the unions, and removing aides accused of being Communists. If he did so, the general believed, Goulart could salvage his term:

"I cannot cast aside the popular forces that support me."

"Then, Mr. President, there is nothing we can do."[84]

Upon which occasion, the general ordered his troops to move on Rio. At night, I was keeping vigil with classmates at Rio's Jesuit Colégio Santo Inácio, in the auditorium of the headquarters of the Marian congregation, beautifully restored by architect Jorge Hue. At midnight, someone burst into the back of the room and announced that Kruel's tanks were arriving in the sleeping city. There was indeed nothing to be done.

Thus began the military regime responsible for grave human rights violations that affected tens of thousands of Brazilians for twenty-one years. The estimates of numbers of people arrested after the coup vary from 10,000 to 50,000. Illegal detention and, in particular, systematic use of torture, resulting in death in many cases, became a common practice of the dictatorship's security forces, made up of officers of the navy, air force, and army, and of the Civil and Military Police. More than 300 young people — students, workers, and militants — were kidnapped, imprisoned, tortured, murdered, and "disappeared." In 1982, three years after the passage of Brazil's political amnesty law, the number of exiles was estimated at 10,000.

Never before in Brazilian history had the state reached such sophistication and scope. Human rights violations were perpetrated by special units of the political police, such as DOPS and its counterparts in the states, the notorious Intelligence Operations Departments/Centers for Operations and Internal Defense (Departmento de Operações de Informações/Centro de Operações e Defesa Interna, DOI/CODI), and corresponding organs in the branches of the armed forces. Operação Bandeirantes (OBAN), named for the Paulista wilderness tamers of the colonial era, was founded during the administration of São Paulo governor Abreu Sodré (1967–71) and financed by São Paulo businessmen. OBAN engaged in kidnapping and torture. The military government's Institutional Act no. 2 (Ato Institucional no. 2, AI-2) of 1965, in the best Brazilian tradition of repression since the *tenentista* revolts of the 1920s and the National Security Court, granted jurisdiction for trying civilians in national security cases to military courts of the armed forces. Article 19 of this model of "exceptional" legislation determined that acts and decisions based on it were not subject to appeal or recourse to the civil judiciary.[85]

In the late phase of the military regime installed in 1964, that of the Abertura, "the slow, gradual, and secure [political] opening" launched by President General Ernesto Geisel (1974–79), the government began to dismantle the parallel organizations of repression and state terrorism, without renouncing illegal violence against dissidents. The leader of the "slow, gradual, and secure" transition himself declared in 1997 that he thought that the practice of torture was acceptable: "I think that torture in certain cases becomes necessary in order to obtain confessions. . . . I do not justify torture, but I recognize that there are circumstances in which the individual is impelled to practice torture to obtain certain confessions and thus avoid a greater evil."[86]

Beginning in the 1970s, the principles and concepts of human rights—civil and political as well as economic and social—emerged with the rise of new actors during the dictatorship. From 1970 to 1980, during the strikes in the ABC region of Greater São Paulo, the heart of the automobile and related metalworking industries, workers and residents united in movements pressing common demands.[87] By the early 1980s, social movements increasingly dedicated themselves to the promotion of social and economic rights among poor sectors of the population, amid growing social insecurity. This was not a mere "importation" of principles but rather the creation of themes and the definition of new strategies that would make civil society in Brazil as well as in the rest of South America and in eastern Europe the "big celebrities of change," in Juan Linz and Alfred Stepan's apt phrase.[88] New and unexpected forms of activism arose, such as the indigenous rights movement, which broadened and extended the agrarian reform agenda. Movements began for the defense of the rights of the most vulnerable groups, such as women, children, Blacks, homosexuals, and the disabled, as well as promotion of rights to housing, health, education, and environmental quality. Civil society's struggle for the restoration of the rule of law had the social movements as its support. These movements, in turn, were based on existing formal structures in society, such as universities, the Catholic Church, and the trade unions. The dictatorship itself had brought on this urgency for creating new means of popular participation in the destiny of the country, with the result that, toward the end of the dictatorship, an extremely dynamic network of social movements was being organized in both city and country.

The administration of President General João Figueiredo (1979–85) was the last military government. In 1982, though still under the exceptional regime, the state governors were chosen by direct elections for the first time since 1964. After 1983, Brazil was shaken by demonstrations in the capitals on a scale equal to those of the 1945 transition. The Direct Elections Now (Diretas Já) movement was launched by the recently elected governor of São Paulo, Franco Montoro (1983–87), who, still during the dictatorship, dared to convene a rally for direct elections in Cathedral Square in downtown São Paulo. On the day of the rally, 25 January 1984 (the birthday of the city), the University of São Paulo (USP) commemorated its fiftieth anniversary. The governor attended the celebration on campus. Upon his departure, as rain began to fall, he heard the news that Cathedral Square was filling up as the "rally of the 300,000" took shape. Congress did not pass the direct elections amendment, but the popular mobilization was the basis for the election of opposition candidates to the dictatorship's Electoral College and set the pace of the transition.

During the Direct Elections Now campaign of 1984, at least two games were being played simultaneously on separate boards. One game was the direct elections campaign: the trademark yellow color (selected by book editor Caio Graco Prado), the rallies and street demonstrations, and the opposition front formed by the Brazilian Democratic Movement Party (Partido do Movimento Democrático Brasileiro, PMDB), the Workers' Party (Partido dos Trabalhadores, PT), and the Democratic Labor Party (Partido Democrático Trabalhista, PDT). Another game was that played by veteran centrist politician Tancredo Neves. "Oh, if only everyone were like Tancredo," President Geisel had vented in 1977. Neves headed a group from the state of Minas Gerais and their São Paulo allies in a game to split the base of the government party with a view to the indirect election in the Electoral College. The government party, the Democratic Social Party (Partido Democrático Social, PDS),[89] was the heir to the official government party of the dictatorship. The PDS had nominated São Paulo governor Paulo Maluf for president. Though a civilian, Maluf alienated many through his coarse style and reputation for corruption. Neves siphoned off disaffected leaders of the PDS and formed the Liberal Front Party (Partido da Frente Liberal, PFL). This ad hoc party joined with the PMDB in the Electoral College, forming the Democratic Alliance (Aliança Democrática) to elect the opposition slate with Neves as president and José Sarney as vice president. Neves's good relations with the military ensured its neutrality in the succession. In spite of the failure of the Direct Elections Now campaign, the Brazilian public happily embraced its first civilian president in twenty-one years.

Neves died from complications from an abdominal infection on the eve of his inauguration. As a result, Sarney constitutionally succeeded him. Sarney was a conservative PDS politician from the Northeast whom Neves had put on the ticket as a political concession to PDS allies and defectors. Even so, Sarney sought to maintain the centrist opposition coalition that had come to power. Brazil's motto could be "Traditione cum transitione semper"—no transition without betrayal. The root meanings of the two Latin terms, "transmitting" and "passing through" respectively, appear to be confused in practice. Amid rumors of a coup toward the end of the Figueiredo administration, English sociologist Ian Roxborough retorted sarcastically, "Coup? What coup? It already happened. It is the Democratic Alliance!"[90]

The Direct Elections Now campaign brought up to date two trends in Brazilian history in every transition to democracy. On the one hand, popular mobilization and independent street demonstrations pressured the rather inert political parties and media, which found themselves obliged to cover that mobilization. This foreshadowed a later rupture. On the other hand, there was the Bernardo Pereira de Vasconcelos syndrome, so called for the liberal politician who was in the opposition in 1827 but became a "regressive" ten years later when he came into the government, compelled to put the brakes on the "revolutionary carriage." "Let's have a revolution before the people have one," as was said in 1930. These threats are almost always mirages, mere fantasies that confuse timid attempts at popular protest with real subversion of the order. In the Brazilian *transitione*, progressive elites thus prefer to reconcile with the former conservatives (now mutated into democrats), ally with them, and gain power through a less risky route. This was the case in the run-up to the 1985 Electoral College set up by the dictatorship. A doubt lingers as to whether the interruption of the Direct Elections Now campaign after the defeat of the amendment was the best course of action for the democratic transition.

The 1985 transition began with the election of an opposition slate by the Electoral College and the inauguration of Sarney as president, and it was completed with the Constituent Assembly's draft of a new constitution. The 1988 constitution incorporated a wide array of guarantees and rights, especially Article 5 with its seventy-seven clauses, constituting an authentic bill of rights, the broadest and most precise in Brazilian constitutional history. The innovations over previous republican periods were its vitality and capacity for the reinvention of civil society. The last two decades of the twentieth century were marked by increased participation of civil society in different areas of societal government, and nongovernmental organizations asserted their role as one of the main foundations for the process of democratic consolidation. There is no doubt that this process, which took shape after the "third wave" of democratic transitions in Latin America, eastern Europe, and the former Soviet Union in the 1980s, fostered the emergence and strengthening of five integrated and mutually sustaining arenas. These five, as proposed by Linz and Stepan, were civil society, political society, the rule of law, state apparatus (a "usable" state), and economic society.[91] It happens that, in the same "fields of force" where there is constant mediation among the five arenas of the process of democratic consolidation, other fields of force survive that are intrinsically opposed to them and that democratization cannot erase. As Linz and Stepan show, these have weighty implications for the possible paths of democratization and for the tasks that the new democracies will face in the process of consolidation.

These elements are present in the "negative arenas" that persist in spite of the transition and the changes in Brazilian social configuration. They are "uncivil" society (political society barely submitted to the control of nonelites and with low prestige), the "unrule" of law for the enthralled majority of nonelites, and an "unusable" state. The unusable state is drowning in clientelism, nepotism, corruption, and, nowadays, organized crime, and it is marked by lack of access to the courts and by institutions that lack accountability, such as the police. To these we add an economic society that flouts regulation and is likewise marked by corruption and illegality, such as systematic tax evasion and fraud.

Today, when, as yesterday, gangs of thugs protect large rural landholdings, in the metropolises the state monopoly on legitimate violence has been so weakened that individual survival in many communities may depend on one's ability to maintain one's reputation by displaying a "credible threat of violence." The increase in criminality after democratic transitions in Brazil, as in South Africa and Russia, has undermined expectations about democracy and helped to legitimate excessive use of force, thus weakening the legitimacy of the political system.[92]

The Paradoxes of Democracy

Two decades after the wave of redemocratization in Latin America, the effective protection of human rights is still an unfulfilled promise. Political regimes are considered democratic because the constitutional government has been restored and because government officials are chosen in free, competitive elections. As we have seen, the former, at least, was never a guarantee of democracy in the Brazilian republic. Evidently, as Lúcio Kowarick has reminded us, one cannot say that "there is a deficit of democracy in the Brazilian political system": compare the mere 7.4 million voters, or 16 percent of the population, in the 1945 election with the 100 million voters in the 1996 municipal elections—two-thirds of the population.[93] *Political* democracy, however, continues to be marked by authoritarian legacies embedded in the governments, the agents of the state.

In South America, this paradox is perhaps most dramatically evident in Brazil. The advent of democracy has not put an end to illegal state violence even though the federal government does not support it. The state does not ignore the serious human rights violations committed by its agents during the "parallel exceptional state" of the oligarchic First Republic or after the 1945 transition and the populist democratic governments. In spite of this, however, in the context of exploding homicide and other crime rates and agrarian conflicts, the agents of state governments continue to commit severe human rights violations. When I served in Montoro's government, my colleague Eduardo Muylaert, special assistant to the governor, with whom I shared an office in Bandeirantes Palace (the São Paulo state government building), asked the Civil and Military Police to communicate to him all of the police killings that occurred each day. To my surprise, we received one day three large envelopes sent to our office by mistake. They contained detailed information from the Civil Police about union meetings and movements, which were ritually sent to the Bandeirantes Palace and piled up, as I later learned, without ever being opened or read by the governor.

Even though Brazil was the ninth-largest economy in the world by the end of the century, it had an annual rate of 25 homicides per 100,000 inhabitants, a rate higher than that of any of the seven largest economies. The United States, the most violent of the G7 countries, has a homicide rate of 12 per 100,000. In 1997 there were in Brazil 40,000 homicides among a population of 156 million. Brazil is the Latin American country with the worst distribution of income, a situation that, if it does not clearly explain it, at least contributes to the endemic violence, in which the victimization is concentrated among the poor majority and disproportionately affects Blacks. Research has shown that countries with racial discrimination and poor income distribution, like Brazil and the United States, tend to have higher homicide rates.

After 1985, the Brazilian government began to reactivate organs like the Council for the Defense of Human Rights (Conselho de Defesa dos Direitos da Pessoa Humana, CDDPH), the first human rights council, established within the Ministry of Justice in March 1964 by Goulart. CDDPH had as its mission to bring perpetrators of human rights abuses to account, an obligation that it had assumed before the international community upon the ratification of human rights treaties in the 1990s. At the end of the twentieth century, many institutions in the sphere of responsibility of state governments contributed to undermining the rule of law, rather than safeguarding it, through the use of brutal and lethal tactics to deal with violence. Evidence of this is the systematic torture from October 1999 to September 2000 of youth offenders interned at the youth detention center of the São Paulo Foundation for the Welfare of Minors (Fundação Estadual do Bem-Estar do Menor, FEBEM), some for having reported such torture. Another example is the massacre of militants of the MST by Military Police and thugs from a security firm in the employ of landowners, as in September 2000 in Mato Grosso do Sul. The police tend to see the rule of law more as an obstacle than as a guarantee of public safety. They act as "border guards," protecting the families of the dominant classes from the poor, the preferential targets of crime and repression.[94] Even though Brazil was one of the first countries to sign the UN Convention against Torture in 1985, systematic torture in the precinct stations still goes on, and summary executions of suspects by the police are an epidemic. "Undesirables" are no longer internally exiled as during the First Republic; they are killed. In 1999, in the city of São Paulo, the Military Police killed 330 civilians. Many of these, as recent research by the São Paulo auditor's office shows, were summary executions. Off-duty police killed another 187. There was a similar number of victims in the city of Rio during the same year. Between January and July 2000 alone, the Military Police of the state of São Paulo killed 449 citizens. If we compare Brazil to other democratic countries (except those where there are insurrection and civil war), the highest rate of lethal police violence in the world is in Brazil.

Other sorts of perpetrators of violence are vigilantes, extermination groups, death squads, and hired guns who kill crime suspects. Another source of violence is the gangs that operate in the peripheries, slums, and favelas of the urban centers, often with the participation or complicity of the Military or Civil Police. This illegal violence is expressed in lynchings, committed by mobs mainly in large cities like São Paulo, Rio de Janeiro, and Salvador. These mobs are incited to act illegally by victims of crime or their families and sometimes by local authorities, such as mayors or council members. In most cases, the lynchings aim to execute criminal suspects caught in the act or, in some cases, even removed by force from jails or prisons.

The judiciary is not considered an institution that protects the rights of the underprivileged but rather an institution responsible for the criminalization and repression of the popular classes. Access to the courts practically does not exist for the poor. Blacks convicted of crimes receive harsher penalties than do their white counterparts, revealing a racial bias in sentencing, as Sérgio Adorno has shown in São Paulo.[95] Judicial authorities have failed to prosecute recent serious violations in spite of irrefutable evidence.

The accomplishments of the Brazilian state in the twentieth century were impressive: a society founded on an agricultural economy recently freed from slavery became the ninth-largest economy in the world by the end of the century.

The state showed extraordinary efficacy in appropriating the country's resources for its transformation. At the same time, these resources were concentrated among privileged groups that succeeded one another throughout the century. We are now faced with "a giant machine for manufacturing poverty," to borrow novelist Arundhati Roy's description of the Indian state. It is a machine for concentrating wealth and tossing crumbs to the poor. In spite of the political transition of 1985 and of Brazil's dramatic changes in the last twenty years of the twentieth century, the pattern of income distribution inequality, one of the worst in the world, is practically unchanged. This inequality has been surprisingly stable, except for a slight decline between 1989 and 1992. After 1994, during the Real Plan, even though inflation had been contained and poverty had seen an important reduction, there was no evidence of any significant reduction of inequality, which reached its highest level in two decades in 1998.[96]

Inadequate protection and promotion of human rights continue to be among the main shortcomings for Brazilian civil society. This situation presents tremendous challenges for human rights organizations, forcing them to evaluate rights and define strategies for the new circumstances, with a view to creating effective, viable mechanisms for safeguarding human rights, particularly those of the poorest. A list of the principle areas of intervention by organizations sounds like complaints from past centuries: absence of the rule of law, inaccessibility of the legal system for nonelites, structural racism and racial discrimination, and the impunity of state agents involved in serious human rights violations. As we have seen, the new democracy continues to be affected by a "socially implanted authoritarianism": a combination of elements present in Brazilian political culture, values, and ideology, in part engendered by the military dictatorship, expressed in daily life. Many of these elements are entrenched in institutions whose roots date to the 1930s. Labor is a case in point. As an indication of the extraordinary longevity and efficacy of the labor laws from the 1930s, the issue put before the labor movement fifty years after its creation, in the 1980s, was to determine whether these laws should be preserved or abolished. The long life and versatility of institutions such as the labor legislation, police structure, and the systems for surveillance of the popular classes constitute a monument to modern strategies of control of nonelites. In spite of public opinion polls that indicate adherence to the values of the rule of law, there is remarkable acquiescence by large segments of the population to the excessive use of force and illegal practices of many state institutions. These include deaths caused by police, torture, inhumane prison conditions, murder of street children and adolescents, and official impunity.

Contemporary civil society in the midst of the endemic violence that has lasted from the military dictatorship into the New Republic finds itself faced with issues that are fundamental for the state: the functions of the state monopoly on physical violence and the search for pacification, the peaceful coexistence of citizens, and a permanent resolution of the problem of controlling private violence. As the twentieth century drew to a close, human rights organizations were confronted with challenges that went beyond simple documentation and indictment of human rights violations that had helped in the resistance to the military dictatorship. In the new century, democratic consolidation demands new ties between autonomous spheres of society and political institutions to exercise the social control of public policies and contribute to their renewal.

In 1996, the government of Fernando Henrique Cardoso (1994–2002) launched the National Human Rights Program (Programa Nacional de Direitos Humanos, PNDH). Prepared for the Ministry of Justice by USP's Center for the Study of Violence (Núcleo de Estudos da Violência, NEV-USP) with hundreds of human rights organizations in Brazil, the program consisted of more than 260 proposals in the areas of civil and political rights. The plan expressed awareness that, to control completely endemic violence, it was necessary to face the structural violence of poverty, hunger, and unemployment. In terms of immediate action, the program envisioned strengthening the rule of law in Brazil. By 2000, a good number of the program's plans had been implemented by the Cardoso government, and the document became a reference point for the mobilization and organization of civil society, often in partnership with state agencies. Currently, Brazilian society has new instruments at its disposal, such as police ombudsmen in São Paulo, Belém, Belo Horizonte, and Rio, as well as a public ministry with renewed powers to fight abuses of power of the state, that Janus-faced god that both protects rights and perpetrates violations. Some relevant laws have been introduced to deal with the authoritarian legacy, including the criminalization of torture; civil jurisdiction over homicides committed by Military Police agents, now tried by a jury of peers; the civilian system of arms control and the outlawing of bearing of arms; and federal jurisdiction over crimes against human rights. Child labor and forced labor have been addressed as never before. In 1997, the government created a secretariat for human rights within the Ministry of Justice that, in 1999, was turned into the Secretariat of State for Human Rights (Secretaria de Estado de Direitos Humanos).[97]

At the same time, structural obstacles persist that need to be overcome to guarantee the implementation of human rights policies. The missing step continues to be institutional reform, for example, of the judiciary and the police. In spite of returning jurisdiction over crimes committed by Military Police to civilian power and in spite of some successful convictions, the efforts of the public ministry charged with prosecuting these crimes, which include murder and participation in massacres, have suffered many reversals. Often, these occur because the crimes committed by Military Police are investigated by amateurish Military Police Inquests (Inquérito Militares Policiais, IMPs) that gather insufficient evidence, as happened in the case of the 1995 Corumbiara massacre, in which police attacked MST families occupying land in the state of Rondônia. Nine of the fourteen Military Police agents charged were absolved in September 2000. The impunity of state agents who commit crimes against poor victims considered "undesirable" or "subhuman" is still virtually assured. Seven years after the 1993 massacre of 111 prisoners in the Carandiru house of detention in São Paulo, none of the more than 100 indicted policemen had been tried. In 2001, the commander of the Military Police operation against Carandiru, Colonel Ubiratan Guimarães, was convicted and sentenced to 632 year in prison for his role in the massacre, but the conviction was overturned in 2006.

Seen from the perspective of human rights, there are more points on which the populist democracy, the military regime, and the current democracy are similar than in which they differ. Just as the 1946 transition did not erase the traces of the Estado Novo, the legacy of the 1964 regime was not eliminated in 1988. In some instances, the legacy was incorporated into the 1988 constitution, as in the case of the public security system. The law enforcement structure set by the military dictatorship was rigidly preserved in the constitution. The authoritarian regime of 1964–85 and the constitutional regime of 1988 run the risk of going down in history as differing expressions of the same structure of domination.

Establishing the rule of law is crucial for democratic governability. Recent experience suggests the need, along with the formal recognition of rights, for institutionalizing public policies capable of preventing human rights violations. A poll conducted in 1999 by Nancy Cardia of NEV-USP in ten Brazilian state capitals shows that Brazilians prefer the law to death squad vigilantism and that a majority oppose torture and police brutality. Most of those interviewed support the legitimacy of strikes and peaceful social protests.[98] These results indicate that, in spite of the authoritarian legacies of the distant and recent past, and in spite of the extremely low rates of support for democracy in some other polls, there is in fact a democratic sensibility in the population.

The democratic government has yet to break with the systematic exclusion of the impoverished majority and eliminate once and for all the structural racism that continues to afflict persons of African descent so as to guarantee civil and political rights to all citizens. When it does, the government will finally have established a state within the full rule of law and thus avoided the risk of simply promoting democracy without citizenship.[99] More than a century after the proclamation of the republic, Brazil still must break with the past.

Notes

I want to thank the State of São Paulo Research Foundation (Fundação de Amparo à Pesquisa do Estado de São Paulo, FAPESP) and the National Council for Scientific and Technological Development (Conselho Nacional de Desenvolvimento Científico e Tecnológico, CNPq) for their support. I also want to thank my friend Michael M. Hall for his generous critical readings among numerous other contributions; Jorge Wilheim for his careful reading of the text and valuable corrections; and Ignacy Sachs and Afrânio Garcia for having suggested the topic, and for their commentaries on the first presentation of the text in their seminar at the School for Advanced Studies in Social Sciences (École des Hautes Études en Sciences Sociales, EHESS), Paris, January 2000. I must give special thanks for the generosity of Paulo Fontes, who did his doctorate in social history at the University of Campinas. His valuable suggestions were inserted into the section of the essay on criminality and police repression during the period of populist democracy of 1950–64. I am most grateful to Ambassador Rubens Barbosa for his generous support for the translation of this book. Of course, responsibility for the final essay is mine alone.

1. Raul Amaro Nin Ferreira graduated in engineering from the Pontifical Catholic University of Rio de Janeiro, where we were classmates. A generous and gentle human being, he was tortured and murdered by the apparatus of clandestine repression of the military dictatorship in May 1971.

2. Murray Kempton, "The Genius of Mussolini," in *Rebellions, Perversities, and Main Events* (New York: Times Books, 1994), 32.

3. Charles Wiener, *333 jours au Brésil* (Paris: Librairie Charles Delagrave, 1911), 22–23.

4. Elizabeth Hardwick, "Sad Brazil," in *Bartleby in Manhattan and Other Essays* (London: Weidenfeld and Nicolson, 1983), 246.

5. Alured Gray Bell, *The Beautiful Rio de Janeiro* (London: William Heinemann, [1914]), 18–19.

6. Ibid., 18.

7. L. E. Elliott, *Brazil, Today and Tomorrow* (New York: Macmillan, 1922), 79–80.

8. C. Reginald Enock, *The Republics of Central and South America* (London: J. Dent and Sons, 1913), 69.

9. See Roberto DaMatta's seminal essay "'Do You Know Who You're Talking To?!' The Distinction between Individual and Person in Brazil," in *Carnivals, Rogues, and Heroes: An Interpretation of the Brazilian Dilemma* (Notre Dame, Ind.: Notre Dame University Press, 1991), 137–97.

10. See Michel Debrun's masterful work *Gramsci: Filosofia, política e bom senso* (Campinas: Editora da Universidade Estadual de Campinas; Centro de Logísitica, 2001).

11. I am using Norbert Elias's concept of configuration. See especially Norbert Elias, *La société de cour* (Paris: Flammarion, 1985).

12. Michel Debrun, *A conciliação e outras estratégias* (São Paulo: Brasiliense, 1983). Also see José Honório Rodrigues, *Conciliação e reforma no Brasil* (Rio de Janeiro: Civilização Brasileira, 1965).

13. C. G. Jung, *Four Archetypes* (Princeton, N.J.: Princeton University Press, 1992), 13. The application of Jung's ideas is my responsibility.

14. Debrun, *A conciliação e outras estratégias*, 15.

15. Here I am using the notion of *trasformismo* coined by Antonio Gramsci. See especially Antonio Gramsci, *Quaderni del carcere*, vol. 2, *Quaderni 6–11 (1930–1931)* (Rome: Einaudi, 1977), §5, 939–40, §36, 962.

16. "With the edge of all food, clothing, and housing problems thus blunted, and the size and strength of his heaven and earth enforcing on the richest inhabitant a certain simplicity of soul, Politics, in the baser sense of the word, became a rather risky, but high class sport." Rudyard Kipling, *Brazilian Sketches* (New York: Doubleday, 1940), 108.

17. John Keane, *Reflections on Violence* (London: Verso, 1996), 63. See also John Keane, *Civil Society* (Oxford: Polity Press, 1998).

18. See Juan Méndez, Guillermo O'Donnel, and Paulo Sérgio Pinheiro, eds., *The (Un)rule of Law and the Underprivileged in Latin America* (Notre Dame: University of Notre Dame Press, 1999), 2.

19. Debrun, *A conciliação e outras estratégias*, 15.

20. Paulo Singer, "Movimentos sociais em São Paulo: Traços comuns e perspectivas," in *São Paulo, o povo em movimento*, by Paulo Singer and Vinicius Caldeira Brant (Petrópolis: Vozes/Centro Brasileiro de Análise e Planejamento, 1980), 218.

21. Emiliano José, *Carlos Marighela* (São Paulo: Sol e Chuva, 1997), 194.

22. W. D. Newman, *The Politics of Aristotle* (Oxford, 1927), 1:223, quoted in Moses Finley, *L'invention de la politique* (Paris: Champs, Flammarion, 1985), 22. In the following argument, I rely heavily and liberally on Sir Moses Finley.

23. N. W. Frederiksen, *Journal of Roman Studies* 57 (1967): 254, quoted in Finley, *L'invention de la politique*, 28.

24. Harold Laski, *The State in Theory and Practice* (London, 1935), 57–58, quoted in Finley, *L'invention de la politique*, 30.

25. Élysée Reclus, *República dos Estados Unidos do Brasil: Geographia, etnographia, estatística* (Rio de Janeiro/Paris: H. Garnier, 1900), 432.

26. José Murilo de Carvalho, *Os bestializados* (São Paulo: Companhia das Letras, 1987), 51.

27. Albert Hale, *The South Americans* (Indianapolis: Bobbs-Merrill, 1907), 231. The Brazilian census of 1890 put the rate of illiteracy at four-fifths of the population.

28. Herman G. James, *Brazil after a Century of Independence* (New York: Macmillan, 1925), 525–26.

29. Reclus, *República dos Estados Unidos do Brasil*, 432–33.

30. P. Taft and P. Ross, "American Labor Violence: Its Causes, Character and Outcome," in *Violence in America*, ed. H. D. Graham and T. R. Gurr, 281, quoted in Michael Mann, *The Rise of Classes and Nation-States: 1760–1914*, vol. 2 of *The Sources of Social Power* (Cambridge: Cambridge University Press, 1993), 664. For more information on this comparison, see Mann, *Rise of Classes and Nation-States*, 650.

31. *Fanfulla*, 4 July 1900, quoted in Michael M. Hall and Paulo Sérgio Pinheiro, "The Control and Policing of the Working Class in Brazil" (paper presented at the Conference on the History of Law, Labour and Crime, University of Warwick, 15–19 September 1983), 4.

32. *Fanfulla*, 11 September 1904, quoted in Hall and Pinheiro, "Control and Policing of the Working Class in Brazil," 3–4.

33. *Fanfulla*, 10 January 1901, quoted in Hall and Pinheiro, "Control and Policing of the Working Class in Brazil," 5.

34. Boris Fausto, *A criminalidade em São Paulo* (São Paulo: Brasiliense, 1984); Boris Fausto, "Urban Crime in Brazil: The Case of São Paulo, 1880–1924" (Working Paper 87, Woodrow Wilson Center Latin American Program, Washington, D.C., 1981), 3–4; Boris Fausto, "Controle social e criminalidade em São Paulo: Um apanhado geral (1880–1924)," in *Crime, violência e poder*, ed. Paulo Sérgio Pinheiro (São Paulo: Brasiliense, 1983), 197.

35. Bell, *Beautiful Rio de Janeiro*, 162.

36. Ibid., 164.

37. Nevin Winter, *Brazil and Her People of To-day* (Boston: Page, 1910), 66.

38. Paul Walle, *Au Brésil: De l'Uruguay au rio São Francisco* (Paris: E. Guilmoto, [1912]), 32.

39. Afonso Henriques de Lima Barreto, *Diário íntimo* (São Paulo: Brasiliense, 1965), 49. For a concise description of the Vaccine Revolt and its context, see Shawn C. Smallman, *Fear and Memory in the Brazilian Army and Society, 1889–1954* (Chapel Hill: University of North Carolina Press, 2002), 22–25.

40. Alan K. Manchester, "Reminiscences of a Latin American Revolution," *South Atlantic Quarterly* 32, no. 1 (January 1933): 78. I am grateful to Michael Hall for pointing out this text to me.

41. Blaise Cendrars, "A revolução de 1924," in *Etc . . . etc . . . : Um livro 100 percent brasileiro* (São Paulo: Perspectiva, 1976), 86.

42. See Decree no. 19398 in vol. 3 of *Coleção das leis do Brasil* (1930), 72, cited in Karl Loewenstein, *Brazil under Vargas*, new ed. (1942; New York: Russell and Russell, 1973), 17 n. 2. This book, first published after the author's visit to Brazil and published in a new edition in 1973, is one of the best studies of the workings of the Estado Novo. At the same time, it is quite possible that the eminent Austrian jurist, a refugee in the United States, was excessively impressed by his treatment by the Brazilian authorities during his visit to the country.

43. Astrojildo Pereira, "Campo de batalha," in *URSS, Itália, Brasil* (São Paulo, 1985), 131–32, quoted in Paulo Sérgio Pinheiro, *Estratégias da ilusão* (São Paulo: Companhia das Letras, 1992), 259. Originally founded as the Communist Party of Brazil (Partido Comunista do Brasil, PCB), the name was changed to Partido Comunista Brasileiro in 1961. It should not be confused with the Partido Comunista do Brasil (PCdoB) founded in 1962.

44. Reynaldo Pompeu de Campos, *Repressão judicial no Estado Novo* (Rio de Janeiro: Achiamé, 1982), 34.

45. Loewenstein, *Brazil under Vargas*, 19.

46. Quoted in Heath Bowman and Stirling Dickinson, *Westward from Rio* (Chicago, New York: Willett, Clark and Company, 1936), 19.

47. Getúlio Vargas, *Diário* (São Paulo: Siciliano/Editora da Fundação Getúlio Vargas, Rio de Janeiro, 1995), 1:456.

48. Loewenstein, *Brazil under Vargas*, 29.

49. For information about repression after 1964, see Archdiocese of São Paulo, *Torture in Brazil*, ed. Joan Dassin, trans. Jaime Wright (Austin: University of Texas Press, 1998).

50. "The first year of the *dictatorship*, 1931, was a year of rigorous economy, cuts in expenses, reduction of payments—beginning with the president of the republic, suspension of works, etc." Vargas, *Diário*, 1:416 (my emphasis).

51. Ibid.

52. Loewenstein, *Brazil under Vargas*, 46.

53. On Estado Novo repression, see Campos, *Repressão judicial no Estado Novo*, and Elizabeth Cancelli, *O mundo da violência: A polícia da era de Vargas* (Brasília: Universidade de Brasília, 1991).

54. Hall and Pinheiro, "Control and Policing of the Working Class in Brazil," 17–19.

55. Carmen Miranda (1909–55), the internationally famous singer and actress, known in the United States as the Brazilian Bombshell, and Felinto Müller (1900–1973), former *tenente* and Vargas's feared Federal Police chief.

56. Laski, *State in Theory and Practice*, 57–58, quoted in Finley, *L'invention de la politique*, 30.

57. Paulo Iumati, *Diários políticos de Caio Prado Júnior, 1945* (São Paulo: Brasiliense, 1998). See also M. L. T. Carneiro, *O anti-semitismo na era de Vargas* (São Paulo: Brasiliense, 1994).

58. Peter Flynn, *Brazil* (Boulder, Colo.: Westview, 1978), 137–38.

59. The first author to use the concept "authoritarian" in regard to the Estado Novo was Loewenstein. See Loewenstein, "A Discourse on Political Terminology: Is Brazil a Fascist State?" in *Brazil under Vargas*, 370–76.

60. Debrun, *A conciliação e outras estratégias*, 16.

61. *Dicionário histórico-biográfico brasileiro, 1930–1983*, ed. Israel Beloch and Alzira Alves de Abreu (Rio de Janeiro: Forense Universitária, Financiadora de Estudos e Projetos, 1984), 1144–45. For the reconstitution of the facts of this period, at several points in this essay I have used Marly Rodrigues, *A década de 50* (São Paulo: Ática, 1996); Maria Helena Simões Paes, *A década de 60* (São Paulo: Ática, 1997); Nadine Habert, *A década de 70* (São Paulo: Ática, 1996); Marly Rodrigues, *A década de 80* (São Paulo: Ática, 1999); and Darcy Ribeiro, *Aos trancos e barrancos* (Rio de Janeiro: Guanabara, 1985).

62. Marco Antônio Coelho, *Herança de um sonho* (São Paulo: Record, 2000), 105, 111, 121. After I finalized this text, Thaís Battibugli's "Democracia e Seguranca Publica em São Paulo (1946–1964)" (Ph.D. diss., Universidade de São Paulo, 2006) appeared. It is a rigorous analysis of the use of illegal violence under a democratic government, a question usually neglected by the studies of this period.

63. Debrun, *A conciliação e outras estratégias*, 16.

64. Cliff Welch, *The Seed Was Planted* (University Park: Pennsylvania State University Press, 1999), 105, 108.

65. J-J. de Santa-Anna Nery, ed., *Le Brésil en 1889* (Paris: Librairie Charles Delagrave, 1889), 202.

66. Gláucio Ary Dillon Soares, *Sociedade e política no Brasil* (São Paulo: Difusão Européia do Livro, 1973), 40–41.

67. Welch, *Seed Was Planted*, 113.

68. All of these records, only a sample of the pattern of illegal repression of the period, are from the newspaper *Jornal da Manhã* of São Paulo. I am grateful to Ana Luiza Pinheiro for collaboration on this research.

69. Flynn, *Brazil*, 140.

70. Alexandre Fortes, "Revendo a legalização dos sindicatos: Metalúrgicos de Porto Alegre (1931–1945)," in Alexandre Fortes, Antonio Luigi Negro, Fernando Teixeira da Silva, Helio da Costa, and Paulo Fontes, *Na luta por direitos: Estudos recentes em história social do trabalho* (São Paulo: Editora da Universidade de Campinas, 1999), 27.

71. *Última Hora*, 25 August 1954, extra edition, 4, quoted in Jorge Luís Pereira, "O car-

naval de tristeza: Os motins urbanos de 24 de agosto," in *Vargas e a crise dos anos 50*, ed. Angela de Castro Gomes (Rio de Janeiro: Relume Dumará, 1994), 72.

72. Paulo Fontes, "Centenas de estopins acesos ao mesmo tempo: A greve dos 400 mil, piquetes e organização dos trabalhadores em São Paulo," in Fortes et al., *Na luta por direitos*, 153.

73. Ibid.

74. Andrei Koerner, "Judiciário democrático, reforma do Estado e cidadania no Brasil." The author kindly shared with me a preliminary version.

75. Paulo Fontes, interview by the author, São Paulo, 2001.

76. Marly Silva da Motta, *Saudades da Guanabara* (Rio de Janeiro: Editora da Fundação Getúlio Vargas, 2000), 46.

77. Nabil G. Bonduki, "Origens da habitação social no Brasil (1930–1954)" (Ph.D. diss., University of São Paulo, 1994), 157.

78. The former Federal District until the move of the federal capital to Brasília. It is now coterminous with the municipality of Rio de Janeiro, within the state of Rio de Janeiro.

79. Bonduki, "Origens da habitação social no Brasil," 62.

80. Carlos Lacerda, *Depoimento* (Rio de Janeiro: Nova Fronteira, 1987), 268.

81. Paulo Fontes, personal communication.

82. "Tenório Cavalcanti," in *Dicionário histórico-biográfico brasileiro*, 1:758.

83. Roberto Kant de Lima, "Bureaucratic Rationality in Brazil and in the United States: Criminal Justice Systems in Comparative Perspective," in *The Brazilian Puzzle: Culture on the Borderlands of the Western World*, ed. David J. Hess and Roberto A. DaMatta (New York: Columbia University Press, 1995), 246.

84. The source of this exchange is Alberto Dines et al., *Os Idos de Março*, 144, quoted in Thomas Skidmore, *Politics in Brazil, 1930–1964: An Experiment in Democracy* (New York: Oxford University Press, 1967), 300, which summarizes the events of 29–31 March 1964.

85. See Archdiocese of São Paulo, *Torture in Brazil*, and Wolfgang S. Heinz and Hugo Frühling, *Determinants of Gross Human Rights Violations by State and State-Sponsored Actors in Brazil, Uruguay, Chile, and Argentina, 1960–1990* (The Hague: Martinus Nijhoff Publishers, 1999), 65–67.

86. Geisel quoted in Maria Celina D'Araújo and Célio Castro, *Ernesto Geisel* (Rio de Janeiro: Editora da Fundação Getúlio Vargas, 1997), 225.

87. Lúcio Kowarick, "Lutas urbanas e movimentos populares," in *Escritos urbanos* (São Paulo: Editora 34, 2000), 65.

88. Juan Linz and Alfred Stepan, *A transição e a consolidação da democracia: A experiência do sul da Europa e da América do Sul* (São Paulo: Paz e Terra, 1999).

89. The PDS should not be confused with the pro-Vargas PSD of the Third Republic

or with the Brazilian Social Democracy Party (Partido da Social Democracia Brasileira, PSDB), the party of Fernando Henrique Cardoso, founded in 1988.

90. Ian Roxborough, interview by the author, New York, 1993.

91. Linz and Stepan, *A transição e a consolidação da democracia*, 25–33.

92. Many studies of South America have demonstrated this. In 2000, South Africa and the city of São Paulo had homicide rates of about 55 per 100,000 inhabitants, more than double the Brazilian national rate of 25 and about five times that of the United States, the industrialized country with the highest homicide rates, as we will see.

93. Lúcio Kowarick, "Fatias de nossa história recente," in *Escritos urbanos*, 108.

94. I owe this image to Aryeh Neier, former director of Human Rights Watch, who used it when he was visiting Brazil in 1987.

95. Sérgio Adorno, "Racial Discrimination and Criminal Justice in São Paulo," in *Race in Contemporary Brazil: From Indifference to Inequality*, ed. Rebecca Reichmann (University Park: Pennsylvania State University Press, 1999), 123–38.

96. For more on the Real Plan, see chapter 3. On recent poverty and inequality, see the seminal article by Ricardo Paes Barros, Ricardo Henriques, and Rosane Mendonça, "Desigualdade e pobreza no Brasil: Retrato de uma estabilidade inaceitável," *Revista Brasileira de Ciências Sociais* 15, no. 42 (February 2000): 135–36.

97. It is relevant for the reader to bear in mind that, after the publication of this chapter, in November 2002, I was appointed secretary of state for human rights, with Aloysio Nunes Ferreira as minister of justice, by President Cardoso. I stayed in the government until December 2003.

98. Nancy Cardia, *Primeira pesquisa sobre atitudes, normas culturais e valores em relação à violência em 10 capitais brasileiras* (Brasília: Ministério da Justiça/Secretaria de Estado dos Direitos Humanos, 1999).

99. I developed these ideas in "Democracies without Citizenship," *NACLA Report on the Americas* 30, no. 2 (1996): 17–33; in "Popular Responses to State-Sponsored Violence in Brazil," in *The New Politics of Inequality in Latin America*, ed. Douglas A. Chalmers, Carlos M. Vilas, Katherine Roberts Hite, Scott B. Martin, Kerianne Piester, and Monique Segarra (Oxford: Oxford University Press, 1997), 261–80; and in "Democratic Governance, Violence, and the (Un)rule of Law," *Daedalus* 129, no. 2 (2000): 119–44.

ASPÁSIA CAMARGO

Federalism and National Identity

Federalism and Federalisms

Ever since the founders of American independence invented the federal system at the end of the eighteenth century as the foundation for unity of the thirteen colonies recently freed from Britain, this New World model has been an established system for organization of the state. It is characterized by the coexistence of two sovereignties: that of the federal union, which maintains control over some common functions, and that of the federated units, the states, which exercise the other functions. This singular accomplishment of political engineering became one trend in democratic states, initially in the United States of America and, later in the course of the nineteenth century, in Canada, Australia, and the young republics of Latin America.[1]

The common colonial origins of these countries seem to have stimulated early on the superimposed structures: one centralizing, inherited from the old metropolis, the other based on regional and local autonomies. These autonomies were fostered by preexisting communication difficulties and by cultural and economic diversity. This overlap or coexistence of sovereignties created a permanent tension between the centripetal forces of centralization and the centrifugal forces of decentralization, expressed in the original, paradigmatic confrontation between Hamilton and Jefferson.

In the evolution of federalism in Brazil in the nineteenth century, as in the United States and in other federations, there were constant systoles and diastoles, as General Golbery do Couto e Silva, the most important political theorist of Brazil's military regime, described them.[2] For Brazil, a continent-size country that had not yet consolidated its territorial settlement or its nation building, this oscillation would be a chronic pathology. One of the manifestations of this pathology, according to Couto e Silva, was the "black hole" of centralization, the control of which escapes even the central authority itself. Other symptoms are political fragmentation and the reinforcement of personal power under the mystique of decentralization.

The vicious circle, in fact, consists of seeking to correct the distortions at the extremes of the continuum, which drags the political system to the opposite extreme, in a repetitive cycle. This is why other authors have characterized these contractions and expansions as a pendulum swing. Behind both extreme distortions lies political patrimonialism, typical of great empires — extensive, heterogeneous political units, politically representing embryonic, rudimentary forms of federalism.[3] Federalism, in fact, is nothing more than a superior, institutionalized form of cooperation between the center and the periphery.

Patrimonialism feeds both the uniformity and the sinecures that excessive centralization yields as well as the ills of radical decentralization: the clientelism, nepotism, and coronelismo — the oligarchic politics — that are typical of local leadership. In spite of the oscillations through time that reveal the greater or lesser strength of central power, the patrimonial arrangement cannot survive without the visceral complicity between the two poles. In fact, centripetal and centrifugal forces are part of the evolution of both patrimonialism and federalism, indeed, of the history of civilization itself.

The relevant point for Brazil and for other, similar countries is to assess to what extent we are referring to federalism or to patrimonialism when we speak of centralization and decentralization. The former presupposes a democratic, institutionalized form of state organization, based on representation; the latter implies traditional forms of power, based on interpenetration of the public and private spheres, in which unstable rules are established only as instruments of co-optation, manipulation, and personal bargaining in the exercise of power. When such mechanisms enter an economic order, mercantilism prevails, setting up relations of complete dependency between the entrepreneurial class and public authority.

Another relevant attribute of federalism is flexibility, that is, the ability to adjust to circumstances in a more or less decentralized way and to resolve regional tensions within the same legal and political frames of reference. The diversity of the arrangement and composition associated with fiscal federalism in the separation of revenues, the distribution of jurisdictions, and the relation among powers constitutes a chapter in the study of "comparative federalism," composed of a broad array of situations that attest to the pragmatic dimension and not just the doctrinaire dimension of this type of state organization. The pendulum swings allow adjustments and solutions to innumerable problems and difficulties. This malleability is, in fact, a special predication of the federal regime that, in Brazil and in other countries, has dampened moments of possible rupture, permitting overt or covert negotiation among the parties in dispute.

Without a doubt, the "original sin" of Brazilian federalism was oligarchic regionalism, which ended up weakening through successive cycles of central government interventionism. Nevertheless, it is always ready to be reborn like the phoenix in every period of political opening. These conditions will continue as long as the pockets of both rural and urban poverty continue to breed a socially needy and politically passive electorate.

In spite of all of its defects, Brazilian federalism in its different phases facilitated the construction of regional identities, whose growth was fueled by their incorporation as common national symbols. A good example of this process was the national patrimony policy spurred on by modernism, which was one of the pillars of the policy of national integration in the first Vargas government.[4] Brazil's regions possessed and still possess quite diverse cultural manifestations, and some of these were more quickly integrated into the nation than others. The history of this integration is one of the most important early chapters of the construction of Brazilian federalism.

The slow weakening of regionalism had as a result the gradual strengthening of the federalism option as a democratic tool. An important continuity throughout the twentieth century was the legal and institutional recognition of federalism as a model of state organization. This principle has been repeatedly renewed ever since it was adopted in the late nineteenth century. Brazilian federalism adapted to the most diverse circumstances, even though it was distorted during the First Republic, called into question by dictatorships, and consecrated in the democratic periods. It came to be an obligatory highlight of the succeeding constitutions, even during the authoritarian periods.

Legally speaking, the federal became a matter of consensus among jurists and legislators, institutionalizing some rules and consolidating a jurisprudence favorable to coexistence of the federal units and the political center. Another indicator of the consensus created around federalism is that, in the frequent agendas of political reform, its elimination has never been included. Such was not the case with two other pillars of the political pact that toppled the empire, to wit, presidentialism and the republic itself. In the plebiscite held in 1993, parliamentarism and monarchy returned to the order of the day, while federalism remained a discreet but unchallenged consensus. The fact is justified by the good offices that federalism — discreetly — has given as an instrument of territorial integration and reduction of regional inequalities, both in authoritarian and democratic eras.

At the same time, one must be clear that rarely have reforms of the federation been the object of global or explicit treatment. This discrimination is surely due to the fact that the matter is of utmost delicacy and, generally, is broken down into digestible pieces, diluted in the topical agendas of public policies. The gray areas and the foci of disagreement around the tacit accords that reinforce federal integration are, in general, skillfully cloaked in the strategy of silence. This, for example, is the case with the heated and dangerous topic of existing distortions in the representation of states in the federal Chamber of Deputies, through which São Paulo is underrepresented and the less populous states of the North and Center-West are overrepresented.

In the final analysis, under what circumstances is federalism indicated as the best solution for strengthening nation-states and, nowadays, even regional blocs? In the course of modern history, up to the present, the federal system seems to be most worthwhile, as both doctrine and practice, in countries with a large area and/or deeply rooted cultural and ethnic diversity, such as the United States, Brazil, Canada, Australia, Germany, and Belgium. Ex-colonies — young nations in the process of settlement or unevenly populated, with large differences in income and infrastructure — benefit as well from federalism. A federal government guarantees fragile states a common fiscal regime and the jurisdiction to ensure investments in national infrastructure and income distribution necessary for the equalization of quality of life. This is known as "cooperative federalism."

In general, separatism and regional autonomy movements originate either in regions annexed in the past or in the more prosperous provinces or regions that do not want to share with the others the fruits of their wealth, which, if kept within their own borders, would multiply. Examples include the north of Italy, Catalonia, and, in Brazil, São Paulo during the First Republic and the present-day Mineiro Triangle in southwest Minas Gerais. In cases of acute asymmetry, as in Brazil and Canada, with extreme differences of income or population distribution among federal units, federalism is the regime most certain to promote political unity and reduction of inequalities. In these cases, setting aside federal resources for such ends is the best way to speed up the process of national integration, as Franklin Roosevelt saw during the Great Depression. The European Union, a federation in the making, invests significant resources in poor and peripheral areas, in association with regional planning, to strengthen political unity.

The best example of the distributive character of federalism is Germany, which has an unprecedented system of income equalization. This coexists, however, with a strong competitive dimension since sovereignty is shared with the states. Autonomy in decision making allows the federation to develop as a veritable laboratory of innovative, creative experiments. A good example of this "official emulation" is the United States, where the binary distribution of jurisdictions between the federal government and the states stimulates a "competitive federalism." This mixture of cooperation and competition affords a federal regime attractive conditions for dynamics, flexibility, and negotiation, whether it is equalizing and integrating or competing and innovating on the level of legislation and public policy.

In the early twenty-first century, the trend toward regionalization and spatial redistribution of power has led many unitary countries subject to serious internal tensions to opt for regimes that tend toward federalism. The establishment of regional autonomies in exchange for their subordination to a higher authority shapes a regime of shared sovereignties, such as the recent development of "devolutions" in the United Kingdom and "autonomous regions" in Spain. In Russia and China, construction of federalism is a challenge inseparable from development of the market economy and democracy. For countries like Brazil, with a century-old option for federation, conditions are much more favorable, since known rules of the game are reinforced. The nation need only perfect it.

The Pulse of the Republican Era: From Oligarchic Federalism to Democratic Federalism

During the twentieth century, Brazil was an extraordinary laboratory for federal experiments, which assumed a wide variety of modes and styles. Brazil began the century fomenting a pact among elites in a frustrated transplant of U.S. federalism to the recently installed Brazilian republic. The people were passive spectators of these changes who witnessed the proclamation of the republic "like beasts" in the well-known phrase of Aristides Lobo. The republic established in 1889 would come to marginalize the cities and the urban population, shifting the dynamic of political and partisan life to the rural world. As we will see, the twentieth century ended with a very different Brazil supporting a new democratic federalism, by means of broad-based social mobilization, with its own, new content. A participatory, trinitary federalism has been created, geared to activity in partnership with civil society and on the three levels of government, with improvements in public policies on the local level, reduction of social inequalities, and, above all, strengthening of civil society and exercise of citizenship.

Between the First Republic and the New Republic, at opposite ends of the twentieth century, there was a long apprenticeship in democracy whose lessons still need to be absorbed fully. The first lesson is that Brazil began with a failed experiment in decentralization promoted by the 1891 constitution that degenerated into exacerbated regionalism. This trauma left indelible marks in Brazilian political memory.

After corrective compensation, Brazil moved toward a centralizing federation that was interventionist and corporatist. Its initial phase, 1930–37, was strongly marked by conflicts between centralists and regionalists. The conflicts finally resulted in the "silent coup" of 1937 that created the authoritarian Estado Novo (New State).[5] The groundwork was laid for the coup by the slow erosion of state leaders not committed to the political reforms that the new federal political elite had decided to impose. The burning of the state flags that ushered in the Estado Novo was the culmination of this discrediting of regionalism, which degenerated into hostility against the paramount symbol of state autonomy. The states were now identified with lesser interests that had impeded the national state from reorganizing to become the true promoter of national progress and development.

In the course of the 1930s, changes on the world stage buried the liberal era and fostered the creation of a corporatist state, which was geared to stimulating cooperation between capital and labor. For intellectuals and reformers of the time, federalism and democracy were the front door of doddering liberalism through which the most retrograde interests of the old oligarchies arrived. In the same way, the social democracy that was expanding around the world (including the labor reforms of the Vargas era) centralized power and ran counter to the debates and doctrines associated with the federation. Still, in this period, federalism existed in the anonymity of silence more than amid hostility or rejection.

Getúlio Vargas's Estado Novo gave the advantage to centralism, but, in practice, it engaged in intense dialogue with the states and regions. It skillfully co-opted state leaders, giving decision-making powers to federally appointed *interventores* who administered unruly states and municipalities. The Estado Novo thus domesticated regionalism and forced it to adjust to the new level of centralization. For this reason, the first Vargas government promoted the administrative capacity of the states' apparatus and at the same time legally recognized and gave value to the municipalities as a means for neutralizing the increasingly menacing power of the state *interventores*. Politically, the Vargas government created conditions for these "satraps" appointed by the dictator to be the embryos of a new generation of state leadership that would be closer to the central government and to the urban masses and therefore further away from the oligarchic model of the First Republic. This is, in fact, what happened when many of the state *interventores* later became legitimate governors in the new constitutional regime after 1945.

The greatest contribution of the Vargas era was the symbolic incorporation of the regions, absorbing their specificities on the national level and treating them as relevant actors, whether by inserting them into the dynamic of the political process or by accelerating their economic development. In many cases, this process made use of peripheral actors to help promote delicate changes in the more sensitive centers of power. Thus was broken the monolithic power of the "café au lait alliance" between São Paulo and Minas Gerais. The interregional dialogue was diversified, reintegrating the Northeast and the South and elevating the status of the Center-West and, to a lesser extent, the North.

Even though it was politically heterogeneous, with discontinuous periods of dictatorship and democracy, in general, the long developmentalist cycle that lasted half a century, 1930–80, was ideologically contrary to the traditional form of parliamentary democracy and to political and administrative decentralization. These had always been tied to the demands of oligarchic regional power that seemed to be revived in democratic periods, because of the value of the vote in the political marketplace and because of the role of traditional politicians as mediators between the federal government and state and local governments. The strategically allied elites who ruled during the developmentalist cycle were more concerned with the efficacy of development than with the markedly traditionalist democratic representation. For these rulers, political regionalism continued to be an obstacle that retarded reforms and required negotiations that were laborious and often costly to the public treasury. For the intellectuals of this period, both in democratic and authoritarian phases, the most important task was to strengthen the reformist national state, which was the promoter of development along with national autonomy and social democracy. Social democracy here meant the incorporation of the masses into the political process and the most equitable distribution of the fruits of development.

Inevitably, the democratic federalism of the 1946 constitution that continued into the 1950s gave rise to sharp conflicts whose backdrop was the populist reformism of the executive branch pitted against the traditionalism of the region-alist elites based in Congress. Another sort of tension crystallized in this period between the president and the more powerful state governors, perennial com-petitors and potential presidential candidates. The fact is that, in this period, Congress was always seen as the privileged locus for resistance to reform and for representation of regional interests as opposed to the executive branch, which was the direct representative of the people and the nation. The "occult forces" denounced by President Jânio Quadros, when contradicted or threatened, were capable, even during a democratic regime, of toppling presidents—as in Qua-dros's sudden resignation in 1961 after less than seven months in office—or even governments, as with the 1964 coup.

During the military regime that came to power in 1964, governors and mayors of state capitals were appointed and Congress was elected, but supervised. The country was led by a body of generals, who chose the president at regular inter-vals. The president was merely the first among equals of this body. Within the framework of a mitigated dictatorship, democratic rituals like the elections of presidents and Congress made this period quite atypical as compared to other manifestations of authoritarianism on the continent. It was an authoritarian form especially well suited for regionalist arrangements and semifederative strategies facilitated by the role of Congress.

These accords coexisted or, indeed, mutually benefited one another with the ad hoc, excessive use of force of the institutional acts that the military govern-ment issued, always within the formal framework of the centralizing federalism of the 1967 constitution. This was the case with the so-called April Package of 1977 (see chapter 6), which subtly strengthened the representation of the North and Center-West at the moment that the military, threatened by the mobilization of the opposition, especially in the Southeast, needed to broaden its base in Con-gress. This expansion, which remained in the 1988 constitution, has facilitated the integration of the Amazonian region, over which hover the threats of territo-rial disintegration and separatism.

During the period in which the developmentalist model and the welfare state prevailed, federalism as a system of state organization was out of fashion, con-demned to the purgatory of association with out-of-date economic liberalism, the politics of local bosses, and the power of large landholders. It was also associated with the private power and matters of family, political clan, and local ties. Con-sidered to be incapable of serving the public interest, the federation was headed in the opposite direction of development and progress.

In the 1980s, everything changed. The developmentalist model and the corporatist state entered a deep crisis, accompanied by the resurrection of economic liberalism in Brazil and in the world as a whole. Liberalism hastened the expansion of transnational companies, market integration, and the coming of the information age to developed countries. In this context, decentralized management of companies and governments grew and spread throughout every continent, along with the promotion of civil society and nongovernmental organizations. The bureaucratic state, which had promoted development, now fostered and coordinated public policies and came increasingly within the orbit of regional and local power.

In the United States during the Reagan era, with economic liberalism came the revival of the decentralized federation, which had undergone decades of centralization. State governors began to pressure the federal government to return to them a number of duties taken over by central intervention.[6] In Brazil at the same time, this movement was significant, though in this instance it was stimulated by the struggle against the military regime and for democratic political opening, which had always been favorable to political decentralization. The revival of Brazilian federalism obliges us to revisit the roots of a national identity that first rejected this political model only later to adopt it. How did it all begin? And why did it take so long to establish it?

Belated Federalism: Utopian Origins and the Construction of the State

The idea of turning Brazil into a federation was one of the country's oldest, yet it was not easy to make it a reality. For a long time, federalism was limited to a utopia mingled with the dilemmas that accompanied the formation of a Brazilian nationality. From the beginning, the federal ideal drove the regional struggles for independence, but it was sidelined by an elite of men educated at Coimbra, Portugal, who feared the risks of disintegration of the former colonial territory.

The various provinces (as the colonial and imperial divisions were called) were distant from one another. They had always communicated directly with the Portuguese court and did not yet recognize a central national authority. Upon independence, the country opted first for a unitary empire, discarding both federalism and republicanism because they had caused so much political instability and interprovincial warfare in the new nations of Spanish America.

The topic returned to the national debate during the Regency (1831–40) with the Additional Act, the constitutional reform of 1834 that put forth a plan for creating in Brazil a federal constitutional monarchy. The bill, approved by the Chamber of Deputies but rejected by the Senate, provoked heated debates between the defenders of American federalism and the Coimbra-educated centralists. The latter argued based on the danger of copying U.S. institutions, citing the disastrous experience of Mexico.

According to Bernardo Pereira de Vasconcelos, a journalist, politician, and jurist who was a major political theorist of the empire, the ill lay not in federalism itself but rather in the stage of civilization in which Brazil found itself, in which the political consciousness of the population was only incipient.[7] Decentralization under such circumstances would mean simply turning power over to the tyranny of the private interests of the large landowners to be wielded against a defenseless population.

In this case, it would fall to the central government to defend public interest and freedom and, moreover, to ensure rotation of local power through use of the moderating power vested in the emperor. This model of the state, which José Murilo de Carvalho calls "pedagogical," would be revived later, with arguments identical to those of another imperial jurist and theorist, Paulino José Soares de Sousa, the Viscount of Uruguai: in such circumstances, it is necessary to educate the people, teaching them little by little to manage their own affairs.[8]

Even though it blocked the election of provincial presidents and the creation of the municipal executive branch, and even though it maintained the moderating power and the lifetime Senate terms, the Additional Act of 1834 instituted a semifederal model that created provincial assemblies and the division of fiscal income, and it abolished the Council of State. This decentralization caused an unprecedented increase in regional uprisings and wars among local factions for the control of the political space that was opening up. As the Count of Suzannet, a French nobleman who visited Brazil in the 1840s, observed, the unity of Brazil was only apparent; all of the provinces wanted separation, and the dream was an American-style republic.[9]

Once more, though, a nascent federalism was aborted, limiting the power of the assemblies and justices of the peace, re-creating the Council of State, and creating judicial and law enforcement systems under the control of the Ministry of Justice. Monarchic centralism was thus fortified along with its greatest legacy: the transformation of the former colony, dismembered into stagnant provinces, into a nation-state, albeit of weak internal circulation. However, this legacy also included a healthy, if embryonic, identity within a vast territory endowed with riches and potential. The national identity, in this sense, appeared to be more virtual and symbolic than real.

The debate about federation returned in the twilight of the empire, and then only after it had become evident that the failure of the demiurge state, whose backward complicity with slavery and other interests of the large landowners was stronger than its plans for preparing the nation to exercise its civil liberties—a sine qua non for self-government and political freedoms. Brazil continued, as the Viscount of Uruguai had warned, with a big head (the central bureaucracy) but with short arms and legs (provincial and local governments). In 1877, 69 percent of public employees were employees of the central government.[10]

The founding of the Republican Party (Partido Republicano) in 1870 was the political line of demarcation of the new era, preparing the ground for what would be, at the right time, the hallmarks of the 1891 constitution: federalism and decentralization. The province of São Paulo, which wanted greater autonomy, led the republican movement and supported the extreme federalism of Alberto Sales, who did not hesitate to say that his true country was São Paulo and that separatism might be a lesser evil than centralization.[11] In its attempt to free itself from the binds of the bureaucratic class, São Paulo led the growing discontent with the excessive uniformity, regulatory furor, and fiscal greed of imperial centralism. The province rose up against the tyranny of administrative centralization, disgusted with having to hand over to the imperial powers export tax revenues collected as a result of the large expansion in coffee production (see chapter 2). What is more, the economic dynamism of the province was based on an immigrant population and a free labor force that, for its part, demanded a process of modernization and more vigorous investment than would be possible for the imperial elite, committed as they were to the old northeastern and Rio de Janeiro alliances.

In fact, the shift of coffee cultivation from the Paraíba Valley to the west of São Paulo, farther from the orbit of the imperial court in Rio de Janeiro, caused a rift between economic and political power. This destabilized the political structure of the empire, making federalism no longer a topic subsidiary to the establishment of the republic but rather, along with the abolition of slavery, the central issue in the Second Empire.

From public enemy number one of national unity, the federal pact was suddenly converted into a great ally. Once the national territory was consolidated, if the stagnant provinces were not "oxygenated," the empire would be doomed, opening the door to a republic, separatism, or both. For the republicans, a condition for national unity was decentralization. The federal ideal circulated at that time as a vision of an old dream, the dream of various failed regionalist movements of the first half of the nineteenth century, such as the Revolution of 1817 and the Praieira Revolution.[12]

The final crisis of the empire did nothing more than revive an old dream of liberty with new trappings, fueled by critical thinking not satisfied with the current contrast between the prosperous ex-colonies of North America and the backward ex-colonies of South America. This shocking difference was especially attributed to the strength of civil society and self-government and to the federal regime that demanded shared sovereignties and guaranteed the states' autonomy in the United States.

In the second half of the nineteenth century, other federations arose on the heels of the successful U.S. experience, notably Canada and Australia. In Brazil, important intellectuals like Joaquim Nabuco and Rui Barbosa were infected with the federalist virus, but no one was more vibrant or passionate than Aureliano Cândido Tavares Bastos, one of the rare thinkers to commit fully to the cause of federalism and decentralization.

Tavares Bastos hailed from the small sugar-producing province of Alagoas in the Northeast. In his first book, *A província* (The Province), he condemned slavery and the unitarism of the empire, militantly engaging in the struggle against tyranny and in defense of liberty.[13] Brazil suffered, he said, from "apoplexy in the center and paralysis in the extremities." Centralism was the "perennial source of corruption." An assiduous reader of Alexis de Tocqueville, he became enamored of the exceptional conditions for the flourishing of democracy in the United States, tied to the idea of self-government, to the fight against tyranny, and to the full exercise of liberty. He advocated the liberal principle of "the eternal struggle of freedom against force and of the individual against the state." Based on this, Tavares Bastos took as a given the importance of combating ignorance and investing massively in education, conferring its management on local governments. For him decentralization was an inseparable part of the concept of a modern republic: "Any prolonged tutelage leads unfailingly to a certain incapacity, and this incapacity serves as a pretext for continuing the tutelage indefinitely. Moreover, these tutors imposed upon us, from where do they come? Do they not come from this same population, which have been declared radically incapable? . . . Aptitudes are not developed in the hothouse of centralization. . . . Without administrative decentralization, the country wilts under the tyranny of uniformity."

The Americanist utopia of Tavares Bastos coincided with the rise of the Republican Party and the proautonomy spirit of São Paulo, typified by the decentralist radicalism of Sales. Recognizing the asymmetry that so bothered the imperial elites, the Republican elites would defend the thesis that the needs of the more prosperous provinces could not be ignored just so they could be adapted to the incipient conditions of the weaker ones. Granting autonomy to the regions, therefore, meant ranking them in a hierarchy based on their living conditions, wealth, and potential.

In the doctrinaire defense of decentralization, Tavares Bastos believed the federal system was "a political fact of the American continent," characterized by a large land area and by natural obstacles that have led to isolation and regional independence. The difficulty of communication among populations isolated by such distance and obstacles, the frailty of ties, and the clash of contradictory interests all conspired to make the unitarism of European monarchies on the American continent impossible.

Federalism would be the solid base for democratic institutions and the foundation for the success of public policies since it was "essential to recognize the municipality's and the province's legislative and executive autonomy in their own affairs." Tavares Bastos lamented, moreover, that the federal monarchy proposed in the 1831 constitutional reform by the Chamber of Deputies had been suppressed by the Senate along with the decentralizing movement of the Regency that was also pushing the Additional Act.[14]

Nabuco introduced the same proposal for a federal monarchy to save the empire, arguing that the federation was a part of Brazil's evolutionary cycle, interrupted during the Regency, since the size and diversity of the country demanded a decentralized administration, closer to local interests and circumstances.[15] Nabuco urgently returned to the subject, fearful that the recently won abolition could precipitate a fall of the empire and lead to three distinct countries in the South.[16]

In fact, the founding father of Brazilian federalism was Rui Barbosa, a liberal politician of the empire who became the principal crafter of the 1891 constitution, in addition to being a major builder and, later, critic of the republic. In his 1882 report, still during the imperial era, he put forth the federal monarchy as the ideal model for government, to avoid the successive crises that had shaken the empire.

Earlier, in 1880, in a speech in defense of the Saraiva plan for electoral reform, Barbosa affirmed that "the basis of our regime, its only basis, is democracy. In the administration of our political interests, the sovereignty of the people is the alpha and omega, the beginning and the end." Clearly linking democracy to territorial representation and to the federative spirit, Barbosa added that the secret of monarchic stability "consists of not trying to superimpose itself on the country or treating the nation as one power to another."[17]

As Bolivar Lamounier shows, Barbosa was, in fact, the only one who, as a theorist and politician, carried to its ultimate consequences the problematic connection, between ideas and practice, of federalism with democracy and liberty. During the critical year of 1889, Barbosa was the great defender, both in the press and within the Liberal Party, of a federal regime. He said that "either the monarchy makes a federation or the federation will make a republic."[18] He believed that the monarchy could not survive the dual pressure from unhappy former slave owners and from the provinces of São Paulo and Rio Grande do Sul. Thus he once again brought up for discussion, now in inverse relation, the old subject of separatism:

> An essentially liberal principle, the federation is, at the same time, in the
> current circumstances of the country, an eminently conservative reform.
> The unitary, centralizing monarchy, parasitically living off of the sap of
> local communities, has created everywhere mistrust, discontent, and
> despair, whose ultimate fruit is separatism. While, in the weak provinces,
> this has not been expressed as a general wish, it has been frankly and
> haughtily articulated in those coming into wealth, including São Paulo
> and Rio Grande do Sul. These provinces warn us that economic develop-
> ment in the other provinces, rather than reconciling them with monarchic
> centralization, will awaken the same centrifugal forces, the disintegrating
> tendencies, whose extreme, though not necessarily distant, result would
> be the transformation of the empire into a group of weak, inconsistent,
> aimless republics, given over to the rivalries of internal and external
> interests.[19]

On various occasions, Barbosa declared that he had supported the republican military coup only when he became convinced that the monarchy would not clear the way for federalism. One month after the proclamation of the republic, Barbosa had affirmed in a telegram that the republican break had been caused "by the aspirations that the Ouro Preto ministry was planning to crush," in order to postpone the full autonomy of the provinces. According to the Viscount of Ouro Preto, president of the Council of Ministers, the provincial presidents should be chosen from a list of three names submitted to the emperor for his choice, as was the case with the senators.[20] Barbosa, instead, preferred that the provincial executives be elected.

Encouraged by the U.S. experience, the United States of Brazil, as the new republic was called, implemented a dual federalism, which strengthened the states at the expense of both the federal and the municipal governments, whose organization was now wholly at the mercy of state government decisions. In Bahia, for example, all of the mayors were appointed by the governor.[21] Another characteristic of the 1891 constitution was to strengthen the functions of Congress as a protagonist in federal government.

Often accused of being an unrealistic dreamer for having created an oligarchic federation that took the country to the brink of disintegration, Barbosa was also identified as typical of the Brazilian elites who used imported ideas in vain attempts to solve the country's problems. As early-twentieth-century intellectual Francisco José de Oliveira Viana argued, the idealism of the 1891 constitution was a failed effort at grafting American-style decentralization because it did not take into account either Brazil's incipient political culture or its social organization.[22]

At the same time, Oliveira Viana recognized that it was thanks to Barbosa that the extremism of São Paulo and Rio Grande republicans was tempered by the republic's monarchist and nationalist foundation. "Without a doubt, we owe to him this great service. With his undeniable authority, he contained the evolution from a federal regime to a confederation—which would have meant the disintegration of our great common homeland."[23]

Moreover, as Victor Nunes Leal recalled, during the Constituent Assembly of 1890, Barbosa fought energetically against the tributary ultrafederalist propositions of the Rio Grande brand of republicanism known as Castilhismo (for its founder Júlio Prates de Castilhos), predicting the "collapse of the nascent federation."[24] Thus the great distortion of the Brazilian federation as compared to American federalism was corrected. While the federal pact in the United States was formed from the bottom up, resulting in the voluntary uniting of the thirteen colonies, the Brazilian federation was formed from the top down, as a process of disintegration of a unitary state. This historical inversion created the singular, and erroneous, situation that, in Brazil, federalism is taken to be a synonym for decentralization.

In the constitutional pact, Barbosa tried to turn back these centrifugal tendencies, drawing Brazilian federalism closer to Hamilton's view and as far away as possible from Jefferson's decentralizing spirit. Although he defended the election of the president by the states, in accordance with the special formula of the American Electoral College—which was eventually rejected by the Constituent Assembly—he also presupposed the federalist principle that the administrative decentralization of the United States would not prevent the country from being as centralized politically as "the European kingdoms that are equal in this respect." The basic issue was that, according to Barbosa, among other federal functions, the constitution guaranteed federal supremacy over the particular interests of the states.[25]

From the beginning, what seemed to be in play was the choice of whether or not to build a nation-state covering a large area, escaping the fate of political fragmentation that, in other countries on the continent, gave rise to political *caudillismo* and bloody local conflicts. There is no doubt that, in the course of history, empires have been embryonic forms of federalism capable of dealing with cultural heterogeneity and social diversity common to large areas with a low degree of institutionalization.

Today, nearly all of the countries with large land areas are federations or quasi federations of imperial formation. In many cases, it was the agglutinative power of the colonizer that caused the integration of territories that were politically and culturally dissociated, as happened in India, Canada, and Australia. The grand institutional mission of the Second Empire was, therefore, to promote within the former colony an embryonic political center that the Portuguese colonial power had not fomented for fear of fueling local separatism. The emperor had assumed the task of forging a minimal state structure for a large territory, applying the moderating power to appease the parties and enforcing the political rotation. Although it did not manage to tame the private impulses of the rural landowners, it softened their excesses and promoted social mobility. In the next phase, it was up to the federation to take the first step in broadening the network of regional representation and strengthening the legs and arms of a body that was lean and out of proportion.

What the partisans of the federation did not foresee was that republican federalism would so soon be put to hard tests. This was palpable for Barbosa, first when faced with the positivist, antiregionalist, antiliberal unitarism of the military men who staged the republican coup. The next test was when power was in the hands of the São Paulo elites who were ill prepared to deal with the rest of the states and with a national party system that was both inchoate and corrupt.

The wars and revolts that dominated the 1890s broke the republic's spell once and for all and obliged some illustrious advisers of the empire to come back onto the stage. For example, the Baron of Rio Branco took up the reins of foreign policy (see chapter 4). Most important, however, was the verification that, in addition to the 1891 constitution, a major political agreement had to be found to ensure the survival of the young republic, which was economically maladjusted and politically adrift. The institutional metamorphosis that afforded a political consensus was accomplished only after serious domestic turbulence — including a civil war in the South between federalists and republicans — that shook the federation in its first years of life. The instability of the 1890s had put at risk not only the recently installed republican regime but also national unity itself, now threatened by both regional divisions and political factionalism.

The Republic of the Possible: Oligarchic Regionalism and Territorial Integration

Thanks to its American influence, the 1891 constitution introduced into Brazil total freedom of state legislation, undoing the central uniformity built up during the empire. Each state, as the former provinces were now called, had its own electoral rules and specific legal codes. They had the freedom to contract international loans and full control of the police and judiciary, under the command of state governors or local bosses. It was in the breaks in this drive toward regionalism that a sort of "country" federalism (*federalismo caboclo*, literally "half-breed federalism") soon developed, which shifted and adapted to the absolute power of the oligarchies that dominated the first decade of the twentieth century.

The price for political stability, achieved by the Campos Sales administration (1898–1902), was the sacrifice of the democratic federalism of which Tavares Bastos and Barbosa had dreamed. The distance between reality and utopia or pragmatism and idealism was exactly the distance between Barbosa and Campos Sales. The Paulista president, who was in the midst of grave financial and institutional crises, discarded the possibility of carrying out a risky constitutional reform and instead stitched together an oligarchic pact that would back up his liberal reforms and international negotiations. His goals were to shore up Brazil's finances, take out loans, and consolidate the dominance of the coffee sector.

As liberal logic would dictate, the accord favored the wealthier states, which received autonomy to conduct their own politics while the poorer and more isolated states, which were more dependent on the federal government, became more submissive. With *coronelismo* confined to its more remote haunts, Campos Sales skillfully revived the moderating power for the president to intervene in the succession process, just as Emperor Pedro II had done during the Second Empire. In exchange, he delegated broad powers to the governors within the narrow boundaries of their own states. With the regional forces fragmented according to the old principle of "divide and rule," it was possible to tame the regionalist excesses.

By the same principle, the official party was regionalized. Each state had its own Republican Party (Partido Republicano, PR), offspring of the national Republican Party. The president of the state PRs was the governor himself. Campos Sales thus freed Congress from the national parties, which were unremarkable but had a strong capacity for political resonance. In Congress, which had been strengthened by the 1891 constitution, Campos Sales took on the coordination of the political process by means of rigid control of the Commission for the Verification of Powers (Comissão de Verificação de Poderes), which was charged with confirming the validity of elections, the outcomes of which were frequently contested by local oppositions.

The pact consisted of offering unconditional support for the candidates nominated by the governors in exchange for their abdication of interference in national questions, which were under the exclusive control of the president. This, in reality, was an old patrimonialist trick: to create or reinforce formal rules only to be purposefully set aside, using their nonenforcement as a bargaining chip. This principle of creating difficulties to sell facility was the central point of the accord between the governors and the president, guaranteeing the latter the freedom to conduct economic policy and the succession process. "A long, flexible leash thus stretched form the federal government to the municipalities, creating the illusion of less distance between the nation and its government and guaranteeing the security of national unity," according to Paulo Mercadante.[26]

Thanks to the ingenious mediation of the "politics of the governors,"[27] the president strengthened the states' public power but left the governors free to exercise power fully and arbitrarily within their domains. This "republican invention,"[28] the result of skill and finesse, reinforced the legitimacy of the federal government and accommodated the regional interests that invaded the national scene, thus taking the wind out of both separatism and congressional factionalism. No doubt the co-optation of regional forces, setting their limits but strengthening their powers, functioned as a retaining wall against the sectional conflicts that had dominated the republic in its first ten years of life.

The disfigured federalism that greeted the twentieth century was, therefore, a mere agent for the promotion and legitimization of regionalism, a variant of patrimonialism, according to which "the regional actors accept the existence of the nation-state but seek economic favoritism and political sinecures from the larger political unit, even at the risk of putting in danger the political regime itself." Whereas federalism is an institutional model of jurisdictions distributed between the federal government and the states, regionalism is a model of exchange of favors between the center and the periphery.[29]

In practice, oligarchic federalism created a hierarchy of well-defined regional status groups, establishing differences among the first-class states, the second-class states, and the pariahs of the federation. On the first level were the three wealthy states that controlled more than half of the population and the gross domestic product: first under the dominance of São Paulo (1894–1906), followed by Minas Gerais, which together formed the "café au lait alliance" that, after 1910, came under the growing pressure of Rio Grande do Sul on the margins.[30]

The integration of Rio Grande do Sul into the Brazilian federation was another major accomplishment of the First Republic. It permitted the definition of a style of governing with continuity of personal power but also with innovations in social policies under the aegis of the positivist authoritarianism of Castilhismo. This integration deepened after 1910, thanks to the state's increased participation in the federal government, especially through the important Ministries of Public Works and Finance.

The ideological moving force of this integration was the idea that the southern state had joined the federation by its "own choice" and that this engagement conferred on it a privileged inclusion within the whole. Integration and inclusion allowed Rio Grande do Sul to develop on the one hand a strong regional identity and on the other a strong commitment to national patriotism and identity.[31] It was this dual ideological militancy that enabled Rio Grande do Sul to arbitrate in the deep regional conflicts that appeared in 1912 and, later, in the conflict between São Paulo and Minas Gerais in the 1929 elections, which dragged the country into the Revolution of 1930 (see chapters 3 and 6).

An official ideology in defense of a demure regionalism, with little vision and little future, oligarchic federalism promoted decentralization, but it weakened society and democracy, institutionalizing the power of the bosses and political clientelism. It also caused important reversals such as a decrease in political participation through the exclusion of illiterates, which kept most of the population on the margins of the political process for forty years.[32] In the succeeding elections, in which there was little real competition among candidates, electoral participation oscillated between 1.5 and 3 percent. In the contested election campaign of

1930, participation barely surpassed 5 percent. This was the consequence of the resumption of the moderating power exercised during the empire, which turned the elections into mere instruments for the ratification of previously chosen candidates.

Perpetuation of the oligarchies in power and their merciless methods ended up causing a slow demoralization, especially in the Northeast, where internal schisms and popular protests, encouraged by the federal government, culminated with the "state defeats" in 1912 and 1913. The destabilization of the oligarchies was a result of the election of a military man from Rio Grande do Sul, General Hermes da Fonseca, as president (1910–14). In opposition to this was born Barbosa's Civilian Campaign (Companha Civilista), which denounced the same legal and institutional distortions that had led him to oppose Campos Sales. Through this campaign, Barbosa criticized the republic that he himself had helped to found.

This was the first sign of the serious political illegitimacy of the Campos Sales accords and of the regime's betrayal of its federalist and republican ideals. The presidential succession would be from then on, as indeed it had been, the focal point of intellectual discontent and the successive crises that worsened in the elections of 1922 and 1930. Electoral fraud and unanimous votes, the famous "throat cutting" (the voiding of the election of opposition candidates), the "electoral corrals," and the "yoked vote"—all allusions to the relation of cattle to their master—only contributed to cheapen the republican ethos and led Barbosa to his frontal attack on the regime.

This picture progressively worsened with the cultural clash between a backward, rural Brazil and an urban society that expanded after World War I. In this clash, the middle classes, intellectuals, artists, politicians, and "lieutenants" (tenentes) mobilized to destabilize the regime with armed sedition that punctuated the 1920s. In isolated and declining regions, clientelism fed pockets of poverty and marginalization of the peasantry from the political process. Under new forms, clientelism prolonged the regime of social exclusion, semislavery, and illiteracy. This was the desolate sight that the revolutionaries of the Prestes Column had of the interior of Brazil, regions traumatized by oligarchic domination and by the passivity and ignorance of the population. In this context, electoral competition and universal vote, freedom of expression and assembly, the separation of powers, and protection under the law—all of the practices of democratic federalism—were cheapened by a realpolitik geared to perpetuating and reproducing regional leadership and its centers of power.

In addition to the farce of the "verification of powers," the general lack of independent civil institutions ended up removing democracy from the republic and federalism from its progress. It was this atavistic commitment that, after World War I, led the emerging intellectual elites to renounce both federalism and democracy, burying them together with the last of agrarian hegemony and coffee monoculture.

"Who Are We?" "What Republic Is This?"

It was not long before the political crises and the obsolescence of the First Republic reopened the old debate in intellectual circles about centralization versus decentralization. This renewed debate focused on the relation between state and nation, stirring up questions of national identity, the territorial and demographic makeup of the country, political culture, and the weakness of the "social body." The heritage of colonization and slavery and the role of elites and their imported ideologies as channels of the "Brazilian political adventure" were not ignored.[33]

At the root of this debate lay a larger issue: discovering the deep reasons for Brazil's institutional failure and a way of overcoming them once and for all. After all, what was permanently wrong with Brazil? Without a clear social identity or a well-developed cultural framework, the country had long suffered from the trauma of not defining its own origins. The rediscovery of Brazil meant, above all, discovering who the "authentic" Brazilian was. At first, the answer seemed discouraging: some sort of degenerated half-breed or mulatto or, at best, a second-class European of Portuguese origin? For many, thus, it was indispensable to "improve the race," which was in increasing need of "whitening" by means of massive doses of immigrants. This was the practical outcome of an ideology based on eugenics and scientific racism that was ascendant in the decades around the turn of the twentieth century.

The culminating symbolic moment that led to a collective intellectual psychoanalysis of national identity was the centennial of independence in 1922, whose commemorations afforded the opportunity of figuring the balance of both Portuguese colonization and the inevitable confrontation between the imperial and republican experiments during the preceding hundred years of independence. The ambiguous relation between the two watershed dates of 7 September (declaration of independence) and 15 November (proclamation of the republic) seemed significant. Both competed for the distinction of paramount symbol of national identity. Another debate of the day was who the true builder of the free and sovereign nation had been.[34]

In the effort of rediscovering Brazil, for many intellectuals of the first half of the twentieth century, it was necessary to return to Portuguese origins: "Intellectual, moral, and material poverty; the absence of social life, and lack of organizational capacity—this is what the colonizers bequeathed to us after three centuries of domination," stated Capistrano de Abreu. Álvaro Bomílcar appropriated Manoel Bomfim's term "parasitism" to sum up the character of Portuguese dominion in Brazil. Others, like Tristão de Ataíde, underscored that Emperor Pedro I "had the intuition of national sentiment" and, therefore, "he had founded the Brazilian nation by guaranteeing its territorial unity and by preventing the 'anarchy' that had accompanied the independence process in other South American countries. The Shout of Ipiranga, when Pedro I announced his intent to remain in Brazil and rule it independently from Portugal, would be the rallying call for all of the scattered forces that were fighting for independence."[35]

The commemorations were the occasion for the unanimous consecration of Paulista José Bonifácio de Andrada e Silva as the patriarch of independence. José Bonifácio was a statesman who defended Brazilian independence from Portugal and supported political centralization. The centralists saw him as an "authentic" Brazilian who had inspired independence, defended order and centralization, and rejected the "liberal idealism" that had later prevailed in the 1891 constitution. For these reasons, he was admired by those who were already in the 1920s advancing authoritarian ideas that would be politically victorious only in the 1930s.

In times of major republican turbulence, 1922 became a landmark year symbolic of breaks with the past and desire for change. Events including the Week of Modern Art (which launched the Brazilian modernist movement), the *tenente* uprising, the creation of the Brazilian Communist Party (Partido Comunista Brasileiro, PCB; see chapter 7), and, finally, a tumultuous presidential election symbolically buried the First Republic and gave birth to a new era. In this context, the definitive "enthronement" of the patriarch José Bonifácio took on enormous significance and was, moreover, encouraged by the mobilization of the São Paulo intelligentsia "as if to remind everyone that the Paulistas had not just begun to govern Brazil today."[36] Taking up the legacy of the generation of the 1870s, this new generation of the 1920s broke away, committed to the enormous task of founding the nation, building the state, and forging national identity, which had been corroded by republican mediocrity that had prevented the awakening of a modern Brazil. In this process, new and old interpretations of the roots of Brazilian nationality came to the fore, "seeking continuities and ruptures, and recreating the country to meet the twentieth century."

Twentieth-century jurist and scholar Francisco Cavalcanti Pontes de Miranda stated that "we need to demarcate the borders of the national spirit just as the territorial ones have been set." For such, the watchword of diplomat and modernist poet Ronald de Carvalho was "Enough of artificial fertilization!" Alberto Torres, Republican ex-governor of Rio de Janeiro, minister of the Federal Supreme Court, was a notable precursor of the critics of the First Republic. His consistent doctrine of state organization would inspire the *tenentista* movement and other influential intellectuals, such as Vicente Licínio Cardoso and Oliveira Viana. Torres reintroduced the old idea that Brazil needed to combat the artificiality of its institutions and Brazilianize the republic. The need for a well-prepared, energetic elite grew insofar as "public opinion does not exist, and the people were incapable of organizing themselves politically."[37] Creating the Brazilian nation, the quest to make a new plan for Brazil: this was the challenge that the intelligentsia of the 1920s undertook.

Everywhere, the same question was circulating: "What republic is this?" Oliveira Viana's words then echoed, "The republic came. Democracy came. The Federation came. And then a great murmur of disappointment arose. . . . This disappointment became accentuated with time as a permanent disillusionment. . . . *This was not the republic of my dreams!*" The disillusionment of the generation of the 1920s was distilled in a significant published collection that intoned the requiem of the First Republic: *À margem da história da República* (On the Margin of the History of the Republic) by Cardoso.

Journalist and author Euclides da Cunha had warned, as early as the turn of the twentieth century, that "this paradise of the mediocre" could not realize the dream of a "civilized, modern" nation. In 1920, the republic no longer was for anyone "that beautiful bust of a strong woman on a pedestal" but rather a "sphinx with a simple hood made of an old newspaper."[38] "Republicanizing" the republic that, according to Álvaro Bomílcar, benefited only half a dozen individuals meant correcting the vices of its origin, inherited from Portuguese colonization.

The first major structural limitations and principal causes of Brazilian problems would be territorial makeup and demographic distribution, noted as serious deficiencies since the empire. Using biological metaphors, Cardoso commented,

The land of Brazil is too big. It shrinks the man; then it wears him out. There is no continuous flow of sap, there is no rhythm in life, there is no follow-through of energy. When the current should flow with greater vigor and experience, the drought comes instead. In successive centuries of apogee and decadence, there is no sequence, no order. The passive attrition of the simultaneity of various and differentiated spaces within the same time is overly violent. There is no regulating pendulum that keeps the balance; no self-sustaining rudder. And, in this way, the acceleration of some organs, in contrast with the retarded movements of other parts of the organism well defines the chaotic situation of the entire system.[39]

Along the same lines, Oliveira Viana argued that through most of the country social conditions were quite poor. Since in vast regions, hungry for greater freedom, there was no order, no justice, and no police, political autonomy and freedom were merely pretexts for covering up the "thuggery of caudillos that deposed mayors and authorities with the same ease that the rubber gatherers struck the rubber tree bark with their hatchets, . . . with their eye fixed on North America and England, on the beauties of self-government and the marvels of decentralization."[40]

Permeating this old debate about the different Brazils that do not relate to one another and that pulse at different rhythms, what stands out is "the inertia of the middle" that confined leadership and programs to "political ostracism." Such programs include those of Tavares Bastos in 1870 and of Barbosa in 1882 and Torres's constitutional reform in 1914 (an indictment of the First Republic meant to strengthen federal power). The reason for this mediocrity was the cultural and educational backwardness of the population that had been criticized by Tavares Bastos and by the entire generation of intellectuals that preceded the Revolution of 1930. Basing his argument on numbers, Cardoso attributed to the empire the "carelessness, inattention, and ineptitude with which it delayed without fomenting the solution to problems of mass education."[41]

Fifty years later, at the end of the 1920s, according to Cardoso, the population was still 70 percent illiterate, making the country void of a real "social body." To criticize the men, the regimes, and the institutions was to ignore that the serious distortions in this social body resulted "from the functional insufficiency of several of its organs for dissecting the organic precariousness of its systems and tissues."

For Oliveira Viana, the thin, dispersed population lacked "a developed political consciousness, the real, lucid sense of its regional unity and of its common interests." It lacked, moreover, "an upper class, sufficiently numerous to assume the wholesale direction of those societies because the truth is that many states in the North and even some in the South feel even now the lack of an administrative aristocracy which had not yet formed when the federative improvisation elevated them, suddenly, to the condition of sovereign entities. This is the primary cause of the stagnation into which the states are plunged—if not of the disorder, of the anarchy, of the disorganization that depresses and annihilates them."

The grand ideas of liberalism, democracy, and federalism, imported from abroad, were of no use without a better educated population and a public opinion able to exercise the citizenship and participation necessary for the republican order, thus guaranteeing greater consistency to both federalism and democracy. According to Cardoso, "A regime of systematic decentralization, of flight from the discipline of the central government, of preponderant localism or provincialism can be, rather than an agent of progress, a factor in weakness and annihilation. Instead of ensuring liberty and democracy, it can actually result in the death thereof."[42]

In the first two decades of the twentieth century, the First Republic showed a precarious political development marked by the social abyss between the elites and the masses and by an incipient, disorganized, backward agrarian society. Moreover, the state was still weak, dominated by mediocre oligarchies. Finally, there was a total lack of a social base for political parties. Brazil lacked relevant social actors and parties molded by class interests endowed with ideologies and plans for modernization. Not by chance, then, intellectuals like Torres, Cardoso, and Oliveira Viana were the main spokesmen for this diagnosis of the First Republic, denouncing oligarchic decadence and the crisis in national identity.[43]

As Oliveira Viana observed, "Our great ill is, on the one hand, the absence of a national ideal, the weakness of collective sentiment and interest, and the frailty of political instinct; on the other hand, there is the exacerbation of localism, of factionalism, and despotism of the local bosses. . . . We are still a long way away from the countries with a high degree of collective integration, like Germany, England, and, perhaps, the United States. . . . Unfortunately, because of our disassociation, our disintegration, our dispersion, we are still nearly at the opposite pole, closer to revolutionary China or Soviet Russia."[44]

For this reason, Oliveira Viana, who was inspired by the pioneering ideas of the Viscount of Uruguai, believed it was essential to separate radically the celebrated concept of political liberty from the prior, indispensable concept of civil liberty. For this, it is necessary to dilute the feelings of clan and family in order to strengthen the collective consciousness, the organization of justice, and its independence from direct political power.[45] Without this, federalism is an aberration and democracy a farce or, at best, a utopia.

This was the challenge that divided the political elites between 1929 and 1937 in a clash that materialized in the following years, pitting the provisional government and the *tenentes* against the states that defended political democracy and regionalist federalism. For the thinkers of this new order, it was a matter of bringing the formal Brazil closer to the real Brazil, of being more concerned with social democracy than with the farce of political democracy. Formal Brazil was divorced from the project of a modern state endowed with a strong executive branch and with technical advisers able to forge a new identity for the "Brazilian archipelago" that would bring state and nation closer together.[46] They were thus restoring the imperial ideal of a demiurge state, a precursor agent of power and public interest, in opposition to unruly private interests and aimless politics.[47]

This was the movement of "translation of ideas" that, according to Oliveira Viana, obliged the country to evolve from a centrifugal federation to a centripetal one "that, by a diffuse movement of the collective unconscious of numerous local centers, is correcting, naturally and spontaneously, the enormous error of political decentralization committed against [the federation's] integrity by the republican constituents. Twenty years ago, political ideas, in the intellectual and partisan centers, both local and federal, did not differ much from these current ideas: they bore the influence of the centrifugal conception of the federal regime. It was provincial liberties, local franchises, state sovereignty, and local autonomy that were in fashion."[48]

Forging an original, Brazilian model that would meet the needs of the nation and not the fashionableness of imported ideals was the challenge that the intellectuals of the 1930s tried to address. In this, initially, they rejected federalism, identified as an exogenous doctrine; later, they supported the politicians in adapting federalism to the centripetal tendencies of a new centralized order. Into this new order was incorporated the irreversible influence of the periphery and of the subaltern regions that, as had occurred in other models of patrimonialism studied by Eisenstadt, had survived embedded within the state itself, whether through the institutionalization of clientelism or through the legitimate regional claims on the distribution of federal resources. The fact is that these traditional

forces accommodated themselves to the new bureaucratic standards, constructing a "political grammar" that promoted the nationalization of clientelism sym-
biotically incorporated into the institutional model of modernity.[49]

The Federation in Chains: Development and Political Instability

The developmentalist cycle was a fifty-year period (1930–80) in which Brazil
abandoned the liberal project of a monoculture export economy linked to the
international market and turned instead to a plan that included strengthening
the central government, building up the internal market, and creating an energy
and communications infrastructure capable of diversifying productive facilities.[50]
Intensification of a network of exchanges, whose absence a range of authors had
indicated as the underlying cause of Brazil's large problems, was the natural consequence of such developments.

The rural world, which had sustained the regionalism of the First Republic,
was gradually drained, siphoned off by an unprecedented urbanization, especially
concentrated in the metropolitan areas of high population density (see chapters 2
and 3). Brazil shifted from an urban population of 30 percent in the 1940 census
to a rural population of 30 percent in the 1980 census. This inversion was accompanied by more cosmopolitan standards of behavior and by an explosion in the
electorate: from 7.5 million in 1945 to 82.5 million in 1990. By the turn of the
millennium, it had exceeded 100 million.

The pace of industrial growth in this period was so high (around 7 percent per
year) that it facilitated significant expansion of the labor market and diversification of professions. In addition, it yielded high rates of social mobility, lower
only than those of the United States and Australia. Mobility and growth created
strong internal cohesion around the national project, which gave rise to the developmentalist pact on a large social base, notwithstanding the persistence of
vast inequalities and many pockets of poverty located in rural areas and urban
peripheries.

Breaking through the social indifference of the oligarchic era, this new movement was accompanied by a centralist "systole." It was marked ideologically by
a preoccupation with social democracy, introduced by the 1934 constitution of
the Second Republic. Strongly defended by the intellectual elites of the time,
this constitution recognized labor rights and the strengthening of the economic
order, which in turn reinforced the power of state intervention. The 1934 constitution was negotiated by centralizing reformists and regionalist federalists.[51]

Regional power that represented state interests, for its part, found itself weakened and scattered. It cast its lot with the "committee of the major parties," that is, with the greater center of the time, to confront the corporatist and centralist steamroller, supported by a class-based constituency. The result of this confrontation was a hybrid constitution that, along with the new chapter in social and economic order, expanded the duties and responsibilities of the national state at the same time that it restricted its powers, now divided among state governments and Congress. The weak point of the 1934 constitution was in not establishing a national party system. This chronic imbalance was one of the main factors leading to the dictatorship of the Estado Novo.

In spite of the pioneering labor legislation (which included a much-debated minimum wage), painstakingly negotiated with the business leaders and implemented during the dictatorship, labor rights were not extended right away to the rural areas, where a majority of the population was found. This was a function of the political weight of the rural landowners. Resistance to rural reform stretched into the administration of João Goulart (1962–64), which succumbed to the impact of the agrarian conflict and confrontations with Congress, which opposed his plans for centralization. In the meanwhile, the crisis created conditions for the adoption of social security and agrarian reform policies even during the military regime. Eventually, there was a policy of minimum income in the form of retirement benefits, extended to the majority who had never contributed.

This unprecedented rise in modernization committed the country to an ambitious process of change, but it had high social and political costs. From the social point of view, in spite of the creation of the Ministry of Education and Health in 1930, educational policy continued to be a political bargaining tool in the hands of regional oligarchies, compromising the country's development model and retarding the formation of a true citizenry. Income inequality, the fruit of socially and spatially concentrated growth, remained at an unacceptable level, even though it was politically neutralized by the high rates of social mobility and by the trickle-down effect that increased the areas with higher rates of human development.

The stability of the developmentalist pact, which held the nation together for fifty years, also contrasted with high degrees of political and institutional instability during that period. Between 1930 and 1985, there were two "exceptional regimes," eight years of the Estado Novo and twenty-one of military dictatorship, and only one constitutional period of eighteen years, 1946–64, not counting the short-lived Second Republic of 1934–35 (see chapter 7). Between the democratic and dictatorial extremes, there were long, extremely unstable "gray periods" of transition, the provisional government of 1930–34, the end of the Estado Novo, the José Linhares administration, and the Constituent Assembly of 1946. The Castelo Branco administration (1964–67) had heralded itself as a short-term "exceptional" period, and the political opening of the military regime took eleven years.

Even in the constitutional era, one of relative stability, the presidential successions degenerated into serious political crises, and, of the five presidents who took office, three were unable to complete their terms. Even the exceptional regimes were riddled with the instability caused by struggles among political factions. The proliferation of constituent assemblies and constitutions in this period ran contrary even to the Latin American tradition; frequent changes in electoral law and in the party system are a serious symptom of institutional pathology that followed the collapse of oligarchic federalism, which still has not found an adequate substitute for articulating the central and state governments. For this very reason, social and economic modernization was not accompanied by desirable political development.

During the first Vargas government, political development was retarded by the new regime's difficulty in digesting formal democracy as a basic value of evolution and progress. Since the practices of political democracies were long confused with oligarchic regionalism, the reformers of the 1930s created powerful antibodies against them. Democratic practices were rejected as instruments of resistance to change, useful only for ensuring an outdated system of privileges. The constitutional pact of 1934, in this case, served only to prove how burdensome the limitations were that the regional elites imposed on structural changes in the economy, the social order, administration, and politics.

The old political elites, who were committed to their regional bases, when they returned to the political game after 1946 and the ostracism of the dictatorship, could not free themselves from an electorate, most of which was poor and illiterate, that depended on small favors. The political and budgetary price of institutionalizing regional forces, giving them strong political representations, as was the case in this period, was therefore high. It retarded the maturation of a citizenry and required in exchange support and financing of the traditional ways of doing micropolitics in its privileged locus: state governments and Congress.

Paradoxically, the revitalization of regionalism usually occurred each time a new constitution was drafted, each time the dictatorships succumbed and the democratic regime resumed its course. As Nunes Leal brilliantly argued in his famous study, the strength of the *coronelismo* of the First Republic was inseparable from the strengthening of Brazil's representational regime, since it gave it the bargaining power of the higher offices of the state, the power to trade resources for votes.[52] This model has survived, point for point, to this day.

The 1946 regime revived federalism in its entirety, freeing it from the corporatist ties created by the 1934 constitution while pushing it into the arms of a reformist, centralizing populism, led by Vargas, Quadros, and Goulart. This regime sought ceaselessly the institutional reinforcement of the central government in the face of clientelist pressure from Congress and the quest for increased autonomy of the states.

For the populist leadership, the distance was the same as ever between the opposing forces; it was only adapted to the urban world and with an inverted significance. The "enemies of the people" also traded legal protection and services for votes. The Achilles heel of the developmentalists was, therefore, the absence of the preconditions of equality as a basic requirement for the exercise of freedom, an essential element of democracy. Unless a mass society, with a significant middle class, was constituted in Brazil, democracy would be limited to a tool to be manipulated by elites.

In practice, hostility against the federal system was bypassed by political accommodations and negotiations among regional actors and those at the political center, who were always defenders of federal decentralization, although disposed to see centralization as a necessary evil and as a bargaining tool for getting resources that their regions could not guarantee on their own.

Democratic Federalism: Municipalism and the Citizens' Constitution

Among the array of political reforms announced at the end of the twentieth century, none are more important or more challenging than the "federation reforms." These reforms have been carried out in stages since the early 1980s, when an irreversible process of political and administrative decentralization began. This broke the long cycle of centralization under the military regime, which the key ideologue of the dictatorship, General Couto e Silva, had denounced as "the black hole of centralization." Behind this incisive metaphor was the process of allotment of resources through which economic groups, professional bodies, interest groups, and regional interests had been appropriated funds from a wide range of sources in the public patrimony, while avoiding federal control. This organized disorder, which coincided with the crisis in developmentalism, was the exposed fracture of a corporatist centralism allied with political patrimonialism. This dragged the country into unbridled inflation, lack of financial and fiscal control, and a slow erosion of the political consensus and national identity.

Decentralization resulted in increased demands from the periphery for greater political autonomy and for less dependence on the federal government. The greatest push came from the movement of municipal and state governments that had taken office after the direct elections of 1982. This precedent of direct state elections, before even the direct elections for president, which did not take place until 1989, was the great ally in the somewhat anarchic decentralization that radicalized the crisis in the state (see chapter 6). Decentralization caused fragmenting tendencies not unlike what Gorbachev was experiencing in the Soviet Union.

As with the Soviet "empire," Brazil opted for a glasnost, not for a perestroika, as happened in China and Chile. This put political reforms and economic reforms seriously out of step with one another. This disconnect radicalized the decentralization and distribution of power among the political parties at the same time that it deepened the fiscal and financial crisis of the developmentalist model, which was strongly resistant to the new liberal economy. In fact, the period was marked by the dawn of civil society's municipality movement within the redemocratization struggle.

The model experiment in decentralization on the state level was the Franco Montoro administration (1982–86) in São Paulo. In an unprecedented gesture of daring, Montoro defended the social democratic doctrine of decentralization based on the principle of "subsidiarity," according to which "anything that can be done by a smaller community should not be done by a larger entity." An enthusiastic supporter of participatory federalism of Christian democratic inspiration, Montoro made a deal with the municipal governments, redistributing jurisdictions, services, and financial resources that revolutionized the administration of public policies in São Paulo.[53]

Another important rupture was the approval of the Passos Porto Amendment, which altered the distribution of constitutional funds in favor of the municipalities and states and unbalanced the preponderance of the federal government on the fiscal level. This political decision, which preceded the Constituent Assembly of 1988, made way for a federative pact that, for the first time in the world history of federalism, gave constitutional status to the municipalities, recognizing their existence as federal entities, equal in condition to the states. Thus the traditional constitutionalist model of "dual federalism," of American inspiration, was broken, and a tripartite model, defined by the jurist Miguel Reale as "trinitary federalism," was inaugurated.

Trinitary federalism was the fruit of the innovation and creativity of Brazilian legislators at this foundational moment in the history of Brazilian democracy. The process of the Constituent Assembly that yielded the 1988 constitution was consolidated in the course of the 1990s. This revolution recovered very old traditions of Portuguese municipalism, inherited from the interior of Portugal and spread throughout colonial Brazil, which lacked strong regional administrations.

The power of local political bosses was a deformed expression of this rural municipalism that, at the same time, was strategically used by the central government as a political force for the neutralization of provincial and state autonomy, during both the empire and the republic. In fact, the first Vargas government recognized the administrative autonomy of municipalities, and the 1967 tax reform, at first, tried to broaden automatic transfers. (Later these were converted into voluntary transfers, freely manipulated by the federal government.)

Fiscal liberation occurred definitively in 1988, with the creation of mutual participation funds (*fundos de participação*, a major form of transfer to state and local governments) that resulted from the growth in liquid revenue. This was more favorable for the municipalities than for the states, and it reduced the federal government's share from 67 to 52 percent, while the state's share rose from 25 to 28 percent and that of the municipalities rose from 9 to 17 percent.

In the meanwhile, the most important change was the transfer of powers, making the municipality, now largely of urban composition, take over definitive leadership in the conduct of social and local affairs, including infrastructure. The practice demonstrated that, whenever the municipality has resources, it competes toe to toe with the state, while states find themselves nearly orphans, decapitalized by the privatization of public service firms and squeezed into a trinity in which the jurisdictions are not yet well defined. Administration of the metropolitan regions, which would have been the states' responsibility, has not yet been assumed because of the tensions among the politically strong municipality of the capital city and those of the poorer periphery, which were ever expanding and had insufficient infrastructure.

Current federalism is characterized by a transitory model of competing jurisdictions that came into force with the 1988 constitution, leaving the federal, state, and municipal governments in an artificial position of equality. These ambiguities, contained in Article 23 of the constitution, continue in the absence of complementary regulatory legislation that, significantly, was never elaborated. In practice, the omission could be something new in Brazilian political tradition, namely the strengthening of the power and legitimacy of local governments. In a legal system with holes in it, it has been possible to speed up decentralization by devolving to the states some control over minimum wage, agrarian reform, and the environment. This also has included the ill-fated transfer of control over metropolitan areas from the federal to the state level. Freely testing the administrative capacity of the three levels and the workings of their respective duties is part of the new rules of the game, which has been favoring municipal initiative.

This decentralization from the bottom up had as a counterpart the broad significance of the voluntary federal transfers to the municipalities' benefit and to the states' detriment. The power of the municipality has stimulated very competitive local elections and helped to energize and "oxygenate" Brazilian democracy. In Brazil, therefore, an authentically republican federalism emerged with a strong democratic dimension. It incorporated into the principle of active citizenship and participatory democracy the modern concept of subsidiarity, based on state–civil society partnerships and on the shared jurisdictions of the several levels of government. In this formula, priority is always given to society over the government,[54] to local power over state power, and to state power over federal power.

The main distortion still to be fixed is chronic civil weakness, inherent not only in the oligarchic federalism that prevailed prior to 1930 but also in the democratic federalism of 1946–64, in which civil apathy and the absence of the exercise of citizenship were distinctive features, complementary to the statism and the populism that have imbued Brazilian democracy. This congenital malaise is caused, of course, by the disorganization and the isolation of a low-density population scattered over a vast territory. Chronic poverty, poor health conditions, and illiteracy among the large masses of rural origin and of recent migration to the cities have also been responsible for the accumulation of a social debt in the course of the development process, generating a chronic deficit in participation and citizenship.

This time, the full resumption of the federal ideal is not merely the result of the choice of the civilian elites in their process of institutional reconstruction, as was the case in the beginning of the republic, which had the strong influences of positivism and the military. The new federalism of the late twentieth century arose as an opposition to the authoritarianism and centralism of the military regime and, for this very reason, drove a form of democracy that was not limited, as it had been in the past, to giving value to the political parties and the system of representation, especially in the national Congress. These systems had been contaminated during the military dictatorship by the practices of the power blocs constituted by the official party, the technocracy, and the military bureaucracy that ruled Brazil for twenty-one years.

The new democracy was the fruit of broad social movements and of an unprecedented participatory process that put value in civil society over a national government that had been weakened not only by the long dictatorship but also by the wave of economic liberalism that swept the world with market globalization and the communications revolution. The rise of the "third sector" of nonstate public entities (see chapter 6) has been accompanied by a growing quest for transparency in public policy, thanks to the Public Ministry, *habeas data* (privacy and freedom of information), and the protection of various rights always geared to the values of citizenship and local power.

More than ever, a municipalism of old Portuguese roots has prospered, in opposition to the military regime and allied with civilian organizations. From the federalist perspective, this has strengthened municipal elections and administrations at the expense of state governments—traditionally the great beneficiaries of political opening and federal weakening. At the beginning of the twentieth century, Brazil had a "federation of the governors," marked by federated state and agrarian power, manipulating the representative system and functioning as a pact among elites that restricted citizenship and democracy by means of a "politics of the governors" and the "yoked vote." In contrast to this older power of oligarchic patronage, Brazil ended the century with an innovative federalism that was more societally based and libertarian, increasingly concerned with controlling public power and restricting the defects of patrimonialism, including clientelism, political corruption, abuses of economic power, and the "election industry."

Local government, for its part, is no longer associated with the image of the isolated municipality lost in the interior of the country, the distorted version of Portuguese traditional municipalism.[55] On the contrary, today local government represents new arenas of local identity, assembled around effervescent nuclei of expanding large and midsize cities that concentrate political and social energy and that harbor most of the Brazilian population (see chapter 13). The old Portuguese municipality, rural, family based, and subject to the church, so influential in colonial Brazil, almost no longer exists.[56] Although they are in their death throes, the old practices still exist, legitimated by the "political grammar" of nationalized clientelism disguised as federalism. Such patrimonialism is not to be confused, though, with the mere distribution of federal resources and government positions.

Notes

1. K. C. Wheare, *Federal Government* (London, New York, Toronto, Oxford: Oxford University Press, 1951).

2. Golbery do Couto e Silva, *Conjuntura política nacional: O Poder Executivo e geopolítica do Brasil* (Rio de Janeiro: José Olympio, 1981).

3. The concept of patrimonialism, formulated by Max Weber, was brilliantly applied to the study of great empires by Samuel Eisenstadt in *The Political Systems of Empires* (London: Free Press of Glencoe, 1963). Raimundo Faoro applied the same concept to the interpretation of the Brazilian national state in *Os donos do poder* (Porto Alegre: Globo, 1958). See also chapter 6.

4. Maria Cecília Londres da Fonseca, *O patrimônio em processo* (Rio de Janeiro: Editora da Universidade Federal do Rio de Janeiro/Ministério de Cultura-Instituto do Patrimônio Histórico e Artístico Nacional, 1997). See also chapter 5.

5. Aspásia Camargo, ed., *O golpe silencioso: As origens da República corporativa* (Rio de Janeiro: Rio Fundo, 1989). See also chapter 7.

6. Paul Peterson, *The Price of Federalism* (Washington: Brookings Institute, 1995).

7. José Murilo de Carvalho, "Federalismo y centralización en el Imperio brasileño," in *Federalismos latinoamericanos, México, Brasil, Argentina*, ed. Marcello Carmagnani (Mexico: Fondo de Cultura, 1993).

8. Viscount of Uruguai, *Ensaio sobre o direito administrativo* (1862; [Rio de Janeiro]: Imprensa Nacional, 1960).

9. Carvalho, "Federalismo y centralización en el Imperio brasileño."

10. Ibid., 64.

11. Alberto Sales, *A pátria paulista* (Brasília: Editora da Universidade de Brasília, 1983).

12. Amaro Quintas, *A Revolução de 1817*, 2nd ed. (Rio de Janeiro: José Olympio, 1985).

13. Aureliano Cândido Tavares Bastos, *A província: Estudo sobre a descentralização no Brasil* (Rio de Janeiro: Garnier, 1870).

14. Ibid., 10, 14–15, 17, 27.

15. Carvalho, "Federalismo y centralización en el Imperio brasileño."

16. Ibid., 67.

17. Rui Barbosa, *Escritos e discursos seletos*, 128–29, quoted in Bolivar Lamounier, *Rui Barbosa* (Rio de Janeiro: Nova Fronteira, 1999), 83.

18. Carvalho, "Federalismo y centralización en el Imperio brasileño," 68.

19. Rui Barbosa, *Campanhas jornalísticas*, quoted in Lamounier, *Rui Barbosa*.

20. Ibid.

21. Lamounier, *Rui Barbosa*, 92.

22. Francisco José de Oliveira Viana, *O idealismo na Constituição*, quoted in Marly Silva da Motta, *A nação faz cem anos: A questão nacional no centenário da Independência* (Rio de Janeiro: Editora da Fundação Getúlio Vargas/Centro de Pesquisa e de Documentação de História Contemporâneo do Brasil, 1992).

23. Francisco José de Oliveira Viana, *Instituições políticas brasileiras*, quoted in Lamounier, *Rui Barbosa*.

24. Victor Nunes Leal, *Coronelismo, enxada e voto* (1949; São Paulo: Alfa-Omega, 1986).

25. Barbosa, *Campanhas jornalísticas*, quoted in Lamounier, *Rui Barbosa*, 86–87.

26. Paulo Mercadante, *Militares e civis: A ética e o compromisso* (Rio de Janeiro: Zahar, 1978), quoted in Lamounier, *Rui Barbosa*, 88.

27. Manoel Ferraz de Campos Sales, *Da propaganda à presidência* (São Paulo: Laemmert, 1908).

28. Renato Lessa, *A invenção republicana: Campos Sales, as bases e a decadência da Primeira República brasileira* (São Paulo, Rio de Janeiro: Instituto Universitário de Pesquisas do Rio de Janeiro, 1988).

29. Joseph L. Love, "Federalismo y regionalismo en Brasil, 1889–1937," in Carmagnani, *Federalismos latinoamericanos*, 181.

30. Joseph L. Love, *Rio Grande do Sul and Brazilian Regionalism, 1882–1930* (Stanford, Calif.: Stanford University Press, 1971).

31. Ruben George Oliven, *A parte e o todo: A diversidade cultural no Brasil nação* (Petrópolis: Vozes, 1992).

32. Maria Antonieta Parahyba, "Participação política na República Velha," *Dados* no. 7 (Rio de Janeiro: Instituto Universitário de Pesquisas do Rio de Janeiro, n.d.).

33. Azevedo Amaral, *A aventura política do Brasil* (Rio de Janeiro: José Olympio, 1935).

34. Motta, *A nação faz cem anos*.

35. Ibid., 20–21.

36. Oliveira Viana, *O idealismo na constituição*, quoted in ibid., 23.

37. Motta, *A nação faz cem anos*, 23.

38. *Careta*, 11 September 1920, quoted in ibid.

39. Vicente Licínio Cardoso, *À margem da história do Brasil* (1933; São Paulo: Companhia Editora Nacional-Coleção Brasiliana, 1938), 198.

40. Francisco José de Oliveira Viana, *Problemas de política objetiva* (São Paulo: Companhia Editora Nacional, 1930), 94.

41. Cardoso, *À margem da história do Brasil*, 202.

42. Ibid., 197.

43. See Alberto Torres, *O problema nacional brasileiro: Introdução a um programa de organização nacional* (Rio de Janeiro: Imprensa Nacional, 1914), and Alberto Torres, *A organização nacional* (Rio de Janeiro: Imprensa Nacional, 1914). These were the bibles of Brazilian intellectuals of the 1930s.

44. Oliveira Viana, *Problemas de política objetiva*, 30.

45. Ibid., 79.

46. On the "Brazilian archipelago," see chapters 1 and 2.

47. Azevedo Amaral, *O Estado autoritário e a realidade nacional* (Rio de Janeiro: José Olympio, 1938).

48. Oliveira Viana, *Problemas de política objetiva*, 89–90.

49. See the excellent work by Edson Nunes, *A gramática política do Brasil: Clientelismo e insulamento burocrático* (Rio de Janeiro: Zahar, 1997).

50. For a more detailed analysis of this period, see Aspásia Camargo, "La federacióin sometida," in Carmagnani, *Federalismos latinoamericanos*.

51. Angela de Castro Gomes, ed., *Regionalismo e centralização política* (Rio de Janeiro: Nova Fronteira, 1978).

52. Nunes Leal, *Coronelismo, enxada e voto*.

53. Antônio Carlos de Mendes Thame and Ricardo Montoro, eds., *Franco Montoro* (São Paulo: Igual, 2000).

54. José Alfredo de Oliveira Baracho, *O princípio da subsidiaridade, conceito e evolução* (Rio de Janeiro: Forense, 1997).

55. Maria Isaura Pereira de Queiroz, *O mandonismo local na vida política brasileira* (1957; São Paulo: Instituto de Estudos Brasileiros/Universidade de São Paulo, 1969).

56. See the brilliant study by Nestor Duarte, *A ordem privada e a organização política nacional* (São Paulo: Companhia Editora Nacional-Coleção Brasiliana, 1939).

9

JOSÉ SEIXAS LOURENÇO

Amazonia:
Past Progress and Future Prospects

Amazonia's Natural and Cultural Diversity

The Greater Amazon Region, or Amazonia, encompasses about 7.8 million square kilometers in northern South America, approximately 60 percent of the combined area of Bolivia, Brazil, Colombia, Ecuador, French Guiana, Guyana, Peru, Surinam, and Venezuela. This corresponds to about 44 percent of the total area of South America and represents 5 percent of the earth's land area. Dominated by the humid tropical forest named Hylea by Alexander von Humboldt, the region covers most of the Amazon River basin. To the north, this forest transcends the limits of the basin; to the south, it is replaced by grassland, savanna, and scrubland known as *cerrado*.

Amazonia includes approximately 20 percent of the earth's potable water, one-third of its broadleaf forest, and 10 percent of its biota. Of its 780 million hectares, nearly 350 million are virgin forest. The Amazon River may be the world's longest river[1] and is certainly the largest in volume — five times the volume of the Zaire (Congo) and twelve times that of the Mississippi. The Amazon and its tributaries form a network of navigable waterways of about 25,000 kilometers. Brazilian Amazonia includes over 60 percent of the larger region, or about 500 million hectares. It includes Brazil's "Legal Amazonia," statutorily defined as including the states of Acre, Amapá, Amazonas, Mato Grosso, Pará, Rondônia, Roraima, Tocantins, and part of Maranhão.

The vast territory is characterized by unusual biodiversity. The number of plant species that have been classified is estimated at more than 1.5 million of a total universe of anywhere from 5 to 30 million species. More than 25 percent of the drugs prescribed in the world today contain active ingredients derived from plants growing in tropical forests. Brazil's indigenous peoples command knowledge of approximately 1,300 plants with antibiotic, narcotic, abortifacient, contraceptive, antidiarrheal, anticoagulant, fungicidal, anesthetic, antiviral, and muscle relaxing properties, among others. Only about 100 of these plants are being used commercially.

Brazilian Amazonia, moreover, is home to more than 20 million human inhabitants. About 60 percent of this population is concentrated in urban centers. The region's economic base ranges from classic extractive activities and mineral prospecting to advanced mineral production and manufacture of household appliances. Regional society includes diverse ethnic groups engaged in an array of productive activities. These include Indians, Blacks, and mestizos (*caboclos*) who are small-scale producers, landless rural workers, urban workers, small and large property owners, and traditional and modern entrepreneurs. Many of these social actors migrated in the last decades from their regions of origin and now contribute to the social and economic diversity of Amazonia.

There are, then, several important diversities to underscore:

(a) physical and natural diversity, expressed in landscapes and ecosystems with distinct features;

(b) biodiversity and its included biomass, which science has yet to research thoroughly;

(c) diversity of settlement, imposed from the outside through expulsion of populations from other regions, and from within through the intense mobility of many of the region's inhabitants;

(d) cultural diversity, a product of the extent, dispersal, and variation of the "people of the forest"—the historical population—faced with large numbers of recent in-migrants;

(e) economic diversity, which has broadened thanks to numerous small public and private projects, public works, and social services, fomented by fiscal incentives and other factors;

(f) social diversity, which results from these growing, multifaceted influences.[2]

This essay analyzes Amazonia's diversity from the point of view of the several cycles of economic activity since the mid-nineteenth century.

The Rubber Cycle

Expansion of the Labor Supply and the Great Northeastern Migration

From 1850 to 1912, the first phase of the rubber cycle, Amazonia went through great economic and demographic changes. When the price of rubber on the foreign market began to rise, the region's population was small. The labor supply had been notoriously scarce in the region since the beginning of the colonial era. Amazonia's indigenous population was employed in the extraction of latex under a regime of slave labor. Black slaves did not participate in rubber production but rather were reserved for domestic labor. The growing international demand for rubber in the 1860s and 1870s made the scarcity of labor in Amazonia more acute. The only alternative for increasing the labor supply for latex extraction was through the migration of workers from other regions of Brazil, especially the Northeast.

The migratory flows from the Northeast were encouraged by problems afflicting that region: the decline in cotton cultivation after 1860, which left a large number of workers unoccupied, and the tragic effects of the drought of 1877–80. After 1880, the flow of migrants from the Northeast swelled the labor supply in the rubber tree groves of Amazonia and continued through the golden age of the rubber boom. Economist Celso Furtado estimates a total flow of 260,000 migrants to Amazonia between 1872 and 1900, and a total of at least 500,000 by 1910.[3] Amazonia specialist Samuel Benchimol considers these estimates too high, believing that migrants numbered about 160,000 by 1900 and 300,000 by 1910.[4] Historian Caio Prado Jr. states that, in 1872, Amazonia had a population of 337,000, and, by 1890, this number had risen to 476,000; by 1906, it was 1.1 million.[5]

Several towns and urban centers arose as commercial centers supporting the latex extraction activity. The cities of Belém, near the mouth of the Amazon, and Manaus, at the confluence of the Rio Negro and the Solimões (as the Amazon is known in Brazil between this point and the Peruvian border) became strategic points for the trade and shipping of rubber to European and North American markets. The occupation of the labor force with latex extraction meant that there was a labor shortage in agriculture to supply foodstuffs to the urban populations. This fact justified the emergence of plans for colonizing the region during the rubber boom years. The failure of these plans contributed to more workers' moving into latex extraction, leading the urban centers to import basic goods from other regions.

From Expansion to Decline

Even though the regional economy was limited to furnishing a raw material to foreign industrial centers, Amazonia enjoyed a period of prosperity until the second decade of the twentieth century. Modernization spread through government investment concentrated on the improvement of services in the larger cities, including lighting, sewers, and theaters. Transportation improved with the construction of ports, canals, roads, and railways. There were, therefore, advancements in urbanization, even including the growth of a modest industrial infrastructure. Nevertheless, agriculture continued to be primitive, with a high concentration of labor in the primary sector and ongoing extractive exploitation, with supplying clients as the primary relation. The wealth generated by the rubber economy remained concentrated in the hands of the rubber plantation owners and of the traders, who, in general, were uninterested in diversifying the region's productive activities.

The period of decline of latex extraction in Amazonia began around 1912 and lasted until the 1920s. High costs of rubber production in the region and price-inflating speculative practices of middlemen ended up stimulating cultivated rubber production in Asia, especially in Sri Lanka, Malaysia, Indonesia, and Thailand. In Brazil, latex was gathered from forest groves, whereas in Asia, rubber trees were cultivated, reducing gathering time and cost. In 1920, rubber, which had previously contributed significantly to Brazilian exchange reserves, represented 3 percent of Brazilian exports.[6] In global terms, Brazilian rubber production fell from 50 percent in 1910 to only 5 percent in 1926.

With this economic defeat in the world market, another migratory movement began within the region, this time from rural to urban areas. The greatest effect of this migration of former rubber workers was on the cities, principally Belém and Manaus. The metropolitan area of Belém at the end of the nineteenth century had a population of 150,000; in 1920, its population was 232,000, making it the fifth-largest city in Brazil. Manaus grew from 50,000 to 75,000.[7] At the same time, other municipalities in the region experienced economic stagnation, and the remaining population returned to subsistence agriculture.

The Period between the World Wars:
Nearly Thirty Years of Stagnation

The Post–World War I Era

The failure of government efforts, such as the Rubber Defense Plan (Plano de Defesa da Borracha) to support and finance latex production as it went into decline in Amazonia, caused the regional economy to stagnate and even regress for almost thirty years. The Amazonian writer Márcio Souza describes the scene:

> In fact, in the period from the early 1920s to the Second World War, the wasting, misery, and corruption affected all sectors. The situation was one of calamity and the state behaved like a colonial region abandoned by the colonizer. . . . Manaus suffered a startling population decline, and the rate of liquidity fell to practically zero. The rural masses returned to the system of subsistence labor and to a regime of barter. The middle-class-turned-working-class lacked available credit for commerce, and, with the high rate of unemployment, it even sank to levels of extreme poverty. The abandoned mansions began to crumble, and the streets filled with potholes. All the infrastructure of urban services began to collapse, and the exodus of the populations from the interior accelerated this process.[8]

Some of the larger merchants, however, shifted their extractive activities to nuts and lumber, thus maintaining the supply system. The rise in the prices of these products created possibilities for employment. The area of Marabá, on the middle course of the Tocantins River, became an important urban and commercial center at a time when most of the other cities of Amazonia were plunged into stagnation. In the south of the state of Pará after the 1930s, a complementary relation between nut extraction and diamond and crystal prospecting emerged, facilitating migratory flows composed for the most part of individuals associated with mineral prospecting coming from other regions of the country. The economic results of mining activity were modest, since almost all diamonds were exported and even traded as contraband. Nevertheless, there arose small settlements of prospectors—known as corrutelas—some of which were the seeds of new urban centers, as was the case with São João do Araguaia. Because of the need to feed the inhabitants of the corrutelas, interest in agriculture and ranching increased. With time, mineral extraction gave way to planting crops and raising livestock. Even so, until the mid-1950s, cattle were imported to the region for local consumption.[9]

World War II and the New Rubber Battle

President Getúlio Vargas's "Speech from the Amazon River," given during his visit to Manaus on 10 October 1940, opened the prospect of a new phase of development in the region, in connection with the "movement of national reconstruction." The development plan needed financial resources for its implementation, though. Taking advantage of the deepening of World War II, with the Japanese occupation of Malayan rubber plantations, Vargas and President Roosevelt signed the Washington Accords, which had the goal of meeting the Allied forces' demand for rubber through an increased latex production effort in Amazonia. For this, a financial and administrative structure was set up, which included several institutions: the Rubber Credit Bank (Banco de Crédito da Borracha), now the Bank of Amazonia (Banco da Amazônia, BASA); the Public Health Special Service (Serviço Especial de Saúde Pública), the present-day National Health Foundation (Fundação Nacional de Saúde); the Agronomy Institute of the North (Instituto Agronômico do Norte); and the Administrative Commission for the Movement of Workers to Amazonia (Commissão Administrativa do Encaminhamento dos Trabalhadores para a Amazônia). Three new federal territories were created: Amapá, Rio Branco, and Guaporé (which much later became the states of Amapá, Roraima, and Rondônia).

Between 1942 and 1945, the rubber battle mobilized around 100,000 northeastern migrants and increased production to nearly 20,000 tons of rubber. This did not mean a sustained phase of economic development for the region as a whole, however. With the end of the world war, the return of Asian rubber supply to Western markets and the increased production of synthetic rubber upset the prices of Amazonian latex production. The Allies had won the war, but Amazonia had lost the rubber battle.

Nevertheless, Amazonia did not return to its previous state; stagnation was partially prevented by putting agricultural settlement plans into action, mainly near the most important urban areas. This would lessen the migratory reflux. Moreover, the monopoly of the Rubber Credit Bank over trade and the setting of prices subsidized by rubber production continued.[10]

Developmentalist Policies of the 1950s and 1960s

In the 1950s, several important changes in the political and economic structure of the country took place, with the growth of the industrial sector and the urban population centered in the Southeast. Amazonia continued to be thought of as a region that provided raw materials, with great natural resource potential, which needed to be incorporated into Brazil's economy. In 1953, the federal government created the Superintendency for the Amazonia Economic Valorization Plan (Superintendência do Plano de Valorização Econômica da Amazônia, SPVEA), with the goals of promoting infrastructure construction, developing agricultural production, and exploiting mineral resources. In the following years, there was economic growth, led by agriculture, mainly the cultivation of jute in the lower Amazon. Between 1955 and 1960, investments in manganese exploration in the Serra do Navio in Amapá and the installation of a petroleum refinery in Manaus were mostly responsible for the growth in gross domestic product (GDP) of the region.

The foundations began to be laid for a new cycle of economic development in Amazonia that would begin in the 1960s. The opening of the Belém-Brasília Highway in 1960 linked Amazonia to the rapidly expanding Center-West. A new migratory flow toward Amazonia began. It included not only northeasterners but also migrants from the regions to the south. Patterns of land settlement changed, occurring now along the highways, which altered long stretches of forest. The highways facilitated expansion of local livestock ranching. Settlement of the region based on federal intervention took shape with the efforts of the military government after the mid-1960s. In 1966, the government launched Operation Amazonia, setting up an institutional apparatus whose aims were regional settlement, development, and integration. The Superintendency for the Development of Amazonia (Superintendência do Desenvolvimento da Amazônia, SUDAM) succeeded SPVEA, and BASA succeeded the Rubber Credit Bank. Both organizations had their headquarters in Belém. A free trade zone, overseen by its own superintendency (Superintendência da Zona Franca de Manaus, SUFRAMA), was established in Manaus. This was to be an area of free import and export, with special fiscal incentives, intended to become an industrial, commercial, and agricultural center serving the states and territories of Acre, Amazonas, Rondônia, and Roraima.

SUDAM launched its first five-year plan (1967–71) with a focus on transportation infrastructure. The paving of the Belém-Brasília Highway, the improvement of the Cuiabá–Porto Velho Highway, and the widening of the state highway systems helped increase the migratory flow to Amazonia from the South. The construction of highway axes and the implementation of fiscal incentives favored the rise of new economic centers in the region, geared to livestock activities and mineral extraction, without the least regard for environmental impacts.

The Policy of "Integration to Avoid Surrender" of the 1970s

The 1970s were characterized by even more pronounced federal government actions in Amazonia, in the name of national security. Another target of government actions was, on this occasion, the excess labor force created by the modernization of agriculture in the southern part of the country. This was a period of generous grants of fiscal incentives and exemptions for entrepreneurs in the agricultural and industrial sectors. The 1970s were marked by the National Integration Program (Programa de Integração Nacional, PIN), the Land Redistribution Program (Programa de Redistribuição de Terra, Pro-Terra), and the building of new highways (the Trans-Amazon, Cuiabá-Santarém, and others). The government also expanded the telecommunications system, promoted official colonization along the federal highways, and began building hydroelectric dams. With these actions, the authoritarian state hoped for profound changes in the economic and social arenas that, in essence, would stimulate the accumulation of capital with the opening of new sectorial or subregional markets.

Programs launched by the Medici government envisioned the settlement of 100,000 families in five years, on land reserves of up to ten kilometers on either side of the Trans-Amazon and Cuiabá-Santarém Highways. The farming villages ended up not taking root for several reasons: the unsuitability of the settlers for the ecological conditions of the region, the rapid decline in soil fertility, insufficient technical assistance, and the difficulties in the storage and shipping of products. The absence of the promised infrastructure associated with unsuitability and conditions so different from those of the place of origin were fatal.

In 1974, the government launched a new special program, the Program of Amazonian Agricultural-Ranching and Agricultural-Mining Centers (Programa de Pólos Agropecuários e Agrominerais de Amazônia, known as Polamazônia), with a total of fifteen centers of growth in the region as foci of development. In these centers, public and private resources were concentrated in large-scale ranching projects, lumbering and mining activities, and hydroelectric projects. Private settlement was privileged, with the installment of large companies attracted by fiscal and credit advantages, to the detriment of the older strategy of colonization by small farmers. The National Institute of Colonization and Agrarian Reform (Instituto Nacional de Colonização e Reforma Agrária, INCRA) implemented the Landholding Projects (Projetos Fundiários) for the installation of large-scale colonization projects as part of a strategy for attracting private capital. Throughout the 1970s, the GDP of Amazonia grew at a rate of 12.2 percent per year, well over the estimated 8.3 percent growth of the national GDP. Nevertheless, the problems of land tenure worsened because the large, capital-intensive enterprises created few employment opportunities and took up vast expanses of land, accentuating the conflicts around landownership. In addition to the social problems, there were environmental ones caused by deforestation, including the burning of broad expanses of tropical forest. This was a result of the effort to establish livestock ranches or to show some evidence of activity on the properties that had benefited from fiscal incentives.

The 1980s: Amazonia as an Urbanized and Industrialized Jungle

In 1981, the Superintendency for Development of the Center-West (Superintendência do Desenvolvimento do Centro-Oeste, SUDECO) launched the Integrated Program for the Development of the Northwest (Programa Integrada de Desenvolvimento do Noroeste, Polonoroeste) in the area around the Cuiabá–Porto Velho Highway. This highway, BR-364, had been recently paved with financing from the World Bank. The original program intended to benefit the small-scale producers already established in the region and paid explicit attention to environmental quality and the indigenous population. The agricultural expansion that had been planned, however, was not successful. Even though the soils of the state of Rondônia were better than those in other Amazonian areas, the land lost fertility after two or three years of use, and brushwood was the natural fate of almost all of the deforested area. As a result, the state's decennial population growth rate fell from about 500,000 according to the 1970 census to little more than 100,000 in the 1980 census.[11]

In the 1980s, given the fragility of Brazilian public finances, support for projects in Amazonia had to come from private international investment. The large hydroelectric projects, such as Tucuruí, Balbina, and Samuel, and the large productive sector projects, such as the Greater Carajás Program (Programa Grande Carajás, PGC) and the Albras-Alunorte complex, had been seeded by the state with the intent of yielding revenues necessary to pay the foreign debt. Thus, in the 1980s, the basic feature of industry in the region was increasingly production destined for the international market.[12] The purpose of the large hydroelectric projects was to furnish cheap energy for the large-scale mining and metallurgy operations.

PGC was founded in 1980 with a grant of tax incentives for undertakings within an area of 900,000 square kilometers in the states of Pará, Maranhão, and northern Goiás (now in the state of Tocantins). The Valley of the Rio Doce Company (Companhia Vale do Rio Doce, CVRD), a public-private company that is Brazil's largest mining and metal producer, began operating the Carajás Iron Project (Projeto Ferro-Carajás) in 1985, thanks to investments of $3.6 billion. The operation mined and processed iron ore in the Carajás Mountains. From there, the iron was shipped 890 kilometers by rail to the port of São Luís, Maranhão, and then by cargo vessel to foreign markets, mainly in Japan and Germany.

In 1985, with $1.4 billion in investment in a joint venture with CVRD and Nippon Amazon Aluminum Company (NAAC, a consortium of thirty Japanese metallurgy companies), the Albras-Alunorte complex began aluminum production in Barcarena, near Belém, Pará. Albras benefited from power generated by the Tucuruí Dam. The Trombetas Project of Rio do Norte Mining (Mineração Rio do Norte, MRN) in the municipality of Oriximiná, Pará, began bauxite production in 1979. MRN was a consortium of CVRD, the Aluminum Company of Canada (Alcan), Billington/Shell, and the Votorantim Group. The bauxite was to be processed into alumina in the Alunorte plant in Barcarena, but its operations were frozen because of a change in strategy by the Japanese partners. Since 1984, MRN has supplied the Alumar aluminum plant in São Luís, a $1.5 billion enterprise of the Aluminum Company of America (Alcoa) and Billington/Shell.

The large mining and metallurgy projects in Amazonia were very important in light of the decline in other segments of the economy in the course of the 1980s. In 1978, the value of exports for the state of Pará was less than $200 million, the main products being black pepper, lumber, and Brazil nuts. In 1980, the value of state exports reached $430 million, with bauxite from Trombetas making up 15 percent of this total. In 1987, with iron from Carajás and aluminum from Barcarena, Pará's exports exceeded $1 billion. In 1990, these three large operations constituted 70 percent of Pará's exports.

Analysis of the production chain resulting from these enterprises shows that they were not well integrated with the local economies. The effects of the chain were insignificant in the MRN and Albras projects. The Carajás Iron Project had some downline effects, such as the establishment of smelting plants and ferroalloys in Pará and Maranhão. The establishment of these companies did not represent a change in their essentially export-oriented character, nor did it unleash a process of industrialization in the region.[13]

Thus the balance of Amazonian development in the 1980s was uneven. On the one hand, the lack of locks in the construction of the Tucuruí Dam made the river unnavigable for about 2,000 kilometers from the Central Plateau to the northern coast. This could have linked the Araguaia-Tocantins waterway with a network of Amazon River waterways and with the Belém and Vila do Conde port complex. On the other hand, the large number of incentives in the Manaus Free Trade Zone led to the formation of an electrical and electronics manufacturing zone that increased exponentially the GDP of Amazonas, of which 95 percent is concentrated in Manaus, causing a strong urban migratory flux. An important economic change took place in Rondônia, which doubled from 5 to 10 percent its share of the regional GDP between 1970 and 1990. This was the result of the intense growth of the agricultural and livestock ranching sector.

The effort to integrate the economy of Amazonia with that of the rest of the country had as a landmark the large infrastructural, industrial, and farming and ranching projects. In the 1980s, considered Brazil's "lost decade," in which the economy grew only 1.9 percent per year, Amazonia's GDP grew at an annual rate of 6.3 percent. The attempts at state action intended to promote greater internal investment of the incomes generated by the large export-oriented operations were not successful on a state level, however. The large projects coexisted with primitive forms of natural resource exploitation, such as prospecting, which absorbed at least 400,000 workers directly engaged in gold extraction, especially in Serra Pelada, the Tapajós River, and the Madeira River. In the state of Roraima, illegal prospecting on Yanomami tribal lands involved about 40,000 prospectors.

The use of inadequate extractive techniques and the abuse of mercury caused increased ecological damage, especially river pollution. At the beginning of the 1990s, gold prospecting, facing the exhaustion of secondary deposits, began to decline and yielded to industrial mining. Consequently, the environmental damage lessened, but serious social problems arose in its place because of the lack of employment alternatives for prospectors. These old mining areas thus lost their economic base.[14]

The 1990s: The Environmental Question

National and international consciousness raising about environmental problems—deforestation and large-scale forest burning, river pollution, and extinction of species of flora and fauna—was on display in June 1992 at the United Nations Conference on Environment and Development (UNCED), held in Rio de Janeiro. The accords that were signed, mainly on biodiversity and climate change as well as Agenda 21, provided a new frame of reference. The environmental variable came to be included in public discourse and in setting policies, as did the concept of sustainable development.

In response to foreign and domestic pressures, international funding agencies, which until then had supported road building and large-scale projects, radically shifted their position by making loans conditional on the completion of environmental impact studies. In this context, the Pilot Program for the Protection of Brazilian Tropical Forests (Programa Piloto para a Proteção das Florestas Tropicais do Brasil, PPG7) was launched. Considered the largest program of international cooperation, it brought about $300 million in donations from the G7 countries and the European Union in partnership with the Brazilian government. It was an innovative experiment that supported a large number of projects and promising initiatives for environmental management and sustainable development.

The Integrated National Policy for Amazonia (Política Nacional Integrada para a Amazônia), approved by the National Legal Amazonia Council in June 1995, is the result of an evaluation of experiences with development in the region. It has as its goal raising the quality of life of the region's population through sustainable economic growth, fuller use of natural and cultural potentials, and regional retention and better distribution of wealth. Based on the reevaluation of the projects already implemented, the redirection of the structure of productions was guided by technological renovation in the economic activities of known environmental impact (mining, mineral prospecting, timber harvesting, livestock raising, and others), modernization and revitalization of traditional activities (fishing, gathering, agriculture, and river navigation), development and implementation of new activities of high economic potential and environmental sustainability (forestry, bioindustry, and ecotourism), and adequately equipping the urban centers with a view to their role in integrating systems of transportation and as sources for innovations in the region.

Within the scope of this integrated policy, two innovative projects with a capacity for yielding positive impact were formulated and incorporated into the Brazil in Action Program (Programa Brasil em Ação) of 1988.

First, the Brazilian Molecular Ecology Program for the Sustainable Use of Amazonian Biodiversity (Programa Brasileiro de Ecologia Molecular para o Uso Sustentável da Biodiversidade da Amazônia, PROBEM Amazônia) has been implemented by the Bio-Amazonia Social Organization (Organização Social Bio-amazônia) in partnership with the Ministries of the Environment, Science and Technology, and National Integration, with support from SUFRAMA, SUDAM, and BASA. PROBEM Amazônia aims to install a group of bioindustries in the region and act in the areas of knowledge production and state-of-the-art technology transfer, through various modes of partnership with research institutions and the private sector. In addition, the purpose of PROBEM Amazônia is to contribute to the diversification of the structures of production in the Manaus Free Trade Zone. Its focus of activity has been the creation of industrial products with high value added and with market potential.

Second, the Amazonian Ecotourism Development Program (Programa de Desenvolvimento do Ecoturismo na Amazônia, Proecotur) was created in partnership with the federal, state, and municipal governments and the organized business sector of the region, with the intent of establishing centers of tourism in each state of the region. Proecotur was designed to receive $210 million from the Inter-American Development Bank (IDB).

Concomitantly, an effort of implementing new businesses connected to renewable natural resources and biodiversity should begin with a foundation in advanced technologies and regional knowledge: natural products agroindustry, fishing industry, and timber and forest agriculture complexes, in addition to bioindustry and ecotourism. The specific natural potentials of the region, including its rich, unique seed bank, offer still underutilized conditions for the multiplication and diversification of enterprises of various sorts and scales. Among the investment opportunities are floodplain agriculture, fishing and fish farming, wild animal breeding, fruit cultivation, and the production of essential oils.

The recent implementation of agroindustrial complexes in Amazonia imposes the need to establish measures that prevent expansion at the expense of deforestation and water and soil resource degradation. Agricultural practices of sustainable management of natural resources should be encouraged, and processing and storage facilities should be incorporated as a way of adding value to regional products, especially those resulting from the labors of small farmers. The challenge of agriculture in Amazonia is to intensify production while maintaining the health of the soil. Some areas of eastern Amazonia that have been foci of deforestation and wasteful practices of natural resource use for more than thirty years are showing signs of agricultural intensification.[15]

In this region one can see a growth in livestock raising among small-scale producers as an alternative for increasing income. Cattle are easy to raise, transport, and sell. They bring a good price, and, at the same time, they provide milk for the producing family's consumption. Specialization and intensification are promising ways to increase profits for both small and large holdings. Some ranchers are rehabilitating old pastures by reseeding them with adaptive forage and fertilization in an attempt to put ranching on a sustainable footing.[16] Income generated by timber harvesting has also had an important role in the recovery of degraded pasture lands.

In the timber sector, there are good prospects on the international market for tropical woods, provided they come from areas under a regimen of sustainable management. Timber harvesting has had a large share in the regional income, but timber companies have often carried out selective and, in general, predatory exploration of species of high commercial value. This makes necessary incentives for forest management as well as investments in consolidation of the entire production chain that vertically and horizontally integrates the timber industry.

From this same perspective, the region must take advantage of advances in mining and metallurgy, vertically integrating and restructuring the economic complexes already created to achieve a better fit with the environmental and social systems of the region. Moreover, mechanisms must be put in place to require of the existing enterprises increased levels of value added to the extracted ore, through its processing in the region, as with pig iron, metallic silicon, and ferroalloys. Mechanisms of another kind must be put in place to integrate mineral production with other production that addresses more directly the needs of the population. As for the implementation of new complexes, it is necessary to establish criteria that assure nonpredatory use of natural resources and the spread of their multiplier effects throughout the region in employment and income.

Locating the free trade zone in Manaus was a strategic factor in continental integration and better insertion into the world economy. On the other hand, in the Manaus Free Trade Zone, mechanisms directed at raising the levels of quality and productivity in industrial firms must be improved, as must the adjustment of processes to the demands of technological "naturalization" and of specialization.

The Outlook for the Twenty-first Century

The development policies implemented in the last decades of the twentieth century fostered accelerated growth in the regional economy and diversification and modernization of the productive structure. Amazonian development now involves diversified activities that range from gathering and extraction to those of the electrical and electronics industries. The most dynamic segment of its productive structure is supported by a tripod: the PGC, the Belém-Barcarena region, and the Manaus Free Trade Zone. There are also important ranching and farming axes in the southwest of Pará, in Tocantins, in the north of Mato Grosso, and in Rondônia. Other experiments in scattered parts of the region point to new possibilities for the use of forest and water resources.

The results of this process in terms of regional development are, however, limited. Internalization of income and employment is insufficient. A substantial portion of Amazonians are excluded from the benefits of economic development. Today, a significant part of the population lives in extreme poverty, especially in the large cities. There is an enormous social debt to be paid.

At the same time, export of the region's natural resources is disorderly and, in many places, predatory. Poverty and assaults on the environment are proven to be associated factors in the same process of degradation. The reversal of this process demands another form of development—socially just, environmentally balanced, economically effective, and linked to an ethical dimension that meets the basic demands of the national project. It is necessary to put the country in tune with the deep and swift global transformations that come especially from the technological-scientific revolution and from the environmental crisis that alter, respectively, the technical-productive base and the organization for the production of labor, and the relation of society to nature and its resources. In this context, nature takes on new meanings alongside the old. For many populations, it continues to be the foundation of their material and cultural life. It also continues to be fundamental as a resource base, indispensable for their economic growth.[17]

The new technologies, however, require the use of elements of nature on a new tier, for example, as biodiversity is a source for biotechnology. In other words, they value nature as capital for current and future activities. Brazil, and Amazonia in particular, brings together the conditions necessary to move forward on a broad front, ranging from basic to applied research, especially on biodiversity. The acceptance of this challenge, if brought to term, will serve as a foundation for the construction of a new form of modern "biomass" civilization, based on sustainable use of natural resources.[18] Therefore, Brazil must recognize the need to acquire, through international cooperation and in accordance with the global

Convention on Biodiversity, scientific knowledge and state-of-the-art technologies to realize the potential in the region, especially in the genetic resources of Amazonia.

Undoubtedly, the new style of development strengthens the strategic importance of Amazonia. This importance derives, most of all, from its comparative advantages in the country and in the world: land area, geographic position, and scale and diversity of its resource base. With regard to foreign challenges, the rapid progress of Mercosul (in Spanish Mercosur) and the succession of bilateral accords and of progressive inclusion in the South American regional bloc are proof that Brazilian Amazonia cannot be isolated from global tendencies. The networking of transportation, communication, and productive processes among the member countries of the Amazonian Cooperation Treaty (ACT) opens channels of access to the Pacific and Caribbean and, thus, to new world markets. Thanks to its privileged position, Amazonia will tend to play a fundamental role in the integration of northern South America and in the future integration of the entire continent.

On the other hand, within the scope of the United Nations Framework Convention on Climate Change, there are now excellent opportunities for Brazil in general and Amazonia in particular to garner international support. These have come to Brazil through the Clean Development Mechanism (CDM) proposed by the Brazilian government and created by the Kyoto Protocol, signed in December 1997, which seeks the reduction of emissions of greenhouses gases and carbon capture and storage. Through this mechanism, projects for recuperation of degraded areas through reforestation for productive ends are eligible for funding. Forest projects are an alternative to changes in land use and thus contribute to a reduction in rates of deforestation. These are important initiatives for the sustainable development of Amazonia, and they also help keep the labor force in the rural areas and create employment there. According to the World Bank, by 2010, the value of this carbon market should reach between $8 and $10 billion, distributed among the main countries where these projects are located—China, India, and Brazil.

At the same time, taking full advantage of these opportunities is conditional on overcoming the necessary challenges. Some of these are inherent in the Amazon region: vast distances and isolation caused by the discontinuity and concentration of settlement and production. These make access to work, goods, services, and markets difficult. Other inherent challenges are the intrinsic vulnerability of the ecosystems and the intense, disorganized migration into the region, accentuated by the internal mobility of its population. Yet another sort of challenge is that of guaranteeing inclusion of all social groups in the benefits of development while respecting their cultural identities. Giving value to the human and social component of Amazonia must be achieved through actions meant to promote the dignity of persons and their access to full citizenship, with the following priorities:

(1) providing conditions for a dignified existence by overcoming the basic shortages in education, health, housing, and transportation, as well as conditions for competitiveness through access to information and training for productive activities;

(2) privileging activities that contribute to the job supply in the region;

(3) implementing regularization of landownership, a differentiated policy of credit, and services of technical aid to stabilize access to land;

(4) guaranteeing the right to difference, through preservation of cultural heritages, with special attention to indigenous communities.

Channeling solutions for the multiple challenges of Amazonia depends, however, on the political ability to choose among alternatives, mobilize the necessary means, coordinate actions, and lead a process of change. This implies, as a consequence, an effort to substitute the fragmented sectorial policies with a policy integrated on the economic, social, and environmental dimensions, as an instrument for regulating the process of sustainable development in the region.[19] This articulation must obey a central purpose: that of promoting retention of the benefits of the development of Amazonia.

Notes

The author wishes to thank Jimena Felipe Beltrão for discussion of the outline and suggestions on the text.

1. According to measurements of satellite imagery by the National Institute of Space Research (Instituto Nacional de Pesquisas Espaciais, INPE), the Amazon River is 6,992.06 kilometers long, about 140 kilometers longer than the Nile. "Estudo do INPE indica que o rio Amazonas é 140 km mais extenso do que o Nilo," Instituto Nacional de Pesquisas Espaciais, 1 July 2008, <http://www.inpe.br/noticias/noticia.php?Cod_Noticia=1501> (accessed 7 July 2008).

2. *Agenda Amazônica 21: Bases para discussão* (Brasilia: Ministério do Meio Ambiente, 1997).

3. Celso Furtado, *Formação econômica do Brasil* (Rio de Janeiro: Fundo de Cultura, 1957).

4. Samuel Benchimol, *Estrutura geo-social e econômica da Amazônia* (Manaus: Governo do Estado do Amazonas, 1966).

5. Caio Prado Jr., *História econômica do Brasil* (São Paulo: Brasiliense, 1956).

6. Roberto Araújo de Oliveira Santos, *História econômica da Amazônia* (São Paulo, 1997).

7. Catharina Virgulino Dias, *Vida urbana na Amazônia* (Belém: Banco da Amazônia, 1972).

8. Márcio Souza, *A expressão amazonense: Do colonialismo ao neocolonialismo* (São Paulo: Alfa-Omega, 1977).

9. Adélia Engrácia de Oliveira, *Amazônia: Desenvolvimento, integração e ecologia* (São Paulo: Brasiliense, 1974).

10. Donald Sawyer, *Ocupação agrícola da Amazônia: Primeiros estudos para a fixação de diretrizes* (Belo Horizonte: Centro de Desenvolvimento e Planejamento Regional [Universidade Federal de Minas Gerais], 1979).

11. George Martine, *A desordem ecológica na Amazônia* (Belém: Associação de Universidades Amazônicas, 1991).

12. David Ferreira Carvalho, "Industrialização tardia e grandes projetos," in *A Amazônia e a crise da modernização* (Belém: Museu Paraense Emilio Goeldi, 1994).

13. Ricardo José Rocha Guimarães, "Nos caminhos do sonho: Grandes projetos e desenvolvimento industrial no Estado do Pará," in *Cenários da industrialização na Amazônia* (Belém: Associação de Universidades Amazônicas, 1995).

14. Armin Mathis, "Garimpagem de ouro na Amazônia," in *Perspectivas do desenvolvimento sustentável: Uma contribuição para a Amazônia 21* (Belém: Universidade Federal do Pará, Núcleo de Altos Estudos Amazônicos, 1997).

15. Angélica Toniolo and Christopher Uhl, "Perspectivas econômicas e ecológicas da agricultura na Amazônia oriental," in *A evolução da fronteira Amazônica: Oportunidades para o desenvolvimento sustentável* (Belém: Instituto do Homem e Meio Ambiente da Amazônia, 1996).

16. Marli Maria Mattos and Christopher Uhl, "Perspectivas econômicas e ecológicas da pecuária na Amazônia oriental na década de 90: O caso Paragominas," in *A evolucção da fronteira Amazônica*.

17. Bertha K. Becker, "Novos rumos da política regional: Por um desenvolvimento sustentável da fronteira Amazônica," in *A geografia política do desenvolvimento sustentável* (Rio de Janeiro: Editora da Universidade Federal do Rio de Janeiro, 1997).

18. Armando Dias Mendes and Ignacy Sachs, *Amazônia 21: Uma agenda para um mundo sustentável* (Belém: Associação de Universidades Amazônicas, 1998).

19. *A política nacional integrada para a Amazônia Legal* (Brasília: Conselho Nacional da Amazônia Legal/Ministério do Meio Ambiente, 1995).

CRISTOVAM BUARQUE

The Northeast:
Five Hundred Years of Discoveries

The Discovery of Brazil in the Northeast

Brazil was discovered in the Northeast. Not only because it was in the north-eastern state of Bahia that the first encounter with what would become Brazil occurred but because it was in the northeastern state of Pernambuco that the new country solidified as a producer of a commodity that required permanent settlement. It was with sugarcane that Brazil began its colonization—in the Northeast—and it was in the Northeast that its first colonial populations with regular, permanent relations among themselves and with the land took shape. Sugar enriched Brazil, consolidated its settlement, created a population of permanent workers, and formed a local elite. Before sugar, Brazil was just a territory to be exploited by pioneers without ties to the land: exporters of brazilwood and restless *bandeirantes*, explorers, in search of precious stones and metals. Wood and minerals were simply goods to be found and carried off, leaving nothing in their place.

For three centuries—most of Brazil's history—the wealth of Brazil was concentrated in the Northeast. Several centuries passed before other, new centers of development took northeastern sugar's place. The first of these, the mining region of Minas Gerais in the Southeast, was short lived, lasting only until the mines were exhausted. Several other economic nuclei formed, but these were also in the Northeast. Only after the early nineteenth century, with the rise of coffee culture in São Paulo, did the Northeast cease to be the economic center of the country. Even then, though, the Northeast had not yet become a problem.

The Discovery of the Northeast by Brazil

Toward the end of the nineteenth century, Brazil discovered the Northeast—as a problem. With the great drought of the 1870s, the imperial crown found it necessary to sell some of its jewels to finance projects to recuperate the region. After that, the Northeast was seen as a problem caused by aridity, a product of nature, as if the region had always been condemned to this fate of backwardness and indigence. Brazil rapidly forgot that it had been born in the Northeast, that there had been its first center of wealth and consolidation as a country. The scarcity of water, the atypical rain patterns, and the consequent poverty of the soil were thus seen as inherently northeastern problems—and the solution was in engineering.

When nature did not "cooperate," Brazil resorted to engineering techniques for overcoming the difficulties, just as a bridge is built to overcome the difficulty of crossing a river. Thus dams were seen as the solution for regularizing the water supply in the region. The task of building dams fell to the National Department of Works against Drought (Departamento Nacional de Obras Contra as Secas, DNOCS), created in 1909. DNOCS became a tool for redeeming the Northeast. For decades this was the cure sought, and for decades it was not found. In spite of the technical success of the work of DNOCS in creating large reservoirs, it changed none of the conditions of striking poverty in much of the Northeast. It was a long time before a new conception would arise. Eventually, economics replaced engineering; exit DNOCS and enter SUDENE.

The Superintendency for Development of the Northeast (Superintendência do Desenvolvimento do Nordeste, SUDENE) was born along with Brazilian economic thought in the 1950s, almost simultaneously with the first large experiment in development in the capitalist world, that of southern Italy. SUDENE arose from a revolutionary analysis of the Northeast Problem: it was economic and social, not natural and technical. Its roots were not in the lack of water but in the lack of savings accounts. The solution was not dams but investments. SUDENE's goal was not to guarantee agricultural production but to create a modern center of industrial production. This organization represented the most important consideration the country had given the Northeast. It was Brazil's largest and most consistent effort to reduce regional inequality. It was also the best example of a consistent, sophisticated, modern policy for confronting the problem.

The underlying ideas of SUDENE had a perfect logic:

(1) The Northeast Problem derives from economic backwardness and not from lack of water;

(2) Its solution should be in industrialization and not in increased agricultural production;

(3) The way to this lies in increased industrial investment;

(4) For this, it will be necessary to create a capital flow from the wealthier southern part of the country to the Northeast;

(5) This capital will come through fiscal incentives; entrepreneurs from all over Brazil will be encouraged to redirect their income tax expenses into investments in the northeastern productive sector;

(6) All of this will be the fruit of an economic architecture planned by the technocrats in SUDENE, with the political support of the governors, under the direct coordination of the president of the republic.

This effort lasted for only a short while, however. The political changes wrought by the 1964 coup entailed a revision of the Brazilian project and caused a radical redirection of SUDENE's plans for the Northeast.

The Discovery of the Northeast in Brazil

Until 1964, underlying SUDENE's plan was a distributive model of Brazil. Since 1930, industrialization had been viewed as a process of distributing wealth more equitably. SUDENE thus sought to work against wealth concentration in the Northeast. The military coup caused a change in direction: Brazil took a route of industrial development that imitated that of the wealthier countries, one that required concentration of income to create a market for luxury goods and a concentration of public investment to increase productivity, that is, to create the necessary economic infrastructure and to support private savings.

In place of regional and social concerns, attention was entirely directed at increasing production more rapidly, which entailed the greatest concentration of wealth possible. Public investment shifted to the more developed southern part of the country, and policies concentrated income in the middle and upper classes. Incentives targeting the Northeast were not entirely eliminated, but they were largely redirected to other regions (e.g., Amazonia; see chapter 9) or to other sectors (e.g., the national tourism agency, Empresa Brasileira de Turismo, EMBRATUR). This was not a matter of directing investment away from the Northeast to other regions because the Northeast had not yet seen results. This was, rather, a matter of investing in certain companies and areas of production even if they were found in other regions.

For this to be done, SUDENE and the Northeast were politically relocated: the regional development agency was moved from the Office of the President and subordinated to the Interior Ministry and, later, to a secretariat of the ministry. Little by little, resources were shifted; planning was abandoned; and, worst of all, resources from the Northeast came to be used more for the capital goods industry of São Paulo than for the consumer goods industry of the Northeast. The incentives became a system of income transfer much more for the developed centers and their wealthy populations than for the Northeast and its poor inhabitants.

After four decades, the results are that the policy of wealth concentration systematically developed by the military government and left unchanged by subsequent civilian governments has served to northeasternize all of Brazil. Poverty has spread through unemployment, migration, low salaries, and lack of public services directed at poor populations. The social and economic policies of the late twentieth century only made the situation worse: uncontrolled liberalization of trade, privatization without criteria, and the primacy of the market turned the dreams of SUDENE into mere memories that seem as distant as the first discovery. Upon reaching its 500th anniversary in 2000, Brazil discovered that, from the social point of view, it was one big Northeast. Brazil has failed both in its policy to reduce regional inequality and in its policies to eradicate poverty.

The Discovery of Brazil by Way of the Northeast

At the dawn of the twenty-first century, 500 years after Brazil began to take shape on the basis of the Northeast, the country is at an important crossroads. The forecast for society in the coming years is a split into two populations. The model of wealth concentration of the last third of the twentieth century reduced regional disparities but increased social disparities and spread poverty. The fact that per capita income in the Northeast is less than that of the southern regions does not show the true drama of inequality. It does not reveal that wealth has become even more concentrated in the Northeast and that wealth concentration in the other regions has made poverty a national phenomenon, not one limited to the Northeast.

The problem of development has ceased being a matter of regional underdevelopment; it is now a matter of wrongheaded development throughout the country. What needs to be changed is not policies targeting the Northeast but policy for all of Brazil. Instead of Brazil discovering the Northeast, Brazil needs to discover itself through the northeasternness of its national poverty, in order to develop new policies to combat the situation. Seen from the point of view of the Northeast, which is spreading throughout the country, the quincentennial and its aftermath are an opportunity for Brazil to revise its future, envisioning the one it wants and the ways to build it.

The Discovery of Brazil as Northeastern Brazil

The Reunification of Brazil

Brazil was "discovered" in 1500 in an encounter between a group of Portuguese navigators who arrived in caravels and a group of natives waiting on the beach. It was "covered up" again thirty years later when these navigators became explorers and exploiters and the Indians became slaves. The divorce between the arriving Portuguese and the Indians who dwelled there transformed the emerging country into a place to be exploited by the metropolis eager for products and profits. The new country was crippled as soon as it arose.

During the following 500 years, Brazil remained covered up, divided between Portuguese and Indians, whites and slaves, the poor and the rich, the included and the excluded. At each moment of the country's history, a new sort of division emerged, hampering the construction of a nation of compatriots involved in the same project of development. The land discovered 500 years ago observed its quincentennial without having yet been transformed into a nation.

The failure of the quincentennial of the "discovery" of Brazil in 2000 as a celebration is proof of the failure of five centuries: one cannot celebrate the birthday of someone who has not yet been born. Five hundred years after the encounter between Europeans and Indians, humanity is still pregnant with a nation called Brazil. It is now time to transform the country into a nation, unifying its population, leaving behind its 500-year-old profile, and giving it a sovereignty that it has never fully had.

In 1989, with the fall of the Berlin Wall, the people of West Germany opted to incorporate East Germany and thus reunite the German people. This decision demanded sacrifices, including the transfer of income from the west to the east, at the cost of reducing the standard of living for those in the west. Investments previously concentrated in the west were redirected to the east. Employment in the west had to be shifted to the east. Pensions and salaries of the wealthier workers in the west were reduced for the benefit of those in the east. Even so, reunification was approved by the German people in the west, who perceived the ethical need for this unification and the political convenience of building a larger country. The financial and economic costs, the reduction of income for some, would be compensated by the benefits to all of constructing a stable nation.

The Brazilian elite needs to have a similar sentiment. In Germany, it was necessary to sacrifice a part of the country that was already integrated into the benefits of modernity in order to incorporate another part that had been excluded. Brazil is divided into a poor part, now spread throughout the country, the excluded republic, and a wealthy part, also now spread throughout the country, the included republic. These labels mean that one part is excluded from, and the other is included in, the benefits of modernity. The Brazilian elite must understand the need to unify the two parts of the country, these two republics, even if this requires income transfer, in exchange for the global benefits to the whole of society.

The Formation of the Brazilian Family

The first lords of the proprietary captaincies who arrived in 1535 did not come with the intention of building a country. They came to enslave Indians and exploit natural resources. After that, Indians were replaced by African slaves, and the African slaves were replaced by exploited workers, and those have now been replaced by disposable workers. Brazilwood was replaced by sugar, sugar by gold, gold by coffee, coffee by manufactured goods, and now manufactured goods by the great global casino that is the financial system. In all this time, Brazilian elites never considered the Brazilian people part of the same national body and family. They were never brought into the educational system, the health system, or urban services. Brazil is no longer even united on the beach, in the street, or in the public square. Even the Portuguese language that unites Brazil is beginning to fragment. At the dawn of the twenty-first century, the concentrated economic growth has turned inequality into a new difference, just as in the past there was a difference between Portuguese and Indians and then between masters and slaves.

The new century presents an even more serious picture, though: difference has become disassembly of a population occupying the same territory. Even though

Brazilians have one flag and national anthem and the same right to vote, they are so differentiated, so disaggregated, that they do not even recognize one another as peers. They are different human species thanks to the use of technical marvels by some and the exclusion of others. The only way to avoid a tragic conclusion is by forming a sense of a Brazilian family.

Exclusion Is Social, Not Regional

Creating a Brazilian extended family does not mean incorporating the Northeast but incorporating the "northeast." The unification process is not regional but social. It is not a matter of enriching the Northeast but enriching the entire country by eradicating the "northeast" wherever it is in the country. One example of the error of economic logic in facing poverty is the continued treatment of regional inequality in Brazil. In the course of forty years, the attempt to develop the Northeast along the same lines as the southern regions has resulted in high rates of economic growth but also increased poverty and social inequality within the region.

The case of the Northeast exemplifies the problem of poverty, not the lack of development. The Northeast Problem is not underdevelopment but the concentration of poverty in higher levels than in the rest of the country. Regional poverty is part of national poverty. The struggle against regional inequality must begin with a struggle against social inequality in the rest of the country. In this struggle against poverty, the poorest regions — that is, the ones with the highest concentrations of numbers of poor — will be the greatest beneficiaries.

Underdevelopment Is an Ethical Matter

For over fifty years, three ideas have prevailed in economic theory:

(1) The world is divided into developed regions or countries, by virtue of being wealthy, and underdeveloped ones, by virtue of being poor;

(2) Wealth and poverty should be measured by the same standard: the gross domestic product and its consequent per capita income;

(3) Underdevelopment is a stage on the way to wealth and, therefore, the end of poverty. The end of the twentieth century demonstrated that this conception does not work from the point of view of the battle against poverty. The economic dynamic no longer lacks cheap labor and it can do without the mass market — it just excludes segments of

the population. Underdevelopment is no longer an economic problem; it is an ethical one.

No economic indicator better defines the picture of poverty than the way a society treats its children. "Abandoned children": this is the most synthetic definition of underdevelopment. Abandoned in the streets, at work, or in schools that lack quality or attraction. This is the ethical definition of poverty.

With the emergence of the concept of "exclusion," poverty ceases to be an economic concept measured by family income and becomes an ethical one: instead of the selection of strategies for development, the choice is between including and excluding the masses. Only an ethical, national coalition against poverty will make a solution to regional inequality possible. Development projects targeting the Northeast will face increasing resistance from members of Congress and governments in the southern regions. Independently of party and ideology, each member of Congress represents his or her state, and each will have difficulty explaining projects that benefit other regions and not his or her own, especially when it is perceived that the subsidies and incentives are benefiting the rich and not the poor of the Northeast. In contrast, it will be easy for them to support a battle against poverty nationwide, which also will benefit even more the regions with the larger concentrations of poverty.

The Brazilian Accord

The Brazilian elite, accustomed to orienting the national project to its own purposes, considers Brazil's problems to be passing crises, needing only quick fixes in the economy, without changes in the purposes of development or in its beneficiaries. The eradication of poverty requires more than economic fixes; it requires a national accord, a common will to include the majority in the benefits of Brazil's economy and potential.

The history of Brazil has all of the ingredients to discredit the hypothesis that Brazil can change an elite corrupted by 500 years of disregard for the people and uncommon selfishness, which has made Brazil one of the most unequal countries in the world. The more so, because the members of the elite were competent enough to incorporate at least part of the population as beneficiaries of the luxury that they themselves had always enjoyed, by guaranteeing high salaries and other rights. This elite knowingly co-opted the middle class with corporatism, much as it had done centuries before with part of the indigenous population.

Even so, today, there are reasons to imagine that this situation can be changed:

the Brazilian middle class senses the loss of these benefits and the probable impoverishment of its descendants. It also feels threatened by the excluded masses. It is searching for alternatives. The oligarchy itself perceives the cost of the status quo of inequality, the weight of maintaining exclusion and the ethical discomfort of opting explicitly for "disassembly." The oligarchy seems tired of the exclusionary model that it itself has created over 500 years and whose upkeep is proving costly: the insecurity of daily life, shame before the world, inefficiency in the functioning of society, and poor quality of life.

Under these conditions, it is perfectly fitting to imagine the eradication of poverty. Such a program would not be the result of a social revolution, nor would it be possible through power vested exclusively in a single party. Whatever the government might be, there would have to be a broad base of support founded less on immediate economic interests than on national survival, just as in the case of the abolition of slavery or the leap into industrial development in the past. It would come from a coalition created more for ethical reasons than for political reasons.

The Discovery of the Understanding of Poverty

Growth Does Not Reduce Poverty

With all of the successful economic growth, there has been no accompanying success in the struggle against poverty. The economic has always been disconnected from the social. Observation of any developing country leads to one conclusion: the last decades of the twentieth century were years of economic growth without reduction in poverty but rather with an increase in inequality. In the Northeast of Brazil, this has been seen in absolute form: after decades of development, there was never such growth and wealth as now, and never has there been so much inequality and abject poverty. The social and economic process of the world and of each country shows that there is a difference between economic growth and the reduction of poverty. This requires that we change our understanding of the fight against poverty and of the tools that must be used in that struggle.

Until the 1970s, for many, economic growth gave the idea of being a distributive tool: wealth appeared to grow laterally. As it grew it would spread throughout society, reducing poverty, and the poor would become less poor at a faster rate than the rich became richer. Under these conditions, if positive growth rates were maintained, the trend would be the continuous reduction in inequality and the consequent elimination of poverty. Thanks to growth, the world would move toward social justice.

In the last several decades, however, one can see a change in these vectors: the rich have enriched themselves at a faster rate than the poor have been lifted out of poverty. Wealth has ceased to grow laterally and rather has grown on the top, like an inverted cone, concentrated in the wealthier portion of the population and condemning the portion in the lower margin to poverty. These two portions of the population are separated by a widening rift.

The Dynamic of Social Apartheid

The dawn of the twenty-first century finds us in a world in which there has never been so much wealth but in which poverty does not retreat. Rather, the distance between rich and poor has grown. The current trend is a continuous increase in social inequality with a worsening of poverty and the threat of a gap between rich and poor so big that soon in every country there will be separate growth, along the lines of that in South Africa under apartheid.

All over the world, there is a curtain that separates human beings with and without access to technological wonders. In place of the iron curtain of the Cold War, we have a gold curtain that separates the rich and the poor. There is no longer a spectrum of economic inequality but rather a break between the included and the excluded. In place of inequality has arisen a separation, a social apartheid.

If this separation keeps up for thirty or fifty more years, with the advances in biotechnology and medicine in the service of a wealthy minority, the social break will be so large that humanity will become like two distinct species. Poverty will indeed disappear, thanks to the invisibility of the poor, just as in the past there was no poverty among Indians or slaves, who were seen as beings different from the elite. This is the humanity that is forming at the turn of the millennium, and Brazil is its best example.

The Brazilian Standard

What is happening on a global scale — the separation of rich and poor — is perfectly reproduced in Brazil in each of its regions, including in the Northeast. Brazil is the perfect picture of worldwide economic development at the beginning of the new millennium. Brazilian social and economic statistics are practically identical to worldwide averages, with the exception of those related to education, in which Brazil is below the global average. As in the rest of the world, Brazil and its Northeast have had surprising technical and economic development, and they have built national and regional societies that are absurdly divided and separated. In Brazil, as in the Northeast, the twentieth century was a technical success and an ethical disaster. Brazil, on a national scale, is already building the future of humanity in a divided globalization, a social apartheid.

Ethical Modernity

To everyone's surprise, the end of the twentieth century came loaded with discontents. The socialist utopia envisioned in the nineteenth century, when implemented in the twentieth, did not yield the answers that humanity had hoped for. It was an unsuccessful experiment, both on the political level and on the level of the people's hopes, dreams, and imaginations. Politically victorious capitalism, once the symbol of individual desires, became a social aberration, creating a humanity more unequal than in any other period of history. In only a few years, this inequality has come to the unthinkable point of distinguishing lives based on access to the means to purchase the right to life. Within this picture of discontent with reality, there is a greater discontent with the lack of alternatives. The world has never been so materially rich yet so poor in dreams. Today it is a world unhappy with the present and with the prospects for the future.

Brazil is the country from which could come a new alternative because no other carries in such degree and dimension the global tragedy of humanity. At the same time, it carries all of the political and moral pressures needed to seek alternatives and the resources to face these problems. Leaders in Europe and the United States are not under the same pressures within their countries, nor do they have the awareness to channel resources to solve the social problems of the world, and, if one of them had the awareness, it would not have the domestic political support. Other countries with poverty similar to Brazil's do not have the recourses necessary for a reorientation of their models of development. Brazil contains all of the tragedy and all of the potential of this moment in history, and it is discovering the need for change.

In contrast to the wealthy nations, which do not have the same need for change, and to the smaller and poorer nations, which do not have the conditions for imagining or constructing change, and to countries like India and China, which do not suffer the same internal pressures, Brazil has all of the ingredients of the crisis and its alternative. At the same time, Brazil has the urgency for changing its failed social model and the resources and potential for correcting its deficiencies. Therefore, it is the locale where a new ethical modernity can arise. An ethical modernity makes the ethical values of society the determinants of social objectives and the latter the definers of economic reasoning, only then using the most convenient technical option. This is a total subversion of the current hierarchy, in which technical advance determines economic rationality, which then determines the social objectives to be attempted, relegating to last place society's ethical values. It is a subversion of the ways in which the policies for the regional development of the Northeast were conceived and executed. Instead of starting with industry, with innovative techniques the central objective would be the eradication of poverty.

The Eradication of Poverty and the Abolition of Social Apartheid

The abolition of social apartheid and the eradication of poverty correspond to an ethical value: elimination of the social exclusion that characterizes poverty. Poverty is no longer defined with a basis in economic indicators, such as family income. What makes a person poor is his or her exclusion from essential goods and social services. The concept of poverty must be demonetarized and made real, less economic and more ethical, less continuous and more discontinuous. To be poor means not to have a guarantee of food, access to education, access to health care, healthy living conditions, efficient urban transport, legal protection, and safety. The road to the eradication of poverty passes through universal supply, whether public or private, of these goods and services rather than through the false promises of an income that would allow these services to be had from the marketplace.

A Change in Logic

Poverty of the Economy

Throughout Brazilian universities, economic theory, just like regional development policy for the Northeast, has concentrated on the idea of increasing wealth while ignoring the routes to reducing poverty. Our young Ph.D.'s, with degrees from countries where the problem of poverty has been solved, brought home an economic theory that was not adaptable to Brazilian needs. By concentrating on wealth, economic theory suffers from a chronic ethical poverty. It is incapable of understanding or confronting the problem of social poverty because it is based on the premise that the market solves the problem. The complements invented to give economic theory a touch of ethics, such as growth with employment, higher salary employment, and growth with income distribution, have all failed. These were the theories that formed the basis of the education of thousands of Brazilian economists in the last several decades. They have been of no use in fighting poverty in Brazil.

Economic growth occurs with the reduction and not the increase of employment; the robotized, globalized economy of the late twentieth and early twenty-first centuries is doing away with human labor. Until recently, increasing investments meant increasing the number of employees to run the new machinery. Now, however, investment means buying new machinery to replace employees. It is of no use to try to impede the use of new equipment by closing borders to technical progress that, besides having its own force, seduces the masses. Blocking this progress, even for the best of social intentions, would require an authoritarian government, and its outcomes would not be positive in the middle and long terms.

Increasing wages is not a successful way to reduce poverty for the simple reason that it works only for those who have jobs. These days, those who have regular, formal employment either have already risen from the most intense degrees of poverty, because they have salaries, per diem and travel allowance vouchers, health insurance, and so forth, or they will not rise out of poverty at their salaries because they are unable to buy essential goods and services.

The same problem happens with income distribution. Just as with water, income can be distributed only to those who have access to "faucets" through which it can flow. One can distribute charity, hot soup, and subsidized foodstuffs, but the distribution of national wealth can be done only through wealth itself, which is not synonymous with income but encompasses land, water, sanitation, education, health services, public transportation, security, and legal services.

Therefore, the first step in eradicating poverty is to be free from subordination to the logic and power of the economists and to choose an ethical option for the end of exclusion. In a way, the national debate returns to the arguments made over a century ago in the case against slavery: first, its indecency; second, its inefficiency.

A Revolution in Point of View

The fight against poverty must be waged from a social and not an economic point of view. This means no longer seeing the reduction of poverty as a consequence of the increase of wealth or even a better distribution of wealth. These do not benefit the truly poor because they occur only among those who are already included in the modern productive sector. For this revolution in facing and defining objectives, one must look at the world from the perspective of the exclusion to be overcome, of the social apartheid to be eliminated. Instead of dividing the world into workers and capitalists and wealth into salary and profits, we must see the world as divided between those who have access and those who do not: access to education, to preventative and curative health care, and to personal security.

The world must be seen, understood, and confronted with the eyes of the excluded: children without a future, especially those out of school, who are usually working; excluded women, upon whom fall most of the consequences of poverty and sexist violence; those who are sick because they lack public and private hygiene and proper health care; and the permanently unemployed.

The Cost of Omission

Prisoners of economic logic in place of ethical values, government leaders consider only the cost of things, the monetary investment, and never the cost of not doing things—the missed investment opportunities when one does not invest in health and education. Changing the point of view on problems and identifying ethical values as the guiding principles in political action and public administration cause government leaders to begin to consider the cost of omission, that is, of not making the right investments. If the cost of omission had been considered in the case of the Northeast, regional poverty would have been eliminated long ago.

The Feminization of Social Policy

Instead of attacking the reality of poverty head-on, regional development policies have all been mediated by the economy, which tried to attack what was taken to be the cause of poverty, the lack of industrial production. Thus the solution to each problem was mediated for a long time by investment, employment, wages, income, and marketplace. This economic logic establishes a period of time between problem and solution. So, for example, if there is no food at home, a man spends days looking for work and a month more waiting for his pay so that he can then go to the market to buy what is lacking at home. From a woman's perspective, though, an immediate response is needed. She looks for a neighbor, friend, or relative, because she cannot wait till the next day, and she asks to borrow the food that she needs.

The fight against poverty in the Northeast and in all of Brazil will require of government leaders a feminization of social policy: a new focus, a policy that goes directly to the problem. Instead of waiting for investments that will generate employment that will pay wages that will increase income that will—finally— put the children in school and the family into the health-care system, the alternative is to offer immediately the health-care, education, and other services that would eliminate the condition of poverty.

Growth from the Base

All strategies of economic development are based on the idea that the effects of production on the wealthy will spread to the base of the social pyramid because traditional economic policy states that poverty comes from the lack of growth. The result of this strategy, however, is a society with growing inequality and economic stagnation. The development policies for the Northeast are examples of this mistaken view. The goals were to eradicate poverty in the Northeast, but the means were to increase wealth through economic growth, with the illusion that this wealth-oriented growth would trickle down to the base of the social pyramid. Brazil managed to achieve complete success in growth, but with a worsening of poverty. Wealth was not distributed, and afterward the growth itself stalled.

In fact, the struggle against poverty can be the route to the resumption of growth. Instead of the eradication of poverty's riding on a growing economy, a reinvigorated economy can ride on a consistent program of poverty eradication. Priority given to the social sectors can stimulate growth from the base of the social pyramid, which can then spread to the top, in an inversion of Brazilian history. Instead of supporting an automobile industry—with the hypocrisy that an automobile sold means more employment for the street child who makes his meager living wiping windshields at the intersection, at great risk to his safety and at the cost of attending school—Bolsa Escola, the recent scholarship program for the families of millions of school-age children, has made it possible for families to buy food, clothing, and other goods without sending their children out to work dangerously on the streets. Bolsa Escola has had an economic multiplier effect from the bottom up. In place of subsidies and incentives for large industries that enjoy tax exemptions, produce goods and services for the wealthy, and do not generate employment, growth can come from an investment in the social sectors, creating employment and energizing the economy. This is growth from the base, the marriage of the economic with the social.

The firm position that the struggle against poverty requires a social focus and not an economic one does not mean that the economy should be forgotten but rather that it should be subordinated to social concerns and to ethical values. The economy cannot be forgotten, first, because the social goals are not limited to the eradication of poverty—that is only the first step. Second, under current circumstances, the economy is important for mobilizing the resources necessary for directly confronting poverty.

Social Productivism

From the 1930s on, in times of crisis, the developed nations used the Keynesian method of creating nonproductive employment as a way of broadening demand and thus jump-starting the stalled production of mass consumer goods. It worked: growth resumed and unemployment declined. Developing countries then imported this method, and it failed because the difference between the developed and developing countries was great. In the developed countries, there was an idle productive capacity in industry, the private sector had a high level of financial reserves, and there was an economic infrastructure. Moreover, social services were available to the population. Upon being employed, workers earned an income, and they already had access to social services such as education, running water, and health.

In developing countries and regions, like the Northeast of Brazil, where these social services did not exist, the population, in addition to being unemployed, was poor. The Keynesian approach proposed the creation of employment for the new industries to produce the goods that would substitute imports from the wealthy countries. The economy did not have a capacity for savings, and Brazilian Keynesianism caused state resources to be directed mainly to implanting infrastructure and financing companies with subsidized capital, making up for the lack of capital in the form of savings in the private sector. As a consequence, social services were not offered to the poor population. Moreover, the public spending resulted in strong, permanent inflationary pressure.

Throughout the twentieth century, one of the greatest ethical errors of Brazil's economists and political leaders who were committed to developmentalism was the false promise that poverty would be eradicated by employment of the poor in the manufacture of products for the rich. In the same way that Brazil had forced slaves to produce export goods in exchange for their food, for fifty years, it asked workers to labor in industries making luxury goods in exchange for a salary that guaranteed—falsely—a way out of poverty.

For the success of the industries, Brazil diverted resources from the social infrastructure to the economic infrastructure. To prevent competition, Brazil prohibited imports. To fulfill the demand for these products, it concentrated income and used public employment. To make up for the lack of private sector reserves, it subsidized credit through development banks. As a result there was neither employment for all nor sufficient wages. The products did not meet social needs, nor did they serve to reduce the poverty of the population. The wealthy came to have domestic products that, now independent of an exchange crisis, allowed them to imitate the wealthy elsewhere in the world, while the Brazilian poor came to have insufficient wages, insufficient employment, and insufficient products and services for getting out of poverty: education, health, housing, water, sanitation, public transportation, and public safety. The situation tended to worsen amid the characteristics of the late-twentieth-century economy: technical progress that did away with labor, production that did not require mass consumer demand, and a liberalization of imports that did away with local production.

Brazil now has an opportunity for a productive, social Keynesianism, to create employment that directly produces the supply of essential goods and services and, at the same time, stimulates the demand for products from the overall economy. The engagement of employment in the direct production of goods and services for the elimination of poverty and for stimulating the economy is "social productivism," in which the poor are employed to produce for the poor. The population is hired to build and maintain schools, to build water and sewage systems, and to improve the public transportation system. None of this is possible, though, if the state does not have enough resources to generate this production of essential goods and services, the lack of which characterizes the poverty of the population. Therefore, the solutions have to be simple, practical, and cheap if they are to mobilize the energy of the idle population.

Mobilizing the Energy of the Population

One of the difficulties in the logic of government workings from the economic point of view is that it does not consider the direct energy of the population as a way of confronting social problems. The labor force is not seen as a resource to mobilize to this end, as a source of idle energy that can be used to confront the problems of poverty; rather, labor unemployment is seen as a problem. Unemployed mothers are ignored; they are not seen as a resource to be mobilized to collaborate in public education. The government does not consider using the unemployed locally for the installation of sewage systems or for building housing. The supply of goods and services necessary for eradicating poverty can be had by the employment of unemployed labor, mobilizing with financial incentives the idle energy that they represent. A prisoner of technological and legal standards, the state has trouble changing the way it deals with problems and does not attempt to mobilize popular energy as a way of solving these problems. It ignores the problems of the poorest population and the transformative power that it has, or it considers the problem of poverty insoluble because of the need for investments. In the same way that governments have trouble understanding how to mobilize social energy, poor individuals have trouble also, caught either in governments' oblivion or paternalism. The eradication of poverty consists in correctly mobilizing poverty itself, without paternalism or "welfarism," through simple, inexpensive measures that can be easily administrated without increasing state bureaucracy.

The Discovery of the Obvious:
Simple, Direct, Concrete Measures

If economic growth does not eliminate poverty, then social plans and programs are also not effective in the fight against it (as has been demonstrated with development policies for the Northeast) unless they are transformed into concrete measures that directly address each one of the links of the vicious cycle that has created the socially segregated society. For decades the population has learned of laws, proposals, purposes, programs, plans, and projects—all frustrated guarantees of full employment, universal education, and universal health care by means of the economy. All mere intentions lacking tangible consequences. At other times, proposals mediated by economic policies that promise and even set out to fight poverty end up benefiting the wealthy and widening the income gap.

A revolution of simple solutions has to be based on measures and not intentions—measures that are concrete, not theoretical; simple, so they can be easily understood and executed; and direct, going to the heart of the problem and not routed based on intermediary policies. The battle against poverty has to be fought through small actions that can solve the specific problems to which they are directed. These are solutions that avoid the strategy of abstract and generic thought and of intentions that serve to hide a lack of direct proposals. These are solutions that pair each problem with concrete measures. If they are not carried out, it is because government leaders and their bases of support have opted for segregated growth and social apartheid.

For Brazil, a set of measures could mobilize the idle population and lead it to produce what it needs to rise out of poverty. This set includes

(1) Bolsa Escola, the school scholarship program that mobilizes parents to ensure that their children do not miss school;

(2) Poupança Escola, school savings accounts, for students in the Bolsa Escola program, into which deposits are made on their promotion to the next grade level, to eliminate the endemic grade repetition that Brazilian schools suffer;

(3) preschool salary and food assistance, so that poor mothers are able to care for their children under six years of age; let us call this a "salary" rather than "welfare," in recognition of the labor that goes into raising a child to school age;

(4) contracting a large contingent of teachers with increased salaries, mobilizing young people for teaching service so that they may be agents of basic education;

(5) agrarian reform, to mobilize millions of workers to increase agricultural production bound for the domestic market;

(6) Bolsa Alfa, a literacy scholarship that mobilizes illiterate adults to become literate in as short a time as possible; whereas a monthly scholarship could become endless, it is possible to award remuneration when the participant demonstrates his or her ability to read; symbolically, the government would purchase the first letter or composition that the student writes in class;

(7) a program of school construction, installation of water and sewer systems, and direct financing of housing construction with employment of poor, idle labor.

As I explain in *A segunda abolição* (The Second Abolition), these and other measures for the eradication of poverty would cost 40 billion reals annually, less than 13 percent of the public budget in 1998.[1] For the entire Northeast, the cost would not exceed 15 billion reals per year, less than 5 percent of the total budget. This is a perfectly feasible amount to correct in 10 years the errors of the previous 500 in regard to poverty.

Note

1. Cristovam Buarque, *A segunda abolição: Um manifesto-proposta para a erradicação da pobreza no Brasil* (São Paulo: Paz e Terra, 1999).

When the Future Arrives

Whence Brazil Has Come

Brazil has been going through a phase of disillusionment and anxiety. Everyone knows that Brazil's late industrialization was carried out within a framework of imitative development that reinforced atavistic tendencies in its society toward elitism and social exclusion. It is natural to ask what has been wrong with the behavior of the country's leaders or to what extent the impasse at which Brazil finds itself can be attributed to external forces that condition the country's decision-making centers. There is now a consensus that Brazilians have been agents of their own history, with leaders who have had a global vision of the reality into which they were inserted. The first level of economic independence was reached in the 1950s, when addressing the problems of the Brazilian economy came to be seen as a politically relevant activity and an object of wide-ranging debate. This essay deals with two fundamental topics on which Brazilians have engaged in relevant theoretical reflection, with repercussions on the political decisions made at the time: inflation and the elaboration of a national plan for development.

As Brazilian economists moved away from traditional monetarist doctrine, which isolated the price system from real productive activities, a school of thought emerged that saw in chronic inflation the reflection of structural tensions generated by conflicts around income distribution. Thus the political factor was relevant. In *The Economic Growth of Brazil*, in the chapter "Two Sides of the Inflationary Process," I stated that "any study of the inflationary process concentrates on two aspects: the rise in the level of prices, and the redistribution of income. Yet it would be wrong to suppose that these are two separate elements. The very word 'inflation' is inducive to such an error, because it stresses the monetary aspect of the process — that is, the expansion of monetary income. This expansion is, however, only the means whereby the system seeks to redistribute real income."[1]

Thus we have seen inflation not as a monetary phenomenon along the lines of the International Monetary Fund's (IMF) view but as a struggle for income redistribution. The difference between the two emphases is that the monetarist view leads to a recessive deflationary policy that favors certain social sectors at the expense of the masses of wage earners. At the same time, the structuralist view allows one to identify the original foci of growing tension and reveal the beneficiaries of the inflationist surge. The utter victory of the IMF's doctrine has led to the present situation, in which a recession is planned to cure price inflation, with the consequences of heavy foreign indebtedness and a high social cost.

The idea that economic planning was a technique that afforded greater rationality in economic decisions, both in businesses and in politically organized society, was widespread after World War II. It was economists in countries under reconstruction who first theorized about the problem, notably in France and Holland. It was easy to see that the reconstruction of an economic system required complementary techniques of forward-looking decision making, beyond the reach of mercantile systems. Reflection on this notion opened the door to the idea that overcoming underdevelopment, which also requires structural transformations, could benefit from the experience of the economies under reconstruction. The first manual of planning technique was developed under my direction at the United Nations' Economic Commission for Latin America (ECLA; now the Economic Commission for Latin America and the Caribbean, ECLAC) in the early 1950s. It served as the basis for preparing the Plan of Goals (Plano de Metas) during the Juscelino Kubitschek government (1955–59), which allowed Brazil's industrialization to advance considerably (see chapter 3).

A few years after the publication of the Brazilian edition of *The Economic Growth of Brazil*, I congratulated myself in *A pré-revolução brasileira*: "Brazil's economy has reached a degree of differentiation — which is distinct from the conventional level of development as measured by per capita income — that has allowed the transfer to the country of the main decision-making centers of its economic life. In other words, the recent development of the Brazilian economy is not only in raising the average real income of the country's inhabitants but it has also taken the shape of a progressive differentiation of the economic system, gaining increasing individualization and autonomy."[2]

The truth is that we all saw that underdevelopment was not a necessary step in the formation of capitalist economies. It is, in and of itself, a particular situation resulting from the expansion of those economies that seek to use raw materials and labor from areas of precapitalist economies. The phenomenon of underdevelopment appears in various forms and in differing stages. The simplest case is the coexistence of foreign companies, producers of a few commodities for export, with a large portion of subsistence economy, a coexistence that can last in balance for long periods. A more complex case is that in which the economy has three sectors: one mainly for subsistence, another geared mostly to export, and a third with an industrial core connected to the domestic market. The connection between this industrial core and the domestic market occurs through the process of substitution of previously imported manufactures; thus this industry exists in a condition of permanent competition with foreign producers. The result is that the greatest concern of the local manufacturers is to put on the market articles similar to the imported ones and to adopt production methods that enable them to compete with importers. That being the case, the productive processes that are deemed the most advantageous are those that allow the most exact reproduction of imported articles and not those that facilitate the transformation of the economic structure so that it may absorb the subsistence sector.

Under these circumstances, the growth in the industrial sector connected to the domestic market and even the growth of its share of the production and an increase in the overall per capita income are not sufficient to cause significant changes in the country's occupational structure. The portion of the population affected by growth remains small, and the relative importance of the subsistence sector declines very slowly. Countries whose industrial production has already reached a high degree of diversification and that have a relatively high share of this production continue with a traditional occupational structure. In this way, underdeveloped economies can experience prolonged phases of growth in their overall and per capita product without reducing the degree of external dependence or domestic structural heterogeneity, which are their essential characteristics.

Where Brazil Is Now

The political authoritarianism that, for two decades after 1964, neutralized all forms of resistance by the excluded portions of the population also exacerbated the antisocial tendencies of Brazil's imitative development. This authoritarianism was Janus faced. If, on the one hand, it favored the interests coming from the economic arena, on the other hand, it aggravated the isolation of the political sphere.

The latter acquired increasing autonomy in the form of technocratic power. The aberrant geopolitical fantasy of Brazil as an "emerging power" took root. One of its roots was the process of incurring foreign debt, which led Brazil to unprecedented ungovernability in the twentieth century.

Development from the inside requires creativity on the political level, and this appears when a strong dose of collective will is added to the perception of the obstacles to be overcome. Refined sensitivity and the state of sharp lucidity evident in some highly gifted individuals in moments of social crisis can leave their mark of exceptional brilliance on an otherwise decadent time. Only imaginative political leadership, however, is capable of bringing out the creative forces for reconstruction of damaged structures and making new progress toward higher forms of sociability.

It might seem paradoxical to speak of decadence to a generation that came of age in a climate of such unbridled triumphalism, but Brazilians must not ignore the lessons of their history. What is Brazil's underdevelopment if not the result of repeated foundering on the shoals of decadence? In the dawning years of Brazil's history, the country was in the vanguard of agroindustrial techniques related to its main economic activities. The decline of the sugar economy was slow, beginning in the mid-seventeenth century, with the calcification of social structures in the Northeast. Later, after its precocious urbanization and preeminence in artistic creation in the eighteenth century, the wealthy mining region fell into lingering lethargy (see chapter 10).

In periods of crisis such as the present, one must put aside many received ideas, especially explanations that seek to ignore the moral responsibilities of the elites. We have the obligation to ask ourselves about the roots of the problems that afflict the people and repudiate doctrinaire positions founded in economic reductionism. How can one ignore that the seeds of the current crises were already corroding the social fabric during Brazil's phase of rapid growth in the productive energies of the country? Might Brazil be one of those cases of bad development that scholars of the subject study today? How does Brazil look after a long period of industrial growth that lasted for near half a century? The answer is apparent: it has accumulated an uncommon foreign debt; it faces an internal debt in the public sector that is leading to disorder in public finances; and half of the population is suffering from lack of food. Globalization has interrupted Brazil's progress in gaining autonomy in strategic decision making. If Brazil sinks into dollarization, it will be regressing into a semicolonial state. If Brazil continues on the road it has been on since 1994, looking for an easy way out of growing indebtedness in both the foreign and the domestic public sectors, in ten years, Brazil's liabilities will swallow up all of the wealth accumulated since the declaration of independence in 1822. It would be foolish for Brazil to ignore that it is on a path leading to a serious impasse.

Socially Pernicious Growth

The immediate cause of the crisis that assails the country was the large imbalance in payments in which several factors, both internal and external, competed. What could one expect from a process of growth that derived its energy from the indiscriminate reproduction of patterns of consumption from societies that had already reached levels of productivity and welfare often many times higher than Brazil's? How could one not see that the high standards of consumption of Brazil's so-called upper middle class have as consequences the neutralization of a substantial portion of savings and an increased dependence on foreign investment? The resulting structural tensions are at the root of uncontrollable inflationary pressures. Under these circumstances, the cost of price stability tends to be recession.

The crisis that now afflicts the Brazilian people, therefore, does not derive only from the widespread process of readjustment at work in the world economy. To a large extent, it is the result of an impasse that was bound to appear in a society that seeks to reproduce the material culture of more advanced capitalism but that deprives the great majority of the population of the essential means of livelihood. Since it was not possible to avoid the diffusion in one way or another of certain patterns of the wealthier minority's consumption, a counterfeit mass society has appeared in the country in which sophisticated forms of superfluous consumption coexist with a lack of essentials within the same social stratum, even within the same family.

Only political creativity driven by collective will can overcome this impasse. This collective will requires the political leadership to rediscover the constant values of Brazilian culture. Therefore, the point of departure for the process of reconstruction that Brazil faces must be greater participation of the people in the decision-making system. Without this, future development will not be fed by authentic creativity and will contribute little to the satisfaction of the legitimate desires of the nation.

Brazil must formulate a development policy by spelling out the substantive goals that it wants to reach rather than by basing its policy on the logic of the means imposed by a process of wealth accumulation that is guided by transnational companies. Overcoming the impasse that Brazil faces requires that development policy lead to an increasing homogenization of society that makes room for the fulfillment of Brazil's cultural potentials.

In an era in which those who hold power are seduced more by the narrow logic dictated by the interests of privileged groups, to speak of development as a rediscovery of the creative genius of Brazilian culture might seem like a mere flight to utopia. In this case, though, the utopian is often the fruit of the perception of the hidden dimensions of reality, a welling up of energies, that precedes the opening of the floodgate of the possibilities available to society. The vanguard action required constitutes one of the noblest tasks for knowledge workers in times of crisis. It falls to these people to deepen the perception of social reality to avoid the spread of irrationality that in turn feeds political opportunism. It also falls to these people to shine a light in the attics of history where the crimes committed by those who abuse power have been hidden. It falls to them to hear and translate the anxieties and aspirations of social forces still without their own means of expression.

The debate about the choices that Brazil faces demands a serene but courageous reflection on Brazilian culture. The absence of this reflection is responsible for the fact that, in trying to diagnose the present situation and look ahead to possible endeavors, Brazilians have contented themselves with conceptual montages that are without roots in their own history. They should instead begin by questioning the existing relations between culture as a system of values and the process of accumulation that is at the base of the expansion of productive forces. This is a matter of contrasting the logic of ends, which the culture determines, with that of means, the instrumental reasoning inherent in purely economic accumulation. How can Brazil preserve the inventive genius of its culture in the face of the need to assimilate techniques that, while they increase Brazil's operational capacity, are vectors for messages that harm its cultural identity? To use a simplifying metaphor, how does Brazil appropriate the computer hardware without being intoxicated by its software, the systems and symbols that frequently dry up Brazil's cultural roots? This problem is apparent everywhere in varying degrees since production of cultural goods has been transformed into a cyclopean business, in which one of the laws that governs it is the imposition of uniformity on patterns of behavior. This uniformity is a basis of the creation of mass markets and, at the same time, a cause of growing social exclusion.

Problems of this degree of complexity have neither a single nor best solution. The goals that drive technological processes are frequently contradictory: some are directed at destruction; others, at preservation. It is a mistake to imagine that technical advances are neutral because they reflect the culturally dominant forces. For example, the military arts are the fruit of the bellicose nature of humans, but not all societies are equally warlike. Too often, technical advances are interconnected and feed off one another. In the century that has just ended, the techniques that advanced the most and that could count on the most abundant financing were those linked to the arts of war. The remaining cultural fields were then exposed to their indirect effects.

Where Brazil Is Headed

Many are the unknowns in the problem to be solved if Brazil is to answer the questions, Where are we now, and where are we headed? If we limit ourselves, however, to the elements that Brazilians can act on, we can easily see that the central question is knowing whether Brazil does or does not have a chance to preserve its cultural identity. Without this, Brazilians will be reduced to the role of passive consumers of cultural goods conceived by other peoples.

It is evident that greater access to cultural goods improves the quality of life for the members of a society. If this process is indiscriminately fomented, however, native forms of creativity are frustrated, and the culture of a people loses its character. Thus a cultural policy that fosters the consumption of imported cultural goods tends to stifle creative activities and put up barriers to innovation. In an era of intense commercialization, of all of the dimensions of social life, the central goal of a cultural policy must be the liberation of the creative forces of a society. Creative activity should not be monitored, but rather room should be made for it to flourish.

Brazilians lack the tools for removing the obstacles to creative activity, whether these come from venerable institutions that call themselves guardians of cultural heritage, from entrepreneurs disguised as protectors of the arts and sciences, or from government bureaucracy. Summing up, this is a matter of defending creative freedom, surely the most surveilled and restricted of all forms of freedom. This will have to be the fruit of effort and vigilance by those who believe in the creative genius of the Brazilian people.

Social Profitability

If Brazil admits that its strategic objective is to reconcile a high rate of economic growth with absorption of unemployment and reduction of income concentration, then it has to recognize that the direction of investments cannot be subordinated to the rationale of transnational companies. Brazilians must start with the concept of social profitability so that the substantive values that express the interests of the collectivity can be taken into account. Only a society supported by a developed economy with a high degree of social homogeneity can trust in the logic of the markets to guide its strategic investments. This discrepancy between the logic of the markets and social interests tends to deepen with globalization. In the case of the automotive industry, the problem seems simple because the companies are based on foreign capital, and technological advance means increased exchange costs. In the case of domestic businesses, however, the same can occur because more advanced technology also translates into increased exchange costs, with increasing pressure on the balance of payments. Nevertheless, this is not the major problem; rather, it is the negative social impact. The traditional Fordism has tended to be replaced by the organization of teams in search of "flexibility." This, of course, reduces the ability of wage earners to organize themselves into unions. This problem is acutely manifest in more advanced capitalism, beginning with the United States, and is at the root of the universal tendency toward income concentration.

We have thus come to the heart of the problem posed by technological advance. The orientation that this assumes translates into a need to diversify consumption in countries with a high standard of living. Technological innovations in marketing have growing importance. The sophistication of patterns of consumption in the wealthy countries tends to guide technological evolution. Only thus can we explain the frenetic waste of goods discarded as obsolete and the brutal attacks on the ecological front.

We return, therefore, to the beginning of our exposition, when we asserted the unforeseeable character of the technical evolution of the capitalist system. Its energy is compulsive and leads to recurring phases of tensions with unforeseeable results. Large-scale destruction by warfare has opened the door to phases of extraordinary prosperity. It is within this picture of uncertainties that we must ask, In what direction is Brazil headed? If we adopt the thesis that globalization is an inescapable technological imperative that will lead all economies to a process of unification of strategic decisions, then Brazil will have to admit that it has even less room in which to maneuver. Brazil is marked by profound social disparities superimposed on regional inequalities in levels of development, and it is therefore fragile in a world dominated by transnational companies that take advantage of these inequalities.

Globalization operates for the benefit of those who are in the technological vanguard and who exploit the uneven development among countries. This leads us to conclude that those countries with great natural resource potential and with accentuated social disparities—like Brazil—are those that will most suffer under globalization. This is because they can fall apart or slide into Fascist authoritarian regimes in response to mounting social tensions. To escape this divide, Brazil must return to the idea of a national plan and recover for the domestic market the dynamic core of the economy. The greatest difficulty is in reversing the process of income concentration, which will occur only through large-scale social mobilization.

Brazil has to prepare its new generation to face these great challenges because it is a matter, on the one hand, of preserving the historical legacy of national unity and, on the other, of continuing to build a democratic society open to foreign relations. Since the possibilities for growth of the domestic market are great, there is room for the positive input of technology controlled by foreign groups. In a word, we can affirm that Brazil will survive as a nation only if it becomes a more just society and preserves its political independence. Then, the dream of building a country that can influence the destiny of humanity will not have vanished.

Notes

1. Celso Furtado, *The Economic Growth of Brazil: A Survey from Colonial to Modern Times* (Berkeley: University of California Press, 1963), 251. Originally published as *A economia brasileira: Contribução à análise do seu desenvolvimento* (Rio de Janeiro: Editora A Noite, 1954).

2. Celso Furtado, *A pré-revolução brasileira* (Rio de Janeiro: Fundo de Cultura, 1962), 9.

GILBERTO DUPAS

The Challenges of the Globalized Economy

The cycle of neoliberal reforms that occurred in the last two decades of the twentieth century accelerated the integration of the large peripheral economies of capitalism into the global market. This cycle was sustained by the rhetoric that it was both inevitable and beneficial. Its objectives were the free flow of capital and the achievements of monetary stability and balanced public budgets. Its principal tools were the opening of trade with an overall reduction in tariffs, internationalization of local production modeled on the logic of fragmentation of production chains, intense privatization of public companies as a way of raising competitiveness, and expansion of the supply of services and reduction of their prices. The political discourse that supported the implementation of these strategies, in addition to arguing for the inexorable nature of globalization, pointed out the possibility of short-term recovery of self-sustained growth as well as some improvement in the chronic income inequality of the countries that were then called "developing."

The main stage of this cycle appears to be over. With rare exceptions, the results of these policies, which ended up coexisting with deep international crises aggravated by the movement of large amounts of volatile capital, were very disappointing. The average unemployment of the thirteen countries of the European Union (EU) grew from 7.5 to 11.0 percent between 1980 and 1998. The cases of the large countries of South America were even more serious. Until then, there was an undeniable average gain in controlling chronic inflationary processes after the implementation of deep reforms consonant with the overall dictates of globalization. This included putting together an economically open regional bloc, Mercosul (Mercosur in Spanish). Nevertheless, Brazil and Argentina went through serious economic crises and still live with the uncertainty of how best to balance their foreign deficits, return to growth, reduce the level of unemployment, and readjust their critical income distribution. In the last two decades of the century, Brazil sustained practically no growth. Its per capita gross domestic product (GDP) grew only 4.8 percent in twenty years, little more than 0.2 percent per year. As for Brazil's perverse income distribution, while there were temporary improvements after the Cruzado Plan and the Real Plan (see chapter 3), 40 percent of the population remained in poverty, and 18 percent, in extreme poverty. Even if one takes as a given the increasing external restrictions that reduce room for autonomous, voluntarist decisions, the renunciation of a national plan that could go beyond the overall neoliberal policies seems to be one of the greatest obstacles for several of these larger peripheral countries in maximizing some of their advantages in their global insertion that might equalize this pernicious distribution.

With this in mind, I intend to study questions that can help to define the possible place of large peripheral countries like Brazil on the world stage. What is the extent of the changes caused by current technologies? Will global capitalism resist the radical future shocks of automation and the fragmentation of information? Will the major powers, especially the United States, have the means to impose and control the forms and the contents of the process of social reproduction? Will they manage to maintain the economic power derived from high rates of capital accumulation earned through continuous technological and productive innovation? Will this innovation thus reinvent labor relations in such a way as to allow at least a minimal supply of jobs worldwide, avoiding an even greater worsening of inequalities? Finally, will countries like Brazil manage to take advantage of globalization without social risks or the rise of intolerable political leaders?

The Information Society's Transforming Paradigms

Even though the twentieth century was a period of exceptional gains, as its final decades approached, the world found itself once again involved with problems that it thought it had eliminated. The enormous triumphs of material progress based on new technologies were questioned amid cyclical depressions, growing unemployment, increased income concentration, and states in crisis.

In fact, after the mid-1970s, the intense socioeconomic phenomena related to the internationalization of the world economy deeply affected the large countries on the periphery of capitalism. This process took on unusual features and enormous drive with the spread of flexibility of production afforded by the qualitative leap in information technology. This radically altered the form of organization of the now globalized productive activity, the role of nation-states, and the paradigm of the labor market.

One of the reasons for the aforementioned paradox is that global capitalism took complete possession of the fate of technology, directing it exclusively to the creation of economic value. Technological leadership basically came to determine the patterns of accumulation. The consequences of technology's gaining autonomy from ethical values and moral norms set by society are among the most serious problems that we must face in this new century. It affects everything from the increased concentration of income and social exclusion to ecological imbalance and the risks of genetic manipulation. It can also entail a slackening dynamic of capital accumulation because of an eventual crisis in demand.

The origins of the information society go back to the end of the 1960s, when revolutionary technologies began to make possible the fragmentation of production chains. This allowed a new design and spatial distribution of productive processes. As a consequence, there arose a sharp change in the correlation of forces among social classes that culminated in the 1980s in new structural relations between capital and labor. This resulted in a substantial loss of power among trade unions, both because these technologies were highly labor saving and because the new relations helped reorganize labor and make it more flexible. As a result, workers' conditions became more precarious. Examples include outsourcing, distance labor, and informal sector activities.

In capitalism today, two key contradictions coexist. The huge scale of investments necessary for technological leadership in products and processes and the need for global networks and media continue to force a process of concentration. Concentration enables only a restricted group of a few hundred gigantic worldwide companies, as leaders of the main production chains, to compete in a fierce contest over market share and accumulation. These corporations decide basically what and how many goods and services to produce and how, when, and where to produce them. Simultaneously and contradictorily, this radical process forces a wave of fragmentation. Outsourcing, franchising, and moving to the informal sector make room for a large number of smaller businesses and flexible labor that feed the central production chain at lower costs.

The second contradiction that drives contemporary capitalism is exclusion versus inclusion. On the one hand, there is growing structural unemployment and instability of employment. On the other, there is the strong dynamic of innovation that drives down the prices of global products, continually incorporating markets that had been at the margins of consumption for lack of income.

Changes deep within the global production chains have altered decisively the way that countries and economic agents relate to one another, appropriate wealth, and change the map of global production. These affect labor demand and the relative strength of various groups of workers. The prospect of widespread fragmentation of the global production chain of a transnational company, made possible by the revolution in information technology, has in turn made possible changes in patterns of production, management systems, and the way labor is used, not to mention progressively breaking down national borders.

In all areas of the economy, we are witnessing a violent process of fusion and incorporation motivated by the new competitive logic that presupposes technological leaps and seeks increasingly global markets. In 1996, the largest 100 corporations in the world held one-third of the global stock of direct investment and were responsible for 80 percent of the international flow of payments in royalties and fees—that is, of technology transfer. The total earnings of the transnational companies in 1992 were $4.8 trillion, having doubled since 1982. This signaled the beginning of a clear increase in concentration, since their rate of growth was much higher than the average growth in the world economy for the same period. In the last years of the century, this trend in concentration remained strong, even though the number of worldwide leaders in the manufacture of products in basic areas of the economy was already very limited.

This means, though, that the room for small and medium-size local companies will disappear. Throughout the Industrial Revolution, these were vital to the development of capitalism and to the creation of jobs. In the global economy, the small and midsize companies will still maintain an important role, especially through outsourcing, franchising, and subcontracting. Basically, however, they will be subordinated to the strategic decisions of transnational companies and integrated into their production chains.

The new logic organizes the production chains into networks of companies, introducing greater flexibility and agility in the face of the need for rapid market responses. These are afforded by the decentralization of the chains' units along with the growing autonomy granted to each one of them. In this way, collaboration and interconnection offer the possibility of multiple structures of partnerships to share costs, risks, and information. Under the conditions of rapid technological changes, the networks, and no longer the companies, are converted into the actual operational units.

The exceptional position of the United States today cannot be considered a paradigm; it derives from its dominant status. In the information society, such hegemony comes about through leadership in the networks around which functions and processes are increasingly organized. These networks are, among others, the global financial flow, the web of political and institutional relations that govern regional blocs, and the global network of new media that determines the nature of cultural expression and of public opinion. They constitute our societies' new social morphology, and the diffusion of this logic radically alters the operations and the outcomes of productive processes, not to mention the stocks of experience, culture, and power. The factors linked to the development and use of new technologies, then, ended up making it possible for the United States to solidify a healthy economic phase that has guaranteed it a long cycle of growth, unequal to the growth of the rest of the global economy. This has allowed the United States to reinforce tenaciously the dominance that it built up after the two world wars.

Technology, Hegemony, and Competitiveness

Hegemonic nations and business leaders in the global production chains currently hold the determining factor of technological innovation. On such innovation is organized global production in search of the most efficient set of factors in labor, capital, knowledge, and natural resources. The new logic of global power derives from competence and confrontation. It is based on a series of power mechanisms in the military, economic, political, ideological, and cultural fields. The fundamental strategic component is control over state-of-the-art technology, essential resources, and a skilled, cheap labor force. In the meanwhile, technological leadership is that which sets the hegemonic condition of both capital and states because it is through it that the overall standards of reproduction and increased accumulation through technological gains are imposed. If technological leadership can be combined with an available labor force and strategic raw materials, a central condition for the exercise of hegemony will be fulfilled. The new dimensions opened up by computer technology and bioengineering have fundamentally changed the concept of appropriation of natural resources. The breakdown and processing of genetic codes have made biological reserves such as those in Amazonia and southeast Mexico valuable again as rich sources of genetic information. The same has occurred with minerals and rare-earth elements used in the manufacture of superconductors and composite substances.

Through the use of the new, flexible, open technologies, the diversity of the international labor market can be converted into a new element of capital superiority. Thus, given the possibilities for widespread geographical fragmentation of production chains made possible by information technology, it is possible for the central countries to use the large reserves of cheap labor in the peripheral countries without having to deal with the infinite demands of social welfare and resulting social tensions if they were to absorb these demands. These pockets of cheap labor are kept in their countries of origin, incorporating their low value added to that stage of production and receiving the increasingly mobile factors of capital, technology, and materials, which can now be brought to where the labor is. The commercial power of natural resources, which are the basic source of export revenues for peripheral countries, is forced to deteriorate because of the greater speed at which technology is incorporated into services and manufactured goods.

With the end of the Cold War, the large flows of direct investment in technological development diminished. These flows had been directed by nation-states, especially the United States and the Soviet Union, to military and related ends. In spite of a noticeable reduction of these flows, the role of nation-states in setting the direction of the technological vectors remains rather important. Although it is estimated that 35 percent of the total expenditures in science and technology in the United States are still bankrolled by the government, the question of the direction of technological development has come to be basically an issue for the private sector. (In these expenditures are included stimuli and incentives, especially for universities and foundations; they are about 2.5 percent of the United States' GDP, compared to only 1 percent of Brazil's.) Thus, since they have been transformed into a basic factor in market competition and in global capital accumulation, the technological vectors have become independent of greater social and public policy considerations.

Through competition with the goal of increasing global market share and accumulation in order to permit new investments in technology and thus to fuel again the cycle of accumulation, technology ended up transforming into an expression of power relations. It is through technology that one gains control of the processes and factors of production and that global wealth is appropriated and concentrated. As a consequence, the United States, because of its land area, the economic power of the transnational companies headquartered there, and its role in broadcasting the dominant cultural pattern, has managed to position itself in the vanguard of this process. In spite of the evolution of its competitors, it outlines the dominant features of globalization and its production chains. As a consequence, the United States produced about 40 percent of the world's new wealth in 1998, compared to 25 percent produced by all of western Europe and 21 percent by all of Asia.

In the meanwhile, paradox is everywhere. The capacity for producing more and better does not stop growing. This process also brings regressions, unemployment, exclusion, and impoverishment. Labor becomes more unstable in this world of power, production, and commodities. Information technologies shrink space. The various "teles" multiply the encounter with the infinite and, at the same time, dematerialize it. On the one hand, nothing seems impossible. On the other hand, the sense of impotence in the face of roadblocks, of instability, and of the precariousness of any gains grows. Technology guarantees the dynamic of capitalist growth, but it also brings complex results in the social arena.

Although most of them do not make the typical products of the new technology, the large companies that have been victorious in the race to global leadership in their sectors are those that have managed to incorporate most effectively these new technologies into the manufacture and distribution of traditional products. What now makes automobile assembly plants; manufacturers of soft drinks, footwear, and apparel; and courier and air transport companies successful is the use of new technologies like computers, automation, real-time data transmission, and the Internet, along with genetic engineering and biotechnology. It is these gigantic, increasingly globalized, concentrated businesses that, for now, sustain the rate of accumulation of the capitalist system. Around the turn of the millennium, the prices of their stocks on the world exchanges maintained a more technical performance infected neither by the euphoria, "the irrational exuberance," of the day that, for a while, dominated the companies of the new economy, nor by the global economic crises. The market identified the solidity of these firms and knew that their performance in the middle term would depend basically on their strategic and operational efficiency, on the condition of incorporating innovations, and on the performance of the world economy. Thus the known logic is affirmed: innovation has been and will continue to be the key to the capitalist dynamic and to the success of its corporations; those that best appropriate innovation will guarantee their future. This once more implies the urgency of national plans that make the development of technological niches viable and allow producers to add value to local production.

Systemic Competitiveness and Localization

Even though global competition is basically a matter for the private sector, there is still a significant role reserved for nation-states in providing a competitive environment for the companies headquartered in them. "Systemic competitiveness" is the set of factors external to the company proper that strongly affect efficiency of operation.

Open and stable national economies can benefit passively from the comparative advantages or develop them actively. At the same time, one needs to remember that the old international division of labor is rapidly losing importance. Today, developing countries have two possibilities: develop dynamic comparative advantages or accept economic stagnation. The former means incorporating new technologies in the areas of agrobusiness, the extractive sector, and processing and service industries. It means perfecting management techniques, creating international networks, using global partnerships, and developing some local technological niches that allow adding value to exports.

Jörg Meyer-Stamer has an interesting approach to systemic competitiveness. He points out the possibility of interaction among the micro, macro, meso, and meta levels. The micro level requires managerial competence and innovation, best practices in all stages of the production cycle (development, production, and marketing), adequate participation in technological networks, and satisfactory interaction among suppliers, producers, and clients. On the macro level, consistent economic policies (and not just those centered on short-term crisis management), coherent monetary and exchange policy, and a fiscal regime in tune with global competitiveness are all needed. On the meso level, which is that of the interaction between the micro and macro levels, it is necessary to guarantee an institutional context that stimulates technological development, legislation that creates adequate conditions for settling labor disputes, and an educational policy that offers ample basic education as well as technical and scientific training compatible with production needs. Finally, on the meta level, it is necessary to develop sociocultural factors and attitudes geared to structural competitiveness through means of a basic model of political and economic organization and the capacity to formulate strategies and policies. It is clear that not even the heavily industrialized countries could dedicate themselves to a strategy of creating internationally competitive companies in all areas. The option is to create dynamic comparative advantages for some key sectors that take into consideration the specific factors of each country. The most difficult issue has typically been the search for sectors with high growth potential in which, given the existing comparative advantages, there are open windows of opportunity that can be leveraged with specific policies. These windows do not stay open for long. Once they have been identified, it is necessary to provide the basic prerequisites rapidly so that the businessmen can keep them open.

During the recent rise in globalization, costs of communication and transportation have fallen, the flow of information and technologies across borders has increased, and barriers to trade and investment have decreased. Productive activities have come to need a global rather than domestic approach. The national identity of the corporation has come to be replaced by a new, borderless strategy. Meanwhile, as Michael Porter reminds us, an important paradox between the global and the local persists. Although companies must compete globally and the factors in production move freely about the world, there is strong evidence that localization continues to play a crucial role in establishing the competitive advantages. Global companies disperse their activities among many countries but continue to concentrate the critical mass of innovation and strategy in one or two locations.

In the peripheral countries, there still predominate commodity export companies based on intensive labor or natural resources and on partnerships with transnationals for production of part of a chain based on low labor costs. In the meanwhile, without final products and services of good reputation, without proper methods of production and the incorporation of some appropriate technology, it will always be difficult to penetrate foreign markets while adding value to the final product. It is fundamental, even for producers of commodities, to enrich the value of their chains, including distribution, marketing, and international supply. For this, the comparative advantages must be made effectively competitive.

Among the critical advantages of localization associated with competitiveness is the idea of clusters. Clusters are geographic concentrations that specialize in certain products or sectors, formed of interconnected companies, specialized suppliers, service providers, competitors, and associated institutions, such as universities, economic development agencies, and trade associations, which compete but at the same time cooperate among themselves. Critical masses of competitive success in certain areas of business have been possible in the more developed countries through the use of clusters. This has been the case with the wine industry in California and the footwear and fashion industries in Italy. In Brazil, one can cite an example in the high technology sector, that of Embraer, whose proximity to the Technological Institute of Aeronautics (Instituto Technológico de Aeronáutica, ITA) and to other activities related to the sector, along with government support through the involvement of the Ministry of Aeronautics, permitted the initial differentiation for competitiveness. In sectors in which natural resources and intermediate technology predominate, one can cite the orange and soy clusters for production, processing, and distribution.

Clusters afford access to inputs, workers, specialized information, complementarity or synergy (as with the tourism industry, for example), institutional support, and a critical mass of technological development. The role of the various levels of government is to provide specialized training and educational programs, agreements and incentives for technological research with local universities, logistics and transportation, regulatory innovations to encourage upgrading, and overall support. This is the case with forest product clusters in Portugal and Sweden. In the world's leading economy, that of the United States, there are a large number of specialized geographic concentrations: biotechnology and software in Boston; engineering and integrated systems services in Colorado; vehicles and parts in Detroit; aerospace defense and entertainment in Los Angeles; hospital administration in Nashville; financial services, advertising, and media in New York; home furnishings and synthetic fibers in North Carolina; hotel management and telemarketing in Omaha; helicopters, semiconductors, and optics in Phoenix; jewelry and nautical equipment in Providence; aeronautics and naval construction in Seattle; microelectronics and biotechnology in Silicon Valley; light aircraft and agricultural equipment in Wichita; and so forth.

As one can see, the phenomenon of clusters well illustrates the paradox of localizing the global economy. At the same time that it rehabilitates the role of public policies in the dynamic of both sectoral and regional development, it also indicates their eminently selective character.

The Role of Regional Blocs

The growth in regional blocs has important, varied effects on the strategic decisions of transnational companies in the formation of their global chains and on their policies of direct investment. The founding of the EU, for example, facilitated an increase in this investment, especially within Europe. This growth resulted from the effort of corporations to rationalize their European production in the quest for economies of scale and efficiency. From the second half of the 1980s on, the portion of intraregional investments in the overall stock of direct investment in Europe grew sharply. A large part of this growth consisted in mergers and acquisitions, in the attempt to protect the European market share from attacks from international competitors.

In the case of the North American Free Trade Agreement (NAFTA), the effects were different. The portions of investments from U.S. firms in Canada and Mexico declined, probably because the removal of barriers made it possible for those companies to export to Canada and Mexico from the United States. On the other hand, the possibility of the intense, flexible use of inexpensive Mexican labor in the maquiladoras introduced a new dynamic into U.S.-Mexican relations that definitively bound Mexico into the structure of that bloc.

The matter of Mercosul is more complex. It appeared to follow a trajectory more like the European one. By adopting open regionalism, the trade among the countries of the bloc grew rapidly from $4 billion to $20 billion between 1990 and 1998. In this period, transnational companies represented about 60 percent of this intraregional commerce, showing that these corporations used the formation of the bloc to their favor, especially those that sought economies of regional scale. In Mercosul they found a useful cushion that adequately compensated the high systemic cost of the region. The total of direct investment in the region increased significantly. European, American, and Asian industries invested in the region with the goal of achieving access to this market through the nuclei of local production.

Unfortunately, the dynamic of insertion supported by the strategy of the regional blocs does not always guarantee favorable balances in trade or in the running transactions for the countries in the bloc. This was the case of recent foreign investment in Brazil, where the main objective of the quest for the domestic market, although that broadened with Mercosul, led to disappointing results in export growth, in addition to entailing continuous increases in the total of dividend remittances. In the case of Mercosul, the adoption of a theoretically healthy open regionalism ended up sharply increasing the importation of intermediate and final products without these amounts' being offset by an increase in exports of traditional and manufactured products to the regional blocs formed by more developed countries. While its total exports grew 41 percent between 1992 and 1998, Mercosul's imports rose 136 percent. If we analyze the character of these flows by origin and destination, we see that the greatest beneficiary of this growth was the EU. While its exports to Mercosul grew 205 percent (compared to 159 percent for the United States and 101 percent for Japan), its imports rose only 31 percent (compared to 43 percent for the United States and 6.5 percent for Japan). As for the strong trade dynamic within the bloc, with imports growing

187 percent and exports 184 percent, it is important to remember that about 60 percent of this trade was made up of exchanges within the intraindustrial matrix, predominantly of transnational corporations, especially European and U.S. companies, established in Mercosul.

One of the consequences of Mercosul's intense insertion into the global economy was the growth in its trade imbalance. In 1997, for example, Mercosul operated with a deficit of $19 billion with the EU and $13 billion with NAFTA in manufactures. This was a result particularly of the increase of its exports connected with the logic of complementarity and specialization of the global chains. On the other hand, the surplus earned in the area of agrobusiness, in which theoretically Brazil is better able to compete, was only $9 billion with the EU and $900 million with NAFTA. In addition to the related deterioration in the terms of exchange, by the continuous addition of value to technological products as compared to commodities, the United States' nontariff barriers and the EU's agricultural subsidies operate intensely as obstacles to the region's expansion of exports.

The future of regional blocs appears uncertain. The global accords for free trade serve to undermine their logic. The main reason is that part of the strategy of the global production chains is to, as radically as possible, eliminate the restrictions on global trade as a way of broadening markets and raising accumulation. In the meanwhile, in the short to middle term, an important frontier of business expansion still can be conditioned to the commercial blocs. A recent change in Brazil's exchange policy and its strong impact on Mercosul, especially on the economic stability of Argentina, will open up new opportunities for the inevitable strategic alliances of Brazilian companies with Argentine and Uruguayan firms, even though these will temporarily modify the complementarities and synergies. Another impact is the involvement of leaders of the global chains of agrobusiness and the industrial and service sectors. The possibility of a new round of offensives on the Free Trade Area of the Americas (FTAA) brings critical new questions about the future of regional agreements on the continent, affecting especially Brazil and its strategy as a global trader maintained up to this point. This is because the drastic reduction in tariffs on imports of U.S. products and the prevalence of cost of production, still significantly higher in Brazil and Argentina, would end up directing a considerable part of new direct investments from transnationals into the United States itself, in those cases, incorporating inexpensive Mexican labor. The United States, then, could easily become an export platform for the large markets of South America, thus strongly inhibiting the growth of the local production base.

Possible Strategic Spaces and the Need for a National Plan

In the face of all of these challenges introduced by globalization and by the role of the technological domain in defining the new hegemonies, it is necessary to interpret very carefully the great transformations that the Brazilian productive and societal structure is undergoing. These changes began with the transnationalization of global production after the 1980s, continued with the radical opening of Brazil started in 1990, and, finally, were consolidated with the monetary stability and change in the exchange standard in the 1990s. Three fundamental processes were the route for the intense internationalization of the Brazilian economy: privatization of the state companies that operated in infrastructure and raw materials manufacture, the purchase of large and midsize domestic companies by foreigners interested in the Brazilian market, and, finally, the expansion of investment from companies that already had local production operations.

In this brief period, beginning when the economic opening started to have real effects, the real liquid operational revenue of the twenty largest foreign groups established in Brazil rose 180 percent, compared to 30 percent for the twenty largest domestic groups. If we limit this to only the ten largest, foreign groups grew 245 percent and domestic groups 37 percent. Aside from the progressive industrial concentration common to globalization, these numbers are evidence of a clear advance in internationalization of the leading companies.

If we pay close attention to the changes in position among international and domestic businesses, we see major modifications. Of the ten largest domestic companies as measured by liquid assets at the end of 1992, eight were no longer in the top ten by the end of 1998. Of those companies that took their place, five were the result of privatization: Tele Norte Leste, Tele Centro Sul, Companhia Vale do Rio Doce (CVRD), Companhia Siderúrgica Nacional (CSN), and Usiminas. If we limit ourselves to the top five companies in this period, three companies were bumped from the list and replaced by state companies bought by local ones.

If we look at international companies, the changes are even more impressive. Among the ten largest in 1992, nine were no longer on the list in 1998. They were replaced by three new groups that came from privatization (Telefónica, Portugal Telecom, and MCI), two groups that bought domestic companies (ABN Amro and Brasmotor), and four other groups already doing business in Brazil that greatly expanded their operations (Fiat, Belgo-Mineira, Volkswagen, and White Martins). If we look only at the top five companies, all of the ones on the list in 1992 were replaced in 1998: Shell, Autolatina, Souza Cruz, Bung and Born, and Alcoa. Two of the new companies came in through the telecom privatization (Telefónica and MCI), two more grew their local businesses (Fiat, Belgo-Mineira), and the fifth was an international financial conglomerate that bought a local bank (ABN Amro). To complete the picture of this revolution, of the twenty largest international companies doing business in Brazil, 75 percent were replaced in this period.

Although these changes are appropriate for the current global model and bring benefits for the local economy, there are several problems to consider. Such a deep transformation in the array of major companies in a country cannot help but have a related impact on the structure of domestic power. Local capital and organization lose ground to the predominance of the leading foreign companies. At the same time, this opens up opportunities for partnerships of domestic companies with these international companies in the capacity of suppliers for the latter's global chains.

The clearest changes in the cast of central actors in the Brazilian economy are in the reduced roles of the state and domestic capital, in the intense natural selection among the surviving major companies, and in the introduction of a new main character: the large transnational company. Several goals of these worldwide companies can eventually coincide with those of the country. This is the case with the general interests in economic growth and monetary stability, which allow remuneration with the lowest risk possible for the large amounts of capital invested by the transnationals. At the same time, it is reasonable to expect future conflicts regarding the rules regulating privatization, tariff policy, contests over patents, environmental aspects, and the various matters involving national sovereignty. Brazilian society needs to reflect on these topics and prepare its institutions for the new realities of power.

A fundamental aspect of the future of domestic productive activity is, evidently, interest rates and, as a consequence, the cost of capital. Creating viable conditions for obtaining capital from third parties who finance production at a cost compatible with the customary rate of return for successful business is increasingly a critical factor in competitiveness. As a point of reference, the average rate of return for an investor in the thirty largest U.S. companies in the period 1988–98 was around 20 percent. This number can serve as an indicator of average remuneration for these businesses. Even if we add in the country risk as an aggravating factor in the expectations, it becomes evident that the cost of capital (or average interest rates for middle- to long-term loans) close to or above the possible rates of return will make investment in Brazilian productive activity un-interesting and unviable in the long term. Therefore, requirements for the future of Brazilian economic growth include reduced, stabilized interest rates on the international level as well as the middle-term availability of domestic capital to be loaned at these rates. This is because it is at this level of international rate that global competitors work to structure their operation with a view to gaining the Brazilian market.

ANOTHER IMPORTANT QUESTION that the process of economic opening brought to Brazil was the radical change in the logic of its foreign transactions and the introduction of a chronic imbalance of payments. As a consequence, under present circumstances of economic opening and insertion into the global system, a strategy of self-sustained economic growth in Brazil is viable only if it has as a basis a significant broadening of exports. This is because, on the one hand, the current degree of opening of the Brazilian economy is a requirement of the logic of complementarity and specialization within which the global markets operate. Therefore, significantly reducing imports could mean a loss of dynamic competi-tiveness in the economy. On the other hand, Brazil continues to need foreign re-serves because of its inability to provide domestically generated long-term funds. It is imperative to change as soon as possible the way of financing the deficit in running transactions, which cannot be reduced in the short term and are today sustained basically by direct investment capital. Thus, considering the aforemen-tioned restrictions, a significant increase in exports is essential for allowing a new healthy cycle to begin.

There are four well-defined periods in Brazil's recent commercial balance. The first was the phase prior to economic opening, 1985–89, in which exports, which were evolving more than imports, were leading to a positive balance trending toward $15 billion a year. The second period, 1990–94, was the immediate post-opening phase. In this phase, imports began to grow more rapidly than exports, and the balance showed a tendency to fall slightly. With the implementation of the Real Plan, which marked the beginning of the third period (1994–98), de-mand showed strong growth, and the anchored exchange was the main tool for controlling inflation. At that moment, imports took a jump, and the trade balance became increasingly negative and progressively unsustainable. It is this factor that, along with the shocks of the worldwide crises of 1997–98 and the flight of large volumes of short-term capital that made up Brazilian reserves, obliged the government to devalue the currency in early 1999. This was the beginning of the fourth period, characterized by a rapid restoration of balance in trade, basically as a result of a significant reduction in imports. A recovery in foreign sales had not, at least by 2000, played a relevant role in this rebalance, because of the absence of a clear and consistent export strategy, the low value added to exports, and the fall in commodity prices.

An analysis of the behavior of imports between 1985 and 2000 shows that their growth only accelerated after the Real Plan. From then on, Brazilian industry inserted itself into the new global economy based on complementarity and specialization of production, even if only in a disorderly way. For this reason, the import of raw materials and intermediate goods jumped from $5 billion in the five-year period 1985–89 to more than $25 billion in the three-year period 1997–99, growing to nearly half of all international purchases. Capital goods and consumer goods also showed strong, though less intense, expansion.

As a result, Brazilian industry came to work with an increasing share of imported products. Its coefficient of penetration leaped from 4.5 percent in 1989 to 10.6 percent in 1994 and to over 19 percent in 1998. Although this growth was generalized, some sectors underwent a more radical process of integration and competition. This was the case of capital goods, which came to work with 57 percent imported components. The durable consumer goods sector tripled its import coefficient to 30 percent in 1998. These new levels of integration are part of a new reality with lessened chances of significant reversal. Therefore, they must be taken into account in the elaboration of a development plan for the country.

On the export side, the first observation is Brazil's difficulty in selling products with greater value added. The share of manufactured products on the export agenda remained in the range of 52–55 percent all through the 1990s. Thus Brazil's exports depended heavily on products with low value added, mostly commodities, whose prices are at the mercy of the world market. The experiences of Korea and Mexico, for example, have been very different. Mexico expected exports to total $150 billion in 2000, five times the 1993 amount. Korea, after recovering rapidly from the crisis of the late 1990s, opted for high-value-added exports, through a more aggressive industrial policy, and expected exports valuing $140 billion in 2000. These two countries thus are excellent examples of the need for large peripheral countries to qualify their insertion in the global system with the support of a national plan that sets guidelines and advocates for policies that maximize national comparative advantages.

The evolution of Brazil's balance of payments, in the meanwhile, has revealed a worrisome situation since economic opening. Until the mid-1990s, the trade balance covered the cost of debt service and the other components of the balance of services. With the subsequent increase in imports, however, the deficits in running transactions were now covered with direct foreign investments. These, which had not been more than $1 billion at the beginning of the 1990s, totaled $77 billion in the 1997–99 period, covering 85 percent of those deficits. As a consequence, the flow of dividends jumped to a new level, and it will continue to grow in the coming years. Surely, this increase in investments reflects a greater confidence in Brazil's economic policy, but it has reached such levels only because of the process of privatization and purchase of Brazilian firms. Since privatization and purchase have tended to decline, it is fundamental for Brazil to develop an adequate alternative to cover this negative flow of reserves. Once more, the path of structural consistency lies in the significant increase in imports. This is because increasing foreign loans does not appear to be a viable path in the long run since Brazil could have difficulties in renewing its debts on a scale much larger than that at present, not to mention that such growth would have an . immediate impact on the debt through increased servicing of the interest cost.

The unstable situation in the balance of trade thus requires a national development plan that seeks to return to self-sustained growth and that reconciles this goal with the issue of imbalance in foreign accounts. The most consistent path appears to be the attempt to sustain a new cycle of expansion by means of exports. In this context, a significant growth in the balance of trade is no longer an option but an imperative. Moreover, in light of the high level of imports, unavoidable because of the logic of complementarity and specialization, it was necessary for exports to reach a level on the order of $80 billion to $90 billion by 2005 to make possible an average annual growth rate in the GDP of 4–5 percent without the risk of an exchange crisis. One can note that, even so, we are talking about a relatively closed economy that would be exporting less than 15 percent of its domestic product. For this model to be successful, it is fundamental to mobilize the country around an export plan that involves various levels and organs of government as well as the entire entrepreneurial class. Such a plan must be sufficiently broad to involve the expansion not only of primary and basic products but also of manufactures, with their various degrees of sophistication and value added. In the near future, the importance of Brazil's exports is such that it cannot miss any chance to broaden them. In the case of manufactures, for example, there must be policies and plans that range from those that created the Mexican maquiladoras, which increase value somewhat, to policies and plans like those of Korea for high-value-added exports.

Of course, in spite of the circumstances of Brazil's balance of payments that have made inevitable the promotion of a growth strategy temporarily founded on a growth in imports, this strategy should not be designed without regard to progressive strengthening of the domestic market, fundamental to the consolidation of sustainable growth over the middle to long term. To some extent, the additional income generated by export activity and the funds distributed by the ample, urgent public programs to combat poverty, as discussed previously, will help reinforce and consolidate this domestic market.

These are some of the huge challenges that Brazil's productive structure will have to face to adjust to the standards of competitiveness in the coming decades. The global companies will maintain their growing interests in local operations to the extent that they manage to create viable competitive conditions for the production of final goods or sufficient value added for their production chains. In these cases the global companies will be making favorable use of the synergies of scale of the local market, natural resources, existing clusters, incorporation of inexpensive labor (when relevant), and systemic advantages eventually available around the country. They will not hesitate to opt for green field operations, acquisition of local firms, or, on a lesser scale, strategic partnerships with domestic companies, in accordance with their best strategic interests.

As for companies with a majority of domestic capital, four possible paths will open to them: they will become partners with or suppliers for the global leaders in local or international operations; they will find specific niches in which their high competence, connected or not with clusters, makes their autonomous growth possible; they themselves will become global companies, in association with international partners or not; or they will sell their operations to global interests. This is the rainbow of standard alternatives over the horizon of strategic possibilities to be explored in the quest for competitive conditions that will allow the growth of Brazilian entrepreneurial activity in the twenty-first century.

IN THE LAST DECADES of the twentieth century, Brazil consolidated a long tradition of intense income inequality and an enormous contingent of excluded population. According to data from the National Household Sample Survey (Pesquisa Nacional por Amostra de Domicílios, PNAD), in 1998, 14 percent of the Brazilian population (21 million people) lived in extreme poverty. This category is part of the 33 percent of citizens (50 million) living below the poverty line. More serious, however, is the trend toward stability in these percentages. Although poverty rates have been momentarily alleviated by periods of growth and economic shocks as, for example, after the Cruzado Plan and Real Plan, when they retreated to 28 percent and 34 percent respectively, the tendency has been for these numbers to return to the level of 41 percent for the poor and 18 percent for the extremely poor, the Brazilian averages since 1977.

As a reflection of the extremely unequal distribution of national income in the last two decades of the twentieth century, the richest 10 percent constantly held 50 percent of the family income, whereas the poorest 50 percent held only 10 percent and the poorest 20 percent, only 2 percent. Among the richest 1 percent is concentrated income greater than that of the poorest 50 percent of the population. Obviously, long periods of high interest rates and inflation have a relevant role in the structural trap that continues to keep income highly concentrated even in periods of economic growth.

What is worse is when Brazil is compared to the rest of the world: while 64 percent of the countries have a lower per capita income than Brazil's, the proportion of the poor in countries with per capita income similar to Brazil's is only 10 percent. As for the concentration of wealth as measured by the Gini coefficient, at the end of the twentieth century, only Sierra Leone, Jamaica, the Central African Republic, Guatemala, and Paraguay had a degree of inequality equal to or greater than Brazil's.

If we add to this picture the paradigm change in the labor market after economic opening—the intense flexibilization and automation of the labor force—we can appreciate fully the challenge that the country will have to face to maintain its global insertion in a climate of social and political equilibrium. The level of unemployment rose from 5 to 8 percent in the 1990s, simultaneous with a growth in flexible labor from 42 to 55 percent of urban dwellers.

As we can see, it is essential that strategies for national growth contain redistributive policies that address the chronic problems of wealth concentration and poverty. This implies policies from the most structural (redistribution of assets, education, and agrarian reform) to the more compensatory (minimum wage). It requires too that the government maintain responsibility for the basic programs covering health, education, and overall social assistance, since a huge contingent of the poor do not have the income available to buy these services in the marketplace. Even if the interaction with communities is imperative, by way of involving them increasingly in the management of these programs, there is no way for the government to run away from the public responsibility of making available the sufficient budgetary resources to support this mass of population on the fringes of the market economy, without the risk of facing serious problems of legitimacy and maintenance of order.

It is essential that Brazil create conditions under which economic growth results in real improvement in distribution of wealth and breaks historical patterns. In fact, the amount needed to put all of the poor over the poverty line would be 7 percent of total family incomes. To free the lowest level from extreme poverty, 2 percent of the income would be enough. This gives us reason for a certain optimism because it shows that facing this problem is compatible with the country's macroeconomic aggregates and that its solution can rest basically on national political will, especially that of the elites.

IN CONCLUSION, it is important to reaffirm that the trend toward globalization of production chains and markets appears to be irreversible, especially for the large peripheral countries with a scale of potential domestic consumption sufficient to fit within the strategic interests of the large transnational corporations and their logic of fragmentation of production. In the meanwhile, the margins of freedom are not great for these countries, and, for this very reason, it is important to articulate a national plan consistent with global insertion. At the same time, these plans must afford at least a minimum of order and bargaining room in monitoring the globalization of the local economy and, at best, a maximum of value added to the local production. In this way, these countries, among other goals, will manage a certain equilibrium in the balance of trade and will not head, in the middle term, toward rendering their economic opening unviable. Without sacrificing other essential policies, this will be possible only with a strong effort in local technological development in several directions: products, processes, and systems, and, in particular, in specialized niches.

The circumstances of globalization and the conditions for turning the insertion into the global economy into a major gain in competitiveness and degrees of freedom in economic development rather than simply a source of unemployment and instability require better awareness of the special character of each country. There is a need to mobilize or remain mobilized around a viable national plan, coupled with a political discourse that can reach the population and recover at least some national enthusiasm. To abandon a plan, imagining that the citizenry will be content to be handed over to the negative freedoms of the market forces and that these will take care of the balanced growth of the country, would mean a serious economic and institutional retreat.

JORGE WILHEIM

Metropolises and the Far West
in the Twenty-first Century

At the beginning of this new century, Brazil offers a varied and attractive panorama. It is the proud home of nineteen metropolitan areas, of which two are high-
profile megacities, São Paulo and Rio de Janeiro. There are thirty more urban
agglomerations with modern metropolitan characteristics. At the same time, the
country is opening up new lands and expanding its economic frontiers beyond
the Central Plateau, entering fragile Amazonia, sowing new cities all along the
new highways that have penetrated the region. In other words, this is a highly
urbanized country that is dealing with large urban areas along with a necklace of
new cities in the Northwest.

This panorama is interesting and diverse because, on the one hand, it requires
dramatic solutions in the metropolises, ingenious ones for the consolidation of
the network of midsize cities, and innovative ones for the new cities. On the other
hand, it offers the energy of a creative, mobile, culturally syncretic, and racially
mixed people.

This exciting picture is a counterpoint to one of chronically anemic urban
planning and an odd omission on the part of the federal government until 2001,
when a new national law — the Statute of the City (Estatuto da Cidade) — was
drafted. Until then, no public policies for Brazil's heavily urban reality had been
implemented on a national scale. In fact, the federal government thought it had
an urban policy because in 2000 it had established a somewhat coherent multiyear budget that dealt with health programs and urban transportation. At the
same time, one cannot think of cities just in terms of their sectors and infrastructure. Cities are the stage on which nowadays we elaborate and display culture,

basic decisions about development, the life of modern society, the fostering of citizenship, and the crucial global connection. They are the seats of innovation and critique. They are the command centers and interfaces among markets, producers, rural production, and global demand. They are the targets of financial interests that are based there as well as actions of organized crime, which is also globalized. It would be difficult for such a reality, crucial to any development strategy, to be understood or to be acted on through a vision limited to isolated issues.

Other chapters of this book have described the social and political trajectories and other phenomena that have transformed the urban network in the course of the twentieth century. Previously, Brazilian urban centers were scattered along the coast, either because they were historically connected to the Portuguese metropolis as ports or because the Central Plateau that dominates the Brazilian interior ends in an escarpment above the narrow coastal strip, always presenting a challenging green wall to overcome. The larger colonial urban areas, all on the coast, were the successive capitals, Salvador and Rio de Janeiro, along with the provisional seventeenth-century Dutch capital of Recife. Several other urban areas, however, resulted from the need to create bases for trade and support services for agricultural and mineral exploitation or the need to establish solidly the military and symbolic values of colonial domination. Examples of these included Vila Rica do Ouro Preto in the heart of the mining region and the *boca do sertão* (literally "mouth of the hinterland") pioneer towns that facilitated the conquest of new lands, such as São Paulo de Piratininga, at its beginning.

The succession of economic cycles led by agricultural exploitation (brazilwood, sugarcane, coffee) and mining corresponded to territorial settlement that was not always marked by important urban areas. The huge size of the Brazilian territory was certainly one of the reasons that Brazil did not have the village life so typical of European urban centers in their early days. The daily going and coming of agricultural workers, conditioned by the rhythms of planting and harvest, with seasonal breaks dedicated to urban tasks, arose only recently, in the second half of the twentieth century, with the *bóias-frias* (migrant laborers; see chapter 2) and the wage-earning rural workers living on the outskirts of midsize cities in precarious preurban circumstances. In the earlier centuries, the rural worker was condemned to live on the farm or plantation itself, whether as a slave in the quarters or, later, as a tenant employee on the property.

At that time, the autonomy of the farm or plantation was relative; it could not do without certain support services and social connections, be they institutional, cultural, or economic, whether for the exercise of power or religious participation. In this way, towns and cities arose in the Paraíba Valley between Rio de Janeiro and São Paulo, on the São Paulo Plateau, in the distant rural South, and punctuating the coast of the Northeast and North. To the extent that greed, adventure, and business pushed pioneers into the continent, there arose the *boca de sertão* towns that were much-needed commercial emporia and refuges for safety. When the trails that Indians had opened in the forest were replaced by railroads, at regular intervals determined by functional necessity and also for the convenience of landowners, service and commercial towns popped up. These were appropriately called *pontas de trilho*, or "rail terminus points."

For four centuries, the construction of the Brazilian urban network obeyed the slow rhythm of exploration and exploitation of the vast territory, always with low population density. At the end of the nineteenth century, with the end of slavery and the heavy influx of immigrant groups, the rhythm of urbanization changed. The speed of transformation and consolidation was startling. São Paulo, now the country's most important metropolis, between 1890 and 1900 grew from 65,000 to 265,000 inhabitants, mostly Italian immigrants. In only 100 years, São Paulo swelled from 265,000 to 10 million. Its completely urbanized metropolitan area of 80 square kilometers grew from 300,000 to 17 million by 2000. Estimates are that it will reach 21 million by 2015, though with much lower annual growth rates.

The cities founded in the west of the state of São Paulo in the 1920s during the expansion of coffee culture into "new" lands are today midsize cities with diversified economies and relatively good quality of life. The towns surrounding Campinas—a medium-size city in Sao Paulo state—which were still small and isolated in the 1950s, now form a new, heavily urbanized metropolitan area, crystallized around Campinas and inserted in a larger agglomeration, the São Paulo macrometropolis. This macrometropolis also functionally includes, though not as a conurbation, the Baixada Santista, the coastal plain region centered on the port city of Santos and the southernmost third of the string of cities in the Paraíba Valley, heading in the direction of Rio de Janeiro.

The vigorous formation of the Brazilian urban network was not simply a result of the increase in the country's population. It was also a consequence of the population's mobility. Therefore, when considering the future of urban Brazil, we cannot simply assert that Brazilian cities will cease to grow and change and that new cities will not be created just because of the sharp drop in birth rates and the prospect of a "modern," that is, low demographic growth rate. The urban dynamic has been heavily fueled by individual will within the Brazilian population to grow, to improve, to enrich, and to consume. Growth—accompanying the growth and development of a city and taking advantage of opportunities that such growth affords its inhabitants—is a common experience of the Brazilian population and its frequent domestic migration. About one-half of the population of the city of São Paulo was not born there. There is not a single city dweller who cannot tell a family story associated with migration and the growth of the city.

WHAT, THEN, are the prospects for urbanization in Brazil? Is it possible to construct a scenario of the future of Brazilian cities for the next several decades? Planning implies, in the first place, dealing with the future and proposing something that does not yet exist but that has the means to come into existence. Scenarios for the future can be constructed and can constitute legitimate proposals, leading to discussions, decisions, cost and time estimates, and plans geared to making the scenario a reality. To work with scenarios for the future, one must use as a point of departure the structure and dynamic elements of the present, string them together according to certain trends, and give to the whole the consistency possible. In choosing various trends and extrapolating them to their extremes, one can set up an intellectual game and set a landmark within which it is possible to make policy choices that lead to decisions about the future that one wants to build.

It is good, however, to heed the warnings of historians and philosophers. Voltaire affirmed that "history does not repeat itself, but man does." Barbara Tuchman and other historians have described the tragic consequences throughout history that have resulted from senseless decisions, decisions that were contrary to the long-range interests of those who made them, the responsibility of the authorities with sufficient power. Examples include the Trojan acceptance of the gift horse and U.S. intervention in Vietnam. Therefore, when proposing scenarios, we can not only make mistakes in interpreting trends but also be surprised by thoughtless decisions and afterthoughts that subvert the apparent logic of the facts.

That said, what are the scenarios that we can visualize for a Brazilian urban world in the early decades of the twenty-first century? Let us posit, as a first scenario, a pessimistic one in which, for many years, a government (contrary to the 2006–10 one) denies the need for a development strategy that focuses centrally on reducing the distance between the rich and poor. In my view, this is a strategic axis full of consequences. In this scenario, economic policy would also remain consonant with neoliberal canons. In this case, Brazil would experience continued dependency on foreign investments, maintenance of relative stability in exchange, growth of the already high public debt, especially the foreign debt, an increase in income concentration, a greater separation of the more cosmopolitan sectors of the population and the excluded sectors, continuation of precarious wages, an increase in industrial unemployment, an increase in the informal sector, and an increase in social tensions.

The rise in frustration in trying to survive and move up economically would worsen social tensions concentrated in the cities and even more in the metropolises. This would increase urban violence and the abandonment of public spaces, considered a dangerous no-man's-land or, rather, a land of the excluded. Dichotomy and fragmentation of the cities could unleash a wave of political movements of civil disobedience, infringing on the norms of daily coexistence, thus leading to the weakening of the state of law and a relatively authoritarian imposition of public order. A state of anomie and absence of government could create a vacuum of power, rapidly filled by caudillo leadership, by recurrent military authoritarianism, or, more likely, by organized crime. The last, moreover, would take advantage of the growing frustration of youths, increasing the drug supply to create dependency, broadening the already present tendency to specialize the effects of drugs according to the demands of the users: sexual excitants, tranquilizers, stimulants, inhibitors, hallucinogens—all creating physical or psychological addiction and social alienation.

The deleterious presence of organized crime, at the moment in which it allies itself with corrupt elements of the public sector, mainly through illicit drug and arms trade and money laundering, could result in a landscape of increasing anomie, of frayed solidarity, and a decrease in civic spirit and action. More subtly, in a setting of increasing civil disobedience and poverty, government sectors would be receptive to "collaboration" with organized crime to gain financial support for the reduction of the risks of weakening governability. The decrease in ethical behavior, especially in the judicial arena, and cynical attitudes in the business arena would complete a picture of decay that could lead to an interruption in the democratic process or even a symptomatic suicidal phase of Western civilization itself. Similar phenomena have already occurred in the history of civilizations, always coinciding with periods in which they considered themselves hegemonic and historically definitive.

To this depressing, dangerous scenario, tending toward heightening social rifts and exacerbating rapine individualism, one must add that society would produce activities of resistance, antibodies destined to compensate for the impotence of the public sector. The "third sector" would produce nongovernmental, nonprofit public institutions that would certainly try to diminish the negative effects described above. These sites of resistance could come to reorient governments, pointing out the public policies suitable for correcting the fractures and social rifts that block development.

If economic growth without a reduction in poverty and ignorance prevailed, the social dichotomy would grow and might crystallize the clear separation into a society of globalized habits, with the training to carry out highly automated activities at a rapid pace of decision making, and an incipient "other society," manipulable because its members lack information, struggle to survive, and live at a slower pace. This social fragmentation or dualism would make the generation of a national development plan difficult because the "modern, globalized" society, while politically dominant, would focus on goals quite distant from those that the "excluded, marginal" society expected. From this first scenario could result revolts out of despair or even a revolution, which, if successful, could invert the power relations, inaugurating a new cycle of uncertainties.

What changes would the Brazilian urban network undergo if this scenario came to be? There would be relatively stable exchange conditions, guaranteeing the pioneering enterprises in the Northwest by continuing the penetration into Amazonia along the highways already built there. A certain decentralization of industrial enterprises favoring midsize cities would also continue. Such a trend would accelerate the in-fill of land adjacent to midsize and larger cities, creating new urban clusters and metropolitan areas. This continued urbanization would present challenges to quality of life if it occurred spontaneously, without the set-aside of public space and green space and provision of adequate sanitation, communication, and transportation around the urbanized area. In the context of the dualism described above, increasingly, cities would be the ideal stage for eruptions of tensions, considerably increasing public insecurity and abandonment of public spaces. Every city, though dynamic, would really be two cities — a rich one and a poor one, one included in the growth and the related quality of life and the other excluded from development and quality of life. It would be a city under siege, dominated by fear.

It is likely, however, that in several metropolitan areas institutions would be created that could direct their growth and plan their development, based on the negative experiences of the existing metropolitan areas. The worst outcomes would be in the rapidly growing cities and metropolises of the Brazilian "Far West," whose unregulated growth has been driven by greed, scant employment opportunities, irresponsible land allotment, deforestation, soil erosion, and compromise of water resources, thus repeating historical errors. This is the case, for example, with the urbanization on both sides of highways with increased regional traffic. In spite of the rich experience afforded by the twentieth-century history of all of the *boca de sertão* and *ponta de trilho* cities (Goiânia, Ribeirão Preto, Londrina, Campo Grande, and many others), we see expansion in the Amazonian Far West as if nothing had been learned from prior experience.

On the opposite extreme, we can try to visualize a second scenario, a more hopeful one, characterized by "inclusive development," what Father Louis-Joseph Lebret, on considering Brazil's potential, called "a civilization of being, with equitable division of having." In this inclusive development, at the beginning, public policies and government actions would correct any neoliberal and deregulatory trends, with the goal of establishing a transition plan of national character, obviously taking into account the necessary global connections, while focusing on the main axis — reduction of the distance between the poor and the rich, the elimination of poverty and ignorance, that is, the homogenization of society. At the same time, the transition plan would take into consideration the economic expansion necessary to make available natural and human resources, with lines of credit designed to meet the needs of businesses, researchers, and innovators, as well as lines of credit for the people. Such incentives would activate the domestic market, which would certainly get a strong push when the social strata that today are out of reach gained access to this market. This is, in fact, what happened immediately after the monetary stabilization as a result of the Real Plan, and this is actually happening at the time of the present edition. The quest for a better trade balance would not be exclusively connected to Brazil's situation of dependency but rather to the potential for the import of inputs for domestic production — in other words, it would be tied to development.

Although this essay is supposed to be limited to the urban environment, our speculation is necessarily expanded to the foreseeable consequences of a greater homogenization of Brazilian society. The upward mobility of the portion of the population rescued from ignorance and lack of opportunities would result in considerable rise in demand, irrigating the economy and forcing its growth. Such increase in the domestic market would have a strong influence on civil construction, because of the need for new housing. It would also generate new economic activity, much of it autonomous. The initial growth in demand for products would be rapidly supplanted by the growth in demand for services. The list of demands for improvements in quality of life would increase, therefore, with pressure on public services provided by the private or public sector. Both of these would be regulated and overseen by the respective agencies and by an auditing system that would be responsible for inspection of both state and private public services providers.

After the period in which demand outpaced supply, urban growth would occur. Where? The best-case scenario of development follows the optimistic path of reinforcement of family agriculture through improving the technical capacity and credit for product elaboration. In this scenario, the highest rates of urbanization would occur in new cities surrounded by diversified rural activities and midsize landholdings. In second place, midsize cities that could process the agricultural products and rapidly expand their service sector would resume growth. These would grow noticeably if there were an increase in local opportunities to acquire knowledge and diversification of education and training of young people, thanks to an expansion in distance education, for which Brazil is ripe. There would be, then, a healthy reinforcement of the urban network as opposed to a mere increase in metropolises, which inevitably would occur to a certain extent.

Thus, in the areas of penetration into the economic frontier in the Central Plateau and the Amazonian Northwest, there could be a repetition of the historical experience of the *boca de sertão* towns, though this time in a modern context that could be easily foreseen and planned. The Brazilian Far West could be rewritten, replacing the chaotic and destructive spontaneous settlement with regional planning that would guide the private initiative of the pioneers and make it less predatory. Such planned development would oversee a roll-out of new infrastructure guided by local governments, financing of credit tied to a rise in technical level of production, a growth in education of the population, and support of a pioneering spirit that hopefully would be void of exploitative and destructive aspects.

During the engagement of development thus understood, the homogenization of society would have a strong influence on midsize cities. These are the ones that present the best conditions for a fruitful functional connection with the surrounding agricultural areas, because of their proximity and because of the nationwide and global connections that most already possess. The demands of the new upwardly mobile classes would be a challenge because these cities would tend to grow and grow together, forming new urban agglomerations. Maintaining the quality of life that they already have, especially in the South and the Southeast, would be a chore that entailed judicious application of resources both to keep and improve urban civility and global connections. Improvement in the quality of life in these metropolises would depend in good part on the educational and cultural development of the homogenized society.

The midsize cities of the Northeast would have a special challenge because their development and improvement in overall level of education and training would become urgent demands. If these needs were met, these northeastern cities would have prospects for a broad diversity of new economic activity in industries of new paradigms, in services with heavy demand, and, moreover, in the important tourism sector.

Aside from the consolidation of the São Paulo macrometropolis, comprising the metropolises of São Paulo, Campinas, the Baixada Santista, and the southwestern Paraíba Valley, the development and the growth of demand in the Brazilian metropolises would occur in diversification of activities in new fields of industry and services. A new period of reindustrialization, occupying little space and offering few jobs, but with high added value and strong ties to research, would increase the importance of global connectivity and would furnish new opportunities for the domestic market. In the meanwhile, within this scenario, the service sector would undergo the most important changes, not only because of demands from new social sectors but also because of sophistication and diversification brought on by the globalization of consumption habits. In an optimistic scenario, in these metropolises, there would be sophistication in culture and research of a global nature, with strong influence in Latin America. For this, networking among research institutions, knowledge producers, organizations that promote technology and patents, and the entities that produce products and services would be important.

The macrometropolises of São Paulo and, to some extent, Rio de Janeiro would strengthen their position as global cities, that is, as metropolises where important international companies and institutions have their headquarters and make global decisions. This aspect of the optimistic scenario would depend, however, on a reversal of the situation of tension and violence, on the recovery of public spaces, and on parallel improvement in quality of life resulting from the nurture of new upwardly mobile classes and a civilizing effort on behalf of urbanity and quality of life of the citizens. Such an undertaking would come with the establishment of decentralized planning and actions, definition of urban areas, a communal policy of public security, recuperation of degraded landscapes, increases in green space and leisure areas, democratization of cultural activities, and improvement in housing conditions with upgrading of favelas and tenement buildings.

More attention would have to be paid to the influx of nonresident users of the Brazilian metropolises. When growing the service sector in a context of high global connectivity and true development, a range of services in lodging, communications, circulation, landscaping, multilingual education, culture, security, and civility should be provided. The unique characteristics, both local and national, of the provision of services would enrich cities appreciably, an increasingly important factor in the competitiveness among global cities. Diversity would be a highly valued quality in the context of globalization of habits resulting from the high degree of global connectivity and standardization of consumption.

In this scenario of planned development, heavy investments must be made in mass public transportation, especially in the São Paulo and Rio subways. The current proportions of modes of transport must be changed. Today, in the São Paulo metropolitan area, of the 30 million daily trips, only a third are made on public transportation (subway, train, and bus), while a third are made by car (private automobile or taxi). The reaming third are made on foot. This proportion reflects the difficulty of transportation for many and the challenge of an increase in both poverty and wealth.

To change such a perverse picture, in a context of inclusive development, in São Paulo, it would be necessary, for example, to build 10 kilometers of subway network per year for ten years to finish the originally projected 140 kilometers. In the meanwhile, this would still be insufficient, insofar as the São Paulo subway must go beyond the limits of the municipality to link up with the urban and suburban rail systems. The extension and consolidation of the subway network could be followed by an increased density of buildings along these corridors, along with an increased centralization of services in the neighborhoods. This would result, physically and socially, in a new "polynuclear metropolis."

Heavy investment should also be made in sanitation in the large cities to solve once and for all the problem of industrial and domestic sewage waste. This would be done by updating the network and implementing decentralized treatment processes or even, through technological advances of a biological and chemical nature, by allowing sewage treatment at the home in which it is produced, eliminating the need for an expensive urban sewage network. On the other hand, industries, which already control their pollution somewhat, could undergo radical changes in their paradigms. They would be decentralized businesses that occupy less space per manufacturing unit, are highly automated, and radically reduce their area of stock. These industries could sell or recycle their waste, to be used as inputs for other products. Within this new vision of industrialization, the São Paulo metropolitan area would probably witness a phase of reindustrialization.

In addition, the drainage of the region, which today is handicapped by the impermeability of the urban area, could be recuperated, creating linear parks along the river valleys that are not yet paved. Drainage, in the optimistic scenario, would have a solution associated with the collection, recycling, and final disposal of solid waste. Finally, the yearly heavy rainfall could be collected and controlled by increasing green space, which would be able to filter the rainwater. Temporary water retention systems could be built, and the use of rainwater could be compulsory for all new construction.

Global connectivity, which created the environment that we call "globalization," leads to a speeding up of all decision-making processes. In the optimistic scenario of inclusive development, citizen participation, whether in pressing that demands be addressed, influencing decisions, or even contributing to the creation of public policies, would also be rapid and would depend on the establishment of a public information network. Its fluidity would be handled by a wide network of interactive terminals distributed in towns and cities that would allow citizens to consult, ask questions and receive answers, engage in self-service, and participate in plebiscites, thus intensifying the contact between municipal government and its citizens. Thus citizen participation in the implementation of development would not be limited to democratic mobilization. It would become a new mode of democracy, resulting in a new format of public administration. The computerization of cities, in theory, would allow a reduction of bureaucracy and facilitate citizens' lives. The degree of civility would rise — one of the basic conditions for competitive advantage in the global network of cities.

The more optimistic scenario, however, would be defined not only by achieving competitiveness among cities but also by regaining solidarity, resulting from the higher degree of consciousness and civility, less tension, greater security and less fear, more hope for the future, better conditions for work and leisure, greater social justice, and greater equity, and by the organization of society.

Brazilian society is still searching for a modus vivendi with the Brazilian state. Historically, the state was constituted after independence from the Portuguese crown before national society could form in a conscious and structured way. The divorce continued amid mutual mistrust throughout the entire imperial period of the nineteenth century; even during the republic, the two spheres appeared to coexist, progressing parallel to one another, without naturally interweaving aspects of the same nation. Thus the common phrase "The law did not stick" is incomprehensible in nations where society generated the state. In Brazil, it is possible for the (apparently legitimate and democratic) state to pass laws far from the daily reality of social life, while society is allowed to ignore them. Moreover, the democratic form of representation has been tainted with vices, corporatism, and patrimonialism, on which recent advances have had some positive effect. Again, in an optimistic scenario, we must assume that these vices, and the very corruptibility of the political system itself, can be largely overcome. In contrast, in the pessimistic scenario, corruption would increase as a result of greater societal fragmentation, anomie, and the more effective presence of organized crime in politics.

What is more, to temper the proposed extreme scenarios, Brazil, like the other countries of Latin America and unlike parts of Africa and Asia, identifies itself as a nation. Even though the original population was decimated, the strong process of racial and cultural miscegenation over five centuries has given birth to a physically beautiful nation with strong elements of national identification. Language, syncretic religious spirit, similar habits easily molded by the media, affection and sensuality, tolerance, superficiality, and adaptability to and acceptance of innovations are general national characteristics. Another feature is the elite class's cynical propensity to hide and camouflage its prejudices.

Therefore, the social fragmentation that one observes is not the fruit of a multiplicity of ethnic and cultural groups in conflict that is difficult to overcome, as on some other continents. It is a matter of fragmentation that is possible to overcome, depending on consistent public policies, on education, and on the establishment of a generous long-term vision that considers development defined as inclusive growth a priority; in other words, more than anything else, a reduction of the distance between rich and poor is the main paradigm for Brazilian development.

IGNACY SACHS

Quo Vadis, Brazil?

There is a misery greater than dying of hunger in the desert:
that is not having anything to eat in the land of Canaan.
— JOSÉ AMÉRICO DE ALMEIDA, *A bagaceira*

Utopia, yes; let us be utopian, very utopian, provided that we do not
make our ideal sterile, expecting its fulfillment from any force
immanent of Utopia itself; let us be utopian as long as we work.
— MANOEL BOMFIM, *A América Latina: Males de origem*

Will Brazil be the eternal "country of the future"? Nearly seventy years after the publication of Stefan Zweig's well-known book *Brazil: Land of the Future*, and notwithstanding a century of especially rapid economic growth and spectacular modernization, in the course of which its population grew tenfold and the gross domestic product (GDP) multiplied by forty, Brazil has not been able to overcome its startling social backwardness. Thanks to successful import-substitution industrialization carried out in the 1950s, 1960s, and 1970s, Brazil rose to the position of ninth-largest economy in the world by the end of the century.[1] It is today a poorly developed country because it has adopted a socially pernicious pattern of growth. It has one of the most regressive income distributions in the world, with abysmal differences between the minority of winners and the great masses of the sacrificed.

According to the 1998 *Human Development Report* published by the United Nations Development Programme (UNDP), the poorer half of the Brazilian population, which held 18 percent of the total annual income in 1960, saw its share sink to 11.6 percent in 1995. At the same time, the richest 10 percent went from holding 54 percent of the domestic income in 1960 to 63 percent in 1995. Once it had managed to stabilize the currency, the 1994 Real Plan brought some improvement. Its effects, however, do not appear to be durable. Data from the Brazilian Institute of Geography and Statistics (Instituto Brasileiro de Geografia e Estatística, IBGE) revealed that, in 1998, the poorer half of the population had 13.5 percent of the income, slightly less than the portion of the income of the richest 1 percent.

Squeezed between the winners and the sacrificed, a rather large middle class has distanced itself from the popular classes and dived into an imitative modernity. It feels, however, increasingly frustrated in its aspiration of maintaining a lifestyle and patterns of consumption similar to those of the winners, placed before it by the omnipresent commercial advertising in the media and on the streets.

Patience and optimism are part of the Brazilian character. At the same time, it is hard to imagine that the successive waves of Brazilians who have been left, generation after generation, on the side of the highway of progress in black plastic shacks, who are added to the others disconnected from the process of wealth-concentrating, exclusive growth, continue to be satisfied with the ever-renewed promises of a radiant future. It is hard to imagine that they will resign themselves, today and tomorrow, to putting up with injustices just because these were inherited from a colonial, slavocratic past. With each passing year, these excuses are less and less plausible.

By persisting on the road of bad development, Brazil will head toward a catastrophic social apartheid. Following the proclamation of the republic in 1889, at the beginning of the "long Brazilian twentieth century," the Brazilian economy grew at the enviable average annual rate of 4.1 percent. From 1950 to 1980, the rate reached 6.7 percent but then plummeted to 2.1 percent in the last two decades of the century.[2] There was a modest growth of 0.5 percent per person, just enough to characterize the paltry performance of the Brazilian economy as going from bad to less bad.[3]

Twenty years of near stagnation in a country like Brazil clearly signal the exhaustion of the prevailing pattern of economic growth. The structural crisis was caused by the coming together of two sets of factors. On the one hand, there are two internal contradictions of wealth-concentrating, exclusive growth: First, the socially pernicious regime, sustained by increasingly greater inequalities in income distribution, finds itself up against a limit in the form of insufficient expansion of the domestic market. About one-third of Brazilians are completely excluded from that market, and another third participate marginally with their low wages. The country has barely begun agrarian reform in earnest and is still straitjacketed by an anachronistic landholding structure. Second, the scurrilous treatment of conflicts generated by this distribution, putting faith in the illusory possibility of dribbling them with domestic financing through inflation and with abusive foreign indebtedness, led to hyperinflation followed by an ultimately successful currency stabilization, the Real Plan, that, nevertheless, was bought at the price of an explosion in overall underemployment and unemployment in the large cities.

On the other hand, there is the clumsy entry into globalization: First, heeding the precepts of the Washington Consensus, Brazil carried out an excessive and too rapid economic opening, appealing recklessly to foreign financing, whose flow requires usurious interest rates and transfers of domestic assets to foreign companies with a consequent denationalization of an important share of the banking system and industrial complex, the privatization of numerous public companies, with the notable exception, so far, of the national oil company, Petrobras. Second, Brazil dismantled the state apparatus without paying due attention to the principal evil that gnaws away at public administration at all levels: the omnipresent patrimonialism that requires, before anything else, its deprivatization and not its shrinkage.

Together with the other countries that undertook to apply the Washington Consensus, which is now repudiated even by its authors, Brazil faces the uncomfortable position of loser in the process of globalization in its current asymmetrical form. Neoliberalism did not fulfill its promise of prosperity shared by all. The invisible hand, to which Joan Robinson attributed a particular dexterity in strangulation, cannot even manage to reestablish the rates of economic growth reached in the past, much less take on the social responsibility of overcoming bad development and putting Brazil on the path of authentic development.

This will not happen unless the visible hand of the state, shriveled but active, starts planning again to overcome the myopia and social insensitivity of the market, to organize the fantasy, in Celso Furtado's metaphor, starting with an original long-term plan, which Brazil once had but now so dearly lacks.

The development potential of a country depends, in good part, on its capacity to think and the self-esteem acquired in going through this process. It is necessary for the country to break the reigning conformity and the intellectual vacuum and to free itself from the bias toward imitative thought that relies on the trans-

position to the country of lifestyles and patterns of consumption of the industrialized countries of the North. The national plan—the selection of values and the
identification of substantive goals in accordance with those values—can arise
only from a broad discussion involving all of the forces alive in the nation and all
of the sectors of opinion, through the consolidation of democracy in daily life.

The observations that follow do not mean to replace this discussion but, rather,
to outline it. A basically heuristic role falls to the social sciences to raise questions, which will be answered by political praxis.

LET US BEGIN with the concept of development for which economic growth
(whose modes and purposes are duly defined) is a necessary but not sufficient
condition. Its objectives are always social and ethical and are, therefore, subordinate to a rationale. Moreover, the recently gained environmental awareness
imposes rules of ecological concern.

Economic considerations refer only to instrumental reasoning, to the clearly
important quest for efficiency, but they are insufficient for prioritizing goals. We
know today that the development process requires aligning five different kinds
of efficiency that do not go together without the influence of the visible hand of
the planner. The first, associated with Adam Smith and the mechanism of competitive markets, is allocative efficiency. Development will not occur, however,
without macroeconomic efficiency, associated with John Maynard Keynes, which
promotes full employment of labor and the productive apparatus. The other three
efficiencies are the distributive, the innovative, and, the ecological.

The indisputable primacy of the social dimension dictates the criteria of
evaluation of development. The rule formulated by Dudley Sears in 1969 has lost
nothing in the present. To know whether a country is developing, we must ask
what is happening with poverty, what is happening with inequality, and what is
happening with unemployment. If there have been improvements in all three of
these central problems, then the country is going through a phase of development. If, to the contrary, the situation has deteriorated with respect to one, two,
or, especially, three of these criteria, it would be odd to call this outcome "development," even if the per capita income has doubled.[4] More recently, Amartya Sen
rightly observed that progress is evaluated more by the reduction of poverty than
by the successive enrichment of the already wealthy.[5]

At the same time, we should broaden the concept of development to include
more than just material consumption. Father Louis-Joseph Lebret said that de-

velopment consists of building "a civilization of being, with equitable division of having."[6] If we move in this direction, we can reinterpret the historical process of development in terms of a struggle for the effective appropriation by all of the set of human rights—political, civil, social, economic, and cultural—without forgetting the collective rights to development, to the city, and to the environment.

The different perspectives mentioned here complement one another, revealing the multidimensional concept of development and justifying its centrality in organizing the discussion about the national plan. This is a matter of points of departure for a concerted reflection. It is good to resist the formulation of abstract ideas, professions of humanist faith, and principles that are sufficiently general to transcend a confrontation with reality.

The potential for Brazil to produce an original plan that is not stale from imitation is exceptional and, in some cases, unique. Gilberto Freyre was right to advocate for the need to build an original tropical civilization in Brazil: "Brazil does not want to be sub-European in its appearance or anti-European in its attitudes but rather to join its European heritage with tropical values to thus form a new style of civilization."[7] Later, in the conclusion to *The Brazilian People*, anthropologist Darcy Ribeiro took this idea up again and broadened it, dreaming of the formation of a single Latin American nation, 500 million today, 1 billion tomorrow, "a tardy, tropical Rome."[8]

Among the various triumphs that Brazil already has at its disposal to head in this new direction are the following:

(1) an enormous reserve of arable land and the largest tropical forest in the world (of which it would be good to keep intact at least two-thirds);

(2) a large variety of climatic conditions for agriculture, giving the different regions the opportunity to complement each other instead of competing with the same products;

(3) abundant and well-distributed water resources, with the exception of the semiarid Northeast;

(4) exceptional wealth in biodiversity;

(5) millions of Brazilians who seek land to cultivate and not jobs on the asphalt;

(6) ample possibilities for rapid advances in land reform, so often postponed, on abandoned land, unproductive large landholdings, or land illegally acquired through claim jumping, making use, through the

measures adopted in the late 1990s, of the arsenal of legal and fiscal tools necessary and of reasonable technical and financial support programs for small family agriculture;

(7) comfortable margins for increased yields per hectare and family farm income, especially on irrigable lands; there are several Californias yet to be created since the potential is estimated at 60 million hectares, and only a little over one-tenth has been equipped so far;

(8) a reasonable capacity for technical and scientific research in the life sciences and agronomy.

No other country brings together the same cast of conditions favorable for exploiting the biodiversity-biomass-biotechnology triad. Making use of the natural advantages of the tropics (Brazil will always have the sun), Brazil can strive to optimize the six uses of biomass—human food, animal feed, biofuels, fertilizers, construction materials, and industrial inputs—integrated into production systems. Brazil can thus be a global leader in the invention of a modern biomass civilization, the heir to the traditional agricultural civilizations.

From this point of view, agrarian reform ceases to be a mere instrument of social policy, aiming to provide small farmers with conditions for subsistence. Land reform leverages modern, knowledge-intensive agroindustrial development, capable of transforming the array of biomass into a diversified range of products. Opportunities for jobs in rural industries would be added to agricultural work properly speaking, beginning with decentralized agroindustry, production units for building materials and biofuels, and, to the extent that rural modernization proceeds, increasingly needed technical services in the commercial, personal, tourism, and social fields. These services are decisive for pulling the rural areas out of their centuries-old and proverbially backward civilization.

This would be the path to market inclusion of those excluded. Acting on the demand for products and services amid the new rural prosperity would thus configure a more harmonious rural-urban relationship, promote growth at the base rather than the peak of the social pyramid, and replace the wealth-concentrating, exclusive model with its opposite, a distributive, inclusive one with a strong social bias.

At the beginning of the nineteenth century, Brazil and the United States were approximately at the same level of development. What Brazil later lacked was the Homestead Act, thus largely explaining the subsequent divergence of the two countries. The question now posed is to what extent a complete agrarian reform accompanied by a resettlement of Brazilian territory based on family agriculture would have the same energizing effect in the twenty-first century as the mobile frontier had in the nineteenth-century United States.

To speak of generating millions of rural jobs through employment and self-employment[9] may not appear fitting in a country that has, in the last ten years, eliminated one-fifth of its agricultural jobs by adopting large-scale mechanized agriculture on the pioneering frontiers that practically dispenses with human labor. No less bold is to think of a development in harmony with nature, a sine qua non of the advent of a new biomass civilization, when all of the successive cycles of the Brazilian economy have been characterized by predatory appropriation of natural resources, by soil exhaustion from wandering agriculture, and by the indiscriminant destruction of forests, which is still taking place: 17,000 square kilometers annually in the last several years of the century. Brazil suffers the negative effects of its continental size and the abundance of its natural resources. These two observations are the measure of the distance that separates the current course of bad development from the route of development founded on the tripod of social justice, ecological prudence, and economic viability.

Despite our emphasis on the rural leveraging of development, the main front of the struggle for employment and self-employment must be in the urban and periurban areas, where a majority of Brazilians live—from two-thirds to three-quarters, according to the criteria of urbanization used here. We should distinguish between those who have already effectively integrated themselves into urban life and the many who are still "waiting to be urbanized," that is, to ascend to a reasonable job, to decent housing, and to effective conditions for the exercise of citizenship. Many are refugees from the country—odd-jobbers, street vendors, *bóias-frias* (migrant laborers), and unskilled construction workers—living in the favelas and the slum neighborhoods on the outskirts, which are veritable precities or, some would say, purgatories.

We know that full employment and self-employment will not increase in Brazilian cities through the mere effect of economic growth, unless this is maintained at the exceptionally high level of 6 percent per year or more.[10] The Brazilian situation differs in two aspects from the experience of today's developed countries when they had a level of development comparable to Brazil's:

(1) A much larger proportion of the population was still in the country; Brazil suffered a premature, excessive rural exodus;

(2) The play of market forces, made possible by the opening of markets and by competition with imported products, was not yet driven with the same violence to the use of highly labor-saving technology as in modern industry and services.

As a consequence, the national plan cannot do without a set of public policies directed at the issue of urban employment. To this end, it is necessary to open up the Pandora's box of so-called informal employment, a comfortable and hypocritical concept, because it disguises the seriousness of the Brazilian social crisis. The real urban economy is made up of a tangle of labor and product markets — formal, informal, and even criminal — in addition to an extensive domestic economy and free public services, both located outside the marketplace.

It is an extremely complex, heterogeneous, and little-known system in which activities useful to society, which deserve support, coexist with others that must be prohibited. What is more, there is no transparency as to the earnings, relations, working conditions (often precarious), forms of exploitation, degree of social coverage, and prospects for the future. As a corollary, we need to abandon the mystifying analyses of labor earnings that use the minimum wage as a unit of accounting as if it were stable. In reality, its purchasing power has eroded almost constantly during the more than seventy years of its existence.

The absence of studies of the real economy conducted from the viewpoint of anthropological economics makes it difficult to identify the sectors of the popular economy that must be protected and assisted by programs of professional training, credit access, and incorporation of small businesses into the formal economy. The participants in the popular economy must, moreover, be provided with social coverage in the same way that was done, and rightly so, in the matter of retirement of rural workers, one of the few social advances in Brazil in the last years of the twentieth century.

Another battlefront against urban unemployment and underemployment involves identifying employment and self-employment niches, which will not materialize in the absence of public policies aimed at this goal. Economic growth is the result of increased labor productivity and the expansion of employment. Private and public companies competing in the marketplace privilege increased productivity, as is natural. It is up to government, therefore, to counterbalance this tendency by promoting employment in the more labor-intensive sectors, such as

(1) public investments in affordable housing, sanitation, water, and mass transit, especially meeting the needs of those social segments without enough buying power to access these services through the market;

(2) support for assisted resident-built affordable housing construction and for urban work crews;

(3) support for social services — education, health, infant and elder care — taking advantage of Brazil's relatively low average wages to meet the enormous latent demand; partnerships with the third sector can open up new horizons in this matter;

(4) jobs geared to the search for greater ecoefficiency; each city is an ecosystem; therefore, it has natural resource potential that is underutilized, poorly utilized, or even wasted.

All of the emphasis in the economic debate falls on labor productivity; efficient use of natural resources appears not to merit the same attention even though it can also contribute to growth. As a result, many opportunities for jobs are lost in energy and water conservation, reuse and recycling of waste, and especially in maintenance of existing infrastructure, equipment, building facilities, and so forth. By extending the life of these items through better maintenance, capital that would have gone to their replacement is saved. In other words, for a determined level of savings, the proportion of liquid investment increases. All of these jobs are self financing in macroeconomic terms through the resource savings that they bring in. We need the public sector only to make these viable in microeconomic terms.

The degree of waste that characterizes the current performance of the Brazilian economy makes it possible to see in the aforementioned activities an opportunity for employment-driven growth.[11] The prospects for employment seem less disheartening than one might imagine in light of the catastrophic statistics for job loss in the formal industrial sector — more than 3 million jobs lost in ten years — on the condition that one explores the suggestions made here.

As Celso Furtado tirelessly proposed, to resume growth and development upon reenergizing the domestic market by means of rural leverage, Brazil must still overcome two obstacles:

(1) the fiscal wars between states and municipalities, which currently erode the federal pact and constitute a game in which the nation as a whole ends up losing;[12]

(2) the fascination with the outward-looking model, which makes little sense in a country of continental dimensions. This is not a matter of promoting an autarky but rather transcending the false dichotomy between outward-looking and inward-looking growth and growing from the inside out, to use Osvaldo Sunkel's phrase. A rapidly expanding domestic market consolidates the international position of the country and reduces the famous but exaggerated "Brazil cost."

Active insertion into the international economy requires selectivity guided by the national plan, the more active presence of the "visible hand" in the strategic interface between domestic economy and world economy, and a closer collaboration with the other countries of the Global South, beginning with India and China, to loosen the ties of dependency on the financial markets, the technological sources, and the markets of the Global North. This does not mean in any way disengaging with the latter, though.

Quo vadis, Brazil? Where are you going? For Hélio Jaguaribe, the leading Brazilian forecaster, "At the close of the twentieth century, Brazil finds itself extremely unprepared to face the challenges of the new century. It is not only the fact that the country, while defying the expectation of the 1950s and 1960s, enters the twenty-first century without having been able to overcome its persistent underdevelopment, though this is part of it. While serious, this limitation is not fatal. The country has reached a sufficient level to meet this old objective, even if belatedly, in a couple of decades, if it adopts in a consistent way the measures required for such."[13]

The future is open because it depends on the actions of people, and the future will tell whether, in the early decades of the twenty-first century, Brazil will remain tangled up in bad development, increasing even more its social heterogeneity with the growing risk of social rupture, or, on the contrary, if Brazil will manage to start down the path of development that is socially homogenizing, distributive, and inclusive.

Put another way, the question becomes, How long will Brazil postpone taking advantage of its extraordinary potential for development, wasting its historic chance to project itself as a world power with a human face? Because of the characteristics of Brazil—its continental size and abundance of arable lands and natural resources—the appropriate metaphor is not Japan but the twenty-first-century United States with an even more human face.

Time is precious, however. With each generation that passes, millions of Brazilians miss the opportunity to live a life of dignity and to realize their human potential. It is an irreparable loss because it is irreversible, and it is ethically scandalous.

Notes

1. After the United States, China, Japan, India, Germany, France, Great Britain, and Italy, and ahead of Russia, Mexico, Canada, Spain, South Korea, and Indonesia. The ranking is based on the 1998 GDP converted into dollars according to the parity of purchasing power of the local currencies. World Bank, cited in *Economist*, 13 May 2000.

2. Marcio Pochmann, *Globalização e emprego: O Brasil na nova divisão internacional de trabalho* (Campinas: Editora da Universidade Estadual de Campinas, 2000). According to Paulo Roberto de Almeida, based on calculations by Angus Maddison, Brazil's GDP was multiplied by 157 between 1870 and 1987, compared to 84 for Japan and 53 for the United States. Paulo Roberto de Almeida, "A inserção econômica internacional do Brasil em perspectiva histórica," in *O Brasil no cenário internacional*, ed. Cadernos Adenauer (São Paulo: Fundação Konrad Adenauer, 2000), 2:37–56.

3. At the Twelfth National Forum on 15 May 2000, President Fernando Henrique Cardoso said that, in the social arena, Brazil was going from bad to less bad. According to Sérgio Abranches, "Integration and social mobility in Brazil explain why Brazilians seem more tolerant of inequalities, to the point of leaving some perplexed and others scandalized." Sérgio Abranches, "De mal a menos mal," *Veja*, 31 May 2000.

4. Dudley Sears, "The Meaning of Development," *International Development Review* 11, no. 4 (1969): 3.

5. Amartya Sen, "Will There Be Any Hope for the Poor?" *Time*, 25 May 2000.

6. "Une civilisation de l'être dans le partage équitable de l'avoir."

7. Gilberto Freyre, *Homem, cultura e trópico* (Recife: Universidade de Recife/Imprensa Universitária, 1962), 75.

8. Darcy Ribeiro, *The Brazilian People: The Formation and Meaning of Brazil* (Gainesville: University Press of Florida, 2000), 322.

9. The report from the International Commission on Peace and Food, presided over by M. S. Swaminathan, put forth the possibility of creating in ten years 1 billion rural jobs and jobs induced by rural prosperity worldwide. This report, *Uncommon Opportunities: An Agenda for Peace and Equitable Development* (London: Zed Books, 1994), went practically unnoticed in Brazil.

10. This is the Economic Commission for Latin America and the Caribbean's (ECLAC) estimate for the whole of Latin America. *La brecha de la equidad: Una segunda evaluación* (Santiago, Chile: ECLAC, 2000).

11. For a discussion of the concept of employment-led growth, see Ignacy Sachs, "L'économie politique du développement des économies mixtes selon Kalecki: Croissance tirée par l'emploi," *Mondes en Développement* 27, no. 106 (1999): 23–34.

12. I. A. S. Prado, "Guerra fiscal e políticas de desenvolvimento estadual no Brasil," *Economia e sociedade* 13 (December 1999): 1–201; C. A. Pacheco, *Fragmentação da nação* (Campinas: Universidade Estadual de Campinas/Instituto de Economia); T. Bacelar, "Dinâmica regional brasileira nos anos noventa: Rumo a desintegração competitiva?" in *Redescobrindo o Brasil: 500 anos depois* (Bertrand Brasil, 1998).

13. Hélio Jaguaribe, "Brasil e o mundo na perspectiva do século XXI," *Política Externa* 8, no. 1 (June–July–August 2000): 12.

Contributors

LUIZ CARLOS BRESSER PEREIRA has a Ph.D. and a *livre-docência* in economics from the University of São Paulo (Universidade de São Paulo, USP). He is a professor at the Getúlio Vargas Foundation (Fundação Getúlio Vargas, FGV), São Paulo, and editor of the *Revista de Economia Política*. He was secretary of government of the state of São Paulo (1985–86) and Brazilian minister of finance (1987), minister of federal administration and reform of the state (1995–98), and minister of science and technology (1999). He has published, among other books, *Development and Crisis in Brazil, 1930–1983*, *O colapso de uma aliança de classes*, *Economic Reforms in New Democracies: A Social-Democratic Approach* (with José María Maravall and Adam Przeworski), and *Democracy and Public Management Reform: Building the Republican State*.

CRISTOVAM BUARQUE has a B.A. in mechanical engineering from the Federal University of Pernambuco (Universidade Federal de Pernambuco, UFPE) and a doctorate from the University of Paris, Sorbonne. He worked for six years at the Inter-American Development Bank (IDB), Washington, D.C. He was a professor and *reitor* (1983–89) of the University of Brasília (*Universidade de Brasília*, UnB); governor of the Federal District; senator (2003–11); minister of education (2003–4); and a candidate for president of Brazil (2006).

ASPÁSIA CAMARGO has a doctorate from the School for Advanced Studies in Social Sciences (École des Hautes Études en Sciences Sociales, EHESS) in Paris. She was president of Brazil's Institute of Applied Economics Research (Instituto de Pesquisa Econômica Aplicada, IPEA); president of the National Association of Graduate Studies and Research in the Social Sciences (Associação Nacional de Pós-Graduação e Pesquisa em Ciências Sociais, ANPOCS); and a professor and researcher at the National School of Public Administration (Escola Nacional de Administração Pública, ENAP) of FGV. She has published several works on federalism.

GILBERTO DUPAS was coordinator of the area of international affairs and member of the council of the Institute of Advanced Studies (Instituto de Estudos Avançados) of USP. He is a professor at the European Institute of Business Administration (INSEAD) in France and at the Kellogg School of Management, Northwestern University. He is the author of, among other books, *Crise econômica e transição democrática*, *Economia global e exclusão so-*

cial: Pobreza, emprego, estado e o futuro do capitalismo, Ética e poder na sociedade de informação, Renda, consumo e crescimento, and *Espaço para crescimento sustentado da economia brasileira.*

CELSO FURTADO (1920–2004) held a Ph.D. in economics from the University of Paris, Sorbonne and undertook postdoctoral study at Cambridge University in the United Kingdom. He was chief of the Development Division of the United Nations' Economic Commission for Latin America (ECLA; now the Economic Commission for Latin America and the Caribbean, ECLAC), executive head of the Superintendency for Development of the Northeast (Superintendência do Desenvolvimento do Nordeste, SUDENE), minister of planning in the government of President João Goulart, and, after returning from twenty years of exile in Paris, minister of culture under President José Sarney. He published more than thirty books and was a member of the Brazilian Academy of Letters (Academia Brasileira de Letras).

AFRÂNIO GARCIA, economist and anthropologist, was a professor in the Department of Anthropology of the National Museum of the Federal University of Rio de Janeiro (Universidade Federal do Rio de Janeiro, UFRJ) from 1978 to 1997 and a researcher for the Brazilian National Council for Scientific and Technological Development (Conselho Nacional de Desenvolvimento Científico e Tecnológico, CNPq) from 1982 to 1995. Since February 1996 he has been a *maître de conférences* at EHESS. He is also codirector of the Centre de Recherches sur le Brésil Contemporain (CRBC).

CELSO LAFER has a Ph.D. in political science from Cornell University (1970), and since 1988 he has been a professor in the College of Law at USP. He was minister of foreign affairs; minister of development, industry and trade; and Brazilian ambassador to international organizations in Geneva. He is the president of the superior council of the State of São Paulo Research Foundation (Fundação de Amparo à Pesquisa do Estado de São Paulo, FAPESP) and member of the Brazilian Academy of Letters. He is the author of, among other books, *Comércio, desarmamento, direitos humanos: Reflexões sobre uma experiência diplomática, Hannah Arendt, pensamento, persuasão e poder, A identidade internacional do Brasil e a política externa brasileira,* and *A internacionalização dos direitos humanos.*

JOSÉ SEIXAS LOURENÇO has a Ph.D. in engineering science from the University of California, Berkeley. In 1991, he received the Anísio Teixeira Prize awarded by the Coordination for the Improvement of Higher Education Personnel (Coordenação de Aperfeiçoamento de Pessoal de Nível Superior, CAPES) for his contribution to the development of education and scientific institutions in Brazil. He is a member of the board of the Fulbright Commission, president of the administrative council of Bioamazônia, special adviser to the minister of science and technology, and member of the administrative council of the International Institute for Higher Education in Latin America (Instituto Internacional para o Ensino Superior na América Latina, IESALC), appointed by the director-general of UNESCO.

RENATO ORTIZ has a Ph.D. from EHESS. He is a professor in the Department of Sociology at the São Paulo State University of Campinas (Universidade Estadual de Campinas, UNI-CAMP). He has published, among other books, *Cultura brasileira e identidade nacional*, *A moderna tradição brasileira*, *Cultura e modernidade*, *Mundialização cultura*, *Ciências sociais e trabalho intelectual*, and *Mundialização, saberes e crenças*.

MOACIR PALMEIRA earned his doctorate in sociology from the Université René Descartes, Paris. He is a professor in the Graduate Program in Social Anthropology of the National Museum, UFRJ.

PAULO SÉRGIO PINHEIRO is Cogut Visiting Professor at the Center for Latin American Studies (CLAS), Watson Institute for International Studies, and Brown University and a research associate at the Center for the Study of Violence at USP (Núcleo de Estudos da Violência, NEV-USP). He served as secretary of state for human rights in the government of President Fernando Henrique Cardoso. As the independent expert for the United Nations secretary-general in 2006, he published the *World Report on Violence against Children* (<http://www.violencestudy.org>).

IGNACY SACHS is a socioeconomist who was educated in universities in Brazil, India, and Poland. Since 1968, he has been a professor at EHESS, where he founded and directed the International Research Center on Environment and Development and is codirector of the CRBC. He was also a founder and member of the International Foundation for Alternatives to Development and special consultant of the secretary-general of the Rio Earth Summit. He has just published his memoirs, *La troisième rive: A la recherche de l'écodéveloppement*.

PAULO SINGER has a B.A. in economics and administration and a Ph.D. in sociology from the School of Philosophy, Letters, and Social Sciences (Faculdade de Filosofia, Letras e Ciências Humanas) and a *livre docência* in demography from the School of Public Health (Faculdade de Saúde Pública), both at USP. He is a professor of macroeconomics at the College of Economics, Administration, and Accounting (Faculdade de Economia, Administração e Contabilidade) of USP. He was a founder and economist of the Brazilian Center for Analysis and Planning (Centro Brasileiro de Análise e Planejamento, CEBRAP) and secretary of planning in the government of the city of São Paulo, 1988–92. He heads the National Secretariat of Solidary Economics (Secretaria Nacional de Economia Solidária, SENAES) in the Brazilian Ministry of Labor and Employment.

HERVÉ THÉRY has worked since the 1970s on the dynamics operating within Brazil's territory, particularly the consequences of state actions. He has been a professor at the École Normale Supérieure in Paris. He is research director at the Centre de Recherche et de

Documentation sur l'Amérique Latine (CNRS-CREDAL) and a visiting researcher at the Center for Sustainable Development at UnB. Among his publications are *Pouvoir et territoire au Brésil, de l'archipel au continent, Le Brésil,* and, with Neli Aparecida de Mello, *Atlas du Brésil.*

JORGE WILHEIM graduated with a degree in architecture in 1952. Among his architectural projects are Anhembi Park, the later buildings of the Albert Einstein Hospital, and the headquarters of the São Paulo Energy Company (Companhia Energética de São Paulo, CESP). He directed about twenty urban plans, including that of Curitiba, and a metropolitan plan for São Paulo. He was the coauthor of the urban renewal plan for the Vale do Anhangabaú in São Paulo. He was state secretary for planning in the Paulo Egydio Martins government, secretary of the environment in the Orestes Quércia government, and the secretary of São Paulo urban planning in the Marta Suplicy government. He was also adjunct executive secretary for the United Nations Habitat II conference (1996). He is the author of seven books on urban issues.

Index

Page numbers followed by (f) indicate figures.

Rio de Janeiro, Protocol of (1942), 102
Rio de Janeiro Stock Exchange, 57, 58
Rio Grande do Sul, 20, 97, 150, 185, 195, 234, 235;
    separatist movement in, 124, 229, 230
River Plate Basin Treaty (1969), 103
Roads. *See* Highway network
Robinson, Joan, 334
Rocha, Sonia, 88
Romero, Sílvio, 147, 148
Rondônia, 16, 208, 253, 258, 259, 261, 263, 266
Roosevelt, Franklin, 76, 111, 219, 258
Roots of Brazil, The (Buarque de Holanda), 26, 147
Roraima, 253, 258, 259, 263
Roxborough, Ian, 201–2
Roy, Arundhati, 206
Rubber Credit Bank, 258, 259
Rubber Defense Plan, 257
Rubber production, 20, 58, 61, 81; Amazonia and,
    255–56, 257, 258; boom in, 11, 255; exports of,
    55, 62, 256; World War II and, 258
Rule of law, 178–80, 193, 200–209
Rural areas, 20–49, 195; chronic civil weaknesses
    in, 248; First Republic's emphasis on, 220, 242;
    future of, 46–49; legacy of social organizations
    of, 27; leverage of development by, 337–38, 340;
    municipalism and, 247; population of, 7(f), 16,
    21, 35, 242; transformational paths of, 33–46,
    242; urban clashes with, 26–27, 35–38, 235;
    urban migrants from, 10, 21, 256, 338. *See also*
    Agrarian reform; Labor, rural; Plantations
Rural Democratic Union, 47
Rural Extension and Technical Assistance Initia-
    tives, 46
Rural Worker Assistance Fund, 44
Rural Worker Statute (1963), 38
Russian Revolution (1917), 177–78, 185

Sachs, Ignacy, 49
Sales, Alberto, 226, 228
Salvador, 10, 22, 89–90, 205, 321
Samba, 127–28
Sanitation, 329, 340
San Tiago Dantas, Francisco Clementino de,
    112–13
São Paulo, 31, 37, 55, 62, 86–87, 177; ABC region
    strikes and, 200; coffee production and, 21,
    22, 23, 31, 32, 57, 62, 147, 222, 226, 271; decen-
    tralization movement and, 226, 228, 229, 230,
    231, 246; Direct Elections Now movement and,
    200–201; dominance of, 16, 226, 234; elites'
    revolt in (1932), 68–69; as film industry center,

125–26; labor violence and, 183, 185, 194–95;
    as macrometropolis, 320, 322, 328–29, 330;
    manufacturing and, 64–65, 66; mass transit
    and, 329; police and, 205, 207; political power
    and, 5, 237; political repression and, 196, 199;
    population growth of, 6, 10, 13, 40, 42; precari-
    ous employment rates and, 89–90; print media
    and, 121–23, 126, 130–31; separatist movement
    in, 124; television and, 131, 132, 136
Sapé League, 44
Saraiva plan, 228
Sarney, José, 85, 103, 159, 162, 201, 202
Sartre, Jean-Paul, 135
Savings, 67, 71; accounts freeze, 60, 86
Schneider, Ben Ross, 157
Schwarz, Roberto, 56
Scientific research, 46, 336
Sears, Dudley, 335
Second Republic (1934–37), 180, 242, 243
Sen, Amartya, 335
Separatist movements, 124, 219, 229, 230
Service sector, 311, 329
"Short twentieth century," 108, 113
Shout of Ipiranga, 237
Simões Lopes, Luiz, 151
Simonsen, Roberto, 63, 64
Slavery, 25–28, 255, 276; abolition of (1888), 25,
    33, 47, 56, 57, 63, 70, 93, 226; continuing legacy
    of, 72, 174–75, 176, 182, 236
Small businesses, 37, 42, 43, 339
Smith, Adam, 335
Soares, Gláucio Ary Dillon, 192
Soccer, 127, 128, 134
Social apartheid, 280, 282, 324, 331, 333
Social democracy, 222, 241, 242, 246
Social Democratic Party, 193
Socialists, 39, 44, 45, 71, 72, 73
Social mobility, 242, 243, 326–28
Social security, 243
Social services, 67, 97, 180, 223, 286; government
    funds for, 44, 318–19; information technology
    and, 305; private programs and, 92
Sodré, Abreu, 199
Soft power, 107, 108
South, 13, 16, 222, 260, 327–28
South America. *See* Latin America
Southeast, 10, 11, 13, 16, 144, 223, 327–28; agricul-
    tural productivity incomes, 33; migrant labor
    and, 35
South Korea, 81, 88, 96, 315, 316
South Sea Bubble, 58

8 148